THE
MAKING
OF
LEGENDS

THE
MAKING
OF
LEGENDS

More True Stories
of Frontier America

R02033 78931

MARK DUGAN

SWALLOW PRESS/OHIO UNIVERSITY PRESS
ATHENS

Swallow Press/Ohio University Press, Athens, Ohio 45701
© 1997 by Mark Dugan
Printed in the United States of America

Swallow Press/Ohio University Press books are printed on acid-free paper ∞

01 00 99 98 97   5 4 3 2 1

Library of Congress Cataloging-in-Publication Data

Dugan, Mark, 1939–
    The making of legends : more true stories of frontier America / by
Mark Dugan.
        p.   cm.
    Includes bibliographical references and index.
    ISBN 0-8040-0995-3 (cloth : alk. paper). — ISBN 0-8040-0996-1
(pbk. : alk. paper)
    1. Frontier and pioneer life — West (U.S.) — Anecdotes.   2. Frontier
and pioneer life — United States — Anecdotes.   3. West (U.S.) —
History — Anecdotes.   4. West (U.S.) — Biography — Anecdotes.
5. United States — History, Local — Anecdotes.   I. Title.
F596.D75   1997   97-4096
978—DC21   CIP

*This book is dedicated to
Kim Andersen Cumber and Sanna Gaffney,
for it is part of them too.*

CONTENTS

List of Illustrations . . . . *ix*

Acknowledgments . . . . *xv*

INTRODUCTION

The Making of Legends 1

CHAPTER I: PENNSYLVANIA
[David Lewis]

Robin Hood of the Cumberland 17

    PART ONE: The Times 17

    PART TWO: The Man 20

    PART THREE: The Legend 36

    PART FOUR: The Aftermath 55

CHAPTER II: NORTH CAROLINA
[Keith and Malinda Blaylock]

Petticoats and Poison Ivy 59

CHAPTER III: TEXAS
[The Hamilton Whites, Father and Son]

Making of an Outlaw 89

CHAPTER IV: CALIFORNIA
[Harvey Bell Mitchell]

Child's Play 102

CHAPTER V: SOUTH DAKOTA
[Laughing Sam Hartman]

Vengeance Is Mine . . . Saith the U.S. Court 108

CHAPTER VI: IDAHO
[Wyatt Earp]
Stampede to Coeur d'Alene 127

CHAPTER VII: OREGON
[Z. G. Harshman]
Golden Eagles and Railroad Ties 145

CHAPTER VIII: NEBRASKA
[The Herron Brothers]
The Bandits' Burlesque 164

CHAPTER IX: INDIANA
[The White Caps]
Matters of Moral Regulation 173

CHAPTER X: WYOMING
[The Powells]
A Legacy of Malice 184

CHAPTER XI: MONTANA
[The Whitney Brothers]
The Ones Who Got Away 213

Notes 237
Index 261

ILLUSTRATIONS

INTRODUCTION

Prominent Confederate guerrilla leaders in Missouri during
the Civil War. 5

Jesse James in 1874 and Frank James c. 1870 7

The outlaw Youngers: Cole, Jim, John, and Bob 9

The well-known photo of Billy the Kid taken in 1880 11

A recently discovered photo probably of Billy the Kid. 11

Butch Cassidy, from the famous "Wild Bunch" photograph 13

Photograph of the Sundance Kid and Etta Place taken in
New York City in 1901 13

Sundance Kid, Etta Place, and Butch Cassidy at their ranch
in Cholila c. 1903 14

CHAPTER I: PENNSYLVANIA

Excerpt from the original 1813 espionage trial of Philander
Noble. 25

Excerpt from the 1816 counterfeiting trial of David Lewis 32

Walnut Street Prison in Philadelphia. 34

Governor William Findlay of Pennsylvania. 35

Charles Huston, defense attorney for David Lewis during his
1816 counterfeiting trial in Bedford County. 35

Bedford courthouse and jail as it looked when David Lewis
escaped in 1819. 40

The Chambersburg jail, scene of David Lewis' final escape, as
it appears today 44

Grave of David Lewis' mother, Jane Dill Lewis, near Benezette,
Elk County, Pennsylvania; the Lewis plot in the Milesburg
Cemetery. 52

Milesburg Cemetery 53

CHAPTER II: NORTH CAROLINA

Tintype of William "Keith" Blaylock taken around 1859. 60

William McKesson "Keith" Blaylock, mid 1870s, and
Malinda Blaylock, late 1870s 62

The Tom Henley house as it appears today 74

Gravesite of Austin Coffey in Coffey's Gap, North Carolina 74

Tombstone of John Boyd, killed by Keith Blaylock, in the
Talbot Cemetery 77

Pardon of William (Keith) Blaylock for the murder of
John Boyd in 1866 80

Last photo of Malinda Blaylock, with granddaughter
Ethyl Blaylock, taken in 1902 81

Blaylock house in Montezuma (2 views) 83

Grave of Malinda Blaylock in the Montezuma Cemetery 84

Tombstone of Keith Blaylock's mother, Mary Coffey 86

Tombstone of Keith Blaylock's second wife,
Martha Jane Hollifield Blaylock 86

Tombstone of William McKessen "Keith" Blaylock in the
Montezuma Cemetery 88

CHAPTER III: TEXAS

A possible photograph of young Ham White taken by
H. R. Marks in April 1877 91

Letter dated July 5, 1867, regarding the death of
Hamilton White II 95

Site of the murder of Ham White's father, Hamilton White II,
on Green's Creek in Bastrop County, Texas 96

The White family cemetery near Cedar Creek, Bastrop
County, Texas 96

San Quentin Prison photograph of Ham White, as
Henry Miller 99

Reward Proclamation for Ham White, 1875 100

CHAPTER IV: CALIFORNIA

Concord Coach, of the type Harvey Mitchell robbed near
Geyserville 104

Indictment against Harvey Bell Mitchell for the stage robbery
near Geyserville on December 25, 1871 106

CHAPTER V: SOUTH DAKOTA

Main Street in Deadwood, June 15, 1876, about the time
Laughing Sam arrived there. 112

Deadwood, c. 1877 113

Harry "Sam" Young, c. 1915 115

Only known photo of Clark Pelton. 122

Detroit House of Corrections in 1881 122

Letter in support of Laughing Sam Hartman's pardon from
U.S. Attorney Hugh Campbell to the U.S. attorney general . . . 124

Application for pardon of Laughing Sam Hartman 125

CHAPTER VI: IDAHO

Wyatt Earp in 1885; Josephine Marcus Earp in 1880;
James Earp in 1881; and Warren Earp in 1888 130

Virgil Earp in 1885 and Morgan Earp in 1880 131

Coeur d'Alene mining district about the time the Earps
were there in 1884 (Two photos) 133, 134

Map of the Coeur d'Alene mining district around 1910 137

Certificate of Sale levied November 10, 1884 on
Wyatt Earp's property in Eagle City, Idaho 143

CHAPTER VII: OREGON

Photograph of the Harshman family taken in Centralia,
Washington, in late 1892 or early 1893 148

Pinkerton's National Detective Agency's reward poster for
the arrest of Bill Miner for the Portland, Oregon train robbery
on September 23, 1903 155

Bill Miner at the time of his capture for train robbery in
British Columbia in May 1906 156

Charles Hoehn after his arrest for the train robbery near
Portland, Oregon in October 1903 158

Oregon State Prison photograph of Charles Hoehn taken in
November 1903. 158

Z. G. Harshman after his arrest for train robbery near
Portland, Oregon in September 1903 159

Oregon State Prison photograph of Z. G. Harshman taken
in November 1903 159

Photograph of Z. G. Harshman taken around 1913. 160

Z. G. Harshman at age 79 162

CHAPTER VIII: NEBRASKA

Nebraska State Prison photo of J. A. (John A.) Herron;
Nebraska State Prison photo of V. (Charles Velson) Herron . . . 165

Bill of Information for train robbery charges against the
Herron brothers. 169

Items used by the Herron brothers during their train robbery
near Arabia, Nebraska in 1890. 170

Sheriff David Hanna in his later years. 170

Receipt from the Nebraska State Penitentiary to
Sheriff David Hanna for delivery of J. A. and V. Herron. 171

CHAPTER IX: INDIANA

James Deavin and Charles Tennyson;
Scene of the lynching on June 12, 1889 177

William and Sam Conrad and their mother, Betsey Conrad . . . 179

The five members of the White Caps who died during
their vigilante raid on the Conrad cabin 181

CHAPTER X: WYOMING

Tom Horn in jail in Cheyenne in 1903. 186

Laramie County Marriage License for Fred and Mary Powell,
dated December 23, 1882. 187

Judgment against Fred Powell in 1894 190

Coroner's Jury verdict in the death of Fred Powell 192

Charges of Burglary against Mary Powell in 1897 198

Information in the 1910 case against Mary Powell for arson . . . 200

Transcript of the justice docket in the 1910 case against
William Powell and William Frazee for stealing livestock 204

Headlines in the January 7th issue of the *Wyoming State
Tribune–Cheyenne State Leader*. 210

Mary Powell in the late 1930s. 211

CHAPTER XI: MONTANA

Hugh and Charley Whitney, c. 1909–1910 215

Charlie Manning, c. early 1900s. 217

Wanted Poster for Hugh Whitney. 221

State Bank of Cokeville, Wyoming, robbed by Hugh and
Charley Whitney on September 11, 1911. 225

Wyoming State Penitentiary photograph of
Albert "Bert" Dalton 227

Hugh Whitney, Charley Whitney, and their cousin,
Clarence Stoner, c. 1909. 232

Newspaper photo of Hugh Whitney, c. 1911 232

Wyoming Governor Frank A. Barrett and Charley Whitney
at Whitney's voluntary surrender on June 18, 1952 235

Tombstone of Charley Whitney in the Whitefish Cemetery . . . 236

ACKNOWLEDGMENTS

Great effort has been taken to ensure the accuracy of this book. Years were spent in researching and hunting down leads, bits of data, old records and photographs. In every stage of this endeavor I received the kind help of many individuals and to each of them I would like to offer my sincere gratitude.

CALIFORNIA: John Boessenecker, San Francisco; Bill Secrest, Fresno; Joseph P. Somora, California State Archives, Sacramento; Robert Olsen, Pico Rivera; Jocelyn A. Moss, Marin County Free Library, San Raphael; Laura L. Smith, Office of the Mendocino County Clerk, Ukiah.

IDAHO: Judge Richard Magnuson, Wallace; Sarah Morris, Leadville Public Library, Leadville, Colorado.

INDIANA: Dan Bays, Corydon Public Library, Corydon; Martha Wright, Indiana State Library, Indianapolis; Staff, New Albany/Floyd County Public Library, New Albany; Madeleine Noble, Wooster, Ohio.

MONTANA: Elizabeth Jaycox, Idaho State Historical Society, Boise; Grove Koger, Boise Public Library, Boise, Idaho; Larry Pointer, Billings, Montana; Jim Dullenty, Hamilton, Montana; Jean Brainerd and Cindy L. Brown, Wyoming State Archives, Museums, and Historical Department, Cheyenne; Linda Thatcher, Utah Historical Society, Salt Lake City; Patricia Yates, Saskatoon Public Library, Saskatoon, Saskatchewan; Arthur and Bernice Robinson, Cokeville, Wyoming; Mary E. Stoner Hadley, Spokane, Washington.

NEBRASKA: Delores Ambroz and Marty J. Miller, Nebraska State Historical Society, Lincoln; Ruth E. Harms, Cherry County Historical Society, Valentine; Peggy Stewart, Clerk of the District Court of Cherry County, Valentine; John B. Greenholtz and Nikki Reisen, Nebraska Board of Parole, Lincoln.

NORTH CAROLINA: Kim Andersen Cumber, North Carolina State Archives, Raleigh; Sana Gaffney, Boone; Betty Burkett, Mike Rominger, Dianna M. Moody, and Suzanne Wise, Belk Library, Appalachian State University, Boone; Edward "Dee" Farmer, Sugar Grove; Lynn and Gail Wilhelm, Blowing Rock; Margaret Farley, Blowing Rock; Sally Collins, Blowing Rock; Rhonda Holifield, Avery County, North Carolina Register of Deeds Office, Newland; Tom Norman and Bertie Burleson, Avery County Journal, Newland; John Hayes, Montezuma; Paul Kardulis, Burnsville; Amy Jones, Caldwell County, North Carolina Register of Deeds Office, Lenoir; Renee Gouge and Patty Young, Mitchell County, North Carolina Register of Deeds Office, Bakersville; Louise Anderson, Burke County, North Carolina Register of Deeds Office, Morganton; Rena Shelton, Marshall; Robert Biggs, Chicago, Illinois.

OREGON: Steven Hallberg, Oregon Historical Society, Portland; James E. Clark, Oregon State Archives, Salem; Wayne Baker, Oregon State Penitentiary, Salem; Walter Kurth, Multnomah County Library, Portland; Chris Childs, Gilliam County Clerk, Condon; Marion Weatherford, Arlington; Sue Miller, Gilliam County Trial Court Clerk, Condon; Lloyd Harshman, Milton-Freewater; Noel G. Harshman, Eightmile; Patricia L. Graham, Parks, Recreation and Cemetery Department, Pendleton; Georgia McNaught, Umatilla County Clerks Office, Pendleton; Barbara Bloodsworth, Morrow County Clerks Office, Heppner.

PENNSYLVANIA: Gladys C. Murray, Centre County Library, Bellefonte; Cynthia A. Drawbaugh, Chambersburg Area School District, Chambersburg; Ned Frear, Bedford Gazette, Bedford; Ward C. Childs, City of Philadelphia, Department of Records, Philadelphia; Bill Lind, Military Branch, National Archives, Washington, D.C.; William S. Crumlish, Fayetteville, North Carolina. A substantial amount of the research and information amassed regarding David Lewis is due to the diligence of the Centre County Library in Bellefonte, Pennsylvania.

SOUTH DAKOTA: Linda Sommer and Laura Glum, South Dakota Historical Society, Pierre; Peggy Dobbs, Hearst Free Library, Lead; Delores Ambroz, Nebraska State Historical Society, Lincoln; Mary Lou Anderson and Terry Harmon, Kansas State Historical Society, Topeka, Kansas; Alice Dalligen, Detroit Public Library, Detroit, Michigan; Rebecca Stuhr, Kansas University Library, Lawrence; Jean Brainerd, Wyoming State Archives, Museums, and Historical Department, Cheyenne; William E. Lind, Military Services Branch, National Archives, Washington, D.C.; Anna L. Vasconcelles, Illinois State Archives, Springfield.

TEXAS: Donaly Brice, Texas State Archives, Austin; Reverend Kenneth Kesselus, Calvary Episcopal Church, Bastrop.

WYOMING: Jean Brainerd, Cindy L. Brown, and Paula West Chavoya, Wyoming State Archives, Museums, and Historical Department, Cheyenne; Ellen Mueller, Cheyenne.

In closing, this work could never have been concluded without the support and encouragement of my wife Sarah.

The Making of Legends

ONLY IN AMERICA has history been pervaded by so many colorful legends based on actual flesh-and-blood characters. The most prominent legends are about those who broke the law, the ones who robbed and killed, which raises the question: Why and how could remorseless killers, robbers, and outlaws, who flourished in the American West during the 1800s, gain such fame throughout the following century, and inspire publishers and the movie and television industries to recreate their fictional careers over and over again?

The core of the answer lies in an examination of the social, economic, and political conditions that existed in the United States during the 1800s. When Leland Stanford pounded in the gold-headed spike at Promontory Point, Utah on May 10, 1869, joining the Central Pacific and the Union Pacific Railroads, the fate of the small farmer and businessman and of the laboring class was sealed. President Ulysses S. Grant's Republican administration gave railroad promoters twenty-three million acres of land and sixty-four million dollars in easy loans. From this point, big business became king, and a select few would earn the title of "robber baron."

In the east the Tweed ring stole over two hundred million dollars from the state of New York. In Washington, D.C., Grant's cabinet and Congress were riddled with corruption. Many of these politicians were connected with the Credit Mobilier Company, Union Pacific's construction company, which siphoned off twenty-three million dollars from the U.S. Treasury. In 1873, Vice President Schuyler Colfax squelched a probe into the company's activities after receiving bribes.

Also in 1873 came the Wall Street Panic, a depression that lasted six years. The major cause was the bankruptcy of robber baron Jay Cooke's banking firm, which overextended its promotion of the Northern Pacific Railway. Over twenty-three thousand small businesses were wiped out. The only winners were the big corporations, which bought up the failed businesses for a song. The "crime of 1873" was the passage of general revisions of the coinage laws demonetizing silver by Congress.

A provision prohibited silver from being freely coined, an act designed to injure the farmer and debtor classes in the west and south.

There was a national slump of farm prices; wheat fell from $1.50 to 67¢ a bushel, corn from 75¢ to 38¢ a bushel, and cotton from 31¢ to 9¢ a pound. The Grange, a secret society designed to act politically for farmers, was founded. The Grange attacked the railroad monopolies, which had initially brought in the small farmers and then charged them such excessive freight rates that profit was nonexistent. Many lost their farms, which were then taken over by the railroads and the process was repeated.

In July 1877, the Baltimore and Ohio Railroad cut wages by 10 percent, the third wage cut in as many years. Workers went on strike, and the Maryland militia marched on the strikers in Baltimore, fired on a hostile crowd, and killed twelve people. The strike spread to Pittsburgh, where the Pennsylvania Railroad had also cut wages. Fifty-seven strikers and soldiers were killed and three million dollars worth of railroad property was destroyed.

The 1880s were just as bad. Statements like, "Law? What do I care about law. Hain't I got the power?" from Cornelius Vanderbilt, and "The public be damned!" from Vanderbilt's son William Henry, helped fan the flames of public dissent. In 1887, the Farmer's Alliance was formed to improve farming conditions through social and legislative actions. This movement evolved into the Populist Party. After years of complaints against the railroads, Congress reluctantly formed the Interstate Commerce Commission in 1887, a government board created to regulate private business and prevent rate discrimination. However, railroad lawyers and the federal courts hampered the commission so effectively that by 1895 it was all but defunct. In addition severe droughts and blizzards in 1886 and 1887 brought the small western farmers and ranchers to their knees.

The "Gay Nineties" is a misnomer; reform efforts were just as ineffective as in the previous two decades. In 1890, Congress passed the Anti-Trust Act, intended to prohibit monopolies from restraining free trade. Adverse court actions rendered the act impotent. The Billion Dollar Congress of 1890 paid off big business by raising tariffs, which raised freight rates, which raised consumer prices, which brought an immense outcry throughout the entire country. People saw the government in bed with big business, and demonstrated their aversion to government at all levels.

In the elections of 1890, the Populists reached their zenith. Their platform proclaimed that organized big business, especially the railroads, was sucking the country dry through monopoly prices, exorbitant railroad rates, and tariffs. The election wrecked the Billion Dollar Congress, and Republicans were swept out of power. The new House had two hundred and thirty-five Democrats, many of whom were tinged with Populism, and only eighty-eight Republicans.

In 1893 the U.S. suffered another depression, one that President

Grover Cleveland blamed on the 1890 Silver Purchase Act, which had mandated that gold be used to buy silver while the rest of the world was on the gold standard. The farmers and silverites opposed Cleveland's efforts to maintain the gold standard. As a result, there was less money circulating in 1890 than when the Civil War ended in 1865, even though the population had doubled and business had tripled.

By 1894, the common man had reached rock bottom. The depression took its toll. Laid-off railroad workers in the west trudged their way east, threatening to march on the capitol. As many as 750,000 went out on strike, essentially for better wages. The straw that broke the camel's back occurred in late 1893, when the Pullman Palace Car Company took advantage of the depression, laid off most of its employees, and hired them back with wage cuts up to 25 percent. The workers went on strike, and in May 1894, President Grover Cleveland ordered regular army troops to Chicago to enforce a federal injunction against the strikers. In the end, twelve strikers were killed and the strike was broken. Similar occurrences would plague the American people for nearly twenty more years. The sad result of this is that in 1900, when the population of the United States was sixty-three million people, eleven million out of twelve million families were living on $380 a year.[1]

The general consensus regarding railroad companies was summed up very well a decade later by Canadians in Victoria, British Columbia, the neighboring big city to Seattle. Bill Miner, an old-time stagecoach and train robber, had been convicted for train robbery, and the popular joke was, "Oh, Bill Miner is not so bad, he only robs the CPR [Canadian Pacific Railroad] once every two years, but the CPR robs us every day."[2] This kind of attitude created the folk hero mantle now worn by the bank and train robbers of America.

The most consequential reason why America's criminals became at the same time its heroes, however, lies within America's social realm. For the most part the American people of the nineteenth century were members of isolated communities, receiving their news primarily from local newspapers. Following the newspapers religiously, the people basically accepted what they read, and grouped themselves accordingly. These newspapers, by unconsciously fanning the flames through biased commentaries, prejudiced the beliefs of the laboring people and must shoulder the blame for helping elevate the criminals of the American West into folk heroes.

Nevertheless, America had one saving grace that other countries lacked: space—the great American frontier. Those stalwart people who, fed up with political and industrial manipulation, accepted the hardships and headed into the distant west, became legendary themselves. Those left behind to work for paltry wages in the crowded cities and for long, backbreaking hours on farms found an outlet for their frustrations—the dime novel. They could read, and imagine themselves in the free, open West, bravely facing the hazards of the frontier. These thrillers, nothing more than fictional hype, glorified the lives of not only the frontiersmen, but the notorious bandits and gunmen of the West. This trend has been carried over into today's mediums of film and television, keeping alive these legendary idols, and the most revered are Jesse James, Billy the Kid, and Butch Cassidy and the Sundance Kid.

The genesis of the Jesse James saga occurred on March 2, 1820. On this day Congress passed the Missouri Compromise, permitting Missouri to become a state that allowed slavery north of 36°30′ north latitude, but mandating that west of the Mississippi River slavery would only be lawful south of the same latitude. Missouri stuck out like a sore thumb, hemmed in from the north and east by free states. The passage of this agreement, twenty-seven years before the birth of Jesse James, led to considerable strife and bloodshed.

Nearly thirty-four years later, on May 30, 1854, when Jesse James was six years old, the next scene of this saga was enacted with the passage of the Kansas–Nebraska Bill. Both of these future states were admitted to the Union as territories; this was a breech of the Missouri Compromise, however, as it left to each of these territories the settlement of the slavery question within its borders. Since Nebraska was basically uninhabited it would not be a fundamental factor in the coming conflict, but Kansas was another matter entirely. If Kansas were to reject slavery, Missouri would then be completely surrounded by free states, and the residents of Missouri did everything they could to prevent this. The following seven years preceding the Civil War would leave both Kansas and Missouri drenched in blood over this issue, giving credence to the assertion that for residents of both states the Civil War did indeed commence in 1854.

Following the declaration of the Civil War two significant events took place that would enhance the legend of Jesse James: the Lawrence, Kansas, raid of August 21, 1863 led by Confederate guerrilla Captain William Clark Quantrill, which left the town in ashes and over one hundred and fifty dead, and the Union's military retaliatory Order No. 11.

There were two basic reasons for the Lawrence raid. First was a payback for the sacking of Osceola, Missouri, on September 22, 1861 by a company of Kansans under the leadership of James H. Lane, resulting in the execution of nine men, property loss in the amount of a million dollars, and the burning of the entire town. The second reason was General Order Number 10, issued on August 18, 1863, from Union General Thomas Ewing's military headquarters in Kansas City, Missouri, which stated in part: "Such officers will arrest, and send to the district provost-marshal for punishment, all men (and all women not heads of families) who willfully aid and encourage guerrillas. . . . The wives and children of known guerrillas, and also women who are heads of families and are willful engaged in aiding guerrillas, will be notified by such officers to remove out of this district and out of the State of Missouri forthwith."

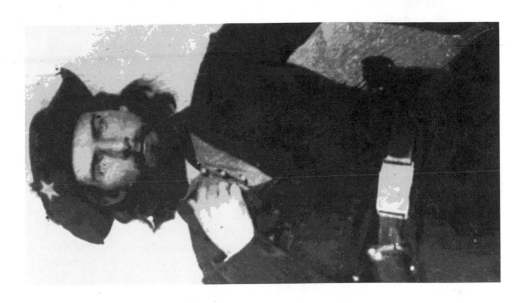

The most prominent of the Confederate guerrilla leaders in Missouri during the Civil War were (left) Captain William Clark Quantrill and (right) Lieutenant William "Bloody Bill" Anderson. Frank James and Cole and Jim Younger rode with Quantrill while Jesse James rode with Anderson. AUTHOR'S COLLECTION

This edict was just a slap in the face following what the Confederate guerrillas felt was the principal justification for the raid. In the spring of 1863 General Ewing began arresting wives, mothers, and sisters of the Missouri guerrillas. By August, eleven women were confined in a ramshackle building on Grand Avenue in Kansas City, which had been reported to the general as unsafe around August 12. Either Ewing was careless, or he deliberately ignored the warning, or, as some reports have it, he allowed the structure to be undermined, for on August 14 the building collapsed. Five women died and several were seriously injured, one of whom, a sister of guerrilla Bill Anderson, was crippled for life. This sealed the fate of the town of Lawrence, Kansas.

Four days following the Lawrence raid General Ewing issued General Order No. 11, an act that would complete the ruin of western Missouri. The order forced all people in Jackson, Cass, Bates, and half of Vernon County who lived more than a mile from Union military posts to leave their homes within fifteen days. As the order was being enforced, all houses, food, stored crops, and forage were burned. The arson was so complete that for hundreds of miles only soot-covered chimneys could be seen. The section was known for years as the "Burnt District." Union soldiers so abused the citizens of Jackson, Lafayette, and Henry Counties that the area was removed from Ewing's District of the Border and put under the aegis of the Central District commanded by Colonel Egbert Brown. The callousness of Ewing's order and his ensuing acts fanned flames of hatred and dissent in the minds and hearts of Missourians, and insured the quixotic adulation of Jesse Woodson James.[3]

For nearly a decade following the war, the vehement anti-southern rule of the Radical Republicans was dominant. The outcast people of Missouri, especially in the western part, were hard pressed to keep food on the table, let alone have any ready cash. Any rebellious acts against the political or economic structure were lauded.[4]

Both Jesse and his brother Alexander Franklin James, known as Frank and four years Jesse's senior, fought with the Confederate guerrillas, and when the bank at Liberty, Missouri was robbed by fourteen ex-guerrillas on February 13, 1866, the legend began to grow. Whether or not Jesse James was present during this initial robbery is irrelevant, for not only was his name soon linked with the succeeding bank robberies, but his stature as the leader of the "border bandits" was firmly established. The majority of the people of Missouri viewed these robberies simply as a continuation of the war against the north, striking a blow against an economic system that closed them out. Jesse James became their instrument of revenge.

In 1873, coupled with the bribery of Vice President Colfax to squelch a probe into the activities of the Union Pacific Railroad and the commencement of the Wall Street Panic, the nationwide depression caused by overextending the promotion of the Northern Pacific Railway, Jesse James and his gang committed their first train robbery in

Jesse James in 1874.
AUTHOR'S COLLECTION

Frank James c. 1870.
AUTHOR'S COLLECTION

Council Bluffs, Iowa. With fervent anti-railroad feelings of the American populace running rampant, it was pure serendipity.

Jesse and his gang also had help from the Missouri press, especially the editorial commentary of ex–Confederate officer John Newman Edwards. With tongue-in-cheek explications such as the following regarding the 1872 robbery of the Kansas City Fairgrounds, Edwards bolstered the tarnished hero status of Jesse James. In the September 27 issue of the Kansas City *Times*, Edwards called the event, "a deed so high-handed, so diabolically daring and so utterly in contempt of fear that we are bound to admire it and revere its perpetrators."

In mid March of 1874 an event occurred that also stirred sentiment for these border bandits. Jim and John Younger were involved in a gun battle with three Pinkerton's detectives, in which John Younger and two detectives died as a result. However, rumors abounded that Younger's death was a result of betrayal.

By the end of 1874, the Radical Republicans were long gone, a decidedly more sympathetic state government was in power, and Jesse's star began to decline. In January, however, it rose again to shine at its brightest when the Pinkerton's Detective Agency completely discredited themselves, and all other agencies of the law in pursuit of the James gang, in a bungling raid on the James home in Kearney, Missouri. A bomb was thrown into the house which, when kicked into the fireplace by Jesse's stepfather, exploded, killing Jesse's nine-year-old half brother and mangling his mother's right hand so severely that it had to be amputated.

Two months later an unprecedented proposition was introduced into the Missouri House of Representatives: a resolution instructing the governor of Missouri to grant full amnesty to Jesse and Frank James and Coleman, James, and Robert Younger. The resolution portrayed them as gallant and principled regardless of their lawless acts. The resolution failed to gain a two-thirds majority by only one vote.

By late 1876, Jesse undoubtedly realized his status as folk hero was precarious, and that robberies of Missouri banks and trains would not be viewed as gallant and daring. So in September he led his gang away from Missouri into the inhospitable North, and met tragedy and defeat in the renowned attempted bank robbery at Northfield, Minnesota.

Cole, Jim, and Bob Younger went to prison while Jesse and Frank went into hiding in Tennessee. The James brothers resumed criminal operations three years later, but Jesse could no longer count on a gang of dashing, hard-riding, and tight-lipped former Confederate guerrillas. He was forced into recruiting the dregs of the criminal element— petty thieves, drunkards, and dull-witted crooks. Jesse began to suspect everyone of treachery, including his brother, and his paranoia culminated in May 1881 when he killed Ed Miller, a friend since boyhood.

Eleven months later, on April 3, Jesse's fears became reality when he was assassinated for reward money in his home in St. Joseph, Missouri by gang members Bob and Charlie Ford. Jesse's status as a folk

The outlaw Youngers (clockwise from top left): Cole, Jim, John, and Bob.
AUTHOR'S COLLECTION

hero was insured forever. This idolization manifested itself again in October 1882 with the deferential and obsequious treatment of Frank James following his surrender to Missouri Governor Thomas T. Crittenden. This veneration carried over into Frank's 1883 trial in Daviess County Courthouse at Gallatin, Missouri for the murder of a train passenger in an 1881 Daviess County train robbery. The jury members were all Southern Democrats, two of whom were ex-Confederate soldiers, and it took them only three and a half hours to return a verdict of not guilty. The view of Jesse James as a symbolic icon of rebelliousness allowed him to ride high, wide, and handsome for sixteen years without capture, and there is no doubt that he will forever remain America's ultimate legendary bandit hero.[5]

Billy the Kid is undoubtedly the most widely known outlaw in America, if not the world. Unlike Jesse James, Billy the Kid became nationally famous forty-five years after his death, his fame gained in a relatively short period of time during the Lincoln County War, the best known of all the conflicts of the American West.

Billy the Kid, in reality a product of the New York City slums named Henry McCarty, was born in 1859. By 1873, he was living in Silver City, New Mexico with his mother, Catherine, and stepfather, a ne'er-do-well prospector named William Antrim. A year later his mother died and the following year Billy was in trouble with the law and was jailed. Escaping through the chimney, Billy lit out for Fort Grant, Arizona, where he stole horses and then killed a man who was roughing him up. On the run again, the Kid hooked up with an outlaw band headed by Jesse Evans in Lincoln County, New Mexico, in 1877.

By this time, the Lincoln County War was in full swing and Billy joined in, choosing the Tunstall-McSween side as opposed to the Murphy-Dolan contingent, which controlled Lincoln County and was supported by the powerful political machine, the Santa Fe Ring. To summarize, the Lincoln County War was simply a power struggle, with both sides ruthless in their determination to be top dog. Although the Murphy-Dolan faction won the campaign, neither side won the war. The conflict lasted several years, took many lives, and left Billy the Kid as one of the few survivors who chose to remain in Lincoln County.

Now an outlaw with a price on his head, Billy the Kid was finally captured by Lincoln County Sheriff Pat Garrett in December 1880. The following April, Billy was tried, convicted, and sentenced to hang for the ambush killing of Sheriff William Brady, in which he was one of the assassins. Within two weeks, with outside help, the young outlaw escaped from the Lincoln County jail, leaving two lawmen dead. At midnight the following July 14, Billy the Kid was finally hunted down and killed by Sheriff Garrett as the young outlaw entered the darkened bedroom of prominent Fort Sumner resident Pete Maxwell.

The legends and tales extolling Billy the Kid abound, when in reality he was much the same as scores of other cattle-rustling drifters who graced the western frontier. In 1882, in a dual effort to make

A recently discovered photo that experts agree is probably of Billy the Kid. AUTHOR'S COLLECTION

The well-known photo of Billy the Kid taken in 1880. AUTHOR'S COLLECTION

money and to dispel rumors that he had killed the Kid without giving him a chance, Pat Garrett made an attempt to present a fictional account of his life in a ghostwritten book. Garrett's tale has the Kid killing twenty-one men, one for every year of his life, when in reality only four killings can be directly chalked up to the young outlaw. Garrett's book was not widely read, and Billy remained relatively unknown outside of New Mexico.

It was in 1926 that Billy the Kid reached his monumental fame with the publishing of *The Saga of Billy the Kid* by Walter Noble Burns, who borrowed much of his material from Garrett's book. The author's characterization of the Kid as a young, likable rogue fighting the big bad wolf became a best seller. This image appealed to Americans living in the lawless and obstreperous decade known as the Roaring Twenties, when a vast number of the population, in disdain, allegorically joined forces with the ever-warring bootleggers and defiantly broke the laws of prohibition by making their own "bathtub gin." Since then an affinity for the young outlaw has not only survived but has grown, spreading his legend throughout the world.[6]

Butch Cassidy and the Sundance Kid are relative newcomers, becoming legendary following the classic 1968 movie, *Butch Cassidy and the Sundance Kid*. While many actors have portrayed Jesse James and Billy the Kid, who can picture anyone else except Paul Newman and Robert Redford as Butch and Sundance?

The careers of these late nineteenth-century bandits have been well documented in several books; nevertheless, the circumstances of their demise have always been in question.[7] The possibility of their escaping from or not actually being the American bandits shot down by the withering gunfire of hordes of Bolivian soldiers has been the subject of at least two books, one of which, Larry Pointer's *In Search of Butch Cassidy*, is classic in its documentation and believability.[8] However, resolute and persistent research in South America by Anne Meadows and her husband Dan Buck has conceivably solved the dilemma.[9] In February 1901, Robert Leroy Parker, alias Butch Cassidy, Harry Alonzo Longabaugh, alias the Sundance Kid, and his paramour Etta Place sailed out of New York City in a British liner for South America. They settled and ranched near Cholila in the Argentine province of Chubut until late 1904 when they discovered the authorities knew their identities and were again on their trail. They returned to their old occupation: banditry.

According to legend, Butch, Sundance, and Etta Place committed several bank robberies in South America; however, the recent South American research by Meadows and Buck revealed that only two banks were robbed. The first occurred in Rio Gallegos, on the southern tip of Argentina, seven hundred miles from Cholila. In early 1905, under aliases, Butch and Sundance checked into a local hotel in Rio Gallegos, claiming to be representatives of a livestock company looking for land to purchase. They deposited 7,000 pesos in the Banco de Tara

Butch Cassidy, from the famous "Wild Bunch" photograph taken in Fort Worth, Texas in November 1990. AUTHOR'S COLLECTION

Photograph of the Sundance Kid and Etta Place taken in New York City in 1901. COURTESY OF PINKERTON'S INC., VAN NUYS, CALIFORNIA

Sundance Kid, Etta Place, and Butch Cassidy (left to right) at their ranch in Cholila c. 1903. COURTESY OF DONNA ERNST

pacá y Argentino Limitado. On February 13 they withdrew all their money. The next afternoon at closing time they entered the bank armed with revolvers and relieved the assistant manager and cashier of 483 pounds sterling. Fleeing the bank, they mounted their horses and sped off at full gallop.

Ten months later and 1,400 miles to the north they struck again. On December 19, four Anglos, three men and a woman, were observed drinking in a tavern in Villa Mercedes, Argentina. When the bar owner was later shown photos from the files of the Pinkerton's Detective Agency, he identified Butch, Sundance, and Etta Place as three of the bandits. From the tavern they rode their horses two blocks to the Banco de la Nación. Leaving Etta to hold the horses, Butch, Sundance, and a third bandit, likely Robert Evans or William Wilson, entered the bank and jumped the counter. Two of the bandits entered the treasurer's office, firing off four reckless but harmless shots, and the other struck the manager on the head upon entering his office. After picking up 12,000 pesos, the four bandits exchanged ineffectual gunfire with a local citizen before riding off in a cloud of dust.

Following the robbery, the bandits spent some time in Antofagasta, Chile, and then moved on to Bolivia where Butch and Sundance obtained mining jobs. Butch was using the aliases of J. P. "Santiago" Maxwell and James "Santiago" Brown while Sundance was known as H. A. Place, Frank Boyd, and H. A. "Enrique" Brown.

At this point Etta Place disappeared, and has since been the subject of much speculation. Author Donna B. Ernst presents the most probable answer to Etta's identity. Pinkerton's files show that there is a register with her signature as Ethel Place, not Etta, and that she became known as Etta because that is how Spanish-speaking South Americans pronounced her name, being unable to vocalize the "th" sound. Also, Etta was reportedly a prostitute as well as a music teacher; an Ethel Bishop, unemployed music teacher, was listed in the 1900 census as a prostitute in a high-class bordello in San Antonio, Texas, right around the corner from Fanny Porter's house of ill fame, a favorite hangout of the Wild Bunch.

As for Robert Evans and William Wilson, on December 29, 1909, they robbed the Compañia Mercantil del Chubut in Arroyo Pescado, Argentina, and murdered the proprietor, Welshman Llywd Aplwan. The two desperadoes met their end in Rio Pico, Argentina on December 9, 1911 in a shoot-out with a police patrol that reads much the same way as the so-called battle where Butch and Sundance die at the hands of Bolivian soldiers.

Two more robberies were credited to Butch and Sundance. Around the twenty-fifth of May 1908, two Americans held up a railroad paymaster of 15,000 bolivianos at Eucaliptus, a way-station about fifty miles southwest of the mines where Butch and Sundance had been employed. On August 19, the same two bandits struck again near Eucaliptus, relieving the paymaster of the South American Construction Company of an undisclosed amount of money. For Butch, now forty-two, and Sundance, at forty-one, the beginning of the end was only three months in the future.

At 9:30 on the morning of November 4, 1908, north of Tupiza in southern Bolivia, the two aging outlaws held up Carlos Peró, mine administrator of Aramayo Francke y Compañia, for 15,000 bolivianos. They also stole a brown mule, and then let Peró, his son, Mariano, and servant, Gil González, continue on to the mines at Quechisla.

Two days later, at 3:30 P.M., a patrol from Uyuni consisting of Captain Justo P. Concha, Police Inspector Timoteo Rios, and two soldiers, Victor Torres and Braulio Munzon, arrived at San Vicente in search of the Aramayo bandits. At 6:30, the two outlaws, armed and riding mules, stopped at the home of Corregidor (chief magistrate) Cleto Bellot for lodging, and were referred to the house of Bonifacio Casasola, where they requested and paid for beer and sardines. The corregidor then left to notify the patrol. Inspector Rios, the two soldiers, and Bellot then headed for Casasola's house to find out who the two men were.

Soldier Victor Torres was in the lead when the four men reached the doorway of Casasola's house, and he received a mortal wound from the revolver of the shorter bandit, ostensibly Butch Cassidy, who shot twice. After firing a reflex shot with his rifle, Torres ran to the home of Julian Saínz where he died within minutes. Rios fired one round and retreated while the other soldier, after firing twice, went to his lodging nearby, obtained more ammunition, and resumed shooting from the doorway. Inspector Rios also reappeared and began firing into the outlaws' refuge. At the request of Captain Concha, who apparently never joined the battle, Corregidor Bellot rounded up several men. As these men were stationed around the besieged house, Bellot reported that he heard three desperate screams from the outlaw's sanctuary. From this point there was no more shooting except for one shot fired by Rios around midnight.

At 6:30 the next morning, the besiegers cautiously entered the house where they found both bandits dead, Cassidy near the doorway with a wound in his arm and one in his temple and Sundance on a bench behind the door, his arms wrapped around an earthen jug, with several bullet wounds in his arm and one in his forehead. After a post-mortem investigation, recovery of the stolen loot, and an inventory of the outlaw's personal effects, the two outlaws were interred in the San Vicente cemetery. On November 20 the bandits were exhumed and identified by Carlos Peró, his son Mariano, and Gil González as the two men who had robbed them.

So, the battle of San Vicente was not a shoot-out with multitudes of Bolivian soldiers, only two plus a police inspector at the outset. However, the theory that Butch killed Sundance and then himself is more than feasible, unless the official reports were not valid, which seems unlikely with all the witnesses who wrote reports and signed the inventory.[10] But we will always see Butch Cassidy and the Sundance Kid dashing from the jacal with guns blazing into the plaza surrounded by Bolivian soldiers. And, in our hearts, they get away. That is the beauty of legends.

This work is written in an effort to bring reality to the forefront, to present the history of the lawless in its true light. It is not meant to deprecate the legends of well-known desperadoes such as Jesse James, Billy the Kid, Butch Cassidy, and the Sundance Kid, for without their popularity and appeal this book would never have been written.

I. PENNSYLVANIA

DAVID LEWIS

Robin Hood of the Cumberland

PART ONE : The Times

DAVID LEWIS' LIFE OF CRIME spanned the first two decades of the nineteenth century, when central and western Pennsylvania was no more than a wilderness that extended through New York to the Canadian border. Documentation and records for this period are generally sparse; however, in Lewis' case, they are quite extensive.

David Lewis became a folk hero and was portrayed as a Robin Hood in Pennsylvania's Cumberland Valley, where his exploits are still vividly remembered. In all probability, he was the first American bandit/criminal to gain this status. To fully comprehend this phenomenon, it is necessary to examine the social, economic, and political conditions in the United States at this time.

A major concern in the United States during the first half of the nineteenth century was the alarming rise in crime. Although reasons for this can be debated, it appears that there were two underlying causes. The first was the birth of the industrial age. Prior to this, rural towns and villages maintained order through public opinion and communal consensus. According to James Q. Wilson:

> . . . industrialization, far from loosening social ties, actually strengthened them by replacing the lost discipline of the small community with the new discipline of the factory and the public school. Work became regular and not, as in the earlier agricultural and handicraft society, episodic. Economic efficiency required punctuality, industriousness, and

habits of cooperative effort: failure to abide by this new regimen condemned the urban worker to destitution or an inhospitable almshouse.[1]

This same disciplne also created unemployment for those who could not adjust to this regimen. Since they could not return to their former society, which was diminishing rapidly, they turned to another desultory lifestyle—crime.

A second cause was the meteoric rise in the production and consumption of alcohol. The annual per capita consumption of alcohol rose from 2.5 gallons in 1790 to seven gallons in 1810 and, by 1829, to ten gallons. The 1810 U.S. census reported that for a population of seven million, 14,000 distilleries produced 25 million gallons of spirits each year. Not counting beer, wine, and hard cider, this was well over three gallons per year for every man, woman, and child in America. In 1819, an English reformer reported that, even in the morning, one could not go into an American home without being asked to drink wine or spirits. Derisively, the United States became known as the "Alcoholic Republic."[2]

A critical factor in the decline of America's economic stability in the 1810s was the failure of the banking system, which ultimately lead to the first great depression in 1819. Following the expiration of the national bank in 1811, the U.S. found itself floundering in a financial muddle. State-chartered banks sprang up like weeds, flooding the market with uncontrolled currency of uncertain value. On March 21, 1814, the Pennsylvania legislature passed an act that established forty-one new state banks, in addition to the existing four chartered banks. Fiscal regulation rapidly declined.

The new banks issued bank notes that passed for currency and unchartered banks leaped into this muddle and issued their own illegal notes. Specie, or hard currency, was almost nonexistent, inflation drastically lowered land values, and "shaving," or reducing the value of bank notes relative to both the distance from and the comparative strength of the home bank, became commonplace. Author William H. Dillistin quoted this complaint from the August 8, 1818 issue of the *Niles Register:* "What a business is this shaving of the bank notes! But the misery of it is, that the loss falls on the productive poor, to pamper the pride and feed the insolence of the dronish rich." By the end of 1819, fifteen of the new banks had closed their doors, and quite often "shaving" rates lowered note values by 50 percent. The only stable currency was the "City paper," issued by the banks in the large eastern cities.

Following the War of 1812, with the election of James Monroe as president, the Federalist Party named the period "The Era of Good Feelings." A misnomer at best, the bubble burst in 1819 with the arrival of a nationwide depression. Because of the soaring price of American cotton, foreign exporters turned to cheaper East Indian cotton, and the price of American cotton dropped by over 50 percent. Businesses had inflated the market with their capricious expansion of credit, and speculators along with settlers had invested heavily in the purchase of western lands.

The banks jumped madly into this mania of get-rich-quick schemes and enlarged their loans far beyond their means of redemption. As a result they failed and closed their doors. The country's money system collapsed, the East's infant industries shut down, causing mass unemployment, and thousands of settlers lost their land. This chaos created a jubilee period for counterfeiters, and David Lewis was primarily a counterfeiter.[3]

Lewis' rise to infamous renown was due to several factors. The monetary and industrial collapse, coupled with local, state, and national government's failure to rectify the problem, instilled deep distrust in the American people toward corporate industry, the court system, and government regulation and authority. These circumstances worked well for David Lewis, who became a symbol of one who fought a system that had failed and then abandoned the people. However, as with many such men as Lewis, this symbolic role alone could not account for his folk hero status. Following Lewis' death in July 1820, his purported confession appeared in newsprint, vaulting him into the limelight.

In Carlisle, Pennsylvania, a disgruntled newspaper editor used this bogus confession as a political tool in the 1820 election against a gubernatorial candidate he opposed. The confession was undoubtedly written by the editor, and he fanned the flames with statements credited to Lewis such as:

> If there were any class or description in society whom I would sooner have robbed than any other, it was those who held public offices, and under color of law had been guilty of extortion; who had plundered the poor, and cheated the widow and the orphan. Against such workers of iniquity my mind had taken a set, and I was determined never to spare them on any occasion that offered. The groans of the distressed, the cries of the widow, and the complainings of the oppressed rang in my ears, and called aloud for vengeance.[4]

The background of Lewis' confession will be examined in greater detail later, but now on to the life and exploits of David Lewis, known throughout Pennsylvania as "Lewis the Robber."

PART TWO : The Man

NEARLY ALL OF THE EVENTS that occurred in David Lewis' life before 1813 must be taken from his confession. For many years the bulk of it was considered bunkum; however, recent research has unearthed documentation that validates portions of it. This lends credence to the undocumented segment. Usually, legends and early undocumented writings are based on actual events, and in Lewis' case, this confession is all that exists.

David Lewis was presumably born in 1788, the date reported as March 4. He was the last of seven boys and one girl born to Lewis and Jane Lewis. The other children, in order of birth, were: Jacob, in 1774, Thomas, in 1776, Sarah, who married Enoch Passmore, Lewis, Jr., Caleb, Guian, and Henry. David's birthplace is Bald Eagle Valley on the banks of Bald Eagle Creek, about one mile from Milesburg in Centre County, Pennsylvania.[5]

David's father, Lewis Lewis, born in 1736, migrated from Wales to America before the Revolutionary War. He settled in York County, Pennsylvania, where, around 1773, he married Jane Dill, who was born around 1750. By 1774, he had moved to Centre County, where he became the county's first surveyor, and afterward served as deputy surveyor for the territory. In 1788, Lewis Lewis paid a large personal tax in Northumberland County, Upper Bald Eagle Township. Lewis Lewis reportedly died in 1790 of injuries sustained when he fell against a tree. His widow remarried twice, and moved to other areas in Pennsylvania.[6]

David Lewis remained at home in Centre County, working for neighboring farmers until 1806. Setting out on his own, he worked for a while in various occupations and then enlisted in the army through a recruiting party at Bellefonte. Discipline was not Lewis' strong suit, and after a short period he committed a petty offense and was punished by his sergeant. He deserted, and several months later, under the name Armstrong Lewis, rejoined the army for bounty money in Captain William N. Irvine's company of Light Artillery at Carlisle. Deciding again that the army was no place for him, Lewis had a lawyer named Metzgar file a writ of *habeas corpus* to get him out of the army. A hearing was held in Carlisle under Judge John Creigh, who decided against Lewis and remanded him back into service.

This led to a military inquiry into Lewis' background, and his prior desertion was discovered. At this time, rumors of war with England were rife. On June 22, 1807, a British frigate fired on an American vessel, killing several men. President Thomas Jefferson favored a peaceful policy and, in December, issued an embargo against exportation from any American ports. It proved to be a dismal failure, and the cry for war was heard throughout the country. These events worked against young David and he was charged with desertion and double enlistment.

A general court-martial was held under General James Wilkinson at Carlisle, and Lewis was found guilty and sentenced to die. Lewis immediately wrote to his mother for help, and she came to his rescue. Borrowing a horse from Judge Jonathan Hoge Walker, who David Lewis would meet later under different circumstances, Lewis' mother rode to Carlisle and obtained the services of attorneys Andrew Carothers and James Duncan, who tried to procure Lewis' release on the grounds that he was a minor. Judge James Hamilton ruled that civil power could not override a military court-martial. However, through the efforts of Lewis' mother, several prominent individuals interceded on David's behalf, and General Wilkinson commuted his sentence to imprisonment for an indefinite time.

At first David Lewis was heavily chained in his cell, but after a week most of the irons were removed. Somehow, Lewis obtained a Barlow knife and managed to cut the chain so he could quickly remove it later. Lewis was allowed an exercise period each day and, as time passed, he gained the complete confidence of his guard. The day came when the guard allowed his prisoner to exercise by himself, and Lewis slipped off his chain and made his escape. He fled to a cave, known as the Devil's Dining Room and later as Lewis' Cave, until late that evening, when he obtained food and lodging at a nearby house. Lewis then made his way back to Centre County.

The preceding account had been regarded as legend until a case for spying against a confederate of Lewis' named Philander Noble was found in the records of the Bellefonte Court of Common Pleas for the year 1813. The records state, "David Lewis is generally understood and known to have deserted some years ago from the army of the United States," with one witness, William Robinson, declaring, "The old woman his [David Lewis'] mother told me that he had been condemned to be shot but that she had got him cleared."[7]

In Bellefonte, David Lewis soon fell in with a Vermont tin peddler who belonged to a band of counterfeiters that was passing bogus bank bills, and returned to Burlington, Vermont with him. The counterfeit gang was likely led by Philander Noble, with whom Lewis would be closely associated until 1816. Lewis took his share of counterfeit bills to New York where he passed them successfully until he met General Erastus Root. At the time Lewis met Root, the general was campaigning for the reelection of Governor Daniel Tompkins, which suggests that this time period was early 1810. Lewis made a deal to buy the general's horse, and paid him in counterfeit bills. Root passed one of the bills and was arrested and thrown in jail. Proving his innocence, Root and a companion trailed Lewis to Troy. The two men found Lewis and hauled him in front of a magistrate who committed him to jail.[8]

Through the daughter of the Troy jailor, Lewis began a romance with her friend, who was called Melinda in the confession. After a promise of marriage, Melinda agreed to help Lewis escape, and one night the jailor's daughter left the cell block unlocked. Lewis fled the jail, met Melinda, and took her to Albany where they were reportedly married. The couple then fled to New York City where Lewis obtained a room, and then went off to join a gang of burglars and thieves.

Lewis reportedly stole a purse from the wife of John Jacob Astor, and had a falling out with other gang members over the division of the spoils. Packing up their goods, Lewis and his wife left for New Brunswick, New Jersey. Finding lodging for Melinda, Lewis took off for Princeton where he fleeced affluent college boys out of three hundred dollars in card games. This was just before Christmas, 1810.

From Princeton Lewis went to Philadelphia, where he robbed, picked pockets, and came up with a scheme to rob a bank vault. Before he could carry out his plan, Melinda wrote that their daughter Kesiah was dangerously ill, and Lewis returned to New Brunswick. He remained there for four weeks and was off again through Pennsylvania. When he arrived in Stoyestown, Lewis received word from a confederate that his wife was dead. Lewis then renewed his connection with the gang of counterfeiters in the Allegheny Mountains of Pennsylvania.[9]

Whether any of the foregoing is fact will never be known. The Bellefonte Court of Common Pleas, 1813, states that after Lewis deserted the army he "eloped to the said province of Upper Canada, from which place he hath made frequent excursions in a concealed and hidden manner to these States and to this County with persons of Suspicious characters."

From this point, documentation supports most of David Lewis' history. The confession claims that from the counterfeiter's camp in the mountains, Lewis traveled to Virginia to obtain paper for counterfeiting bank notes. This is confirmed by witness William Robinson's statement at the 1813 Common Pleas Court, "D. Lewis said he had been through Virginia." Returning to the counterfeiter's camp, Lewis had a falling out with his fellow criminals and hurriedly left with the spoils during the night.

Lewis then passed through Fayette County, Pennsylvania, where he struck up a romance with a young woman. After leaving for a short period, he returned and married her. This presumably occurred in the latter part of 1811. A man who knew David Lewis reported in an article published in the *American Volunteer*, "He got his wife in Fayette county, Pennsylvania, when he run from there, his brother Thomas went and brought her to his house in the vicinity of Bellefonte, where she remained for a considerable length of time, and was well known there." From Thomas' home, David's wife went to live with his mother. In testimony before the Bellefonte Court of Common Pleas, 1813, witness Aaron Ellis both confirms this statement and gives David

Lewis' wife's name: "Margarate Lewis who lives with Mrs. Leathers says she is the wife of David Lewis."

This period was during the summer of 1812, for David's brother Thomas stated in the 1813 Common Pleas Court, "I saw David Lewis last summer [1812]—saw him down where I live." Another witness, Isaac Buffington, stated, "Saw him [David Lewis] about two years ago last winter [1811]—Met him on the road between Thos. Lewis's and Daniel Billew's Mother's."[10]

There can be no doubt that Lewis then headed for Canada, for some of his actions were unveiled by Philander Noble in his examination trial at the 1813 Bellefonte Court of Common Pleas. Noble, the leader and engraver of the counterfeit ring, was also the mentor of David Lewis.

Philander Norton Noble, according to the *American Volunteer*, was "about 5 feet 10 inches high, corpulent, bald headed, fair hair cut short, about 45 or 50 years of age, is fond of grog, and supposed to be a native of one of the eastern states." In his 1813 trial, Noble claimed he was from Westfield, Massachusetts, and left there for Middlebury, Vermont, in 1803. Here Noble organized the counterfeiter's ring and undoubtedly met and recruited David Lewis. Apparently things got too hot for Noble and he left Vermont in 1810, claiming to have spent the next three years in both the United States and Canada.[11]

The War of 1812 was officially declared on June 18, 1812; however, a detachment of troops under General Henry Dearborn marched from Ohio to Detroit and Fort Niagara on June 1. The confession states that David Lewis hired out to the army to drive a wagon, and it was undoubtedly with this detachment of troops that Lewis headed north toward the Canadian border. At the American camp, Lewis stole both money and property from officers and enlisted men, and then absconded with a team and wagon and headed for the Allegheny Mountains of Pennsylvania where he sold them. From here Lewis headed for Centre County, as reported by his brother Thomas.

David Lewis returned to Canada in early fall of 1812, and undoubtedly met with Philander Noble, who had been there since the summer. Canada was a melting pot for American criminals fleeing the states, causing British General Isaac Brock to write from his Ontario headquarters in early July that Upper Canada was full of "the most abandoned characters who seek impunity in this province from crimes committed in the states."

Apparently the British caught Lewis fleecing the troops or passing counterfeit bills around the first part of October. General Brock vented his wrath on Lewis, threatening to hang him so high from the gallows that he could see his own country from it. The general ordered the sheriff to take all Lewis' money before tossing him in jail at Fort George. General Brock did not live to fulfill his promise to David Lewis. On October 13, six hundred Americans crossed the Niagara

River to occupy Queenstown Heights, but were repulsed by the British. General Brock was killed during this raid.[12]

Lewis languished in jail until the British at Fort George began shelling American troops across the Saint Lawrence River at Fort Niagara on November 16. The Americans responded with their own artillery, resulting in a five-day battle. During the bombardment, the jail at Fort George caught fire and Lewis escaped. He made his way northward along the shore of Lake Ontario until he reached the banks of the Saint Lawrence River across from Odgensburg, New York. Here Lewis met Philander Noble, and the two crossed the ice to Odgensburg in mid February, meeting a confederate named Brown. All three obtained passes from Major Benjamin Forsyth, commander of the American forces, and headed south.

Noble caught the measles on the road, so he and Lewis stopped at the home of Bastion Jones, around fifty miles from Bellefonte. Noble remained at Jones' recuperating while Lewis was absent about five weeks. When Lewis returned to Jones', both men headed to Centre County, arriving there around noon on March 28. About a mile from Thomas Lewis' home, David Lewis gave Noble a note to his wife and then sent him ahead to his brother's house. Within a half hour David Lewis arrived.

Noble gave Thomas Lewis a story about wanting to buy some land in the area, and then went to stay at Lewis' mother's home, telling her he wanted to board there for a week. David Lewis disappeared for about four days. On April 3, David Lewis returned to his mother's house for supper, spent the rest of the evening at his brother Thomas' home, and disappeared again.

David Lewis was fortunate, for the next day Noble was picked up and jailed on suspicion of being a British spy. In an examination trial held on April fourth through the sixth, Noble admitted that he had lived in Canada, had been drafted into the militia, but was released because of his age. He said he took an oath of allegiance to the King of Great Britain, but stated it was an old-fashioned oath that was good only in Canada. He told of his experiences in Canada and with David Lewis, and said his wife had been dead for five years and he had three children in Middlebury, Vermont. Four witnesses, Aaron Ellis, William Robinson, Isaac Buffington, and Thomas Lewis, testified in the trial, but gave no testimony against Noble. The examination records show no further action, so Noble was apparently released without a trial.[13]

David Lewis' actions from April 1813 until September 1815, are unclear. Historian Mac Barrick reports that during 1813 Lewis was in Pine Grove, Cumberland County, Pennsylvania with an accomplice called Crosby Howard, whose real name was Rufus Crosby. Howard and Lewis first convinced a few settlers to pass counterfeit money for them, and then committed a burglary at David Dull's sawmill on Mountain Creek. In 1814, Jacob Cook, a tavern owner in East Berlin, Adams County, became an associate of the two robbers, who apparently headquartered at his tavern.

Excerpt from the original 1813 espionage trial of Philander Noble in the Centre County Court of Common Pleas, Bellefonte, Pennsylvania. CENTRE COUNTY LIBRARY AND HISTORICAL MUSEUM, BELLEFONTE, PENNSYLVANIA

According to the confession, Lewis fled to Virginia to avoid capture. It may have been at this point that Lewis, who later admitted to this, drove a wagon from Baltimore to Charleston where he passed a thousand dollars in counterfeit notes. The *Bedford Gazette* stated Lewis was arrested and later broke jail at Morgantown, Virginia. The confession continued with Lewis heading for Emmittsburg, Maryland, where he stole a horse and fled to Shippensburg, Pennsylvania. He then traveled through Cumberland to Walnut Bottom, near Carlisle. Here Lewis tried to pass counterfeit bills to a store owner named Martin. The owner confronted Lewis with the evidence, and the two men headed for the bank in Carlisle to have the bills examined. When the bank declared them counterfeit, Lewis swore he could prove his innocence through a respected resident of the town. Martin and the bankers foolishly allowed Lewis to go alone in search of his witness and the crafty swindler made his escape.[14]

By 1815, David Lewis was a member of an extensive counterfeiting ring headed by Philander Noble. As previously noted, the Pennsylvania legislature passed an act in March 1814 to establish forty-one state banks, all issuing currency of their own. The market became flooded and the counterfeiting gang took advantage of the situation. The *American Volunteer* outlined the workings of this vast organization:

> The club of counterfeiters, and their regular agents . . . is known
> . . . to consist of upwards of one hundred members [one of the counterfeiters later stated there were only twenty members]—They princi-

pally reside in New York; New Brunswick in the state of New Jersey; Philadelphia, Bristol, Lancaster, York, Berlin, Hanover, Harrisburg, Pittsburg, and in Bedford county, Pennsylvania; Steubenville, Ohio; and Berkley and Fredrick counties in Virginia.

Their paper-maker resides in Virginia. They have on hand an immense quantity of paper, on the following banks, to wit: Five dollar notes of the Elkton Bank, Maryland; tens of the Farmer's Bank of Lancaster; twenties tens and fives of the red impression of the Bank of North America; tens and twenties of the Bank of Maryland; fifties of the Bank of Pennsylvania; hundred dollar notes of the Philadelphia Bank; twenties of the Union Bank of Maryland; fifties and twos of the Hagerstown Bank, and tens of the Mechanics' Bank of New York.

The newspaper reported that Noble engraved most of the plates at Berlin and Pine Grove Furnace outside Gettysburg. The printing was done three miles north of Miller's tavern on Allegheny Mountain in Bedford County. There were at least thirty wagoners engaged in circulating the bogus bills, and the gang employed several "affidavit men" who would "swear off their employers" (provide alibis and testify in court). The gang also had crooked gamblers stationed in taverns across the country. The *American Volunteer* listed the following members of the gang: the principal engravers were Noble and a woman named Tabitha from Upper Canada; James Smith, twenty to twenty-five years old, who signed the notes; Alberson Ward, gambler, from Bedford County; twenty-eight-year-old James Murray, alias James Crawford, of Lancaster County; McGolrick, Gibbs, and Miller, noted gamblers and swindlers; Cela Coal from Philadelphia; Robert Allison, gambler and wagoner between Philadelphia and Pittsburgh; John Dubs, age thirty, associate of Allison; James Rowley, age twenty-five, from Philadelphia; John Osburn and one Casey, circulators for the gang; and Daniel Jones of Harrisburg, an expert at altering bank notes.[15]

Other members of the gang were James R. Reid of Juniata Crossings, a dozen miles east of Bedford; Rufus Crosby, alias Crosby Howard, a fiddler; a gambler named Barker; Pegleg Smith; and two men named Goldsby and Covert. William Drenning and his sons Samuel, William, Jr., and Lewis, who lived in Bedford and were reported as uncle and cousins of David Lewis, were also considered members of the gang.[16]

On September 5, 1815, David Lewis and the gang's forger, James Smith, arrived at the tavern of Michael Miller located on Allegheny Mountain, about sixteen miles northwest of Bedford, and asked for boarding. Lewis was now using the aliases of David Wilson, Phillips Green, David Lewis Wilson, and D. L. Phillips. The pair told Miller they were surveying land. Philander Noble and Rufus Crosby showed up the following day and the four spent the night at the tavern. The next day they set up camp three miles north of Miller's tavern.

On Sunday, the tenth, Noble and Crosby brought a wagon and two trunks and left them in the tavern. During wet weather the four counterfeiters remained at Miller's tavern, otherwise they were at their camp printing bogus bills. On September 26, they left the area heading northeast. Miller later described the camp, "I never was at the camp whilst they were there. . . . Saw it 3 weeks after they went away. It was small saplings built like a house. Open in front. Poles put up as a camp, no chinking. Had been covered with Limbs and Leaves. . . . No bench or table. Poles put up to sleep on. Roof would not turn rain."[17]

By late November, David Lewis began passing the bogus bills hot and heavy in south-central Pennsylvania. He knew that greed would be in his favor as the counterfeit hundred-dollar notes he was passing were "city paper" on the Philadelphia Bank and would not be shaved. Around the twenty-ninth, he passed a hundred-dollar note to a merchant named Anderson at Landisburg. From there he headed south to Newville where on the thirtieth he had another hundred-dollar note changed in Geese's Store by John Piper. On December 1, clerk James Schoaf at Roxbury changed another counterfeit hundred for Lewis and on the fourth he got the same results from Samuel Wallich in Waterford.

On December 10, Henry Weaver, a clerk at Barndollar's Store, shrewdly refused to accept a fifty-dollar note when Lewis tried to buy some cord. Lewis told him to give the goods to another clerk named Taylor and he would pay for it later. On the fifteenth, Lewis had better luck.

Using the alias of Phillips, Lewis bought a black silk handkerchief from shopkeeper Thomas McClellen at McConnelsburg, offering a bogus hundred as payment. At first the shopkeeper was suspicious, but after looking at the signature he thought it was valid and took the bill. Lewis asked for his change in western paper, stating he was going toward Carlisle, and then bought some shawls at a discount, using McClellen's desire for "city paper" as leverage. When Lewis left the store, he headed straight for a tavern.

When David Lewis returned to Barndollar's Store on the eighteenth, Weaver refused a twenty-dollar note Lewis tried to pass. The disgruntled swindler had to pay up with small bills he retrieved from his saddlebags. On the same day Lewis was flanked again when Hugh Denison, who kept the George Washington Inn at Martins (now Breezewood), refused to change a twenty-dollar note. On the morning of the twenty-first, Lewis returned to Martins by stage and met Denison who asked him how he made out with the counterfeit bill. Lewis admitted the bill was bad and jokingly replied that he owed the innkeeper a treat because of it.

The next day Lewis bought a horse from Raney Breathed at the Sideling Hill Tavern, paying the man two hundred dollars in counterfeit fifty-dollar notes. Lewis spent Christmas day at a shooting match at Woodbury, and passed a bogus twenty-dollar note to William Hipple of Morrison's Cove. That evening, at Martinsburg, Lewis met John Lytle, a friend of his brother Thomas. Learning that Lytle was in debt, Lewis gave the man a counterfeit twenty as a gift. The two men then went to a gambling house and afterward spent the night together at a tavern. The following day, in Bedford, Lewis passed a spurious fifty-dollar note on the Hagerstown Bank to a man named Baxter.

On December 26, Lytle used the twenty-dollar note to pay a debt to innkeeper J. H. Bridenthal at Morrison's Cove, who later checked the note and found it to be counterfeit. Lewis and Lytle returned to Bridenthal's later that week and talked about selling a horse to a man named Stewart. After Bridenthal told Lytle about the bogus bill, Lewis claimed the rest of his money was good and had been drawn on the bank at Bedford. Lytle later stated at Lewis' trial: "I am easy deceived in notes, don't handle many notes of large size."[18]

Unknown to David Lewis, the net was closing in fast on the counterfeiting gang. During Christmas week of 1815, John R. Reid was arrested in Hagerstown, Maryland. He confessed that he was a member of a gang of twenty counterfeiters who had at least two hundred thousand dollars in counterfeit money to circulate. Lewis' turn was next.[19]

Around December 29, Lewis stopped at the tavern of Hill Wilson at Bloody Run (now Everett), ten miles east of Bedford. He asked Wilson to either keep his dark bay horse or sell it for $150, saying that the horse could beat any horse in the county in a race. Promising to give the tavern keeper's hostler a dollar to take care of the animal, Lewis left on the outgoing stage.

About dusk on the thirty-first Lewis returned to Hill Wilson's tavern, riding another horse. Entering the tavern, he asked for a drink of gin. Wilson told Lewis the sheriff had confiscated his horse, and Lewis asked, "For what?" The tavern owner replied that he was suspected of passing counterfeit money. Wilson added that John Reid had been captured and confessed, stating Lewis had bought the horse with counterfeit money. Lewis laughed it off, stating he had not bought the horse from Breathed but had borrowed him from a man named Leeper. A tavern patron named Jim Peoples spoke up and said the animal was not one of Leeper's horses unless he just got him. Lewis irately answered that he did not care when the devil Leeper got him, the man gave it to him.

Wilson then told Lewis he was their prisoner, and would have to stay the night, and then told a hired boy to take Lewis' horse and lock him up. Nonchalantly, Lewis asked for another gill of gin, and remarked, "Do you consider that I am the man?" Both Wilson and Peoples answered in the affirmative. Lewis laughed again and said he would give up peaceably, and then added a grim warning that he would kill anyone that laid hands on him. Lewis then took off his greatcoat and asked, "What did you think when I came in?" "I considered you damn safe and pitied your case. I knew you could not get away," bluntly replied Peoples. Lewis replied that no man had a right to touch him without a precept, and asked Peoples what name Reid gave him. The man replied, "A different name." Again Lewis laughed and said his name was D. Wilson, and drolly remarked to the tavern owner, "I am a namesake of yours."

Leaving Peoples with Lewis, Hill Wilson slipped out and rode to Leeper's house, telling the man to find Breathed and the sheriff, Thomas Moore, and bring them to the tavern.[20] Wilson described the scene:

> Mr. Breathed and others came, the Sheriff foremost. [Sheriff] catched him by the wrist and begin to shake him a little. Said [Lewis] was his prisoner.
>
> I told him [the sheriff] not to use him rough, he had given himself up. [Lewis] said yes, more than two hours ago. He let him go. I asked Breathed if [this was] the man. He [Lewis] walked out on the floor, told Breathed to be certain. So did I tell him. Breathed said he was the very man. I had no more to say. I told the Sheriff I gave him up to him.[21]

The arrest of David Lewis is undoubtedly one of the strangest on record. Wilson went into another room while the rest of the men, including Lewis, sat around drinking gin for the next hour. Then the sheriff went to Wilson and said, "I must tie this man [Lewis]," and asked for a rope. Wilson said it was not necessary, but Moore insisted, and the tavern owner gave him a bed cord. Returning to the tavern room, the sheriff asked Lewis if he was armed. Lewis said no, and Moore put his hand in Lewis' pocket and pulled out a dirk. Lewis quickly pulled out a pistol, snarled at the sheriff, "Your life is mine," and snapped the trigger, but the pistol did not fire. A mad struggle commenced, but the men could not bring Lewis down. A man named Fletcher struck Lewis several times on the head with a stick, but still the prisoner continued to fight. Hearing the noise of the scuffle, Wilson grabbed a candle and came running. He gave this account of the fight:

> He [Lewis] had a pistol, in his right hand. I asked why they did not pull him on his face, offered to do so. McDermott and the Sheriff and Peoples held him. I pulled out the left arm. They got his right out and the pistol under him. As I caught him and gave a jerk, his pistol burnt priming.
>
> I asked, why would he shoot me? He said, if it was his own brother, he would kill him rather than be tied. I said [it] would have hit my legs. He said it was pointed upwards.

Sheriff Moore added, "Mr. Wilson came in and caught him by the back of the neck and pulled him down. He said afterward he would have been sorry to have killed me but he was determined to kill any person who would attempt to take him." Wilson finished the story with this classic understatement, "They searched him, found money. I went to bed."

Nearly $1,900 in good bank paper was found on Lewis and he was kept overnight at the tavern. The next morning he was taken to Bedford and, following an examination trial, was bound over for trial and lodged in the county jail. During the trial Lewis stated he was David Lewis Wilson from Philadelphia; however, his identity was verified that day. Lewis' hideout, his uncle William Drenning's house just south of

Bedford, was also discovered on January 1. A search warrant was issued, and according to the *American Volunteer*, "The same evening, suspicion attached to a house in the neighborhood, in which, on being searched, three pair of saddle bags were found, containing a variety of elegant goods."

The newspaper also reported that William Drenning's son Lewis was arrested while another son, William, after hearing of his brother's arrest, made his escape on an elegant horse presumably bought with counterfeit bills. The *Volunteer* stated that Lewis Drenning, like his cousin David, "was examined, and committed for trial."

On January 4, true bills were lodged against Lewis for passing counterfeit bank notes and against William, Sr., William, Jr., and Lewis Drenning as accessories. Lewis' trial was scheduled to commence the next day. A reward was posted for William Drenning, Jr., describing the wanted man as around six feet in height, with sandy hair and light complected, with some freckles on his face. David Lewis and his cousin, William Drenning, were said to look very much alike. The Bedford County Court nol-prossed the indictments against the Drennings in early April because the Philadelphia Bank failed to send proof that the passed notes were counterfeit.

By the end of January, Barker, another member of the gang, had been captured and jailed at Uniontown. The shame was too much for this young man of a good family, and he attempted to cut his throat during his examination trial. When this failed, Barker sang like a bird, confessing all he knew, bringing the heat down on other members of the gang. By June, James Murray, Pegleg Smith, Covert, and Goldsby had been arrested in New York with over $20,000 in counterfeit money, and in Frederickstown, Maryland, Casey had been sentenced to ten years in prison.[22]

David Lewis' case enticed one notable Pennsylvania personage, State Attorney General Jared Ingersoll, who would prosecute along with local attorney, Samuel Riddle. Lewis engaged Charles Huston and George Burd as defense counsel. It was reported that by trial time Burd had filched around six hundred dollars from the defendants. The trial judge was six-foot four-inch Jonathan Hoge Walker, depicted seventy-some years later by local historian and jurist William M. Hall as a man more remarkable for his size than his brains. Ironically, this was the same Judge Walker who lent David Lewis' mother a horse when Lewis was on trial for desertion from the army.

David Lewis was indicted on three charges: (1) on January 4, a true bill for passing counterfeit notes to Raney Breathed on December 22; (2) on February 14, a true bill for passing counterfeit notes to William Hipple, Baxter, and John Lytle on December 25 and 26; (3) on February 21, a true bill for passing counterfeit notes. On January 5, the court continued Lewis' trial on the first indictment until February 13 because of absence of defense witnesses.

When the trial began on February 13, there were twenty-seven witnesses for the prosecution and only four for the defense. The jury wasted no time, for by the end of the day a verdict of guilty on the first indictment was brought in. On the seventeenth, after four days of trial, Lewis was found guilty in three counts on the second indictment, and not guilty on the fourth count, passing counterfeit notes to Lytle. Judge Walker felt it improper to find Lewis guilty on the charge of passing the counterfeit twenty-dollar note to Lytle because Lewis had not intended to deceive him. On February 21, Lewis was found not guilty on the third indictment.

David Lewis was reported to have $1,500 deposited in the Bedford Bank at the time of his trial, and a sizeable amount, if not all, was reportedly paid to his defense counsel, Charles Huston. If so, Huston did his best to earn it. On January 20, Huston entered an arrest of judgment on the two guilty verdicts because the language of the indictment was technically flawed in naming the bank. He managed to get the strongest case, the first indictment, reversed, and Judge Walker charged the jury to find Lewis guilty on the lesser charge of making (uttering and publishing) counterfeit notes instead of passing them.

On February 22, Judge Walker sentenced Lewis to ten hours in the Bedford jail and fined him one dollar on the first indictment. In the second indictment, however, the arrest of judgment was overruled in the first three counts and David Lewis was fined one dollar and sentenced to six years at hard labor in the penitentiary at Philadelphia (Walnut Street Prison). Huston immediately entered an appeal to the Pennsylvania Supreme Court.[23]

David Lewis had no intention of going to prison or waiting out an appeal. At 8 A.M. on February 27, ten days after he was found guilty, Lewis escaped from the Bedford jail. The counterfeiter was last seen when he robbed a traveler on Ray's Hill within twenty-four hours after his escape. Legend has it that he, like Jesse James, then gave money to a destitute widow and, in disguise, joined his pursuers in the chase for the wily David Lewis.

The combination Bedford courthouse and jail was built between 1771 and 1780. In 1906 the *Bedford Gazette* said, "It was an unusually extensive building for that day, being massively constructed of limestone. . . . The jail, with its windowless dungeon for convicts, its cell, looking out into the high-walled yard, for ordinary criminals, and its debtors' prison, with grated window, in front, occupied the lower story to the left of the entrance. The balance of the first floor, to the right, was the sheriff's residence. . . . The courtroom occupied the entire second story. . . . The jail yard, enclosed by a high limestone wall, held a whipping post and a pillory."

Mystery and controversy surround the escape of David Lewis. *Bedford Gazette* editor Ned Frear wrote that Bedford attorney J. W. Sharpe stated, "He [Lewis] could easily have escaped, but his lawyers assured him of an acquittal, and as he did not want to lose the fifteen hundred dollars in the bank, he stood trial." The confession states, "I [Lewis]

Excerpt from the 1816 counterfeiting trial of David Lewis in the Bedford County Court.
CENTRE COUNTY LIBRARY AND HISTORICAL MUSEUM, BELLEFONTE, PENNSYLVANIA

could easily have made my escape from the jail of Bedford, but Samuel Riddle and Charles Huston, Esqs., the lawyers to whom I gave the balance of money to clear me, flattered me with such encouraging assurances of acquittal that I was induced to see it out." This indicates that the Bedford jail was not secure, which is substantiated by an April 13, 1816 article in the *Bedford Gazette* reprinted in the *American Volunteer:* "Until our penny-wise Commissioners shall see fit to erect a stronger jail, and the rulers of our county to appoint more vigilant officers, there is but little use in committing any offender to custody in this county. For the last five or six years we have not heard of any person being detained in our prison, contrary to his wish."

Regarding Lewis' escape, one account has him cutting through the oaken floor and burrowing under the walls while another points to collusion. Following Lewis' break for freedom the *Gazette* reported, "No doubt can exist but that the doors were thrown open, and assistance was given in cutting the irons." On April 13, the same newspaper explicitly blamed the sheriff and his staff for the escape, "David Lewis, who was lately convicted in this place and sentenced to the cells, and afterwards let out of prison by some one or more of those who had charge of him." The sheriff was in control of the $1,900 confiscated from Lewis plus the loot found at the Drenning's house.[24]

Two days following the the escape, Sheriff Moore offered a three-hundred-dollar reward for Lewis. These specifics were given:

> Lewis has frequently visited the principal cities of the Union, and has been long engaged in passing counterfeit money. He has passed by the names of Wilson, Phillips, Green, and Irwin, and once drove a waggon between Baltimore and Charleston, and, according to his own account, distributed upwards of $1,000 of counterfeit paper in the course of his trip. . . . It is probable that he will make for Kentucky or Orleans, as it is understood that [James] Smith and others of his fraternity have gone in that direction, with a large supply of counterfeit paper.
>
> The manner of his escape from the county, is at present the subject of legal investigation, and it is hoped that whoever may have aided in it will be brought to justice.

According to Frear, Bedford lawyer Joseph Morrison wrote the following to a Harrisburg friend, John Tod, "This morning at eight o'-clock Lewis the Money Man took his departure from Smithburg [the jail] by way of Larry Harmin's and past the spring toward the hill without molestation. Although seen by several—myself, Larry, and Mrs. Harmin among the rest—How he got the instruments to take off his irons is not yet fully ascertained." A week later, Morrison wrote Tod, "Though no one individual is charged with the crime of liberating him yet strong suspicions are founded against your friend Betsy Ray." (This person has not been identified.) Morrison added, "Your man John Young has been in town several times after the money the sheriff had collected [from Lewis and the Drenning house] but has not got it yet." Morrison would also drop this bombshell, "Dr. Anderson and Sheriff Moore had made a large trade. Moore was to give him 35,000 dollars for the Sprinkleburg property and his property in this place to boot—afterwards however Moore was persuaded by his friends to get a real bargain out of the Doctor which he says he accomplished, the only thing which saved his bacon from entire destruction." Dr. John Anderson was a large land developer and businessman who bought and sold vast tracts of land. Thomas Moore, who had been sheriff for four years, would soon build and operate the Rising Sun tavern.

Nothing happened for three weeks, so on March 18 the *Gazette* goaded the sheriff:

> Our Sheriff and his party returned some days ago, from the pursuit of Lewis—they heard nothing of him. Nothing satisfactory has been done toward investigating the causes of his escape. This is certainly not as it should be. No doubt can exist but that the doors of the jail were thrown open, and assistance given in cutting off his irons. We blamed the sheriff much for suffering the prisoner to remain so long in our jail, after conviction. He should have been in the penitentiary, in Philadelphia, at the time he made his escape. We trust the affair will be investigated, and we conceive it to be the bounden duty of the sheriff to have it done thoroughly and fairly, so that the guilty may be punished, and the innocent, if possible, cleared.

Presumably, Sheriff Moore then drew up a report that cleared everyone and filed it in the courthouse, where it vanished. That ended the investigation and the search for Lewis. There is no concrete proof that anyone collaborated in Lewis' escape and apparently no one was ever charged with aiding and abetting him in his jailbreak. However, innuendo and circumstantial evidence hint strongly that in exchange for the spoils Sheriff Moore allowed David Lewis to escape.[25]

For nearly three months David Lewis ran free, until about mid May, when he was captured in Ohio. The crafty counterfeiter again managed to escape, only to be captured around the first of June by an alert New York constable who had read a reprint of the April 13 *Gazette* counterfeiter article in another newspaper. Six hundred dollars in gold eagles and half eagles was found on Lewis, so possibly a deal had been made allowing Lewis to keep part of his loot when he escaped from the Bedford jail. Lewis was immediately taken to the penitentiary in Philadelphia.[26]

David Lewis entered the Walnut Street Prison on June 8, 1816, listing his age as twenty-eight. Apparently counterfeiting was not considered much of an offense for it was listed under the Crimes column as a "misdemeanor in passing counterfeit Bank notes."[27]

There are two substantiated descriptions of David Lewis. The first was printed in 1816 in the *Bedford Gazette* and the *American Volunteer:* "He is about 27 years of age, six feet high, slim, straight, and well made; ruddy complexion, large sandy whiskers, sandy or yellow hair cut in the fashion: Genteel in his appearance, easy in his gait, polite in his manners, serious in his conversation, and seldom seen to laugh."

Contemporary drawing of the Walnut Street Prison in Philadelphia, where David Lewis was imprisoned from 1816 until he was pardoned by Governor William Findlay in 1819.
AUTHOR'S COLLECTION

The second, shorter depiction comes from the Walnut Street Sentence Docket: "A white man 5 ft. 10¾ in. high. born in Penna., intends going to the Western Country, by trade a painter, Sandy hair, light complexion, blue eyes."

These descriptions clearly point out that David Lewis was a polished gentleman of his time. He would leave prison a completely changed man. Prisoners confined in American penal institutions in the nineteenth century were not coddled and did not reap benefits from reform programs, they learned to survive—and to change. David Lewis was no exception.[28]

If Lewis had high hopes of an appeal they were dashed on September 4, 1816 when the Supreme Court affirmed the judgment of the Bedford Court. However, David Lewis was not destined to serve out his six-year term. Like most penitentiaries in America at the time, the Walnut Street Prison was overcrowded, and failed to provide industrial occupations for the inmates. This led to rioting in 1817 and 1819, and Lewis used this to his advantage. Apparently he leaked news of the 1819 riot to the prison authorities, for the *American Volunteer* reported that Lewis was "recommended after 3½ years confinement, to the governor for pardon in consequence of his giving information to the keepers, of a conspiracy to break the jail." Because of overcrowding, a general policy of the prison was to offer executive clemency as a reward for good behavior. On September 9, 1819, David Lewis reaped the benefits and was pardoned by Governor William Findlay "in compliance with the recommendation of the Inspectors of the jail of the City and County of Philadelphia." This act would launch the legend of David Lewis and destroy the political career of William Findlay.[29]

WILLIAM FINDLAY.

Left: Governor William Findlay of Pennsylvania, who lost his bid for reelection in 1820 because of his alleged association with David Lewis. Right: Charles Huston, defense attorney for David Lewis during his 1816 trial for counterfeiting in Bedford County. AUTHOR'S COLLECTION

PART THREE : The Legend

IN LESS THAN A MONTH, Governor Findlay would have good reason to regret pardoning David Lewis, for prison had transformed the genteel counterfeiter into a coarse and hardened highwayman. He would launch a crime spree and demonstrate remarkable escape abilities that would equal any dime novel thriller.

According to the confession, Lewis came back to Bedford to get his money from the Bedford bank, but the bankers refused his checks. He then fell in with two villains who persuaded him to become a highwayman. Lewis did take up with two criminals, John M. Connelly and James Hanson, but it was undoubtedly by choice. Both were said to be ex-convicts. If so, Lewis had likely known them in prison, and joined them following his release.

The *American Volunteer* described Connelly as "better than six feet high, not fleshy but weighs 230 or 240 lbs. He has dark hair, little or no whiskers, and not much beard—rather long or lantern jaw'd [jawed], and has a down look. He is an Irishman by birth, but speaks tolerably good English, though somewhat broad."

Judge William Hall claimed Connelly was an alias, stating, "The man's real name was Rumbaugh. He was a large, coarse looking man, of low grade of intellect, and was completely under Lewis' influence." Other sources maintain that Donnelly was his legitimate last name. The third crook, James Hanson, was a much smaller man, but was also reported to be an Irishman.[30]

David Lewis and his two confederates were first seen in Bedford on or about September 27, 1819. They obviously had devised a robbery scheme, and had set up camp about a half mile north of the turnpike on Sideling Hill. They struck six days later. The *American Volunteer* reported:

> Early last week he [Lewis] and two of his associates were seen in Bedford, where they purchased pistols. On Wednesday [September 29] he got into the stage below town, and went to the Crossings [Juniata Crossings]. About two o'clock at night he was seen on the road one mile east of the Crossings. On Thursday he got into the stage between the Crossings and Bedford and rode a few miles. Between that time and Sunday he was several times seen near the place where the robbery was committed.

On the evening of October 2, Pittsburgh merchant John McClelland took lodgings at Christian Reamer's tavern at the bottom of Sideling Hill in Bedford County. As there was no bank exchange system, McClelland was carrying $1,500 to Philadelphia. The confession stated that Connelly and Hanson had traced McClelland from Pittsburgh to Bedford, and knew he was carrying considerable currency. The next morning, on horseback, McClelland took the turnpike on Sideling Hill. Around 9 o'clock he observed a man walking ahead of him. As McClelland started to pass him, the man suddenly turned, drew a pistol, and told the merchant to stand and deliver his money. Just as the victim started to hand over his money, two men rushed from the side of the turnpike. Sighting a man and a woman on the path, Lewis and Hanson quickly pulled McClelland off his horse and dragged him a short distance into the woods. Connelly jumped on McClelland's horse and rode up the hill into the woods. Pointing their cocked pistols at the merchant, the two robbers forced him to lie down, swearing they would send him to eternity if he moved or uttered a word. They need not have worried, for the couple on the turnpike were too intoxicated to notice anything.

The highwaymen then marched McClelland to their camp, where the hapless merchant observed a hut, a fire, a pot, and a wagoner's bucket. Here the robbers rifled his saddlebags, and took from him his watch, some clothing, and $1,500 from his letters. Hanson then proposed killing McClelland, but Lewis and Connelly opposed this. Around 3 P.M., the three robbers left the hut, ordering the merchant, on threat of death, not to look out or leave the hut until sunset. The *Volunteer* reported:

> After the robbers had gone a short distance from the hut, the leader [Lewis] returned—told him they were going to attack the mail stage, and gave back to Mr. M'C. his watch and thirty dollars, and said that if they had good luck they would return him his money. Some time after their departure, Mr. M'C. ventured out, mounted his horse and galloped to the turnpike road, and gave the alarm at the first tavern. Several of the neighbors well armed, went in pursuit.[31]

From Sideling Hill, the three highwaymen rapidly made their way northeast. In Huntingdon County they passed and greeted Thomas T. Cromwell who was returning from a meeting held in the neighborhood. They then passed James Lockart, who had heard news of the robbery and immediately suspected the three men. Early Monday morning, October 4, Lockart passed the news to Richard Ashman, who immediately got Cromwell and began trailing the robbers. At Shirleysburg they were joined by Patrick McCarey and James Ramsey, and in Mifflin County, Waynesburg residents Ephraim Enser and William Price swelled the ranks of the determined posse.

By the next evening, Lewis and his crew had put quite a distance between themselves and the scene of the crime, and may have attempted another robbery near Linglestown. Somehow Lewis had heard that two maiden sisters by the name of Steen supposedly had a substantial amount of money hidden in their house. Lewis and Connelly, entering the house at night, failed to secure one of the two women, who grabbed a hunting horn and blew it lustily into the night. Soon several neighbors barged into the Steen house only to be threatened and forced to sit on the floor. One man named Hefflefinger was relieved of his rifle. Presently Captain James Cowden and his dogs came plowing noisily through the woods. Thinking a band of men was approaching, the two robbers fled into the night. Unknown to the fugitives, however, the self-appointed lawmen from Huntingdon and Mifflin Counties were right behind them.

From Harrisburg, the *Oracle of Dauphin* gave the story:

> These gentlemen pursued the trail of the three men whom they supposed to be the robbers and who had robbed one or two spring houses in the course of the proceeding night. At a small tavern or dram shop one mile and a half or two miles below Lewistown and 60 or 70 miles from the scene of the robbery, it was ascertained that the three men had taken lodging for the night. Some guarded the house and others rushed in and before the supposed robbers were completely awakened they were secured. No doubt there would have been bloody work had the three robbers had their pistols and knives at their command, which it does not seem they had, though all three were well armed, when traveling there being found in their sleeping room two large light horse pistols, a small one, and two very efficient carving or butcher knives which it is believed were stolen by Lewis and one of his companions out of Mr. Snively's tavern at Snake Spring a few days previous to the robbery.

The rifle taken from Hefflefinger was reportedly in Lewis' possession when he was arrested. That night the prisoners were taken to Lewistown and given a meal. While eating, Lewis spotted a pistol one of the men had carelessly placed on a table. Leaping to his feet, Lewis grabbed the pistol, dashed for the door, knocked one man down, pushed another aside, and sprinted down the street. Price and Enser were right behind him. Overtaking Lewis, Price grabbed him, but the fugitive proved too strong and threw him off. Enser then jumped on the robber but failed to knock him down. Seeing he was evenly matched, Lewis pushed the pistol into Enser's chest and pulled the trigger. When the pistol misfired, Lewis pulled the trigger again, with the same results. Enser then brought Lewis down hard, rendering him senseless. The three robbers were secured in irons and lodged in the Lewistown jail for the night. Legend has it that Lewis told the Lewistown sheriff, "No jail can hold me." Whether Lewis said it or not, it would certainly prove true.

The next morning the prisoners were taken to Bedford by Price and Enser. With nearly all of McClelland's money recovered and the robbers behind bars, the town of Bedford treated Price and Enser to a community supper. Upon receiving the news of the robbery but not of the capture, the embarrassed Governor Findlay issued a three-hundred-dollar reward for the robbers on October 7.[32]

In the early morning hours of October 25, Lewis, his two confederates, and two runaway slaves broke out of the Bedford jail. The two black men were in the robber's cell, and with their help, the slippery prisoners burned out the staples holding their irons, burned a large hole in the prison floor, dug their way through the jail wall into the jail yard, and broke a hole through the wall around the prison yard. At a sink hole near Bedford it took until daylight for them to remove their irons with an ax and a frow (a cleaving tool with a handle at right angles to the blade) that they grabbed from the jailer's woodpile.

Unfortunately for the escapees, a large amount of snow had fallen, hindering their progress, and around 11 A.M. John Reiley and Dr. William Van Lear spotted them in the woods seven miles west of Bedford. Lewis instantly shouted that they would be shot with a rifle if they followed, and then all five escapees ran down a small stream. Van Lear took Reiley's horse and passed the alarm throughout the area while Reiley went for a man named Wertz who had a rifle. As Reiley and Wertz pursued the robbers they were joined by Abraham Kerns and another man. They plunged on over rough terrain for two miles before they captured the two black runaways. Leaving one man with the captives, the others took off after the three outlaws.

The three escapees were climbing a ridge when Reiley caught up with Hanson and ordered him to stop or be shot. "I don't give a damn for you or your militia!" cried Hanson, so Reiley closed in on the robber, warned him again he would shoot, and the tired fugitive gave up. Reiley then took off after Connelly, who had taken refuge on a ledge of rocks. Fearing that Reiley would shoot the outlaw, Kerns climbed up and knocked Connelly off the ledge with a club. The outlaw was then tied up. Lewis was still on the move but the four pursuers were too exhausted to continue. Coming down the ridge they met Joseph Harbolt and a boy named McGibbons. Enticed by the promise of a reward, they each took a rifle and started in pursuit of Lewis. When the jaded outlaw saw two fresh men and their rifles on his track, he turned back and surrendered. The fugitives had run more than seven miles in the snow and crossed a 2,460-foot ridge before they finally ran out of steam.

The escapees were taken to Colvin's Tavern, given refreshment, and put in a wagon and returned to jail by that evening. Bedford citizens met at Thomas Bonnet's tavern the next evening and agreed that two men would guard the jail every night until the robbers came to trial. It proved to be a futile effort, for in less than two months David Lewis made his third escape from the Bedford jail.[33]

That the jailbreak was possible was due to the critical eye of John Connelly, who, according to the *American Volunteer*, "observed a flaw in the point of his bolt, which he forced into the steeple that fastened him to the floor, which he succeeded in breaking off—having got his hopples [hobbles] off, the bolt was a very formidable instrument, and which he made use of, to break every prisoner in the room from their steeples, which held them fast to the floor, except a black man, whose hopples were so carelessly made, that he pulled his feet through them!"

The jailbreak occurred around suppertime on December 16. Any prisoner who wanted to escape was allowed to go, except a man named

McCurdy who had robbed a poor widow. He was locked inside the jail with the jailer and his family. No reason was given why James Hanson did not escape, which indicates that he decided to take his chances in court.[34]

During the January term of the Bedford County Court, David Lewis, in absentia, was indicted for robbery and breaking jail. During this court term, James Hanson was convicted of robbery and sentenced to seven years in the Walnut Street Prison in Philadelphia. It was at this point that the legend of David Lewis and the condemnation of Governor William Findlay began.[35]

In January 1820, the *American Volunteer* reprinted an article from Pittsburgh's *Gazette* that first gave David Lewis the nickname "Lewis the robber" and the mantle of a folk hero/bandit:

> Lewis, the rober [*sic*]—Many little traits in the character of Lewis are spoken of, and prove him to be a man of no common order. With all his villainy, there is something magnanimous in his conduct: there is every reason to suppose, that after Mr. M'Clelland was seized on the winding ridge, he owed his life to Lewis, as the others evinced an evident disposition to murder him. [At the time of the robbery, the *American Volunteer* of October 14 stated only Hanson wanted to do away with McClelland.] Whilst in jail in Bedford, a man of the name of M'Curdy was imprisoned for robbing a poor widow. Lewis made use of this fellow in extracting himself from his irons, but refused to let him escape with his company, swearing that any man who would rob a woman, was not fit to associate with gentlemen! M'Curdy was obliged to remain.[36]

Contemporary drawing of the Bedford courthouse and jail as it looked when David Lewis escaped in 1819. AUTHOR'S COLLECTION

The press would not be so kind to Governor William Findlay. Chief among his detractors was John McFarland, editor of the *Carlisle Republican*. The pardon, Lewis' subsequent crimes, and the reward proclamation played right into McFarland's hands. The *Centre County Heritage* states: "McFarland saw in the governor's embarrassment useful ammunition for the coming campaign. When Lewis obligingly kept the issue before the public eye by repeatedly escaping from jail after repeatedly getting himself caught—McFarland turned Lewis into a symbol of Findlay administration blundering."[37]

The following tirade is typical of McFarland's vendetta:

> Lewis is the same old offender . . . who shortly after his confinement received the pardon of Governor Findlay in 1818 [*sic*], and was again let loose upon society, to plunder and rob.
>
> Alas! We have fallen indeed on evil times when the pardoning power of the Executive is thus ignorantly and improperly prostituted to the dangerous purpose of liberating infamous cut-throats, robbers and counterfeiters, for the sake of acquiring a short-lived popularity, or obtaining the reputation of a false humanity.[38]

There is no doubt that David Lewis had been "let loose upon society." On December 21, he was reportedly seen in Stoyestown, pursued by a large company of men. A week later the sheriff of Indiana County was in Lewistown and stated that Lewis and Connelly were discovered in a house near Pittsburgh, and that Connelly was captured but Lewis escaped by jumping out a window. It was also rumored that Lewis had been shot in the thigh and captured.

According to the confession, after breaking jail Lewis and Connelly proceeded to Doubling Gap in Cumberland County, then to Petersburg in Adams County, and finally to the Conewego hills in York County, where they committed several petty robberies. From there they made their way back to East Pennsboro in Cumberland County, a prosperous German settlement, where they made plans to rob Jonas Rupp, who they heard had gathered a considerable amount of money to build a mill. This is likely factual, for the *Carlisle Republican* reported that during the week of April 10, 1820, the robbers attempted but failed to plunder the house of a wealthy farmer in East Pennsboro, and failed again on the evening of the sixteenth to rob a young man two miles from Harrisburg. The victim refused to dismount and was struck on the head with a stone. His horse became frightened and ran with him a mile before the man recovered.

The confession states that they then planned to rob one Krietzer, who owned a tavern in Cumberland County, but this also came to naught. However, while in Krietzer's tavern, they overheard some of the patrons remarking that a man named Beshore of Good Hope Mills had "more ready money than all of his neighbors put together."[39]

On the night of April 19, Lewis and Connelly attempted to rob Beshore's house. During the preceding three or four weeks they had frequently been seen in the neighborhood, and the *American Volunteer* reported that "from enquiries made by them of the neighbors of Mr. Beshore, concerning his pecuniary circumstances, a suspicion was excited, that they intended to rob him, of which he was informed: it was thereupon agreed, if an attempt was made to rob him, that he should sound a horn, and his neighbors would hasten to his assistance." Apparently that is what happened, although more detailed accounts state that it was Mrs. Beshore who blew the horn and then sat on a trap door, keeping the robbers inside until the neighbors came. During the resulting fracas, Connelly grabbed a rifle and escaped, but Lewis, who was supposedly intoxicated, was captured.

The confession claims that Lewis was tied up and then struck by one of his captors. A footnote reads, "An old resident of the neighborhood, named Samuel Miller, was with the party making the arrest. After they were arrested Miller struck with his fist and kicked Lewis, whereupon Lewis swore that he never killed a man in his life, but if he ever had an opportunity he would kill him (Miller)." The next morning Lewis was taken to Carlisle and locked up in jail. The *Volunteer* added:

> After his [Lewis'] confinement in the jail of this county, which was affirmed by some, to be insufficient, for his safekeeping, he was removed thence on Tuesday morning last [April 25], by Sheriff Ritner, to the jail of Franklin county [Chambersburg], which is said to be the strongest in the state.[40]

The Cumberland County jail in Carlisle, built of stone in 1754 and enlarged in 1790, was sufficient to hold Lewis. However, though the authorities were likely influenced by his record of escapes, others, like editor John McFarland, saw only corruption and political impropriety:

> We have seen it stated in several places, since the apprehension of Lewis the Chambersburg Jail is "the strongest in the state." This is not the fact, for although the good people of Franklin County were pretty well milked of their money during the building of it and although its pretty brick walls and fog heats [steam heating rooms at great expense] are more inviting and comfortable to the luckless tenantry within its gates, yet Mr. David Lewis was ten times more secure in the Jail at Carlisle than in the new jail of Chambersburg. The windows and bars of the Chambersburg jail form no security, for even less expert Jail Birds than Mr. Lewis.[41]

Ironically, McFarland's words proved true, adding to the store of venom that the editor would spew at the system and Governor Findlay. However, McFarland was not the only editorial enemy of Findlay, and his actions shortly after Lewis' transfer to the Franklin County jail would cause him undue problems, as demonstrated by this *Harrisburg Chronicle* article dated May 8, 1820:

> David Lewis has been removed from Carlisle to the Chambersburg Prison, as a place of greater security. What is the use of a secure prison, when William Findlay so liberally exercises his pardoning prerogative?

Shortly after the removal of Lewis to Chambersburg, William Findlay departed on a visit to the same place; to ascertain, we suppose, by his own senses, whether Lewis is so great a rogue as people represent him, or whether he is not a reformed man, since he had the benefit of his excellency's pardon. Should the latter be the case, in the "great man's" judgment, Lewis may expect another pardon after the conviction.

There would not be another conviction, for between midnight and 2 A.M. on May 25 he made his fourth, and final, escape from jail. That evening the jailer, named Leader, had been locking up the prisoners when a fight broke out near the jail, and a woman came screaming for help. He quickly bolted the door, but forgot to come back later and lock it. The *American Volunteer* reported:

> During the day the prisoners had fixed a string over the top of the door, which they had waxed so as to make it concealed in a crack on the outside of the door—on the end of this string was a loop of slip knot, which they artfully fixed up with wax around inside of the staple on which the hasp of the little window is fastened, so that when drawn it would pull out the key, or whatever it was fastened with. This plan succeeding, they unbolted the door through this window. Having thus got to the entry, and having the necessary key, they liberated Lewis. Being joined by this master spirit, they quickly found means to spring the lock of the door leading into the women's apartment—the door leading hence into the yard, and of the gate leading into the street!

One prisoner, a woman, refused to escape and told the sheriff the details. The courthouse bell was rung before 3 A.M., and a search was begun, which continued until the next day. Lewis was the only prisoner in irons, and just after daylight his hobbles, along with a chisel and ax, were found in a pine thicket half a mile from town. The escapees, Lewis, Felix McGuire, John Meyers, a black named Peter Pendelton, and a mulatto named Caesar Rodney, hid all day in a grain field outside Shippensburg. That night, Pendelton, and apparently Meyers, split from the others as they stealthily crossed the countryside to a spot above Doubling Gap where they made camp. The next evening, John Connelly, with arms and provisions, joined the fugitives at the camp. During the night they navigated down the mountain to a cave at Doubling Gap north of Newville. Pendelton was caught but the others remained free.

In Chambersburg, a three-hundred-dollar reward was issued for Lewis, and rewards of twenty-five dollars each were offered for the others. On May 31, Governor Findlay, now doubly embarrassed, offered a reward of one hundred dollars for the capture of David Lewis.

John McFarland was not one to pass up an opportunity like Governor Findlay's visit to the Chambersburg jail just prior to the escape of the notorious David Lewis. The rancorous newspaperman no doubt took great delight in printing this bit of virulent editorialism in the *Carlisle Republican*:

The Chambersburg jail, scene of David Lewis' final escape, as it appears today. AUTHOR'S COLLECTION

Let us ask, why, after Lewis' apprehension and confinement in the prison at Chambersburg, did Governor Findlay pay him a formal visit? If he did not aid and abet his escape from that prison, why did he, through motives of interest or a childish curiosity, lend his countenance to gratify the vanity of this hardened robber? A visit from a Governor! and in a jail too! Why the mere act itself was enough to inspire Lewis with new hopes, new life, and new resolution; and if the Governor did not lend him money and assistance or otherwise effect his escape, he read in the friendly demeanor of his distinguished visitor, at least a partial approbation of his deeds of crime and successful attempts at general jail delivery.[42]

The hideout at Doubling Gap, locally well known as "Lewis' cave," was not actually a cave, but a deep recess under a shelf of rock, with a spring at the entrance, that was well sheltered and capable of lodging five men. It was located 255 feet above the valley floor along Flat Rock Trail. From this vantage point, David Lewis could clearly see the hotel of his friend, Nicholas Howard of Newville. According to tradition, Howard would hang a flag from an upper window if the coast was clear for Lewis and his comrades to come down in the evening to join their friends.

Frear writes that the *Bedford Gazette* gave this report regarding one of Lewis' friends: "The road passes through a gap; a short distance up the mountain on the north side of the road there is a small house, the owner's name Bob or Robert, a small man with two children who entertains Lewis and Co., finds them provisions, etc., and gives them news of the day." This man was undoubtedly Robert Moffitt, and likely the same Robert Moffet [*sic*] who was convicted of stealing a gelding and sentenced to the penitentiary from Cumberland County in 1807. He was still living in Doubling Gap in 1853 when he gave this interesting statement printed in the confession:

When Lewis was here he generally concealed himself in the cave up the Gap. Some rods up the cave is a beautiful spring that breaks out more than halfway up the mountain, which is about sixteen hundred feet high. I frequently visited, and sometimes stayed with him at the cave. We had the stream running from the spring brought to the mouth of the cave. Everything was so comfortably arranged in and about the cave that it was quite a comfortable home. I remained about the Gap and cave some six or eight months, with the exception of a few short intervals. A friend named K____ [Kuhns] lived in the hollow at the sulphur spring, in a small house that he built, and which we called our tavern. We could see his door from the cave, and having an understanding with "our host," we could always tell when there was any danger, as on such occasions he would hang out a red flag. If all was clear, and it was considered safe to come down, a white flag was hung out. There were some persons in the valley who were our friends; one particularly, who was an endless talker, and sometimes talked too much. Lewis was a great favorite with the ladies. Some of them used to furnish us with the comforts of life, and several times visited us at the cave. We had a number of little parties at the tavern, and had great times. A number of the mountain ladies would come, and some of the men, and we would every now and then have a dance. This was the way we carried on whenever Lewis was here. The cave was neatly fitted up, and would accommodate five of us comfortably; there was just that number of us acting together that stayed at the cave. We did not rob in the neighborhood of the Gap, except to get such things as were necessary to live on. We lived on what we got in this way, and what was brought to us. I shall never forget.

On the night of June 15, Caesar Rodney slipped away from the robbers and went home to his wife. On the nineteenth he was caught in Bedford and returned to the Franklin County jail. He was carrying a well-made shotgun, a brass watch, and some clothing, all reported stolen. Rodney agreed to take the officers to the cave, stating that Lewis, Connelly, and McGuire would be gone as they had been talking about robbing a rich man between Doubling Gap and Huntingdon and then escaping to Canada. The *Franklin Repository* continued:

On the head of this information a large party started on Tuesday last [June 20] in pursuit of them, in hopes that they had not yet left it—The cage was found but the birds were flown. Caesar had described everything correctly—the bark where they had made up their bread on, pieces of crocks, egg-shells and many other symptoms of **good living** was found, and a few rods from the cave, two blankets taken from this jail with them and several fragments of old clothes. . . .

It appears they were at no loss for friends at this place to supply them with such articles as they could not rob or steal. A shoemaker in whose house Connelly slept on Thursday week last [June 8], made him a pair of shoes on that day.

The three fugitives, undoubtedly figuring that Rodney would get caught and confess, wisely left the hideout shortly after he skipped out.[43]

Following their exodus from the cave at Doubling Gap, Lewis and company launched a furious crime spree. The confession was obviously correct in stating that they hid out in East Pennsboro Township, across the river from Harrisburg, where they plotted to rob Jonas Rupp, Conrad Reiniger, and a Mr. Eberly. The *Harrisburg Chronicle* confirmed part of the above when it reported that on the seventeenth of June an attempted raid was made on Eberly's house, near Krietzer's Tavern. Apparently the household put up a strong resistance, for the robbers had to make a hasty retreat. The *Chronicle* also reported that several spring houses in the area had been broken into and "robbed of meat, butter, milk, and bread, and other provisions to the great annoyance of the owners."

Several other robberies occurred in the area during this time. One was committed on Peter's Mountain, and the houses of William Armstrong and Michael Boyer, six miles north of Harrisburg, were pilfered of small sums of money. Two attempted robberies were also reported; one in Cumberland and the other on the house of Hugh Steven, deceased, five miles west of Harrisburg. Three women were occupying the Steven house when several armed and disguised men broke in. They ransacked chests and drawers, but missed a hidden six hundred dollars. They left after taking only two shotguns.

Lewis' escapades gave the anti-Findlay newspapers more ammunition to besiege the governor. The *Harrisburg Chronicle* had a field day with barbs like, "The citizens of Harrisburg have been much amused, since the escape of Lewis, with the stories that have been invented and swallowed wholesale by our most penetrating Governor," and "The country is kept in continual alarm for which the citizens have to thank the humanity of William Findlay, in letting loose so many hardened malefactors, to prey on society." The newspapers defending Findlay vainly fought back, reporting that the prison inspectors had recommended the pardon after Lewis informed on his cellmates who were planning a prison escape. This did little good because the smear campaign against Findlay was growing in momentum.

One of these "stories that have been invented and swallowed wholesale" may have been factual. Several respected citizens of Harrisburg would gather of an evening at the corner of Front and Market Streets to discuss the affairs of the day, including the crimes of Lewis the robber. Unknown to these men, David Lewis was hiding behind some boxes and barrels in front of the John C. Bucher & Co. Store. Author John Blair Linn wrote that after listening to their conversation for some time, "David Lewis rose up and exclaimed, 'I am Lewis, the robber, take me if you dare!' putting the whole squad to flight, running helter skelter over tar-barrels and grindstones, skinning shins," as graphically described by "H" in the *Bellefonte Patriot*. According to this account, David Lewis "was looking and watching for Dr. Peter Shoenberger, of Huntingdon County, a rich iron-master, and his return from

Baltimore and Harper's Ferry with a large some [sic] of money, received for iron sold the United States for gun-barrels."

The reference to the planned robbery of Shoenberger gives credibility to the story. Another contributing factor is that David Lewis may have made a visit to his family, for his wife, Margarate, and seven- or eight-year-old daughter, Mary Ann, presumably were living on Locust Street in Harrisburg. They most likely left the Lewis homestead near Milesburg and moved to Harrisburg following David Lewis' imprisonment in Philadelphia in June, 1816.

The highwaymen then moved west into Cumberland County and, on June 18, robbed the McCullough store near Waterford of a substantial amount of goods and money. Connelly was recognized by someone who knew him from when he was incarcerated in the county jail. The highwaymen then headed north.[44]

Two days later, in Centre County, the thieves got a break. According to author John Blair Linn, who collected the information from a member of the posse that pursued Lewis' gang:

> Hammond and Page, merchants of Bellefonte, were receiving at that time a stock of goods. They had three teams hauling them. One in particular, being loaded with the costliest goods, in crossing the seven Mountains, broke down, and it being late, they drove on to John Carr's [Kerr's] tavern at Potter's Mills, with the remaining wagons. Lewis and his party overhauled the goods and took such as suited them, and then started for Potter's Mills, with the intention of robbing Potter's store.[45]

The goods plundered from the wagon reportedly were valued at $1,200, a costly loss to suffer during those depression days.

The next morning, June 21, Connelly went into John Kerr's tavern in Potter's Mills and asked if anyone slept at James Potter's store next door. The robber was told no one slept there but that someone would be there soon. When the store opened, Connelly bought some cigars and left.

Before dawn the next day Kerr was awakened by his dogs, and observed Lewis, Connelly, and McGuire trying to break into Potter's store. Kerr woke several men sleeping at the tavern, who, when told of the pending robbery, charged into Potter's store with foolhardy abandon. The thieves tried to fire at their adversaries but their pistols misfired, except for one shot that missed. For several minutes the three robbers remained inside the store, and then bolted through the doorway. The robbers were quickly pursued, and in Linn's words, "Paul Lebo, a very active man, outran the rest so far that Lewis and Connelly, who had secreted themselves, captured Lebo, and Connelly had him nearly choked to death, and only at the earnest request of Lewis released him." Linn continued, obviously overstating the situation: "The terror in that neighborhood for some weeks was unbounded, and its shadows still linger in the traditions of the valley. Night after night men patrolled the valley, while the women shuddered and trembled at any approaching footstep."

Nothing was heard from the highwaymen until Saturday, June 24, when they raided a spring house of bread, radishes, pies, cakes, and herring at Hoeman's farm on the south side of Nittany Mountain, seven miles from Potter's Mills. They made their way to the William Riddle farm in the Nittany Valley, where they stole a horse, which they soon turned loose. On Sunday morning the robbers entertained themselves by shooting at marks near the home of Colonel McKibben near Porter Township. The trio were seen as they crossed Muncy Mountain (now Bald Eagle Mountain).

Reaching Bald Eagle Creek, they stole a canoe, paddled upstream to Great Island (now Lock Haven) in the Susquehanna River, and camped that Sunday night. Apparently tired of hauling the spoils from the Hammond and Page wagon, they burned a portion of them near the Great Road. The *American Volunteer* continued:

> The smell having drawn some persons to the spot, a discovery took place which ended in the taking of M'Guire. He did not tell his real name until after he was committed to prison [Chambersburg jail]—he then acknowledged to it—and that he had escaped from Chambersburg prison with Lewis—refused to give any information about his companions, other than that they were actually Lewis and Connelly, with others. A quantity of the goods were found near the road, distant a short space from those burning, the same day, and among them was a check shirt, seen on M'Guire the day before, which gave the clue to his certainly being one of the robbers. That night some guns were heard to go off, in the adjacent hills, and loud whistles were repeatedly heard. This, no doubt, was the concerted plan in case of separation, to find one another again. The next morning Lewis and Connelly crossed the River [Bald Eagle Creek near Beech Creek], and at a house nearby, got their breakfast and run some bullets.

On August 29, 1820, Felix McGuire was tried, convicted of robbery, and sentenced to two years in the penitentiary at Philadelphia, to be served following the completion of his term in the Franklin County jail. Ironically, McGuire turned out to be the most fortunate of the three robbers.[46]

Lewis and Connelly then headed deep into the wilderness of the Sinnemahoning, and undoubtedly visited Lewis' mother's home on Bennett's Branch of Sinnemahoning Creek. Apparently the Lewis family were also victims who suffered for the infamy of David Lewis.

Following the death of her husband, Lewis Lewis, in 1790, Jane Lewis remarried. According to *The Elk Horn*:

> In 1792, Jane Dill Lewis, widow with eight children, married Frederick Leathers, who owned land adjoining the Lewis property [in Bald Eagle Valley]. Then in 1796 Leathers died. In 1800 Jane Dill Lewis Leathers took her eight children and her belongings and migrated into the area that later was Clearfield County. She crossed the mountains on horseback over an old Indian path and settled her family on the bank of the Susquehanna where the city of Clearfield now stands. . . .
> After Jane's family had all left home, she returned to Bald Eagle

Valley to settle the estates of her husbands, Lewis Lewis and Frederick Leathers. Then she married for a third time. In 1820, Reese Stevens and wife Jane were living in the valley of Bennett's Branch of the Susquehanna.

The *History of Clearfield County, Pennsylvania* corroborates the above, showing Jane Lewis Lathers [Leathers] and sons Thomas, David, and Lewis Lewis listed on the 1806 Clearfield County tax rolls as living in Chincleclamousche Township, which is now Clearfield. Jane Lewis spent her last years at her son Thomas' home near Benezette, and according to her tombstone, died in 1842.

In December of 1817, David's brother Thomas moved his family up Bennett's Branch, near the villages of Benezette and Medix Run, in what is now Elk County. The move took place exactly a year and a half after David Lewis entered the penitentiary at Philadelphia, so it is probable that the pressure of being family of the notorious David Lewis took its toll.[47]

Word that the robbers had been seen on Muncy Mountain reached Bellefonte on Monday night, June 26. Presuming the fugitives would head for Lewis' mother's home, a posse was quickly formed. It consisted of Centre County Coroner James McGhee, John Hammond, part-owner of the plundered wagon, Joseph Butler, William Armor, Paul Lebo, and Peter Deisal, a one-armed veteran of the War of 1812. Former Sheriff William Alexander headed down Nittany Valley to collect men to go to Great Island, but apparently failed to induce anyone to join the manhunt.

The plan was for both posses to meet at the home of Lewis' mother. On the way McGhee's posse picked up a guide, Andrew Walker, and reached the town of Karthaus on the night of the 27th. Here they were joined by Samuel Carnel, William Hannah, John Kuhns, and Peter Roder. The next night they camped out in the wilderness.

Although the *American Volunteer* does not include Centre County Sheriff John Mitchell in the posse, both author John Blair Linn and compiler Michael A. Leeson include him in their publications. This may have been a deliberate omission by the newspaper, as controversy surrounds the conclusion of the hunt. The accounts from Linn, who got his information from a member of the posse, and the *American Volunteer* and the *Patriot*, contradict that reported by Leeson, who got his information from John Brooks, a resident who witnessed the grand finale of the manhunt. The accounts from both sides are given here, allowing the reader to judge their relative validity.

The posse reached the home of Lewis' mother and her husband, Reese Stevens, on the evening of June 29. Walker and Carnel went ahead of the others to question the woman as to the whereabouts of her son and Connelly, but received nothing for their efforts. According to Leeson, the posse then visited the nearby home of David's brother Thomas and got the same results. That night they camped on Bennett's

Branch, about four miles below Lewis' mother's home, intending to return by way of Great Island. At noon on Friday, Sheriff Mitchell and his twelve-man posse reached the junction of Bennett's Branch and Driftwood Branch. Crossing the latter, they discovered that two men answering the description of Lewis and Connelly had eaten breakfast at a nearby house that morning.

Continuing about four miles down the Sinnemahoning to Grove Creek, they ran into a young man named David Brooks gigging in the stream. Brooks told them that Lewis and another man had passed that way earlier. With Brooks as a guide, the reinvigorated posse turned around and headed four miles back up Driftwood Branch. There, according to Leeson:

> After having reached Tanglefoot run, about a half a mile below the residence of Samuel Smith, they met William Shephard, who lived at the mouth of Bennett's branch, and who was on his way home from Smith's, where he had been all forenoon with a party, including Connelly and Lewis, firing at a target and indulging in potations of old rye. . . . Obtaining advices of the whereabouts of the robbers, they detailed Shephard to return to Smith's and to privately inform him so that he might keep his family in the house and avoid danger, while Brooks was detailed to conduct the posse, by a path through the woods, to a point on the summit of a hill commanding Smith's residence and about one hundred feet therefrom. Shephard arriving at the house about the time someone called "treat," and delayed his message to gulp a bumper or two, when he perceived a motion in the bushes at the top of the hill, he wildly and with gesticulations exclaimed, "Take care of yourselves, the sheriff and his men are here," upon which the whole posse charged down the hill firing as they ran.

Linn and the newspapers report that the posse arrived at the house of Samuel Smith about an hour before sundown. Brooks led the posse around the house to the top of a steep bank that concealed them from below. Here they saw Lewis and Connelly shooting at marks with several other persons. Spotting a lone man some distance from the house, the posse told Brooks to tell the man to secretly get the women and children into the house. When confronted by Brooks, the man, William Shephard, swore "that not a hair of Lewis' head should be hurt." He then rushed back to the house, giving warning to the two robbers.

Following their probable visit to Lewis' mother's home, the two highwaymen made their way up Driftwood Branch. They apparently had no fear of being followed, as they were found casually shooting at marks when they were taken unaware by the posse. At Shephard's warning, the posse clambered down the embankment, shouting at Lewis and Connelly to surrender, and that they would be well treated.

Linn and the newspapers contend that the battle commenced in earnest after Connelly swore by his Savior that he would blow them all to hell. The *American Volunteer* reported:

> Lewis seized a gun and snapped twice, but [it] did not go off. Connelly at the same moment fired his point blank at one of the posse [the

shot missed]; and Lewis having got another gun fired also. The volley was quickly returned by the posse, and another request was made them to surrender; but uttering threats of defiance they refused. . . .

"Shoot and be damned! We'll shoot back," roared the two highwaymen, as they fired again at their adversaries. The posse returned fire, and Lewis dropped. Connelly fled across the creek and was running through a grain field when he was fired at and wounded by the one-armed Peter Deisal. He was found nearly a mile away hiding in a treetop. At first he denied he was Connelly, but shortly afterward admitted his identity.

Connelly's wound was serious; a bullet had penetrated the left side of his groin, below the stomach, causing his entrails to protrude, and plowed downward, exiting through his right thigh. Lewis was wounded in the left thigh and in the right arm above the wrist.

During the shoot-out, the robbers were handed loaded weapons from inside the Smith house. Following the fight some of the stolen goods were found with the wounded bandits, and more were discovered hidden under a bed in Smith's house. Apparently Smith and Shephard were neither arrested nor charged for their part in the conflict. The *American Volunteer* added:

> Having dressed their wounds, with all the care of which they were capable, they purchased a canoe and prepared to move down the River. . . . Then they pushed off with their prisoners, whom they treated with all possible care, tenderness and humanity, and on Sunday the 2nd of July instant, landed near the Big island [Great Island], in Lycoming county. They carried the prisoners to Mr. Carscadden's Tavern, being the nearest public house; where they were attended by three Physicians and a minister of the gospel. Everything in the power of man was done for them; but Connelly's wound having produced a mortification, he died that night in gloomy sullenness. Lewis' wounds were dressed and appear to be doing well; his recovery, however, is considered doubtful.

Leeson recounts an entirely different scenario:

> Connelly seized his gun when the alarm [Shephard's warning] was given, Lewis surrendered, and was shot in the arm afterward. Connelly was shot in the abdomen; he bounded across the field and the river, leaping the fences until, having reached the potato field of Benjamin Brooks, on the opposite side of the river, he wheeled about, presenting his gun through the fence toward his pursuers, saying, "Gentlemen, I will have shot about with you." His gun was, however, unloaded, and he had dropped his ammunition. He soon retreated a few rods into the bushes and was lost from sight. . . . After the party . . . concluded that the wounded robber had made his escape up the mountain, and as they were about abandoning further search, one of the party . . . observed a glimpse of clothing of the wounded man through the bushes, where they found him asleep, being faint and exhausted from loss of blood, he having crawled into the top of a large red oak tree, which had been recently blown down by the storm.
> Procuring a bed-sheet and pillow from Mrs. Brooks, they carried the wounded man into a canoe, which they had procured from one of

Above: Grave of David Lewis' mother, Jane Dill Lewis, near Benezette, Elk County, Pennsylvania. Upper left: Original gravestone. Upper right: Monument erected by the Boy Scouts of Caledonia, Pennsylvania. PHOTOGRAPHS TAKEN BY SARAH CASKEY OF ST. MARYS, PENNSYLVANIA

Below: The Lewis plot in the Milesburg Cemetery, where David Lewis is undoubtedly buried. There is no stone to mark his grave, probably because of the shame and to discourage grave robbers. The gravestone in the middle is presumably that of Reese or Rees Lewis, son of David's brother Jacob Lewis. The stone reads: "Rees, Son of J. & M. Lewis, DIED Oct. 27, 1841, Ag 30 Ys 7 Mo 8 ds." PHOTO TAKEN IN AUGUST 1996 BY JAY AND KAY JONES OF DANVILLE, PENNSYLVANIA

the neighbors . . . and having placed both robbers therein, they descended the Sinnemahoning and the west branch, stopping at some point on the river over night, where they left the wounded men lying in the water in the canoe, keeping guard over them, and on the next day arrived at some of the farm houses, where the city of Lock Haven is now situate, and from thence they assayed to convey the prisoners by wagon to Bellefonte. Connelly, however, died at Carskadden.

Following an inquest held on July 3 by Justice Irvine, the body of John Connelly was buried just outside the Great Island Cemetery at Lock Haven.[48]

Lewis was conveyed by litter to Mill Hall, and then to the jail at Bellefonte where crowds of curious onlookers came to view the notorious highwayman. Lewis made his peace with God, and told a local minister, Reverend Linn, that he hoped for mercy as he had never killed a man. The dying robber was concerned about a satisfactory burial, leaving instructions to obtain the money that the Bedford bank had refused to give him five years before, when he was arrested for counterfeiting.

In jail at Bellefonte, Lewis was examined by Dr. C. Curtin, a skilled surgeon. Lewis' right arm was fractured at the wrist and gangrene had set in, so Dr. Curtin proposed amputation. Lewis adamantly refused, evidently preferring death to amputation and imprisonment. If so, David Lewis got his wish, prompting these comments by the *York Recorder* as a final epitaph to the renowned robber:

Entrance of Milesburg Cemetery, Milesburg, Pennsylvania, established in 1804, the final resting place of David Lewis. PHOTO TAKEN IN AUGUST 1996 BY JAY AND KAY JONES OF DANVILLE, PENNSYLVANIA

DAVID LEWIS, for the last time.

This notorious offender, the Robin Hood of Pennsylvania, died in the jail of Centre county, of his wounds, on the evening of the twelfth inst. in the 30th year of his age. . . .

Here we see, that the vengeance of the offended justice, must sooner or later fall upon the heads of the guilty. He was the terror of the mountainous parts of Pennsylvania, and even when apprehended always contrived some means of escape. But in his "present prison house, the grave," where neither bolts nor bars, but the strong hand of death holds him in detention, he is secure.

On July 13, an inquest on the late David Lewis was held in Bellefonte under William Petriken and the following jurors: Andrew Gregg, Thomas Burnside, John Blanchard, Joseph Miles, James Dundass, Henry Vandyke, Patrick Cambridge, John Rankin, James Rothrock, Evan Miles, Thomas Hastings, Jr., Richard Miles, William Alexander, and John Irwin, Jr. They found that the actions of James McGhee and his posse "were performed in pursuance of and agreeably to the laws of the country."

David Lewis was buried on the same day in the Milesburg Cemetery. Although no detailed newspaper report of Lewis' funeral appeared, no doubt family members picked up his body and buried him near his boyhood home on Bald Eagle Creek.[49]

This leaves a few nagging questions. If the robbers were aided during the fight at the Smith house, why was no one charged or arrested? Secondly, did the posse, as witness John Brooks claimed, shoot down unarmed David Lewis after he had surrendered? If so, would a posse that held that much animosity give the two wounded robbers as much tender care as they professed; or did David Lewis die as a result of malicious neglect? Those who read this will have to draw their own conclusions.

PART FOUR : The Aftermath

THE PEN IS MIGHTIER THAN THE SWORD! However, in the case of David Lewis it was a draw: He was brought down by the sword, but was resurrected by the pen. David Lewis may have been dead in body, but he was certainly alive in spirit, all because two vindictive men, editor John McFarland and attorney James Duncan, made very sure of it. Their purpose was the political defeat of Governor William Findlay; the end result would be the so-called confession.

The sixty-page confession of David Lewis was purported to have been written by Lewis while confined in jail in Bellefonte in July 1820. And all of it written in the course of ten days or less by a man dying of gangrene. This, of course, is ludicrous. The confession, when published in pamphlet form in 1890 as *The Life And Adventures of David Lewis, Robber And Counterfeiter. The Terror Of The Cumberland Valley*, was eighty-four pages in length, with additions.

There are different schools of thought as to who actually wrote the confession; some say McFarland, and some say Duncan. After a thorough study of all the material, it seems logical that both men contributed to its composition. McFarland was a writer, a newspaperman who was familiar with words, and the confession resounds with the vocabulary of professional writing of the early 1800s. But McFarland would have had no knowledge of the details of Lewis' early life and career. James Duncan, however, was a family friend and served as David Lewis' lawyer during the robber's trial as a deserter from the U.S. Army. He would have had no trouble furnishing McFarland with this vast amount of information. The confession is undoubtedly the combined work of both men, who had the same purpose for wanting it written.

The *Centre County Heritage* explains the reason for McFarland's animosity toward Findlay:

> John McFarland, editor of the *Carlisle Republican*, was one of the "fighting editors" of the early 19th century. The previous year he had been taken to court by a fellow Carlisle editor, Michael Holcomb, for knocking him down "with a cowhide." McFarland's decision to oppose the candidacy for governor of William Findlay in his hometown in 1817 cost McFarland his job as editor of the Chambersburg weekly, *The Republican*. Findlay supporters simply bought the paper out from under him. Findlay was elected governor despite McFarland in 1817, and was running again in 1820. McFarland meanwhile had set up a paper in Shippensburg, carried it to Carlisle, permitted it to fold, and taken over as editor of the *Carlisle Republican* in late 1819, just in time for the next gubernatorial campaign. His views about Findlay had not mellowed.[50]

James Duncan's reason, on the other hand, is ambiguous. Duncan, who was from Carlisle but reportedly living in Bellefonte at the time of David Lewis' death, was running for Congress on the same party ticket as William Findlay. Nonetheless, two prominent men, Judge William Hall and historian John Blair Linn, credit Duncan with the confession. Furthermore, both men give veiled clues to Duncan's input: Hall claims that Duncan "prepared" the confession whereas Linn was likely correct when he wrote that Duncan "edited" the work. Apparently Duncan had an unknown grudge against Governor Findlay, yet could not openly condemn or oppose him. Furnishing McFarland with information and editing was the only solution. To add credence to the theory of Duncan's involvement, the next year he was appointed to public office by Findlay's opponent, probably as a reward.[51]

The death of David Lewis ended McFarland's use of him as an active anti-Findlay symbol. The confession filled the gap: eight installments in the *Carlisle Republican* that began on August 1, continuing up to the election on October 10, keeping the heat on Governor Findlay. The preface of Rishel's 1890 publication of the confession points out McFarland's intentions: "While Lewis apparently professes to feel himself under deep obligations of gratitude to Governor Findlay, he nevertheless takes several opportunities of covertly assailing him and of making both him and his party odious to the public."

Here are examples of the confession's satiric and sardonic references to Governor Findlay. The first regards Lewis' pardon:

> I remained here [the penitentiary] about a year, during which time I began to have serious thoughts about reformation, when the powerful intercessions of my friends, and the knowledge I had of the weak side of Governor Findlay in favoring applications of this nature suggested a pardon as the best means of restoring me to liberty. As I expected, his excellency received my petition for a pardon in a manner that gave my friends no doubt of the success of the application; and they did not remain many hours in suspense before the Secretary delivered them a paper under the great seal of the state, granting me full forgiveness for all my crimes, and a complete remission of all the penalties of the law.

There is some basis for this insinuation, as Governor Findlay had pardoned 144 felons by the end of his term, 26 more than any of his predecessors.

The following account, also from the confession, is full of innuendo, and reads like a meeting between two colleagues rather than a gubernatorial visit to a jail.

> I was lodged in the jail in Chambersburg [May, 1820], where I was shortly after my confinement gratified with a visit from his excellency, Governor Findlay, who opportunely had arrived in Chambersburg nearly about the same time. He condoled with me on my present misadventure, and after the jailors and spectators had left the room, we had a private interview, during which we conversed freely on different subjects, not necessary now to mention, but any person will wrong his excellency, if he supposes the conversation related to an office. He never

promised me any such thing, nor did I ask one of him. His excellency did not remain with me longer than half an hour, and in leaving the room, he gave me an affectionate squeeze of the hand.[52]

Not everyone was taken in by the purported confession, as is demonstrated by this rebuttal in the *American Volunteer*, written by an irate citizen from Centre County.

> David Lewis never uttered one sentence, word, or syllable of this FORGED confession, to any human being. The only thing he uttered like a confession, was to the clergyman who attended him occasionally during his confinement in our prison. . . . I was puzzled to conceive what could be the object that any depraved wretch could have in view, in inventing such a collection of falsehoods; but as I progressed the mystery unfolded: It was to make a malignant thrust at Mr. Tompkins [U.S. Vice President Daniel Tompkins] and governor Findlay that dictated the whole of these palpable falsehoods to the poisoned mind of the inventor.[53]

Whether or not McFarland's biting editorials had anything to do with the election, the end result was Joseph Hiester's defeat of Governor William Findlay by a total of 1,597 votes. Ironically, in the election of 1817, Findlay had defeated Hiester by 7,005 votes. Political plum or not, James Duncan was appointed Auditor General on April 2, 1821, by the new governor. This may be the only time in history when a dead criminal was used to defeat a political opponent.[54]

One would think that in order for a criminal's pardon and escapades to prove useful as political weapons, the criminal in question would have to be a dangerous, vicious, and utterly despicable individual. Incongruously, David Lewis was depicted as just the opposite, which is confirmed by these opening lines of a January 1820 article in the *American Volunteer:* "Many little traits in the character of Lewis are spoken of, and prove him to be a man of no common order. With all his villainy, there is something magnanimous in his conduct." Even in death, the symbol was affixed to his name by the *York Recorder:* "This notorious offender, the Robin Hood of Pennsylvania, died in the jail in Centre County."[55]

No, David Lewis is a folk hero, whose exploits became legends. And all because of the wrath of a disgruntled newspaper editor. As time passed, these legends grew. The most comprehensive compilation of these legends can be found in historian Mac E. Barrick's article, "Lewis the Robber in Life and Legend." There is the ever-popular tale, usually credited to Jesse James, of the widow who is going to lose all to the mean-spirited tax collector, or landlord, or constable. Lewis gives her the money, she pays the collector, and Lewis, in turn, robs the collector. Another is about a proposed victim who gives Lewis a ride on his wagon, and when the robber finds out the man is poor, gallantly gives up his plan. There are numerous others.[56]

Basically, these legends spring up through the people of rural areas, who saw the outlaw as a symbol of resistance to corrupt business, authority, and/or government. In Lewis' case, the poor economy of the times fostered the growth of the legend.

In spite of the tragedy of this story, there is a sidebar of happiness: "Mary Ann Lewis, a daughter of the robber Lewis was considered one of the handsomest girls in Harrisburg. She was rather slender and delicate looking, but had a sweet countenance and dark brown hair. In the loveliness of her face there were indications of resolution, and yet she was modest withal. She resided with her widowed mother on Locust street. She married a shoemaker named Halfman, and left Harrisburg many years ago."[57]

With this somewhat pleasant conclusion, David Lewis' calamitous story ends. His legend, however, will live on in central Pennsylvania, where to many he will always remain the Robin Hood of the Cumberland.

II. NORTH CAROLINA

KEITH & MALINDA BLAYLOCK

Petticoats and Poison Ivy

AT THE HIGHEST POINT IN NORTH CAROLINA'S Blue Ridge Mountains lies Avery County. Located in the northern tier of the mountains and bordered on the west by Tennessee, this naturally beautiful rural county is known as the Christmas tree capital of the east. It also abounds in mountain legends; the most prominent concerns a one-eyed man, reportedly an egregious bushwhacker who served in both the Confederate and Union armies during the Civil War, and his wife, who allegedly joined the Confederate army as a man to serve alongside her husband and later rode with him as a bushwhacker. Sound like a typical tall tale? It is not. However, there are controversies, and they start right at the beginning.

First, the physical setting for this narrative is shrouded in confusion. The area that is now Avery County was formed in 1912 from the counties of Mitchell (formed 1862), Watauga (formed 1849), and Caldwell (formed 1841). If this is not confusing enough, part of this area before 1862 was Yancey County, and before 1833 it was Burke County.[1] To obtain all pertinent information and documentation, records from these six counties had to be examined.

The birth date of William McKesson Blaylock, commonly known as Keith, has been erroneously recorded as June 21, 1836; however, his tombstone gives the date as November 21, 1837, which corresponds with his listing in the 1850 Caldwell County census and Confederate troop records. Keith was born in Burnsville, Yancey County, North Carolina.[2]

Tintype of William "Keith" Blaylock taken around 1859. COURTESY OF SYLVIA MOORE, FORT PAYNE, ALABAMA, GREAT-GRANDDAUGHTER OF KEITH BLAYLOCK

Next is the question of the legitimacy of Keith's birth. There is no doubt that Mary A. Blaylock (born March 25, 1818) was his mother. She was born in what was Burke County and is now Yancey County, the seventh child of Revolutionary War veteran John Blaylock (born September 4, 1762—died March 10, 1846) of Brunswick County, Virginia, and Mary E. "Polly" Dorman (born 1782—died October 7, 1856) of Yancey County, North Carolina.

Who, then, was Keith's father? From all indications he was an ex–Mexican War soldier named Alfred F. Keith, a noted rough and tumble fighter throughout western North Carolina. Keith served as a lieutenant under Keith Blaylock's uncle, Tilman Blaylock, during the war with Mexico. John Preston Arthur reported in his *History of Watauga County* that young William Blaylock was a fierce scrapper from an early age; the youngster's companions began calling him

Keith, after Alfred Keith, in deference to his prowess as a fighter, and the name stuck with him the rest of his life. However, it is traditionally thought that his young contemporaries goaded him by calling him Keith after his father, and consequently turned him into a formidable fighter.

There also are rumors that Keith's father was either a Gragg or a Burleson; however, these are names from the area including the counties that were at one time Mitchell, Caldwell, Watauga, and Avery. Keith Blaylock's birthplace, Burnsville in Yancey County, was the stomping grounds of Alfred Keith, who was also a known womanizer. Alfred Keith was seventeen, two years younger than Mary Blaylock, when Keith Blaylock was born; if indeed Alfred was the father, his youth may have been the reason he and Mary Blaylock did not marry. The 1850 Yancey County census shows widower Alfred F. Keeth [sic] with six children, the oldest of whom was aged nine, which would indicate that he had married in 1839 or 1840. His wife, Emaline R. Keith, died on January 20, 1850 of typhoid fever at age thirty-two. Shortly after midnight on October 29, 1859, when Keith Blaylock was twenty-one, Alfred Keith was stabbed to death in an affray in a hotel room in Burnsville, North Carolina.[3]

The first record of Keith Blaylock is found in the 1850 Caldwell County census, where he was listed as living with his stepfather Austin Coffey, a well-known farmer (born 1818), and his mother Mary, who married Coffey around 1844. Also in the household were Keith's eight-year-old sister, Mary Blaylock, who was also born out of wedlock, his stepsister Margaret Ann Coffey (born August 22, 1845), and nineteen-year-old Henry Pritchard. Although they were not related by blood, Austin Coffey treated Keith as his own son and the two became extremely close. The Coffeys had three more children, all sons: David, born August 22, 1853; Thomas A., born June 3, 1854; and Jesse Fillmore, born October 22, 1858.[4]

On December 14, 1844, Austin Coffey and Arthur Pritchard were granted two hundred acres on John's River in Caldwell County for five dollars per hundred acres. This grant in the John's River District is known as Coffey's Gap and is located around six miles west of the town of Blowing Rock. The whole area, which now includes parts of four counties, is known as the Globe. It was here, from age seven, that Keith Blaylock was raised.[5]

On June 21, 1856, Keith Blaylock and Malinda Pritchard were married near his home in Caldwell County. Malinda, born on March 10, 1839 and named Sarah Malinda, was the daughter of Alfred Pritchard (born 1802) and his wife Elizabeth (born 1801), who also lived in John's River District. Malinda had two sisters, Harriet (born 1832) and Nancy (born 1836), and two brothers, John R. (born 1835) and James (born 1859). The Henry Pritchard living with Keith's family in 1850 was likely Malinda's brother. On April 29, 1857 Keith and Malinda had a son, William R.; however, the boy died before 1862.[6]

Left: William McKesson "Keith" Blaylock, from tintype c. mid 1870s;
Right: Malinda Blaylock, late 1870s. Note Keith's blind right eye and that Malinda is holding the same tintype of Keith.

Within four years after Keith's marriage he was granted two tracts of land on John's River near his family and in-laws. On January 27, 1858 he was granted one hundred acres at 12½¢ an acre and on December 29, 1860 another thirty-seven acres at the same cost per acre. In 1860 this area was listed as the Blue Ridge Township in Watauga County, and the census included William "Keith" and his wife, Sarah Malinda Blaylock. For six years the Blaylocks lived as typical western Carolina mountaineers, and then came the Civil War.[7]

Keith Blaylock was a Union sympathizer in a Southern state, as were many throughout the mountains of North Carolina where slavery was not an issue. However, when war broke out there was a division of support and Keith realized that the western mountains would be a hotbed of conflict and that it would be best to sell his land. On April 16, 1861, four days after the war commenced, Keith sold a tract of land to his stepfather for fifty dollars.[8]

During the first year of the war Confederate troops strongly championed the war effort, but the tide of support shifted dramatically with the enactment of the Confederate Conscription Act on April 16, 1862. The act called for all males between the ages of eighteen and thirty-five to serve in the army for three years, and those already in service to serve out three years regardless of when their enlistment was up. In September 1862, the upper age was raised to forty-five. The Confederate soldiers considered this a breech of faith on the part of the Confederate government, and desertion became a serious problem. Keith Blaylock found himself between a rock and a hard place.[9]

By March of 1862 rumors that the Confederate Army would soon enact the Conscription Act rapidly spread across the mountains. Realizing that he would soon be subject to conscription, Keith decided to beat the draft and join a company of his choice. He selected Colonel Zebulon B. Vance's 26th Regiment, North Carolina Troops. Malinda Blaylock was determined not to be separated from her husband, and it was decided that she would accompany Keith and enlist as a man. They both enlisted in Kinston, North Carolina on March 20.[10]

According to *The Histories of the Several Regiments and Battalions from North Carolina*:

> When the Twenty-sixth Regiment was in camp in and around Kinston, after the battle of New Bern [March 14, 1862], many recruits joined the command. Among them were two young men, giving their names as L. M. [sic] and Samuel Blalock [sic]. They enlisted in Captain Ballew's company (F) and were brought to the regiment by private James D. Moore, of Company F. On the way from their home, in Caldwell County, to join the regiment, Moore was informed in strict confidence by L. M. (Keith) Blalock, that Samuel was his young wife, and that he would only enlist on the condition that his wife be allowed to enlist with him. This was agreed to by Moore, who was acting as recruiting officer, and Moore also promised not to divulge the secret. Sam Blalock is described as a good looking boy, aged 16, weight about 130 pounds, height 5 feet and 4 inches, dark hair; her husband (Keith) was over 6 feet in height.[11]

Posing as a male, Malinda Blaylock apparently played her part as a soldier well, and there are several references to "Sam's" actions while in service. In one, Samuel A'Court Ashe reported, "Her disguise was never penetrated. She did the duties of a soldier well and was adept at the manual and drill." John Preston Arthur wrote, "She wore a regular private's uniform and tented and messed with her husband. . . . She stood guard, drilled, and handled her musket like a man, and no one ever suspected her sex." In 1927 Rupert Gillette stated in an article in the *Charlotte Observer,* "It seems in those days soldiers were not stripped and given the rigid physical examinations to which they are now subjected, for Mrs. Blaylock kept up the masquerade for months [one month]. She used to sit on the banks of the creek while the other soldiers were in swimming, but she never went in herself." In contrast, *The Confederate War Veteran* implied that she was not as zealous as her fellow servicemen.[12]

From the beginning Keith was determined to find a way to get out of the Confederate army. Perceiving that desertion would be foolish as well as dangerous, he reportedly devised a method that would guarantee his discharge: he covered himself thoroughly with poison ivy. This is the local folklore; however, Keith was discharged exactly one month after his enlistment on March 20, 1862, and poison sumac, not poison ivy, was listed as a contributing factor, although the major reason was that Keith had a hernia.

Malinda, of course, was not about to remain in the army without her husband, and immediately informed her commanding officer and/or Colonel Vance that she was a woman. Malinda "Sam" Blaylock was discharged on the same day as her husband, but not until, as Rupert Gillette delicately stated, she "gave proof 'as strong as the holy writ.'" Military chronicler John W. Moore endorses this reason for Malinda's discharge:

> Blaylock, Mrs. L. W. [sic], enlisted March 20, '62; dg. April 20, '62; Caldwell County; dg. for being a woman. . . . This lady had done a soldier's duty without a suspicion of her sex among her comrades, until her husband, L. M. [sic] Blaylock, was discharged, when she claimed the same privilege, and was sent home rejoicing."[13]

John Preston Arthur continues:

> They returned to their home under the Grandfather [Grandfather Mountain], but it was not long till Keith had cured his infirmity by the frequent application of strong brine to the affected parts, brine being nothing more or less than strong salt water. Then Confederate sympathizers wanted to know why he did not return. Keith showed his discharge, and they answered by trying to arrest and conscript him.[14]

For the next two years Keith lived precariously. Legend has it that the Blaylock cabin was besieged by Confederate conscripters and Keith was wounded in the arm, but quickly dodged behind a tree and made his escape. This incident, however, likely occurred at a later date and will be recounted in full later. Whatever the case, it is presumed that Keith and Malinda retreated farther up Grandfather Mountain where they lived in a rail pen. Supposedly, they also hid out in caves on the side of the mountain. On January 14, 1863, a son, Columbus Fillmore ("Lum"), was born to Keith and Malinda, so apparently they periodically occupied their cabin when not on the run. With a newborn child, Malinda would have had to live in the cabin.[15]

On July 7, 1863, the North Carolina General Assembly established the Confederate Home Guard, a unit composed of all males between eighteen and fifty years of age, to be utilized for home defense. This added to Keith's perilous lifestyle until the emergence of Major George W. Kirk, who would become a scourge to Confederate forces in western North Carolina.[16]

The mountain people of western North Carolina were not analogous with their counterparts in the flatlands to the east. They were an isolated people, without slaves, who traveled down the mountain only when they needed supplies that they could not produce, and were divided in their sentiments regarding the war. The area was prime for guerrilla warfare, more commonly known as bushwhacking.

Guerrilla warfare was prevalent in all the border states, especially during the last half of the war, and John Mosby of Virginia, William Quantrill and Bloody Bill Anderson of Missouri, Sue Mundy (Jerome Clarke) and Sam "One-armed" Berry of Kentucky, and Champ Ferguson of Tennessee are familiar names to students of Civil War history. All were Confederate guerrillas who fought in northern states or northern-held territory, such as Missouri, whose Confederate government was in exile. North Carolina was an exception to the rule, a southern state where the prevailing guerrilla force was Union, and Keith Blaylock would become its best-known proponent.

Conforming with the prevailing pattern of this story, Keith Blaylock's service record is atypical. Arthur writes that in early 1864 "Keith Blaylock was passing back and forth between the lines and keeping the federal authorities informed of conditions around his home 'under the Grandfather,'" and that "Keith . . . became a recruiting officer for a Michigan regiment stationed in Tennessee." Federal records show that on June 1, 1864 at Strawberry Plains, Tennessee, Keith, as William Blalock, enrolled in the U.S. Army for three years as a private in Company D, 10th Regiment, Michigan Cavalry, commanded by Captain James Minihan. However, the records also show Keith was not mustered into the company until a year later, on June 23, 1865. The first and only time Blaylock's name is recorded on the company rolls is for the months of May through August 1865; thus these rolls support the concept that much of Blaylock's military career was spent taking recruits across the mountains to the Union lines in Tennessee, scouting, bushwhacking, or riding with Major George Kirk. Ironically, Blaylock's date of enlistment coincides with Kirk's intrepid dash across the North Carolina mountains and raid on Camp Vance in Burke County.[17]

George Washington Kirk was born near Greeneville, Tennessee on June 23, 1837, and was married near Greeneville on February 29, 1860 to Mariah Louesa Jones. Kirk's ascension in rank was rather meteoric, from private to lieutenant colonel in just over two years. Waiting a little over a year after the war commenced, Kirk joined Company I, 4th Regiment, Tennessee Infantry on August 1, 1862, and on the following January 4 he was promoted to lieutenant. On February 13, 1864, General John M. Schofield granted Kirk authority to form a regiment of troops from eastern Tennessee and western North Carolina; Kirk was mustered out by reason of consolidation on April 15, 1864 and transferred to the 2nd North Carolina Mounted Infantry on April 30. On June 11, 1864, Kirk was mustered in and promoted to captain in Company A, 3rd Mounted North Carolina Infantry. On the following September 20 he was promoted to lieutenant colonel.

The first action Kirk likely saw in North Carolina occurred on October 22, 1863 when he led a probing force of six to eight hundred men just across the Tennessee line to Warm Springs, Madison County, and dug in. The closest Confederate force, a battalion of troops led by Major John Woodfin, was located in Marshall, around fifteen miles from Kirk's encampment. Woodfin foolishly led his troops into battle with Kirk's forces, who held the high ground. Two of the Confederates were wounded, one mortally, and Woodfin was shot off his horse and instantly killed. The rebel force wisely retreated back to Marshall. The next day a group of citizens from Asheville, who went out to recover Woodfin's body under a flag of truce, discovered Kirk's command was gone. However, what brought Kirk's name to the attention of the Confederate forces in North Carolina, and undoubtedly launched the career of Keith Blaylock, was the raid on Camp Vance.[18]

In mid June 1864, on orders of General Schofield, Kirk left Morristown, Tennessee with a small force, superiorly armed with the new Spencer repeating rifles and made up mainly of Madison County Unionists, to lead a strike on Camp Vance, a Confederate training camp six miles south of Morganton, North Carolina and seventy-five miles behind Confederate lines. The total distance was around 115 miles, mainly through the inhospitable Blue Ridge Mountains. Near the state line a local Unionist named Joseph V. Franklin led them into North Carolina and up the Toe River near Minneapolis, a few miles south of the village of Cranberry. To successfully pass through this remote area a guide would have been essential, and undoubtedly this guide was the newly recruited Keith Blaylock, since the route led straight through his home turf of what is now Avery County. John Preston Arthur gives a concise but thorough description of the raid:

> With 130 men, including twelve Cherokee Indians, on foot and carrying their rations and arms and blankets, Kirk left Morristown, Tenn., June 13, 1864, and marched via Bull Gap [Bulls Gap], Greeneville, and the Crab Orchard, all in Tennessee, crossed the Big Hump Mountain and went up the Toe River, passing the Cranberry iron mine, where

from forty to sixty men were detailed by the Confederate government making iron, where they camped near David Ellis' [local Unionist] house and where rations were cooked for Kirk's men. On the 26th they scouted through the mountains, passing Pineola and crossing Linville River. The following day they got to Upper Creek at dark, where they did not camp, but keeping themselves in the woods all the time, got to Camp Vance at daylight. Here they demanded its surrender, where it was agreed to. [In actuality a small skirmish occurred, resulting in ten Confederate conscripts and one officer killed.] It had been Kirk's plan to take a locomotive and cars and such arms as he might find at the Camp and go to Salisbury, where the Federal prisoners confined there were to be released. Failing in that, he wanted to destroy the bridge over the Yadkin, but a telegram had been sent before they could cut the wire and that part of their scheme was abandoned. They captured 1,200 small arms, 3,000 bushels of grain, 279 prisoners, thirty-two negroes and forty-eight horses and mules. Kirk also got forty recruits for his regiment, and then, after destroying the locomotive he found there, three cars, the depot and commissary buildings, he started to return. R. C. Pearson shot Hack Norton, of Madison County, one of Kirk's men, at Hunting Creek, but Kirk got over the Catawba River and camped that night. The next day they crossed John's River and Brown's Mountain, where they were fired into by pursuing Confederates at 3:30 P.M. Kirk put some of his Camp Vance prisoners in front, and one of them, B. A. Bowles, a drummer, was killed and a seventeen year old boy was wounded. Colonel [Captain] Kirk was himself wounded [in the arm] here with several others of his command. This was at Israel Beck's farm. They camped that night at top of the Winding Stairs Road, where they were attacked next morning. [Confederate] Col. W. W. [Waightstill] Avery and Phillip Chandler were mortally wounded, Col. Calvin Houck was shot through the wrist and Powell Benfield through the thigh. The attacking party then retreated and Kirk continued his retreat, passing by Col. J. [John] B. Palmer's [Confederate commander of the Western District of North Carolina] home and burning it that morning. Kirk and all his men escaped without further mishap.[19]

From the spring of 1864 until the end of the war guerrilla activity escalated throughout the border states, and the North Carolina mountain district was no exception. The inhabitants suffered harassment not only from deserters but from raiders from both sides. A body of men from John C. Vaughan's Confederate cavalry unit, which had been defeated in a battle at Russellville, Tennessee, on October 28, came to the Boone, North Carolina area for safety. They soon covered the countryside, stealing horses, mules, and anything else they saw, destroying what they did not want or could not carry. On the other side, the Unionists were bolstered by the raid on Camp Vance, and Keith Blaylock commenced his retaliation against his Confederate neighbors and enemies.[20]

Keith probably spent some of the time between July and August leading recruits or other Unionists across the line into Tennessee and was reported as seeing action near Knoxville, Tennessee on August 23 and 24, but his first strike as a bushwhacker occurred at the end of August. Blaylock stated on his federal pension application that on August 30, 1864 he was wounded in the wrist during action near Lenoir,

North Carolina. Contemporary sources state that Keith was wounded in the left arm while being hotly pursued near his hideout on Grandfather Mountain, and that he had to take refuge with hogs that had bedded up under some rocks. Legend has it that Keith's arm became inflamed, and he cured it by puncturing his flesh with slippery elm splinters to let the poisoned blood drain out.

Keith Blaylock believed that Robert Green, who lived in the Globe but also had property in Blowing Rock, was one of the attacking party. Subsequently, Blaylock met Green driving his wagon from the Globe to Blowing Rock. Whether or not Blaylock was with companions is unclear, but when Keith told Green that he was going to kill him, the frightened man either took off running down the mountain or tried to hide behind the wagon while begging Keith not to kill him. Nevertheless, Keith shot Green in the thigh and left him where he fell. After Keith left, Green managed to climb back into the wagon and reach safety. Supporters of Blaylock state that after Keith shot through the side of the wagon and wounded Green, he then put the unconscious man into his wagon, turned it around, and started the team toward Green's home. [21]

Apparently the wound in Blaylock's wrist was not too serious, for two days later, on September 1, Keith was involved in the first of two murders he would later be charged with, the murder of William Coffey, brother of his beloved stepfather. Here is a prime example of divided loyalties during the Civil War. There were four Coffey brothers: Austin, McCaleb, Ruben, and William. Austin, a Union man, lived almost within sight of the home of his brother McCaleb, who was a southern sympathizer with a son in the Confederate army. Both were moderate in their sentiments. Ruben and William, however, were avid Confederate sympathizers, and one can only imagine the dissension that plagued this family, especially between Keith Blaylock and these two Coffey brothers.

There is no record specifying a reason for the killing; however, since it occurred two days following the wounding of Keith Blaylock, it indicates that Blaylock felt his stepuncles were involved. Blaylock, with George Perkins and William Blackwell, first sought out Ruben Coffey. Not finding him at home, the trio then went to William Coffey's house, found him in his fields, and forced him to go to James Gragg's mill, half a mile away. According to written sources, Coffey was seated on a rude bench and was shot and killed, Blaylock turning the act over to Perkins as he could not kill his stepfather's brother. The court records, which plausibly report the true facts, state that all three men shot Coffey, as there were numerous wounds in his chest. To escape retaliation and the turmoil, Ruben Coffey moved from the Globe to Meat Camp in the northern part of Watauga County. [22]

No other actions of Keith Blaylock are recorded for the next four months, so apparently the murder of William Coffey forced him to flee the area. He undoubtedly joined the ranks of George Kirk's unit that had been operating off and on out of Shelton Laurel in Madison County, North Carolina since the previous April. On September 20, on the date he was promoted to lieutenant colonel, Kirk issued orders for a raid into Madison County to capture his Confederate counterpart, Lieutenant Colonel James A. Keith. The result would be disastrous for three members of a family who were members of Kirk's units. All other members of the detachment are unnamed, but Blaylock very well may have been involved. In almost every account this incident, known commonly as the Granny Franklin affair, has been misstated and distorted, even to the actual names of the family members involved; however, supported by documentation, it is presented here as a prime example of guerrilla warfare in the mountains of North Carolina.[23]

"Granny" Franklin was in reality Nancy Shelton, born in Madison County in 1826 and likely the daughter of James "Old Jim" Shelton. Around 1842 she married Drury Norton, settled in a cabin near White Rock, and gave birth to five sons, Bayliss in 1843, James in 1845, George in 1847, Josiah in 1849, and Dillard in 1853. During the week of May 21, 1854 Drury Norton was driven from his house and beaten to death with rocks by two Sheltons, James and either Rodrick "Stob Rob" or David, and Tillman Landers. James was probably Nancy's brother, being the son of "Old Jim" Shelton. Although no reason was given for the killing, the brutal method implies family abuse by Norton.

Prior to the Civil War Nancy married George Franklin. Nancy Franklin, also called Nance, had problems in choosing suitable husbands, for Franklin, who was addicted to the bottle, left all the farm work to Nancy and her sons within a year after their marriage. During the war he deserted from the Confederate army, joined the Union side, and was wounded sometime before the fall of 1864. He was unable to work, obtained a pension, and later divorced Nancy.

When George Kirk was recruiting for the 2nd and 3rd Regiments of North Carolina Mounted Infantry in 1864, Nancy's sons joined up. Bayliss, James, and George enlisted in Company E, 2nd Regiment, while fifteen-year-old Josiah went to Company G, 3rd Regiment. In all previous accounts Nancy Franklin was erroneously reported to be a Confederate sympathizer, while her sons, who were misnamed Franklin instead of Norton, were inaccurately described as Confederate bushwhackers.

Captain H. A. White of Company C, 3rd Regiment, was the recipient of Kirk's order for the Madison County raid, and, in an affidavit for a Federal Invalid Pension for Nancy Franklin, he stated:

> That on or about the 20th day of Sept. 1864 affiant was detailed by the Colonel of his Regt. Geo. W. Kirk to make a raid into Madison Co. N.C. to try to effect the capture of Col. Keith & his rebel scouts then operating in said Co. That James, Bayliss, and Josiah Norton, sons of the claimant Nancy Franklin, having been cut off from their Co. & Regt. were at the time doing service in the 3rd Regt. They, with about 17

other men, were detailed to go with me upon said raid into Madison Co. N.C. I having orders to gather up any men of either the 2nd or 3rd Regts. who might be in N.C. & add to my force. After entering N.C. in order to increase my force, it not being safe to remain in a body, I told the men to meet me at Walnut Creek on a certain day & we would capture the rebel scouts. One of the men being captured was drunk betrayed the whole plan & immediately the rebels surprised & captured me [on September 24] and carried me to Salisbury, N.C.

When Captain White dismissed the troops, the four Norton boys went home to visit their mother. On the morning of September 24 George Norton was away, but Bayliss, James, and Josiah Norton were at the cabin when it was surrounded by the Confederates. Legend has it that the three boys ran from the cabin and opened fire on the rebels, wounding some of them. Returning fire from the superior force killed Bayliss and James, but Josiah succeeded in scrambling under the house. When two of the rebels tried to crawl after him he shot and killed them both. The Confederates then set fire to the house and when Josiah finally crawled out his head was crushed with a rifle butt. Not only did Nancy supposedly witness the killings of her sons, but also lost a lock of hair when shot at by one the Confederates. This account was dramatic, but untrue according to a Federal House of Representatives investigation report of the incident for Nancy's pension, which includes a statement by Nancy Franklin herself.

The records show that on the morning of September 24, Bayliss, James, and Josiah Norton were eating breakfast when the cabin was surrounded by the Confederates. Bolting from the doorway, Bayliss and Josiah were immediately shot down and killed while James ran some distance before he was killed. There was no returning fire from the Norton boys. The Confederates then set fire to the Franklin house. Nancy Franklin stated in her deposition, "I heard the shooting and saw them after they were dead. They were all buried in one grave without a coffin. I did not see them actually shot down. I could not see it done." As an aside, Nancy got her federal pension for the death of her three boys.[24]

In early December as Keith Blaylock, with William and Elijah Estes, Daniel Marcus, Joseph White, Noah Clark, W. Reid Linsey (sometimes spelled Lindsey), and his brother-in-law, John R. Pritchard, attempted to make their way to the Federal lines in Tennessee they met a Major Davis who was a Federal recruiting officer. None of the men, except Blaylock, were authorized U.S. soldiers, so Davis convinced them to line up and receive the oath of allegiance, and then gave them one-and-a-half days' rations. Blaylock and his now recruited band of soldiers continued to attempt to reach federal lines, but finding that all the bridges and fords were guarded by Confederate soldiers, gave up their attempt.[25]

Keith Blaylock resurfaced on his home turf in early January 1865. Arthur gives a probable reason for this: during autumn of 1864, Levi

Coffey, son of Elisha, who apparently was a relative of Keith's step-father, escaped arrest by Benjamin Green and his men in what is now Foscoe in Watauga County. Coffey was shot and wounded in the shoulder as he ran out of a Mrs. Fox's house, but managed to elude capture. He immediately joined the forces of Keith Blaylock. According to John Preston Arthur, "This caused the bushwhackers, as Blaylock and his followers were called, when they were not called robbers outright, to turn against the Greens."[26]

Keith Blaylock had another score to settle before taking on the Greens: to attack the Carroll Moore house on the John's River in Caldwell County. This action would leave Keith with a reminder he would have to endure until his dying day. According to Moore descendants, this was Blaylock's second attack against the Moores, the first allegedly occurring during the last week of November 1864, when they stole some of Moore's horses. The raiders in this first attack were Keith and Malinda Blaylock and possibly J. D. English. Malinda reportedly was wounded in the shoulder during the affray. Although there is no supporting documentation, this attack probably did occur; the only charge ever brought against Malinda was for forcible trespass, brought to trial in 1868 in Mitchell County. However, the court record does back up the claim that Malinda rode with her husband and his raiders.[27]

The area around Carroll Moore's house was headquarters for the Confederate Home Guard, and two of the Moores, Carroll and Jesse, were known members. On the evening of January 7, 1865, Keith Blaylock and his aforementioned squad of seven men, which may have also included Milton Webb and Lampton Estes, Jr., were ordered by 1st Lieutenant James Hartley of the 2nd Regiment of North Carolina Mounted Infantry to raid the home of Carroll Moore and capture members of the Home Guard who were known to be there. That night, on the banks of John's River, Blaylock split his men into two groups, sending one up Graveyard Hill behind Moore's house and the other down the road in front of the house.

Between daybreak and sunrise the raiders approached the house, but were seen by Carroll's sons Jade and Billy Moore and his nephew Pat Moore, and Jesse Moore, who armed themselves and fled the house into the orchard. As the Unionists shouted "Halt! Surrender!" firing broke out on both sides. Jesse Moore was wounded in the heel but continued shooting. One of his shots hit and blinded Keith Blaylock's right eye. Moore descendants claim that the three boys then ran up Graveyard Hill where Pat Moore was wounded in the thigh while the other two escaped, although the official court records did not report this.

As the firing continued, Carroll Moore's daughter, Rebecca Moore Estes, who was visiting her parents, ran to the orchard and helped Jesse hobble into the house. Then, with two servants, she hiked up Graveyard Hill and brought Pat down on a litter. Carroll and Jesse Moore took axes and went upstairs to fight a last-ditch stand. But the raiders were through, likely disheartened by Blaylock being blinded, and they took Moore's horses as a parting tribute.[28]

Keith's half brother, David Coffey, related an interesting story about Keith and the Moores that occurred following the war:

> I was with Keith one day when he went to Zachariah Coffey's place down under the Grandfather. Jesse Moore happened to be there when he called, and as Keith went in the front door, Jesse started to run out the back. Keith called him. "Don't ever run from me," Keith said, "I have nothing against you, because that fight we had at the Globe during the war was a fair man-to-man fight, with no hard feelings on either side." Jesse came back and began spinning war yarns.
>
> That's the kind of man Keith was. But it would have gone hard with that man who shot at him from ambush, if he had ever met up with Keith Blaylock again.[29]

Keith Blaylock was made of stern stuff, and, not letting the loss of his eye impair him, was back in action within a month. On or about February 5, Keith turned his attention to the Greens. No official records describing this confrontation exist, but the reliable John Preston Arthur states:

> . . . finding that Lott Green, a son of Amos, was at his home near Blowing Rock, they went there at night to arrest or kill him. Lott was expecting a physician to visit him that night, and when someone knocked at his door he, thinking that the doctor had arrived, unsuspectingly opened it. Finding who his visitors really were, he drew back, slamming the door to. It just so happened that there were at that time in the house with Lott his brother, Joseph; his brother-in-law, Henry Henley, the latter of the Home Guard, and L. L. Green, afterwards a judge of the Superior Court, then but seventeen years old, but also of the Home Guard. The bushwhackers were said to have been Keith Blaylock, Levi Coffey, Sampson Calloway, son of Larkin, Edmund Ivy of Georgia, a deserter from the Confederate army, Adolphus Pritchard, and _____ Gardner of Mitchell. Blaylock demanded that all in the house surrender, whereupon Henley asked what treatment would be accorded them in case they surrendered, and Blaylock is said to have answered, "As you deserve, damn you." Henley then slipped his gun through a crack in the door and fired, wounding Calloway in the side. The bushwhackers then retired, and the Green party, who followed, saw blood. Calloway was left at the house of John Walker, two miles above Shull's Mill. Henley led the party at Green's house, excepting L. L. Green, to Walker's and surrounded it. Henley was at the rear and shot Edmund Ivy as he ran out, killing him. Blaylock called to a woman to open the gate, and Mrs. Medie Walker, born McHaarg, did so. Through the gate Blaylock and his company escaped. [Two other men, Milton Webb and Taylor Green, were likely involved in this affray.][30]

During this same month a tragedy occurred that saddened and enraged Keith: the murder of his stepfather, Austin Coffey. But Keith would bide his time and ruthlessly avenge this act. On February 26, a small band of Confederates under Captain James Marlow of Colonel

W. W. Avery's battalion came through Coffey's Gap and stopped at Mc-Caleb Coffey's house where they arrested Thomas Wright, who was a brother-in-law to Keith's half brother, David Coffey. Austin Coffey was standing near the house talking to his wife when recognized by John Boyd, who was with Marlow's group. Boyd told Marlow to arrest Coffey as he was also a Union man, and when both prisoners were secured, Boyd left for his home in the Globe. While the prisoners were being taken to the Tom Henley place, a vacant house between Shull's Mill and Blowing Rock, Thomas Wright managed to escape.

Upon reaching the Henley house, the party lit a fire and Austin Coffey went to sleep on the floor. David Coffey later stated that Captain Marlow ordered Coffey killed as retribution for Wright's escape. Whatever the reason, John Preston Arthur writes: "While he (Austin Coffey) was sleeping John Walker was detailed to kill Austin Coffey, but refused. It was then that a base born fellow, named Robert Glass, or Anders, volunteered to do the act, and while the old man slept shot him through the head. The body was taken to a laurel and ivy thicket nearby and hidden. One week later a dog was seen with a human hand in his mouth. Search revealed the body."

Glass was reported to have suffered severe mental anguish over the killing and died in Rutherford County sometime before 1882. Austin Coffey was buried on a rise behind his house in Coffey's Gap.[31]

For the next two months there is no record of Blaylock's activities, so it is probable that he crossed the lines into Tennessee in time to join Colonel Kirk's companies before they marched into North Carolina as part of a major raid. On March 21, 1865, Major General George Stoneman left Knoxville, Tennessee with a command consisting of a division of cavalry and a battery of artillery, crossing the Blue Ridge Mountains into North Carolina on the twenty-seventh. The command reached Boone at 11 A.M. the next day and divided, the first brigade heading for the Yadkin River while part of the other brigade left for Wilkesboro through Deep Gap.

Colonel Kirk, in charge of the 2nd and 3rd Regiments of Mounted Infantry, left Tennessee on April 5 and reached Boone the next day, where he was joined by Brigadier General Davis Tillson. On the morning of the seventh the 2nd Regiment left for Deep Gap under Major Bahney, and two hundred men from the 3rd Regiment, commanded by Major W. W. Rollins, went to Blowing Rock. Kirk, with 406 men, remained in Boone, headquartering at the home of J. D. Councill, where the men reportedly conducted themselves like barbarians, stealing personal property from citizens, tearing up flower beds, throwing garbage in the road, and urinating in the yard. To the relief of the citizens of Boone the 2nd and 3rd Regiments were moved toward Asheville on April 27, arriving there three days later. However, Keith Blaylock was not with them as he had one last score to settle with the Moores.[32]

On April 12, before Kirk's command left Boone, the war had ended, so Keith Blaylock had no grounds to execute any more raids.

The Tom Henley house as it appears today (1996), site of the murder of Keith Blaylock's stepfather, Austin Coffey, by Confederate soldiers on the night of February 26, 1865.
AUTHOR'S COLLECTION

Stone marking the gravesite of Keith Blaylock's stepfather, Austin Coffey, in Coffey's Gap near Blowing Rock, North Carolina. AUTHOR'S COLLECTION

Nevertheless, On May 27, Blaylock, David Moore, William Estes, and John R. Pritchard attacked the residence of Judson Moore and "took a quantity of bacon against his will."[33]

Governor Jonathan Worth, in his papers which were published later, reviewed the Judson Moore case and gives a little more insight into the conditions of the times and the case itself. Under the dateline Lincolnton, North Carolina, August 3, 1866 and using David Moore as an example, Worth's report stated:

> Caldwell County.
> David Moore, Indicted for stealing bacon. The "report" charges that he was a Union man and was with U.S. soldiers when the bacon was taken and that it was probably his own which had been taken a short time before by the "rebels."
> Answer: If the bacon was taken by U.S. soldiers under orders and Moore merely present, it is clearly not larceny or any offense at all, and if any such evidence is produced on trial, the case will certainly not be further prosecuted. But the evidence submitted to me was quite the contrary and made out a case larceny and forcible trespass.
> David Moore never complained to me or the grand jury, as I am advised, of any criminal wrong; if he had, the grievance would have been examined in the course of law.[34]

Keith Blaylock then headed for Knoxville, Tennessee where he was officially mustered into Company D, 10th Regiment of Michigan Cavalry on June 23. Keith remained in camp the remainder of his service period, being mustered out in Memphis, Tennessee on October 21, 1865.[35]

Although the war was over and he was discharged from service, Keith Blaylock was not through with his enemies. He had made a vow to kill John Boyd, the man he held responsible for the death of his stepfather, and he intended to keep it. According to John Preston Arthur, Blaylock "swore he would kill Boyd if it took forty years after the war to do so. It did not take nearly so long."

There are conflicting dates given for the killing of sixty-year-old John B. Boyd. The court record shows April 1, 1866; historian John Preston Arthur records it as February 8, 1866. Apparently the court record is incorrect, for Arthur's date and the date recorded on Boyd's gravestone in the Talbot Cemetery in the Globe correspond. On that date, Boyd and his son-in-law, William T. Blair, were building a chimney at the Boone Moore house near the Globe. That evening as they were leaving they heard a shot they thought was a signal and soon after met Keith Blaylock and Thomas Wright on a narrow path. Blaylock asked, "Is that you, Boyd?" Boyd quickly took the offensive: upon answering, "Yes," he struck out at Blaylock's head with a stout hickory walking stick. Blocking the blow with his left wrist, Blaylock backed up a few steps, raised up his Sharp's rifle, and shot Boyd. Blaylock then forced Blair to turn Boyd's body over. Satisfying himself that the man was dead, Blaylock turned and left the scene, stopping by the house of Noah White to report the incident.

Arthur reported that Keith was examined before the provost marshal in Morganton, who turned the case over to Judge Mitchell in Statesville, Iredell County. The Caldwell County Superior Court minutes show that Keith was indicted by the Grand Jury, taken into custody by Sheriff R. R. McCall, and brought into Superior Court around April 15, 1866, where he pled not guilty. Keith was released on bail.[36]

The papers of Ex-Governor Jonathan Worth, published in 1909, summarized the murder case of John Boyd under the dateline of Lincolnton, North Carolina, August 3, 1866:

> Caldwell County.
> 1. It is charged by the report of Major Wolcott that William Blaylock is indicted for the murder of John Boyd, done *since* the war. The report declares that Blaylock had been in the U.S. service, that he carefully examined the case and "a clearer case of justifiable homicide could not be made out," yet "it is believed that an unprejudiced trial could not be had, etc."
> The report admits that the homicide was since the war, does not allege that it grew out of the discharge of any military duty or order on the part of Blaylock. So it is simply an indictment against a citizen for killing another citizen in time of peace. Whether it is a case of "clear justifiable homicide" is for the courts to determine upon *sworn* testimony and the laws of the land.[37]

It would not take long for other transgressions to catch up with Keith. Indictments issued from both Caldwell and Mitchell County began to pile up and for the next two years Keith would find himself constantly in and out of court. On or about October 15, 1866, Keith was indicted by the Grand Jury in Caldwell County for the murder of William Coffey, taken into custody by Sheriff R. R. McCall, and brought into Caldwell County Superior Court in Lenoir where he pled not guilty and was released on bail.[38]

Also on October 15, Mary Coffey was appointed administratrix of the estate of Austin Coffey in Caldwell County, and Mary, William "Keith" Blaylock, and Reid Linsey were "bound unto the State of North Carolina in the sum of eleven hundred dollars." These administration bonds, which were "performance" bonds guaranteeing that the estate would be fairly and justly administered, were usually set at an amount equal to two times the value of the estate.[39]

On this same day, October 15, Keith Blaylock pled not guilty to an apparent charge of forcible trespass in Caldwell County Superior Court. This likely referred to the May 27, 1865 raid on Judson Moore in which a quantity of bacon was taken. Keith was found guilty, fined ten dollars, and placed in custody of the sheriff until the fine was paid.[40]

On the sixteenth of October, Keith, along with William Estes, David Moore, and J. R. Pritchard, was back in Superior Court to answer another charge of forcible trespass in the Judson Moore affair. All were found guilty, fined twenty dollars each along with court costs, and

Tombstone of John Boyd, killed by Keith Blaylock, in the Talbot Cemetery in the Grove area near Blowing Rock, North Carolina. AUTHOR'S COLLECTION

appealed the case to the Supreme Court. All were granted bonds and released.[41]

Keith, his brother-in-law, John R. Pritchard, William and Elijah Estes, Daniel Marcus, Joseph White, Noah Clark, and Reid Linsey, after pleading not guilty, spent the next three days in Superior Court vainly fighting a charge of affray for the January 8, 1865 attack on the Carroll Moore family. Only Blaylock, White, Linsey, and William Estes were found guilty and fined twenty-five dollars, which they appealed to the Supreme Court.[42]

Keith had a respite from court for six months, but the month of April 1867 would be a busy and crucial one for him. On the fifteenth, Keith, William Estes, and Lampton Estes, Jr., returned to Caldwell County Superior Court and pled not guilty to a charge of assault and battery in the Carroll Moore case. They were found guilty, but according to the court record, "discharged under the amnesty act on the payment of costs and in custody of the sheriff until the cost is paid. Defendant William Blaylock and Mary Coffey Security and William Estes and Joseph P. Estes Security and Lampton Estes and Madison Estes Security confesses judgment to the State for the cost."[43]

On the same day, Keith pled not guilty and amnesty to a charge of forcible trespass in the Carroll Moore affair. He was found not guilty.[44]

Next, Keith, David Moore, William Estes, and John R. Pritchard appeared on the charge of assault and battery for the attack on Judson Moore. All pled not guilty and only Blaylock and Estes were found guilty. They were "discharged under the amnesty act on the payment of costs and in custody of the sheriff until the cost is paid. Defendant William Blaylock, J. R. Pritchard, W. R. Linsey, Joseph White, Arthur Pritchard Security and William Estes and Joseph P. Estes Security confesses judgment to the State for the cost."[45]

Although both murder cases against Keith were on the docket, neither came to trial. The ensuing case against Keith was for forcible trespass, apparently for the February 1865 attack on Lott Green. Keith entered a plea of not guilty but to no avail; however, the court arrested judgment and the defendant was discharged.[46]

Keith, William Estes, and Lampton Estes, Jr. then faced another charge of forcible trespass, apparently again for the attack on Carroll Moore. The plea and results were the same: not guilty and found guilty, followed by "discharged under the amnesty act on the payment of costs and in custody of the sheriff until the cost is paid. Defendant William Blaylock and J. R. Pritchard and Mary Coffey Security and William Estes and Joseph P. Estes Security and Lampton Estes and Madison Estes Security confesses judgment to the State for the cost."[47]

The last two cases during the April court term were additional charges of assault and battery against Blaylock, William Estes, David Moore, and John R. Pritchard for the Judson Moore affair. The men were found not guilty in both cases.[48]

Again, Keith was given another rest from the hassle of court appearances, but it was not over yet. During the week of October 7, Keith, Milton Webb, Taylor Green, and Sampson Calloway were tried in Caldwell County Superior Court on the probable charge of affray for the attack on Lott Green. All pled not guilty, and all but Sampson Calloway were found guilty. In the now familiar court jargon, they were "discharged under the amnesty act on the payment of costs and in custody of the sheriff until the cost is paid. Defendant William Blaylock and W. R. Lindsey Security and the Defendant Milton Webb and Thomas H. Barber and Enoch Coffey Security, and the Defendant Taylor Green and W. R. Lindsey Security each confesses judgment to the State for the cost."[49]

At the same time Keith was tried alone on the likely charge of assault and battery, feasibly for the Lott Green affair. He was found guilty, discharged under the amnesty act on payment of costs, with W. R. Lindsey as security.[50]

On February 7, 1868, Keith Blaylock got a break; he was granted executive clemency and pardoned by Governor Jonathan Worth for the murder of John Boyd.[51] Since there is no disposition in the case against Blaylock for the murder of William Coffey in the court records of Caldwell County, it was undoubtedly dismissed under the amnesty act as an act of war.

Keith wound up his court appearances in Caldwell County with John R. Pritchard on April 6, 1868, on another charge of forcible trespass, again likely for either the Carroll Moore or Judson Moore affair. Both were found guilty, ordered to pay a fine of sixpence each and costs. Thomas Pritchard acted as security for both defendants.[52]

Keith's last court appearance occurred during the fall term of Mitchell County Superior Court in Bakersville, North Carolina. Along with his wife Malinda and J. D. English, he was charged with forcible trespass. A *nolle prosequi* (unwilling to prosecute) was entered in Malinda's case, but Keith pled guilty, paid the costs, and judgment was suspended. It is likely that this charge was for the first raid on Carroll Moore; however the court record is unspecified.[53]

In retrospect, most of the court cases against Keith Blaylock and his companions occurred during the Civil War when he was officially a soldier in the service of the United States, and could be deemed unjust. However, the acts themselves were of a personal nature and not executed under official orders. Nevertheless, Keith was undoubtedly fortunate to come out of it with so little punishment.

It was time now for the Blaylocks to settle down and raise their family. On August 28, 1869 their third son John H. "Jack" was born. The 1867 Mitchell County Tax List for the Cranberry and Linville Districts lists Keith with a state tax of 50¢ and a county tax of $1.50. According to the Mitchell County census, the Blaylocks were living and farming in Jonas Ridge Township in 1870. In 1872 Keith Blaylock was using the post office in Childsville, near present-day Ingalls.[54]

The Blaylock family kept growing; a son, Isaac William, called Will or Willie, was born on November 21, 1874, followed by another son, Samuel Washington on April 17, 1877. In 1880, Keith was still listed as a farmer, but living in Snow Creek Township in Mitchell County. For some reason a remark that William (Keith) Blaylock was insane was entered in the Miscellaneous Information column of the census.[55]

On a more sanguine note, on November 15, 1871 Keith made two claims against the U.S. Government for actions taken during the Civil War: The first in the amount of $447 for "Provisioning. Taken by the [U.S.] army in N.C.," and the second, $150 for a "Horse. Taken by the

Pardon of William (Keith) Blaylock for the murder of John Boyd in 1866, granted by North Carolina Governor Jonathan Worth on February 7, 1868. State v William Blaylock, Murder: Executive Clemency, Caldwell County, North Carolina Minute Docket, Superior Court 1867–1868, C.R. 017.311.2 (Fall Term 1867), p. 7. DIVISION OF ARCHIVES AND HISTORY, NORTH CAROLINA DEPARTMENT OF CULTURAL RESOURCES, RALEIGH

Last photo of Malinda Blaylock, with granddaughter Ethyl Blaylock, taken in 1902.
COURTESY OF MABEL BLAYLOCK SMITH, GRANDDAUGHTER OF MALINDA BLAYLOCK

[U.S.] army in Tennessee." Both claims were presented to Congress in December, 1874 and on March 4, 1875, the claims were approved and Keith was allowed $80 on the first claim and $125 on the second.[56]

There is not much information about the later life of Keith and Malinda Blaylock. On January 9, 1879, Keith filed for a government pension for his military service during the Civil War. The pension was granted and he received fifty dollars a month for the rest of his life. In 1880 *The Mountain Voice* in Bakersville related the following tongue in cheek item: "The irrepressible Keith Blaylock was in town this week and his benign countenance was radiant with smiles over the election." Writer Walter Clark claimed that Keith endeavored to be a merchandiser and made an unsuccessful bid for the legislature on the Republican ticket. There is supposition that Keith ran a general store in Montezuma, North Carolina, and it is also rumored that he ran a house of prostitution above the store. All this is unconfirmed, and there are no charges against him in the court records. It is also reported that Keith worked in the area's various tree and garden nurseries throughout his life.[57]

Keith, however, made additional court appearances in his later life. He was brought into court under the name "Keith" Blaylock during the fall 1874 term of Mitchell County Superior Court, but the unnamed charge was dropped and a *nolle prosequi* was entered.[58]

Keith's last appearance as a defendant in court was in 1881. Apparently Keith and his son Lum got into a brawl early in the year and were charged with affray under "State vs Columbus Blaylock *et. al.*" during the spring term of Mitchell County Superior Court. The case proceeded on October 27, and quoting from the docket, "The defendants Columbus Blaylock and William Blaylock come into Court and acknowledge themselves indebted to the State of North Carolina in the sum of Two Hundred Dollars but to be void on condition that Columbus Blaylock shall make his personal appearance at the next term of the Court and shall show to the court that he has paid the costs in this behalf incurred." The court's instructions were evidently carried out as there was no further action in the case.[59]

The land holdings of the Blaylocks were numerous, as can be confirmed by the Mitchell County Deed Books. From 1870 until 1894 there were thirty-one listings in the Grantee Index totaling nearly 1,700 acres of land under the names of William, Malinda, and S. M. (Sarah Malinda). The most important was their purchase of their house and lot in Montezuma on March 7, 1894 from C. C. Banner and wife, and by 1902 they owned around fifty-five acres in the town. Starting in 1874 and continuing until 1907, nearly one thousand acres of this land was sold by Keith, Malinda, and later with their son Samuel.[60]

The town of Montezuma, where Keith and Malinda choose to spend their later years, was just a scattering of a few settlers in 1850. *Avery County Heritage* reports, "Ranging cattle roamed the fields once grazed by buffalo, the bulls scraping the ground with their hooves to

The house in Montezuma, North Carolina, purchased by Keith and Malinda Blaylock in 1894, as it appeared in the late 1920s. COURTESY OF MARGARET FARLEY, BLOWING ROCK, NORTH CAROLINA

Photograph taken in 1994 of the house in Montezuma, North Carolina that Keith and Malinda Blaylock bought in 1894. AUTHOR'S COLLECTION

show superiority. Hence, the community was named Bull Scrape." The locale was in Watauga County until the Civil War when it incorporated within the borders of newly created Mitchell County. In June 1883, when a post office was established, the community was renamed Aaron. In 1891 the town of Aaron was incorporated and, through an election, renamed Montezuma. By 1900, Montezuma was a thriving community.[61]

It is family conjecture among the Blaylock descendants that Keith and Malinda went to Texas sometime in their later life, but returned in about two years. By examining the Mitchell County Deed Books there are three two-year periods in the 1890s that are free of any transactions by Keith and/or Malinda, and it is probable they went to Texas sometime during this time. The period between 1890 and 1892 is the best guess for their Texas venture, as they bought their home in Montezuma in 1894. A family anecdote is that while in Texas Keith got so sick from eating bananas that he could never again stand the sight of them.[62]

In December 1902, an ailing and aged Malinda Blaylock went to visit her oldest son, Lum, who was U.S. Postmaster in Hickory, North Carolina. She returned to Montezuma the last week in February, but her condition continued to decline. Malinda died on March 9, one day before her sixty-fourth birthday. She was buried in the Montezuma Cemetery, high on the hill that overlooked her home.[63]

Apparently Keith, at age sixty-five, could not stand the life of a widower for by June of 1903 he was involved with twenty-five-year-old Martha Jane Hollifield of Blowing Rock.[64] On February 4, 1904, Martha gave birth to Keith's child, a boy she named Aaron Paul Blaylock, but was called Paul.[65] Four years later, on May 10, 1908, William "Keith" Blaylock and Martha Jane Hollifield were married by Reverend W. H. Calloway in Saginaw, North Carolina, in the extreme west-

Grave of Malinda Blaylock in the Montezuma Cemetery. AUTHOR'S COLLECTION

ern part of Burke County that lies high in the Blue Ridge Mountains.[66] Martha had given birth to another son out of wedlock in 1901 who was named Edward Jerome Hollifield; however, there is no indication he was Keith's son.[67]

The year 1905 was a tragic one for Keith Blaylock. First was the death of his eighty-six-year-old mother, Mary Blaylock Coffey, on January 19, 1905.[68] Four months later Keith's son Will died. Thirty-year-old Will Blaylock was a barber in Montezuma, and was locally known as a bully. Seemingly, he enjoyed picking on younger men, physically pushing and kicking them around. On May 7, Will jumped on the wrong person, twenty-year-old Bun Ledford.

John Bunyon Ledford, known as Bun, was born in North Carolina to Marion and Ruth Clark Ledford and grew up a slight man of short stature. At the time of the incident he was living a short distance away, near Newland. Will Blaylock, who had been drinking, spotted young Ledford in Montezuma and decided to have some fun running him out of town. Blaylock followed Ledford across the road and then began kicking him. Apparently this was not the first time Blaylock had abused Ledford, and the latter turned and said something like, "This is the last time you'll ever do that to me!" Ledford then pulled out a pistol and shot Blaylock, instantly killing him.[69]

Legend has it that Ledford hid out in the woods along the Linville River and that his family brought food to him. Factual or not, Bun Ledford was in Mitchell County Superior Court in Bakersville when his trial for murder began on May 29, 1905 under Judge W. B. Councill. Prosecutor W. C. Newland, apparently judging the mien of the people, gave notice that he would not "ask for a verdict of murder in the 1st degree but only for a verdict of second degree or manslaughter." The rest of the day was used forming a jury. The next two days were spent in the giving of testimony and closing arguments. On the morning of June 1, the jury reached a verdict of not guilty. Bun Ledford married and spent the rest of his life in Avery County, passing away at age fifty-six on July 24, 1941. He was buried in Montezuma.[70]

As Keith settled into old age and became known as "Uncle Keith" to many, his legends lived on. They have been engagingly presented by Marrion W. Ward in an unpublished short history of Keith Blaylock. Since Ward researched these stories, let his words stand:

> Howard Gragg, whose grandfather bought Keith and Malinda Blaylock's land, remembers several stories his father told him about Keith Blaylock. Across the road from where Howard lives now is the "Keith field" where Keith raised corn. He carried his corn 6 or 7 miles to the Globe to the mill. Problems arose there, however, because the miller, probably James Gragg, was a Confederate sympathizer who did not think highly of Keith and his Union activities. Getting the corn ground and back home safely was a challenge for Keith.
>
> Gragg's father also told him that during one of the periods when Keith had to hide out in the rocks under the Grandfather, he had only one fry pan for cooking. Mr. Gragg said Keith had killed a bear and

Tombstone of Keith Blaylock's mother, Mary Coffey, in the White Springs Cemetery near Blowing Rock, North Carolina. AUTHOR'S COLLECTION

Tombstone of Keith Blaylock's second wife, Martha Jane Hollifield Blaylock, in the Boone's Fork Cemetery in Blowing Rock, North Carolina. AUTHOR'S COLLECTION

stayed under the rocks the length of time it took to cook the entire bear in that one skillet.

Not far from Keith and Malinda's cabin was a temporary hideout Keith used. The present road was just a path then, and Keith had a wonderful lookout atop a large granite boulder. Onto the boulder had fallen other large rocks creating a cave about 10 feet long and 4 to 5 feet wide. Rocks still lie there that Keith wedged in to close up one end. He could hide there by walling up the other end or he could shoot from the end of his natural fortress. These rocks are still called the Keith Rocks or Keese's Rock House. . . .

Judge [J. Ray] Braswell also remembers his father's telling of one group of youngsters who got the best of Keith. An old man, Keith was sitting in the Baptist church at Montezuma with his hands resting on the top of a cane or walking stick with his head resting on his hands. He may have been dozing a little during the sermon, but the youngsters sneaked up and yanked on his beard, causing him to lose his balance—a prank Keith may not have appreciated at the time, but most certainly would have enjoyed in his earlier days.[71]

Another legendary action of Keith's reportedly occurred at the funeral of his victim, John Boyd. According to Keith's half brother David Coffey, "The next day Keith went to Boyd's funeral and told the people present, 'I've always come and gone in the Globe as a free man, but yesterday I was attacked and had to kill a man whose funeral you are witnessing. I expect in the future to come and go here as freely as I have in the past.'"[72]

According to Keith's granddaughter, Mabel Blaylock Smith, there was one chief passion in Keith's life, fishing. The *Morganton Herald* supports that assertion in this June 1913 article, "Uncle Keith Blaylock, of Montezuma, has been catching some fine fish in the river [Catawba River] here—some 19 and 17½ inches long. But his son, C. F. Blaylock, broke the record yesterday, the 9th. He caught one 22½ inches long."[73] But Keith's fishing days were nearly over, for in two months he would be dead.

On the morning of July 18, Keith decided to go fishing in the Linville River near Pineola. As he reached the railroad spur that led down the mountain from Montezuma to Pineola he encountered several youngsters from the area, Lloyd Suddreth, his future wife Belle Pritchard and her two sisters, Edna and Estelle, and Bob Robbins, who were boarding a railroad handcar, or flat dump car. Keith accepted the offer of a ride on the railroad car down the spur to Pineola. As the rail car picked up momentum the young people began horsing around, jumping on and off the car. In their amusement they either broke or lost the wooden brake stick, which had to be inserted between the metal floor and the wheel and pulled back to stop the car. The runaway car continued on the downgrade until it crashed into some boxcars at the Pineola siding. Most of the young people jumped or were thrown clear except the septuagenarian Keith, whose ribs were broken when he was hurled from the car and fell on Edna Pritchard, also breaking her ankle.

Keith was rushed to the Pineola Hotel and according to Marrion Ward, Martine Pritchard Davis, a great-niece of Malinda Blaylock and sister of the three Pritchard girls involved in the accident, remembered as a young child a horse and buggy stopping in front of her house and that "The driver bore the news that three of Tina's sisters had been on a 'dump truck' that had wrecked. Her mother had been baking and dropped everything to run out of the house to be taken near Pineola where the accident occurred."

Keith was soon brought to his home in Montezuma where he suffered for nearly a month. Retired Judge J. Ray Braswell related that his father, Warsaw Braswell, was walking by the Blaylock home when Martha Blaylock rushed out and asked him to help as Keith was having great difficulty breathing. Braswell did what he could, lifting Keith to a sitting position, but to no avail, and Keith died in his arms. The date was August 11, 1913. Keith was buried next to Malinda in the Montezuma Cemetery, the death date on his tombstone reflecting the date of the accident and not of his death.[74]

Keith and Malinda Blaylock were an enigmatic couple. Much of their lives and their escapades during the Civil War are shrouded in mystery. Their trip to Texas and what Keith did for a living, besides drawing a fifty-dollar Civil War pension, are prime examples. It is only fitting that even Keith's death escaped the local newspapers. The reason was that no death certificate was filed, and also that he died at home and his wife and family did not report it. Nonetheless, there is enough for a good story, legend or not.

Tombstone of William McKessen "Keith" Blaylock in the Montezuma Cemetery erected by his son Paul Blaylock. Note the incorrect initials, L.M., which were taken from Histories of the Several Regiments and Battalions from North Carolina in the Great War 1861–65, *and that the date of death reflects the date of the rail car accident and not the correct death date of August 11, 1913.* AUTHOR'S COLLECTION

III. TEXAS

THE HAMILTON WHITES, FATHER AND SON

Making of an Outlaw

EVERY ENTHUSIAST WHO PROBES into the history of American outlaws is undoubtedly intrigued by what launched them on their criminal careers. In many cases the cause seems ambiguous; in others it is legendary and untrue. For example, legend has it that the James brothers became robbers because the railroad took their land; that Billy the Kid became a killer to avenge the murder of his best friend and ended up killing twenty-one men; and that William Quantrill became a Confederate guerrilla because his brother was murdered by Kansas "jayhawkers." In stage robber Ham White's case, however, the motive is clear-cut: he became an outlaw by avenging the murder of his father.

When this author's biography of Ham White, *Knight of the Road,* was published in 1990 there were many unanswered questions regarding the 1867 murder of Ham's father, Hamilton White II. Since that time documentation has been discovered that establishes the motive behind the killing, the positive identity of the killer, and the manner of death of Hamilton II. Young Ham White's thirst for revenge for this murder started him on his path to notoriety.

Ham White was descended from a long line of respected and affluent people. His great-grandfather, Jeremiah White (c. 1740–1788), was born in Dinwiddie County, Virginia and moved to the eastern portion of Pittsylvania County, Virginia in 1778. Ham's grandfather, Hamilton White I (c. 1770–1832), remained in Pittsylvania County; his son Hamilton White II was born in about 1808. Hamilton II married

Tabitha Hutchings (born c. 1815), and had one child in Pittsylvania County.[1]

By 1835 Hamilton II had decided to emigrate and in January 1836 he arrived in Bastrop County, Texas and staked a claim on Mayhaw Creek in the Cedar Creek community, about ten miles west of Bastrop and around twenty miles southeast of Austin. The Whites picked a very inopportune time to settle in Texas because the Anglo-Texans had begun their revolution against Mexican rule the previous November. When news reached Bastrop that the Alamo had fallen on March 6, a general panic spread and families hurriedly packed what they could and fled eastward for safety.

Since most of the men were serving with the army, a company of rangers aided the women and children in their flight. Although Hamilton White's name does not appear as a member of the army, it was likely he had enlisted in Bastrop's "Mina Volunteers." The rangers remained at Bastrop until Mexican General Gaona with around seven hundred troops arrived on April 1, 1835. The Mexican troops entered the deserted village and after plundering it, departed for San Felipe. Following the departure of the Mexicans, the Indians destroyed what was left of Bastrop. After the defeat of Santa Anna's Mexican Army at San Jacinto on April 21, the refugee families returned to Bastrop and began rebuilding the homes they had lost.

From late 1837 until April 1839 the towns of Bastrop and Waterloo (now Austin) vied for the seat as capital of the Republic of Texas. On April 25, 1838, in a report to the Second Congress, Bastrop citizens pledged over ten thousand acres of privately owned land on condition that the capital be located in Bastrop. One of the signers was Hamilton White II, who offered three hundred acres of land located within twelve miles of Bastrop. It was a vain effort, for on April 13, 1839 Waterloo was chosen as the capital site.

During Bastrop County's early years no one was exempt from the danger of Indian raids. During the late 1830s Hamilton II had contracted to supply lumber for building construction in Austin. In the fall of 1839 he sent a slave to Austin with a load of lumber and, on the return trip, the slave was shot and killed by a band of Indians. Life in Bastrop County was not always troublesome, however, and Hamilton II contributed to its brighter side. Horse racing was a popular pastime and in 1840 Hamilton II, as proprietor of the local race course, advertised in Austin's *Texas Sentinel* the three-day Bastrop Fall Races, scheduled to commence on October 15.[2]

Hamilton II also held public office three times during the period of time Texas was a Republic. To serve in these positions he posted bond on the following dates: February 24, 1845 as constable, August 13, 1846 as justice of the peace, and August 18, 1846 as surveyor. In the spring of 1847, during the war with Mexico, he served for six weeks as a private in the Bastrop County Mounted Volunteer Company's expedition to San Antonio and was honorably discharged. He was also post-

Although there is no confirming documentation, it is probable that this is a photograph of young Ham White taken by H. R. Marks in April 1877. It is titled "Unidentified Biography" in the H. R. Marks collection at the Austin History Center, Texas Public Library, Austin. In 1987 the North Carolina State Bureau of Investigation in Raleigh compared this photograph to White's 1891 San Quentin Prison photograph. Although the bureau was unable to state positively that both photos were of the same man, John Neuner of the Latent Evidence Division wrote to the author on November 17, "As an untrained observer, a consistency in the bone structure of the face is apparent."

master of Cedar Creek from September 12, 1859 through August 1861. Hamilton White II is considered one of the prominent early pioneers of Texas.

Prior to 1867 Hamilton and Tabitha White had acquired a large amount of land, totaling 3,887 acres, with their first deed being registered on December 23, 1837. Four tracts of 320 acres each had been obtained by patent under the Pre-emption (Homestead) Act of 1845. According to the 1860 census Hamilton II's Bastrop County land holdings amounted to $10,760 with personal property valued at $5,900. The Agricultural census for 1860 listed Hamilton II as owning 890 acres of land, 250 acres of which was improved acreage valued at six thousand dollars. Apparently the Whites found the buying and selling of land profitable, for by 1867 they had sold 3,172 acres of their land. They were also slaveholders, owning five in 1850 and eleven in 1860. Hamilton White was alleged to be the second wealthiest man in Bastrop County.[3]

While the Whites lived in Bastrop County, seven additional children were born to them. Hamilton III, the sixth child, was born on April 17, 1854.[4]

The Whites had the distinction of living in one of the twenty-three original counties of the Republic of Texas, which hosted the settlement of Stephen F. Austin's first colony in Texas in 1829. At that time Bastrop County contained all of the fifteen present-day counties. In 1874, the last boundary change occurred, reducing the county to its present size of 867 square miles. Until the early 1880s the county remained chiefly agricultural with cotton, produced under a plantation system, as its main crop. Approximately twelve miles east of White's homestead stood the unusual forest called the "Lost Pines of Texas." This isolated stand of loblolly pines, so named because of its eighty-some-mile separation from the eastern limit of the main pine belt, constituted Bastrop County's first commercial product—timber, used in many early buildings in central Texas.[5]

That the elder White was well respected and esteemed by the community is borne out by this passage in the diary of well-to-do Bastrop County socialite Mary Ann "Molly" McDowell regarding White's death in 1867: "The father of my good friend Ham White was killed Wednesday night, he was going to his home 12 miles from town when a man shot him in the back. (He was in a buggy—Mr. W.)"

The same sentiments were not held by Freedman's Bureau Sub-Assistant Commissioner Bryon Porter. The Freedman's Bureau was set up by the United States Congress on March 3, 1865, a little over a month before the Civil War was officially over. It began operation in Texas in December 1866, with its function to manage freedmen, refugees, and abandoned lands in the conquered Southern states. According to the *Handbook of Texas,* Volume I:

> The function of the bureau which was most offensive to the white population, however, was that of giving protection to the freedmen in the

courts, in the process of which regular court procedure was blocked. Insolent and officious bureau agents frequently withdrew the freedman's cases from the regular courts and themselves assumed the rights of adjudication. After a stormy existence, marked by bitter conflicts with the regularly constituted state authorities, the bureau ceased to operate in Texas in 1868.

Porter's report from Bastrop states, "The death of White caused no surprise in the community for he was well known as a bad, violent man who has killed several men and wounded more." Porter's statements were obviously biased, and were likely based on White's undoubted support for the Confederacy during the Civil War and hearsay, for the records of the Bastrop County District Court do not substantiate the agent's report. There were only two incidents of violence in which White was involved.[6]

In mid June 1859, the *True Issue* in La Grange, Texas quoted this article from the *Bastrop Advertiser*: "An encounter took place between Mr. Ham White and a Scotchman [Douglass], at the residence of the former on Cedar Creek, on Wednesday last [June 5], in which the latter was shot by the former, two buck-shot out of three, with which the gun was loaded, taking effect—one in the right and the other in the left shoulder."[7] There are no details that explain the cause of the confrontation, but Hamilton II was indicted for "assault with intent to kill and murder one Douglass" and posted bond on October 7. The case was continued on October 12, and state witnesses W. H. Dixon, Carroll Billingsley, and Antonio Schmidt were subpoenaed. On March 11, 1860, the case was again continued, and on April 8 of the following year the court minutes stated that the court was still trying to locate witness Schmidt. Since there is no further mention of the case, the charges were apparently dismissed.[8]

Hamilton II's death resulted from lawsuits and criminal charges between White and a neighboring family named Rowe. Thomas Rowe and his wife Mary had been neighbors of the Whites since moving from South Carolina in 1846. Although the Rowes had several children, only twenty-seven-year-old James Rowe and his father figured prominently in the feud.[9]

The first recorded incident occurred on October 19, 1859, when White, as administrator of the estate of M. A. Craft, brought suit, presumably for debt, against Thomas Rowe in Bastrop County District Court for forty-six dollars. White won the case.[10]

Seven years later, on March 6, 1866, the Rowes charged White with assault and battery. On the following December 18, White had James Rowe indicted for stealing cattle and trial was set for the following June 17. On June 12, 1867, White's trial for assault and battery was held. The Rowes lost the case but White was ordered to pay the court costs. On his way home from court this same day, Hamilton White II would die.[11]

James Rowe likely attended the trial and, with or without his father's concurrence, followed White until a perfect opportunity to kill him presented itself. This cold-blooded murder occurred on Green's Creek, about four miles from White's home. According to the *Houston Daily Telegraph:*

> We regret to announce that Mr. Ham White was killed on Wednesday evening last, on his return to his farm on Cedar Creek from the town of Bastrop. It appears that he had reached a small creek in the neighborhood of Mr. Alexander, some eight miles west of town, and had gotten out of his buggy to make an examination of the water to see whether it had swollen too much to prevent his crossing, when he was approached by some person or persons and shot through the head, the body, and the wrist. His body was discovered a very short time after the occurrence took place, by Mr. George Moore, who was returning to his home in the neighborhood where the occurrence took place, from town. We have learned that parties have already been suspicioned as connected with the affair, but we will not mention any names until facts are fully developed in the premises. Mr. White was an old resident of Bastrop County, and was well acquainted through this section. He leaves a large family to mourn his loss.[12]

A more detailed account came from Bryon Porter of the Freedman's Bureau, who was stationed in Bastrop, Texas:

> He [White] was on his way home from town alone, in a buggy, and stopped at a small stream which had been swollen by the constant rains. Here, it is supposed, he got out, tied his horse to a tree and leaving his pistol on the seat of the buggy, went to examine the stream for a fording place. It was evident from the tracks and other indications found, that some person mounted, rode up and cut him off from his buggy, and while White dodged around a tree, rode around several times after him discharging his pistol at him. White was found a short time afterwards, lying by the tree quite dead, shot in three places, the head, the chest and the wrist.
>
> A woman living about five hundred yards from the scene of the murder heard five shots fired.
>
> There is not much doubt but that he was killed by a young man named James Rowe who was seen riding a short distance behind White and who immediately left the country and has not been seen here since.

Porter reported that Rowe, in company with Charles Barnett, who was also wanted for murder in Bastrop County, was seen in Waco a few days before July 5. Rowe was thought to be headed for Shelby or Panola, Texas, where he had relatives, and Porter wrote the sub-assistant commissioners of the Freedman's Bureau in those districts to be on the lookout for him. Rowe was never apprehended. Porter also gave this vivid description of the fugitive: "James Rowe . . . is about 5 ft. 9 or 10 inches in height—very light straight hair—blue eyes, has a slight impediment or catch in the throat when speaking—has an habitual grin or drawing up of the nose like one looking at the sun (this last is his marked peculiarity). Is about 25 [twenty-seven] yrs. of age. His general appearance is simple or green."[13]

Needless to say, when Rowe's trial for cattle theft came up on June 17, he was long gone. His bond was forfeited and the case was contin-

Bastrop, Texas, 5ᵗʰ July 1867.

Lieut J. T. Kirkman
a. a. a. Genl.
Bu. R. Fan A. L.
Galveston, Texas.

Lieutenant.

I have the honor to submit the
following general report for the Month of June
1867

On the 14ᵗʰ of June Ham White an old
and well known citizen of Bastrop County,
living on Cedar Creek, — was murdered about
five miles from Bastrop. He was on his way
home from town alone, in a buggy, and stopped at a small stream which had been
much swollen by the constant rains. Here,
it is supposed, he got out, tied his horse to a
tree and leaving his pistol on the seat of
the buggy, went to examine the stream for
a fording place. It was evident from the track
and other indications found, that some person
mounted, rode up and cut him off from his
buggy, and while White dodged around a
tree, rode around several times after him
discharging his pistol at him. White was

---

*Portion of letter dated July 5, 1867, regarding the death of Hamilton White II, from Freed-
man Agent Bryon Porter to Lieut. J. T. Kirkman, Bureau of R. F. and A. L., Galveston,
Texas.* FREEDMAN'S BUREAU RECORDS, BASTROP COUNTY, TEXAS STATE ARCHIVES,
AUSTIN

Site of the murder of Ham White's father, Hamilton White II, on Green's Creek in Bastrop County, Texas. The murder occurred on June 12, 1867. PHOTO TAKEN BY DONALY BRICE IN MAY 1986

The White family cemetery near Cedar Creek, Bastrop County, Texas. Large tombstone marks the grave of Ham White's brother, John White. The cemetery is located just east of the old homestead. PHOTO TAKEN BY DONALY BRICE IN MAY 1986

ued. He was never tried for this case nor was he indicted for the murder of Hamilton II.[14] This indicates that the Rowe family were in good favor with the United States authorities, and later with the Reconstruction rule in Texas established through the election of Radical Republican Edmund Jackson Davis as governor of Texas in 1870. Davis formed the hated and corrupt State Police, virtually the only law in Texas until the Texas Rangers were reformed under Governor Richard Coke in 1874.[15]

As the eldest son and namesake, Ham White was closely attached and devoted to his father. He was barely thirteen years old when he was devastated by his father's tragic and brutal death, and it took eight long, agonizing years for young Ham to avenge his father's death. The tragedy and aftermath of his father's death created an overpowering desire for revenge which so engulfed young Ham that it ultimately altered the course of his life, bringing about his criminal career. His devotion to and memory of his father's image would also emerge and clearly manifest itself when he attempted to add honor to his unhonorable deeds. In a newspaper interview years later, White described his feelings at the time:

> I, child as I was, over the bloody corpse of my murdered father, took a solemn oath to devote my whole life, if necessary, to avenge his death, and to kill his cowardly and treacherous assassin. This cold blooded, and as far as I knew unprovoked murder, changed me at once from the innocent confiding boy to an avenging Nemesis. My entire thought and objection in life appeared to be to meet and slay this man who had so abruptly despoiled our family. . . . My desire for vengeance appeared to "grow with my growth and strengthen with my strength." Nothing short of "an eye for an eye and a tooth for a tooth" would satisfy me. . . . Upon the day that I arrived at maturity I visited my father's grave, and there renewed my oath of vengeance, and vowed that ere another sun would set I would kill his murderer.

About two years after the murder of Hamilton II, James Rowe returned to Bastrop County. Shortly after his return the White farmhouse mysteriously burned to the ground, forcing the White family to move to "the river farm" closer to the town of Bastrop. Ham's mother forbade him to return to the old homeplace for fear he would kill Rowe. For the next eight years Ham White lived in a completely female-dominated household with thoughts of revenge festering in his mind.[16]

In August 1875, his pent-up emotions broke loose and the twenty-one-year-old White committed his first crime, stealing a herd of cattle in Caldwell County and driving them north. An indictment was issued from Bastrop County for which bond was immediately paid, likely by his mother. In late September he was captured in Milam County and incarcerated in the Rockdale jail. A few days later he was turned over to a Milam County deputy sheriff for return to Caldwell County, from whom he escaped. On December 1, six additional indictments for cattle theft were issued.[17]

Now a fugitive, White set out determined to fulfill his vow of vengeance and made his way back to Bastrop County. At dusk on October 7 he rode to a spot near the Rowe house and waited patiently for James Rowe to appear.

According to White's version, as soon as he saw Rowe he started walking toward him. Sighting his adversary, Rowe began running in the opposite direction. Continuing to advance toward Rowe, and knowing he was armed, White ordered him to defend himself. Ignoring the command Rowe continued running. White then opened fire with his revolver, his first shot breaking Rowe's right arm. The next shot entered Rowe's back and came out his throat, immediately killing him. On hearing the gunshots James' younger brother, thirty-two-year-old Alexander, rushed to the scene and began firing at his brother's killer. Rowe fired eight times, wounding White in several places. White held no animosity toward Alexander and refused to return his fire. Seeing that his horse had been killed, White painfully hobbled away from the scene of conflict.[18]

The *Bastrop Advertiser* and the *Daily Democratic Statesman* in Austin, however, gave a somewhat different version of Rowe's killing. The *Bastrop Advertiser* ran the following piece:

ANOTHER MURDER—Just as we go to press we learn of another horrible murder which occurred on Ceder Creek, 12 miles west of Bastrop, on Thursday evening. The particulars as we got them from Mr. Norgrath, one of the jury of inquest, are that about dark Thursday evening, while Mr. Jas. V. Rhoe [*sic*], was in his lot feeding his horse, a man rode up to the fence and began shooting at him with a Spencer rifle. Mr. Rhoe, in the effort to evade the shots, ran around the corn crib, the man all the while continuing to shoot at him. He finally got into the crib, as he thought for security, where he was shot to death, no less than twelve or fifteen shots being fired at him. We are told that Rhoe called lustily for his six-shooter, but there being no one at the house, or in hearing, but his aged mother, it was not carried to him. The jury of inquest fail to elicit any evidence [as] to the murder, though strong [feeling] amounting to almost certainty, exist among the people as to who did the deed. As usual, as of date, the murderer escaped.

The *Daily Democratic Statesman* had this report:

Two travelers from Colorado county, who arrived in this city yesterday, report that on Tuesday [*sic*] evening a man named James Rowe was killed while at work at a corn crib by an unknown assassin. Rowe was shot five times, the last ball passing through his neck and causing instant death.

Since writing the above as we are informed by Mr. J. J. Allen of this city that a boy named Ham White was supposed to have done the killing, as he swore he would kill Rowe, who had killed the boy's father twelve years ago.[19]

Basically, White's account and the newspapers' versions agree that White shot Rowe as he was trying to get away. The major difference was that White failed to point out that the killing took place in a corn crib. As neither newspaper account mentions the shooting of White by Rowe's brother, evidently the Rowe family did not report it. By March of 1877 the *Daily Democratic Statesman* had obtained all the details of the killing and gave the following report: "Ham White, the notorious highwayman . . . has one stiff knee, caused by a shot from the brother of the man Rowe, who was killed by White about a year ago."[20]

San Quentin Prison photograph of Ham White, as Henry Miller, taken in 1891. COURTESY OF CALIFORNIA STATE ARCHIVES, SACRAMENTO, CALIFORNIA

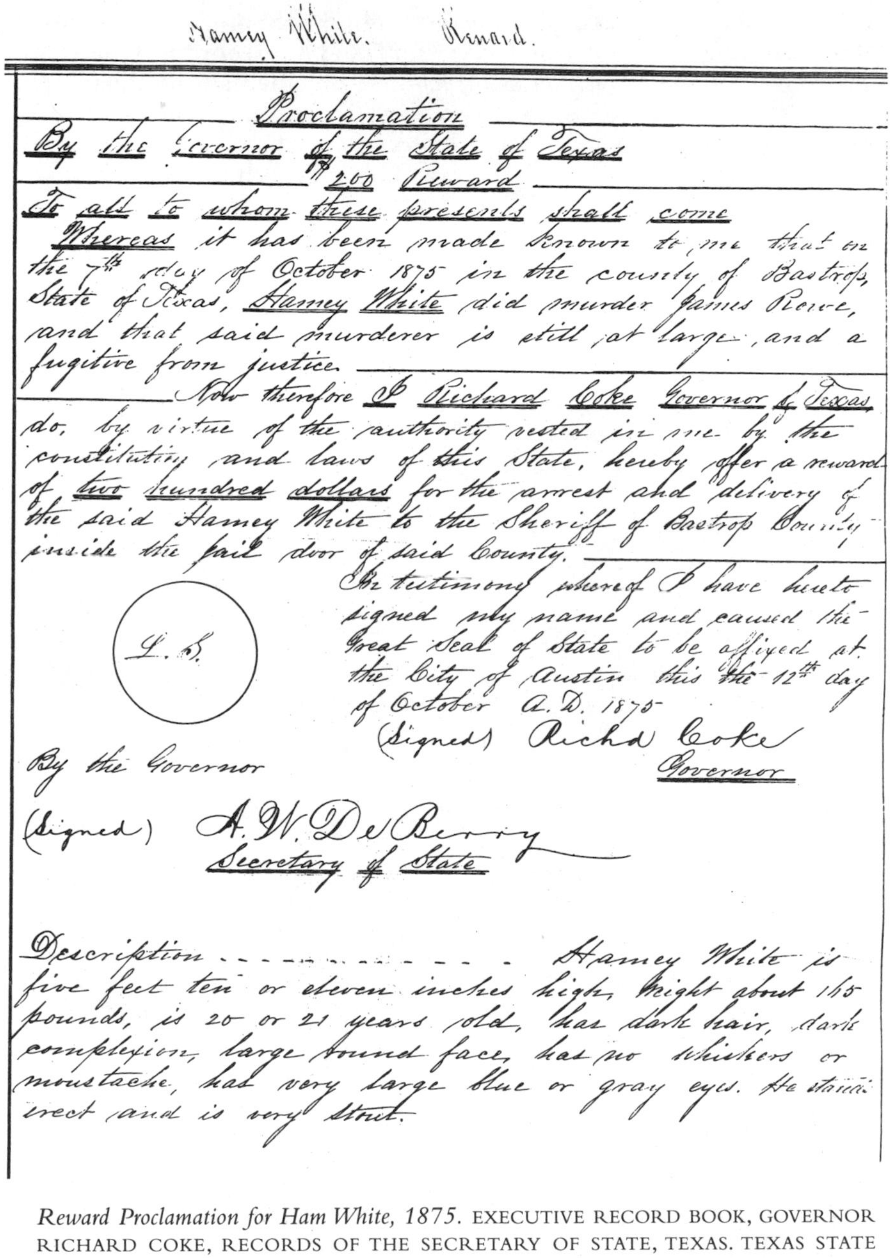

Proclamation

By the Governor of the State of Texas

$200 Reward

To all to whom these presents shall come
Whereas it has been made known to me that on the 7th day of October 1875 in the county of Bastrop, State of Texas, Hamey White did murder James Reeve, and that said murderer is still at large, and a fugitive from justice.

Now therefore I Richard Coke Governor of Texas do, by virtue of the authority vested in me by the constitution and laws of this State, hereby offer a reward of two hundred dollars for the arrest and delivery of the said Hamey White to the Sheriff of Bastrop County inside the jail door of said County.

In testimony whereof I have hereunto signed my name and caused the Great Seal of State to be affixed at the City of Austin this the 12th day of October A.D. 1875

(L. S.)

(Signed) Richd Coke
Governor

By the Governor

(Signed) A. W. DeBerry
Secretary of State

Description — — — — — — — — — Hamey White is five feet ten or eleven inches high, weight about 165 pounds, is 20 or 21 years old, has dark hair, dark complexion, large round face, has no whiskers or moustache, has very large blue or gray eyes. He stands erect and is very stout.

Reward Proclamation for Ham White, 1875. EXECUTIVE RECORD BOOK, GOVERNOR RICHARD COKE, RECORDS OF THE SECRETARY OF STATE, TEXAS. TEXAS STATE ARCHIVES, AUSTIN

On October 12, 1875, Texas Governor Richard Coke issued a two-hundred-dollar reward for Ham White.[21] Following his recovery from wounds received in the Rowe shoot-out, Ham escaped to West Texas. In March of 1877, he was returning to Bastrop County when he robbed his first stagecoach near Waco, Texas. From this point on there was no stopping Ham White. He developed an unabated obsession for robbing stagecoaches, and became the premier stage robber in U.S. history. He was in and out of various jails and penitentiaries for the rest of his life. The image of his father was always with him, however, and the highwayman attempted to live up to this image by adhering to a code of honor while committing his crimes. This was manifested in the grudging admiration and respect of the lawmen who pursued him. Who can say what Ham White's life would have been if not for the cowardly murder of his father.

IV. CALIFORNIA

HARVEY BELL MITCHELL

Child's Play

DURING THE 1870S STAGECOACH ROBBERIES were no novelty in the western United States, especially in central and northern California. The typical scenario, depicted in films, books, and quite often in reality, is a group of armed, masked men swooping down on the stagecoach, demanding the treasure box, lining up the passengers who are relieved of their money and possessions, and then riding off in a blaze of gunfire, hooting with shouts of glee. In this story, however, the scenario is much different: a child in the dead of a winter's night in 1871, armed with only a redwood fence picket, relieving a terrified stage driver of the treasure box.

To fully understand the dramatics in the second scenario, it is necessary to give a brief history of some previous, typical stage robberies. They undoubtedly set a precedent for the young boy's actions.

During the early 1870s, a series of at least seven stage robberies were committed in Sonoma County, California. The most spectacular holdup occurred at 9 P.M., August 16, 1872, near Healdsburg. Four outlaws attacked the stage and met armed resistance. In the ensuing gunfight, one passenger and the driver were wounded and another passenger and one of the bandits were killed. The robbers got nothing for their efforts.[1] For two months law officers carried on an exhaustive investigation. They finally learned the bandits' identities through Billy Curtis, a drunken ex-member of the gang, who agreed to work with the lawmen in exchange for immunity.

The leader of the gang was John L. Houx, a Missouri hardcase who lived in Cloverdale. The other members were Elisha William "Bigfoot"

Andrus, Tom Jones, Lodi and Johnny Brown, young sons of a stock rancher in Sanel (Hopeland) in Mendocino County, and Jack "Rattling Jack" Brown, who was killed in the August 16th robbery. On November 9, 1871, Houx was arrested, and to save his own neck, agreed to turn state's evidence. The rest of the gang were quickly captured, and all but Curtis, Jones, and Houx were tried, convicted, and sentenced to terms in San Quentin Prison.[2]

So what does this have to do with a child robbing a stagecoach? Plenty. The child in question, Harvey Bell Mitchell, later known as Matt Lynch Bully, was a thirteen-year-old "Digger Indian" boy from Mendocino County. The term "Digger Indian" encompassed several Indian tribes, and the area the boy came from was the Pomo Indian district. In 1872, the boy's father was reported as a resident of Big River in the northern portion of Mendocino County. This would indicate that Mitchell was a Northern Pomo of the Buldam group.[3]

Mitchell was born on July 22, 1858, and his childhood apparently was one of little play and much work. Life in the Indian village left much to be desired, so several years before 1871 the young boy went to live at the home of Daniel Sink near Cloverdale, likely for food and lodging in exchange for hard work. During the summer of 1871 he moved to the home of Charles Brown, father of stage robbers Lodi and Johnny Brown. Here Mitchell overheard the Browns discuss various stage robberies they had committed, and began to devise a plan of his own.[4]

On Christmas night, 1871, young Mitchell made his way to a spot about one and a half miles south of Geyserville. With a whittled-down redwood fence picket resembling a rifle, he settled down to await the arrival of the down stage to Healdsburg.[5]

The driver of the stage that night was J. D. "Doc" Curtis, and his actions that evening were vividly depicted, if not embellished, by this report in the *San Francisco Examiner:*

> "Doc" Curtis was driving between Healdsburg and Cloverdale. "Doc" was inclined to blow some, now that the band [Houx gang] had been gathered in, and what he wouldn't do if any knight of the road undertook to "hang him up" wasn't worth talking about. All the same he was "hung up" one night about three miles from Healdsburg.[6]

As Curtis reached the spot where the young Indian boy was waiting, he slowed the stage to maneuver around a downed tree in the road. At that moment, Mitchell stepped out and ordered Curtis to halt. The driver ignored the command at first, but upon a second command to halt, and thinking the boy had a rifle, he complied. Mitchell then demanded the treasure box which Curtis hastily threw to the ground. The boy told Curtis to drive on and then took the box to the side of the road where he opened it with a dull ax. Finding nothing in the box, Mitchell made his way back to Cloverdale.[7]

Humorously, the *Examiner* described Curtis' actions following the robbery:

*Concord Coach, of the type Harvey Mitchell robbed near Geyserville, at the Stewart &
Gray Depot Hotel in Redding, California around 1872.* AUTHOR'S COLLECTION

He was considerably excited when he reigned up in front of the So-
toyome House, Healdsburg, and related his adventure, taking pains to explain how "they got the drop on him" and how he "looked down the
Barrels of that shotgun for some time before he would hand out the
box." It was afterward revealed that the robbery was committed by a
fourteen-year-old [*sic*] Indian boy raised by old man Brown, father of
Johnny and Lodi. In lieu of a shotgun the youngster had whittled down
a picket to the rough shape of a gun, and it was down the "double barrels" of that picket "Doc" Curtis gazed.[8]

On Christmas night, the news of the robbery reached Sonoma
County Deputy Sheriff William B. Reynolds and his brother Hedge in
Healdsburg. The *Daily Territorial Enterprise* stated:

Sheriff Reynolds and his brother, who were tripping the light fan-
tastic at the time at the ball at Liberty Hall, Healdsburg, when the news
was brought in, immediately left the assembly of fair women, to find
some clue, if possible, to trace the robbers. They spared not their steeds
till they reached the spot where the stage was stopped. They found the
box but no trace of the bold Claude Duval. There was nothing in the
box to reward the highwaymen or man.[9]

The day following the robbery, young Mitchell turned up at
Daniel Sink's, his former home near Cloverdale, and foolishly told
Sink's black hired man that he had robbed the stage. The hired man
told Sink, who immediately headed for Cloverdale and had an arrest
warrant issued by Justice of the Peace Morgan. On December 28,
1871, Deputy Sheriff Thomas Crawford arrested the young Indian in
Cloverdale and took him by stage to Healdsburg.

Mitchell readily admitted that he had robbed the stage and told
Crawford that he had heard the Brown brothers discuss various stage

robberies they had committed. He offered to take them to a canyon where type for the *Mendocino Press* had been dumped and the express box cut open. The boy also stated he could show the deputy where the bandits had buried their fellow outlaw, "Rattling Jack" Brown.[10]

On the morning of the twenty-ninth, Mitchell was conveyed to the jail in Santa Rosa, and was indicted on January 4, 1872. His bail was set at $1,500, which apparently was never posted. Mitchell's trial was held in Sonoma County Court in Santa Rosa on January 12, Judge A. P. Overton presiding. District Attorney Barclay Henley prosecuted the case and C. W. Langdon handled the defense. The jury, under foreman J. H. Holman, found Mitchell guilty the same day.

On January 15, Mitchell's attorney filed motions to arrest judgment and order a new trial. At the time of the trial, no one knew that Mitchell was only thirteen years old, and on these grounds Langdon filed his motion. The motions were denied the next day; however, Judge Overton leniently sentenced Mitchell to one year's imprisonment.[11]

Four days later, the thirteen-year-old boy was delivered to San Quentin, and when he passed through the prison gates he became the youngest convict to serve a term in the prison. He was erroneously registered as Henry B. Mitchell.

San Quentin had a reputation as one of the worst prisons in the United States at the time; a major problem was sexual abuse. It was not until 1877 that any type of reform program was initiated. When Mitchell entered San Quentin, it was like throwing a lamb to the wolves.[12]

The following description of Harvey Bell Mitchell is taken from the prison register: "Age: 13 years-old; Height: 5 feet; Complexion: dark; Eye color: brown; Hair color: black; Remarks: Full face, straight nose, large eyes, two moles on center of breast, double toe on right foot, stout build." The *Daily Territorial Enterprise* added that Mitchell only weighed seventy-five pounds and was old for his age.[13]

The only official punishment meted out to the boy occurred on February 29, 1872, when he spent "7 days in the dungeon for being unruly and disobedient to superiors." Mitchell was released from the dungeon on March 7. In late October, 1872, the *Daily Territorial Enterprise,* quoting from the *Sacramento Union,* reported that Mitchell was to be pardoned on October 25 by Governor Newton Booth, and stated, "He is said not to be really a bad boy, and should be assisted, as he is without relatives to give him aid."[14]

The newspaper was wrong, for young Mitchell was discharged without pardon on November 25, 1872. The *Gold Hill Evening News* quoted the following from the *San Francisco Bulletin:*

> [Mitchell] was released from State Prison last Monday and sent to his Father, a resident of Big River in Mendocino County. Harvey was a model boy while in the prison, and promised to become an honorable member of society. Several generous gentlemen interested themselves in the lad's case on the day of his release, and saw that he was provided with a considerable sum of money and an outfit of clothing.[15]

Indictment against Harvey Bell Mitchell for the stage robbery near Geyserville on December 25, 1871. State of California v Harvey Bell Mitchell, Robbery, Sonoma County Court Case 627. CALIFORNIA STATE ARCHIVES, SACRAMENTO

This act of generosity in a day when stage robbery was common-place was likely prompted by concealed feelings of admiration for the young Indian. Popular pulp writers and dime novelists glorified the western bandits, and the act of helping a gutsy thirteen-year-old kid who robbed stages with sticks of wood must have appealed to these gentlemen.

However, young Mitchell's promise to become an honorable member of society was a hollow pledge. San Quentin and its inmates had a profound effect on the young Indian boy, as did the influence of the Brown brothers in 1871. Following his release from prison there is no record of Mitchell until 1877, when he was arrested under the alias of Matt Lynch Bully.

On the twenty-second of January, 1877, the now seventeen-year-old Indian boy entered the house of Thomas Cox in Mendocino County to commit burglary. He was immediately caught. On March 7 an indictment was filed and the next day Bully was arraigned and pled guilty to second-degree burglary in the Mendocino County Court at Ukiah. On the tenth, Judge Thomas B. Bond sentenced him to one year's imprisonment. Bully was delivered to San Quentin on March 12 and was discharged on January 20, 1878. The young teenager had grown to a height of five feet, five inches, but gave his age as twenty-one.[16]

Five days after his release from prison, Bully was back in the bur-glary business. During the night of January 25, he broke into the store of W. W. Thatcher in Mendocino County. Around eleven o'clock Thatcher caught the youngster inside his store with his pockets stuffed with a small hairbrush with a mirror on the back, two pencils, a bar of soap, a knife, a comb, and some sugar. Bully was apparently held in jail nearly five months, for he was not indicted until June 4. His arraign-ment and trial for first-degree burglary were held the next day in Mendocino County Court, where he again faced Judge Bond. Bully pled guilty to the charge and was given a one-year sentence.[17]

Matt Lynch Bully entered San Quentin for the third time on June 10, 1878; however, he was not destined to leave the prison alive. On July 27, a little over a month after incarceration and five days following his twentieth birthday, Mitchell/Bully died in the prison hospital and was buried in the prison cemetery. There was no cause of death given, but in all likelihood the boy died of tuberculosis, the most common cause of death of prison inmates in the 1800s. It was Wells, Fargo de-tectives James B. Hume and John N. Thacker who discovered that Mitchell and Bully were one and the same, and wrote in their *Wells, Fargo Robbers Record,* under the segment for Henry [sic] B. Mitchell, "Served two terms subsequently of one year each from Mendocino County, and died in prison July 27, 1878." Little did the young Indian know, or probably care, that he was an historical first—the youngest person ever to be locked behind the walls of San Quentin.[18]

V. SOUTH DAKOTA

LAUGHING SAM HARTMAN

Vengeance Is Mine . . .
Saith the U.S. Court

SAMUEL S. HARTMAN WAS A dour, uncompromising individual, quick to take offense and even quicker to retaliate. The rollicking denizens of Deadwood, in the wide-open Black Hills region of the Dakota Territory, displaying their characteristic wry humor, dubbed him "Laughing Sam." Even his notoriety, like his nickname, was unearned, and he was charged with crimes he never committed. To cap it all off, the U.S. court system vindictively made an example of him.

Laughing Sam was born in 1847 but his birthplace is questionable. Under the nativity section in his prison record, he gave Indiana, but the *Black Hills Daily Times* gave Mercer County, Illinois as his birthplace. In contrast, the 1850 Iowa census reports he was a native of Iowa; however, the 1860 Atchison County, Kansas census indicates his state of birth was Maryland.[1]

Samuel S. Hartman was the son of James B. and Sarah J. Hartman, who, according to the 1860 Atchison County, Kansas census, were age thirty-six and age thirty-seven, respectively, and were reported as being born in Maryland. In 1850 the Hartmans were living in Wicondah Township, Davis County, Iowa, and the census, enumerated in October, lists James as twenty-four and wife, Sarah, as twenty-seven. Their firstborn, Sam, was age four, his sister Elizabeth was age three, and his sister Martha Ann was shown as having been born the previous March. The entire family was listed as born in Iowa. Sam's age in both censuses corresponds with the age Laughing Sam Hartman reported on his prison record.[2]

In late 1850 or early 1851 the Hartmans left Iowa for Illinois, settling for a short time in Tazwell County. On November 6, 1851, James Hartman purchased from George M. and Mary Hinkle a parcel of land located in Duncan Township in the northern portion of Mercer County, which bordered Iowa in the northwestern part of the state, for one thousand dollars. Thus the reference to Sam's birthplace as Mercer County in the *Black Hills Times*.[3]

The Hartmans apparently were related to the Hinkles, for there were several Hartmans living with them, according to the 1850 Mercer County census. George M. Hinkle was a noted figure during the Mormon movement in the 1830s. In late June of 1838, the Danites—the fighting force created by the Mormons to repulse the Gentiles, or non-Mormons—were organized in Far West, Caldwell County, Missouri; Hinkle was elected colonel. During the conflict between the Mormons and the Missouri militia in the fall of 1838, Hinkle was the highest ranking officer, but he soon fell into disfavor and was accused of betraying Joseph Smith into the hands of the Missourians. For this he was expelled from the church. Around 1840 he settled in Mercer County, Illinois, where he preached the doctrine of the Mormon church in Millersburg Township. After selling the land to James Hartman in 1851, the sixty-eight-year-old Hinkle went to Iowa where he spent his remaining days.[4]

In 1853, a third daughter, named Lenorah, was born to the Hartmans. Just two months short of two years after purchasing their land, James and Sarah Hartman sold it at a profit to John Braught for one thousand, seven hundred dollars on September 9, 1853. The Hartman family returned to Iowa, likely Davis County, where three more children were born; Mary F. in 1854, Idaletta in 1856, and William in 1858. Around 1859, the family moved to the city of Atchison, Kansas, located on the Missouri River about halfway between Kansas City and St. Joseph, Missouri.[5]

Prior to and during the first year of the Civil War, Atchison was headquarters for the northern segment of jayhawkers, quasi-military bands of men, who journeyed to Missouri where they plundered goods and slaves from the inhabitants. These bands were held in high esteem by the free-state Kansans until late 1861 when the military support for these raids withdrew. The jayhawking activities continued and became acts of rank outlawry under civilian leaders who pillaged indiscriminately. The leader of the Atchison raiders was Jim Hartman.

Hartman's band, which included his fifteen-year-old son Sam, not only crossed the Missouri River and raided Missouri residents, but looted Atchison as well. By the spring of 1862, the Atchison residents had had enough. On April 2, 1862, young Sam Hartman, either sensing the growing resentment or through a flash of patriotism, enlisted for three years in Company I, 7th Cavalry, Kansas Volunteers, at Lawrence.

Company I had been recruited by Major Albert L. Lee in October 1861 in Doniphan County, Kansas, and was mustered into the United States service on October 28. Sam's patriotism didn't last long as he deserted on April 13, just in time to be thrown into jail with his father a week later.[6]

Jim Hartman and his son were arrested on the charge of jayhawking during the week of April 21, 1862 by the provost guard. The Hartmans, like most of the jayhawkers who were arrested at this time, were held only a few days and released. Jim Hartman continued his raiding until late summer of 1864. Sometime after that, according to the *History of Atchison County*, a small group of Atchison residents dealt out their own brand of justice:

> . . . a fellow named [Jim] Hartman, was the worst of the gang, and was guilty of so many and such flagrant outrages upon the prominent citizens that in sheer desperation, four men . . . met and drew straws to see who would kill Hartman—(1) Jesse C. Crall, . . . (2) George T. Challiss, . . . (3) James McEwan, . . . (4) The fourth was a prominent physician. Each of these had suffered outrages at the hands of Hartman. He had visited their houses and terrified their wives by notifying them that unless their husbands left Atchison within a specified period they would be mobbed. Even the children of two of the victims of persecution had been abused. They met at the physicians office, and after a prolonged conference at which it was agreed that neither would leave until Hartman had been killed, proceeded to draw straws to see which would undertake the work. Crall held the straws, McEwan drew the short straw and the job fell to his lot. Atchison is bisected by two or three brooks, one of which traverses the northwest section of the town and runs into White Clay creek. This ravine has very precipitous banks, and was crossed by several foot bridges. At the east approach of the bridge was a tall elm tree. McEwan took his position under this tree, and awaited the appearance of Hartman, who necessarily passed that way going home at night. When Hartman was half-way across the bridge, McEwan stepped out, dropped to his knee, leveled a double-barreled shotgun and turned loose. He filled Hartman with buckshot from his head to his heels, but strange to say, the fellow did not die for months afterward.[7]

By the summer of 1864, jayhawking was dying out and Sam was now the head of the family. He probably began working as a muleskinner and teamster, the line of work he would follow from then on. However, he apparently joined the military again, enlisting as a private in the Irregulars attached to the Second Regiment of Kansas State Militia on October 11, 1864 at Topeka. The enlistment was no more than a short service to safeguard the town, for he was mustered out on October 28. For the next decade, his history is unclear.[8]

The only record of Hartman's life before his arrival in the Black Hills is this 1878 report on his trial in the *Black Hills Daily Times*:

> Hartman was put on the stand, and upon cross-examination gave a history of his life's wanderings . . . that . . . carried him all over the western States and Territories, from Illinois, Mercer County, the place of

his birth, to Mexico, Colorado, Salt Lake and the Buffalo country. He has been engaged in all kinds of business from driving government mules to hunting buffaloes, and from his statement it has been a hard, laborious one, and from the sweat of his brow has he earned his bread.[9]

Like thousands of other disillusioned men in 1876, Sam Hartman, soon to be known as Laughing Sam, was drawn like a magnet to the booming gold fields of the Black Hills in Dakota Territory.

There had been miners in the Black Hills and rumors of gold as early as the 1830s, continuing off and on for the next forty years. The Sioux Indians let the secret out by trading gold for goods at Fort Laramie and the Red Cloud Agency. In July 1874, General George A. Custer led one thousand troops into this area and many found traces of gold. Upon their return, reports of the expedition leaked out and by mid August newspapers in Chicago and New York sensationalized their findings.

The U.S. Army tried to stop all migration into the area to avert hostilities with the Sioux Indians. However, nothing would deter the quest for riches; the first group of gold-seekers, twenty-six men and one woman, left Covington, Nebraska in October 1874 and succeeded in reaching the Black Hills. From that point on there was no stopping the deluge of the would-be-rich, and the influx continued to grow.

Although the gold rush had not reached its peak by mid summer of 1876, the embryonic Deadwood was showing signs of the hell-raising, volcanic town it would soon become. Stores and saloons sprang up so fast along the one street in Deadwood that the newspaper gave up trying to list them. Two sawmills could not supply enough lumber and the bakery used 1,500 pounds of flour a day, which was still inadequate to feed the hungry hordes. Into this pandemonium of whiskey, gambling, music, and women came Sam Hartman.[10]

During the summer of 1876, Sam was probably given his nickname while working as a mule-skinner or teamster in the Deadwood area. He was described as a man whose looks were not repulsive, having dark hair and a heavy mustache with a face somewhat powdermarked.[11]

The first mention of Laughing Sam in the Black Hills was in late August 1876, when, because of Sam's volatile temper, an innocent man died in his place. The encounter took place in the Number 10 Saloon in Deadwood, owned by Carl Mann and Jerry Lewis. The saloon had already gained notoriety as the scene of the assassination of Wild Bill Hickok by Jack McCall earlier in the month, and owner Carl Mann did all he could to prevent Sam from causing another violent incident.[12]

Sometime during the summer, Laughing Sam and Harry Sam Young, known as Sam, the bartender at the Number 10 Saloon, had a falling out over an "occupant of the badlands," a colloquial Deadwood term for a prostitute. The girl had dumped Sam for Young and the enraged Hartman let it be known throughout Deadwood that he intended to kill the bartender. On August 19, Sam went to see Young's

Main Street in Deadwood, June 15, 1876, about the time Laughing Sam arrived there. HARRY GARLICK COLLECTION, ADAMS MEMORIAL MUSEUM, DEADWOOD, SOUTH DAKOTA

Deadwood, c. 1877. Possibly one of the bearded men in the foreground is Laughing Sam.
MORROW COLLECTION, UNIVERSITY OF SOUTH DAKOTA MUSEUM

employer, Carl Mann, and asked to borrow a pistol. The saloon owner refused and twice tried to persuade the irate teamster to stop making threats and causing trouble. Hartman replied that it was not Mann he was after but, "Sam Young, the son of a bitch; I will kill him."

On the evening of the twenty-second, rumors of impending trouble between the two men again circulated throughout the saloon. To prevent a showdown, Mann told Young to "go into the dark," and then headed for a dance hall where he confronted Laughing Sam. Mann told the belligerent teamster that if he killed Young "he would go up in a second." Laughing Sam retorted, "He won't speak to me; I have only a little while to live, and I will kill that Young and whore if they hang me tonight."

Around 10 P.M., Hartman went to Mann's saloon and asked to see the owner. At this moment, a Deadwood vagrant and roommate of Sam Young's named Meyer Baum came into the saloon, borrowed Laughing Sam's overcoat, and headed toward the rear door. Unknown to anyone, Sam Young had secured a weapon and stationed himself in back of the saloon. As Baum reached the door, Young took him for Laughing Sam and fired two quick shots, killing the man almost instantly.

At this time, the Black Hills region was still Indian domain under the Red Cloud Treaty of 1868, and was not part of Dakota Territory. There was no organized government at Deadwood except the Board of Health. Young surrendered to this agency claiming self-defense, stating he mistook Baum for Laughing Sam. The next morning a miners' meeting organized a court at the Langrishe Theater, and a judge, jury, and counsel for both sides were chosen. The defense raised the question of jurisdiction, but the court countered that the offense was committed within the boundaries of the U.S. and that was law enough for the court. After three days, Young was found not guilty. The killing had a sobering effect on the two antagonists and their conflict abated.[13]

If anyone could have shed some light on the activities of Sam Hartman it would have been Sam Young. In 1915 Young had his autobiography published, but only listed Laughing Sam as a Deadwood character. Apparently Young did not want to publicize the conflict he had had with Sam over a prostitute and his accidental killing of an innocent man.[14]

During the winter of 1877, Laughing Sam's combative nature created more trouble for him. He was reportedly wounded in a shoot-out in Sidney, Nebraska, which might account for his powder-marked face. It is possible that shortly afterward he commenced his brief criminal career. Following his arrest in October 1877, the *Omaha Daily Bee* reported that Sam was wanted in Deadwood for additional charges of highway robbery. A search of the *Black Hills Daily Times* reveals three unsolved robberies of the type he would commit the following September. Sam no doubt turned to crime for the same reasons others like him did: unsavory associates, adverse environment, bad attitude, and a desire for easy money.[15]

Harry "Sam" Young, c. 1915. AUTHOR'S COLLECTION

In late winter or early spring, 1877, two men held up a man named Moran near Custer, Dakota Territory. After relieving Moran of his money, the bandits derisively remarked that since they knew him everything would be all right, and to consider the robbery a temporary loan which they would repay when convenient. A second robbery was committed at 11 A.M. on April 16, on the Cheyenne Road twelve miles north of Custer, when two men stopped a resident of Deadwood and demanded his money. The hapless victim threw down a purse containing three ounces of gold dust which the robbers snatched up and then quickly disappeared.

The last robbery occurred around the first week of June. The previous week, F. M. Darling and four others from Cheyenne headed to Deadwood with two wagonloads of goods. They reached their destination safely and then headed back to Cheyenne. Arriving at the mouth of Red Canyon, they camped for the night. Around midnight, Darling woke up to find a man standing over him with a leveled pistol. On a demand for money, Darling handed over fourteen dollars in gold dust and was relieved of his watch, rifle, and pistol. The robber then joined his confederates and raided Darling's wagon, taking all of his provisions.[16]

Among the crimes Laughing Sam was accused of during this period was stage robbery, which was untrue but understandable considering his choice of associates. Stage holdups became a dominant Black Hills crime in the late 1870s, and in view of the course that Hartman's life was taking, he may well have joined the ranks of stage robbers had he remained free.

On March 25, 1877, the first of a rash of stage holdups occurred in the Black Hills. The gang's leader was Joel Collins and one of its members was Sam Bass. They committed a total of six robberies by mid July. Following in their footsteps were Duncan Blackburn and James Wall.

Blackburn was a twenty-eight-year-old ex-sailor from Halifax, Nova Scotia and Wall, at twenty-one, was a teamster hailing from Saint Paul, Minnesota. Their gang included Bill Bevans, a formerly affluent resident of Montana who had lost all his money gambling, a vicious hard-case from Ohio named Robert "Reddy" McKimie, who had been ostracized by the Collins gang for the needless killing of a stage driver, and a twenty-two-year-old known variously as the Kid, Kid Webster, William Webster, and William Clark. The Kid's real name was Clark Pelton, and he had come to the Black Hills from Cleveland, Ohio to work as a laborer. Laughing Sam's undeserved notoriety would come from his association with Webster.

Three consecutive stage robberies occurred near the Cheyenne River in Wyoming beginning on the night of June 25, 1877. The gang split up and Bevans was immediately arrested near Lander and taken to Cheyenne, where he unsuccessfully attempted to break jail on July 28. He was ultimately tried, convicted, and sentenced to ten years in prison.

Blackburn and Webster escaped and were not seen until they appeared on July 21 at the Six Mile Ranch, a combination bar and stage station near Fort Laramie, Wyoming. The next day Blackburn was recognized by Deputy Sheriff Charles Hays who promptly arrested him. Deputizing Adolph Cuny, Hays left him in charge of the prisoner and went looking for Webster. Unnoticed, Kid Webster walked into the dining room behind Cuny and ordered him to drop his gun. When Cuny whirled around, Webster fired. Cuny shot in defense but Webster's second shot killed him. Both outlaws fled the building and escaped.

Around midnight on August 17, near Old Woman's Forks, the two outlaws unexpectedly ran into Frank Whitney, a well-known freighter, on the Cheyenne Road. The three held a friendly conversation and when the question of Cuny's killing came up, Webster told the freighter, "No, Blackburn didn't shoot Cuny. Here is the rifle that did it, and I am the man that fired it." Blackburn and Webster then headed for Fort Pierre where they separated.

Blackburn again teamed up with James Wall and, with two others, held up the Sidney stage on August 23, 1877. During the robbery, the stage line's division agent, Ed Cooke, was slightly wounded in the ear. On the night of September 26, Blackburn and Wall stopped the stage from Deadwood near the Cheyenne River in Wyoming. In a shoot-out with the stage guards, the highwaymen wounded messenger Scott Davis in the leg. A one-thousand-dollar reward was issued for the arrest of the bandits and two hundred dollars if they were killed.

On the night of October 2, the robbers struck again, stopping the Sidney coach near Buffalo Gap. This time there were four bandits. The gang split up, and the following night Blackburn and Wall held up the Deadwood stage five miles from Eagles Nest. Continuing their depredations, the two bandits stopped both the up and down coaches on the night of October 9. These were their last stage robberies, although they did rustle seventeen horses from the Lance Creek stage station on the night of November 10.

An intensive manhunt was launched and after a grueling three-hundred-mile search across Wyoming, Wall was wounded and captured at the Alkali stage station on the night of November 19. Blackburn escaped in his underwear but was captured the next night in a store in Green River, still in his long johns. Both men were tried in Laramie and convicted on December 8 on charges of stage robbery, attempting to kill and murder, grand larceny, and aiding in a jailbreak. Blackburn was sentenced to ten years and Wall to eight years. They entered the Wyoming Penitentiary at Laramie on December 25, 1877, and were transferred to the Nebraska Penitentiary at Lincoln on June 21, 1878. Blackburn was discharged on March 8, 1885 and Wall the following June 26.[17]

Following his separation from Blackburn at Fort Pierre, Kid Webster fell in with Laughing Sam. In late August 1877 the two were joined by a villainous character called Lame Bradley. This large, forty-year-old, grizzled and heavily bearded Irishman had killed an outlaw partner named Powell in a dispute at their hangout near Crook City in July. Bradley, with Cornelius "Lame Johnny" Donahue, then joined up with Blackburn and Wall in the August 23 holdup of the Sidney-bound stage. It was Bradley, who held a grudge against Division Agent Cooke, who shot and slightly wounded him in the ear.

By the second of September, Hartman, Webster, and Bradley reached the Cheyenne River. Here Laughing Sam would commit his first and only documented criminal act, the robbery of three Omaha residents who had been mining in the Black Hills.[18] The *Omaha Daily Bee* gave this excellent account of the robbery:

> On Saturday afternoon [September 22], Henry A. Homan, C. T. Sweeney and A. [Albert] A. Jones arrived in the city from Deadwood, having come in by the Elkhorn Valley route by mule team and wagon; Mr. Homan having made the trip over this route several times before without meeting with any adventures worthy of note, but this time proved an exception, as the party were corralled by a trio of bold road agents who relieved them of their ready cash.
>
> Homan and his two companions left Deadwood on the 29th of August, and met with no trouble until they arrived at the Cheyenne river. At sunset of 2nd of the present month as they went into camp, three men on horseback put in an appearance on a hill some little distance off, and the travelers supposed them at first to be Indians, and accordingly got their guns ready.
>
> The horsemen, however, made no hostile demonstrations that night, but went into camp half a mile below Homan's outfit.
>
> At sunrise next morning as the three returning miners were going over the hill at Cheyenne river, they noticed the three mysterious strangers gathering up their horses at the bottoms; a mile and a half further on they saw them again, and then supposed them to be pilgrims. Four miles further on the horsemen overtook them and came up within twenty feet of the wagon and said "good morning." They then closed in on the wagon, two on one side and one on the other, and as soon as they had got into this position, they suddenly drew their revolvers, and one sang out with an emphatic oath; "Put up your hands and stop that team." [The *Black Hills Daily Times* of October 8, 1878 reported that the robber said, "Hold up your hands damn quick; get out of the wagon on the left hand side."]
>
> The order was obeyed. The prisoners . . . were then commanded to get on the right side of the wagon in a row, which they did. Two of the road agents . . . covered the three prisoners with cocked revolvers, while another searched them, taking about everything they had. Homan had to give up $300 in money, while Jones and Sweeney lost a small amount each.
>
> The wagon, boxes, carpet sacks, etc, were all searched, and even the flour sack was examined, for more plunder.
>
> The thieves wore no masks, and could be easily identified by their victims at any time they should meet them again. The man who did the searching was recognized by Jones as Laughing Sam, a notorious character of Deadwood. While he was searching, Jones said to him, "Hello, Sam! For God's sake leave me my watch, as I think the world of it."
>
> Sam sprang back in great surprise and said, "where have you ever seen me?"

"In Deadwood," was the reply. Sam gave him back his watch.

The road agents took the arms of the party, notwithstanding their earnest entreaties to be allowed to keep them as they might meet with Indians, but the heartless scoundrels replied that they needed the shooters in their business. They also took Jones' horse, a fine animal, and left an almost valueless critter in its place. They then allowed their victims to pursue their course but followed them to White River, seventeen miles distant, and there left them. The three unlucky miners hurried on to Young's ranch, where they thought they would wait for a larger party whom they expected. The morning after they arrived there they saw a man on horseback at some distance, who wheeled and ran, and the place where two men had stayed overnight was discovered. These men were undoubtedly the same ones who had robbed them. Homan followed them from Young's ranch to Wounded Knee, on the old Fort Randall road, where they took the Kearney road.[19]

Jones's recognition of Sam forced him to leave Dakota in a hurry, and he and the Kid headed east after parting company with Bradley. Traveling hard, they wound up around forty miles northeast of Omaha at Harlan, Iowa, and hired out to a farmer at eighteen dollars a month. After working for nearly a month, Sam was convinced they were safe and quit his job. He began sporting and loafing around Harlan while Webster remained in the farmer's employ.

On the morning of October 3, 1877, Omaha City Marshal Butler received a telegram from Shelby County Sheriff John Long in Harlan that Laughing Sam and the Kid had been arrested. The sheriff requested that members of the Homan party come to Iowa and identify the two prisoners. Homan was contacted and immediately left for Harlan.

The two highwaymen were arrested after Sam was identified by a neighbor of their employer. The man was passing the field where they were working and recognized Hartman as the man who had allegedly robbed him on a moonlit night a few weeks before. He informed Sheriff Long who promptly arrested Hartman in town. Long went to the farm where Webster was working and arrested him on suspicion. The arms taken from the Homan party were also found by the sheriff.

Following Homan's identification of Sam and Webster, the U.S. authorities quickly got into the act. Accompanied by Homan, the officers brought Laughing Sam and Webster to Omaha on the evening of October 5. The next morning, a preliminary hearing was held and the two prisoners, in handcuffs and chains, appeared before U.S. Commissioner Watson B. Smith on the charge of highway robbery on the Sioux Indian Reservation in Dakota. The complaint was incorrectly filed against S. S. Houston (Hartman) and William Clark (Pelton). Both Homan and Jones testified that the accused took around one hundred dollars, some blankets, revolvers, rifles, and other articles. It was the revolver stolen from Jones that ultimately would be Laughing Sam's undoing.

The question of jurisdiction was the major issue and the case was continued until Monday, October 15. The court decided that since the crime was committed in Dakota, the prisoners would have to be tried at Yankton; Sam was indicted on a charge of robbery in U.S. District Court at Rapid City in Pennington County, Dakota Territory.[20]

Laughing Sam's problems mounted when the *Cheyenne Daily Leader* reported that the stage from Sidney was robbed on the night of October 2 by Blackburn, Wall, the Kid (Webster), and Laughing Tom (*sic*). This was impossible as both Hartman and Webster were under arrest in Iowa, over five hundred miles from the robbery site. Nevertheless, Sam was indicted for the robbery during the November term of the Dakota Territorial District Court at Rapid City. The likely culprits were Lame Bradley, who had split with Sam and the Kid after the Homan robbery, and Lame Johnny Donahue. Bradley escaped to Texas where he was killed no more than a year later by a youth of nineteen whom he had tried to rob; Lame Johnny was lynched by Black Hills vigilantes on the night of July 1, 1879.[21]

Both Laughing Sam and Webster remained in jail at Omaha until November 18, when the Kid was taken to Deadwood by a U.S. marshal. In Rapid City in 1878, Webster was tried and convicted for grand larceny and began serving a one-year sentence in the Minnesota Penitentiary on June 15. Upon his release on May 21, 1879, Sheriff George Draper arrested him on the charge of murdering Adolph Cuny and took him to Laramie for trial. He was tried on December 22, 1879, found guilty of manslaughter, and two days later was sentenced to four years in the Wyoming Territorial Penitentiary. Clark Pelton, alias William Webster, entered prison on January 25, 1880 and was pardoned by Governor John W. Hoyt and released on April 29, 1882. Following his release, Pelton turned over a new leaf. He remained in Laramie where he began working as a building contractor, married, and raised a family. Pelton became a leading citizen in Laramie, serving as a school board member and becoming a friend of the University of Wyoming. Pelton died while on a fishing trip near Laramie on June 30, 1930.[22]

Laughing Sam's troubles continued to compound. In mid October, City Marshal Butler received a letter from Sheriff Seth Bullock in Deadwood informing him that Hartman was wanted on other charges of highway robbery and that he was coming after the prisoner. Bullock never got Sam because the U.S. authorities had already indicted him and had no intention of releasing their prisoner. A month later, he was taken to Dakota for trial. On November 28, the *Omaha Daily Bee* reported: "Deputy United States Marshal Perkins of Dakota, left Omaha today for Yankton with that villainous stage coach robber and highwayman, 'Laughing Sam.'"[23]

The Second Judicial District U.S. Court at Yankton found that it had no jurisdiction in Hartman's case since the ratification of the Sioux Treaty in 1877 established that the crime had been committed in an area that now came under the authority of the First Judicial District

Court at Rapid City, Dakota Territory. On January 4, 1878, he was taken back to Omaha and jailed for the night. The next day, U.S. Marshal John B. Raymond took Sam into custody and headed for Rapid City via Yankton. The *Omaha Daily Herald* made this comment about Laughing Sam: "He was in good spirits, however, yesterday, although in irons, and the Marshal says he behaved himself excellently." Raymond left Yankton with his prisoner on January 9, 1878. Traveling most of the way by stage, they arrived in Rapid City on January 16 and Sam was turned over to Sheriff Frank Moulton. Laughing Sam would cool his heels in jail at Rapid City for the next nine months.[24]

Sam was finally brought to trial in U.S. District Court in October 1878. The government knew it had no case against him for stage robbery and apparently dropped the charge. On October 3, Sam was indicted on two charges, highway robbery of an individual in Indian lands and robbery of a pistol that was United States property. Laughing Sam was tried for the robbery of the pistol, which carried a more stringent sentence.

The case was tried under Judge Gideon C. Moody and prosecuted by District Attorney Hugh J. Campbell. Sam was defended by attorneys Allen and W. H. Parker. On the fourth, he pled not guilty. The next day a jury was selected and Sam's trial commenced. As to Hartman's defense, the *Black Hills Daily Times* of October 7 reported:

> No man ever tried has been more faithfully defended than he. His counsel, Col. Parker and Mr. Allen, have fought every inch of ground, have taken advantage of everything that presented itself, have objected to everything, and had exceptions noted when ruled against, and have made a splendid fight.

At 11 P.M. on the sixth, the case was given to the jury and within one hour they came back with a verdict of guilty.

On the seventh, Sam's attorneys made a motion for a new trial and sentencing was postponed until 2 P.M. on October 9. The sentencing was again continued to give Hartman's attorneys time to prepare a bill of exception. On the eleventh, the motion for a new trial was overruled and sentencing was continued until October 16.

At 2 P.M. on the sixteenth, Laughing Sam was brought back to court and was asked if he had reason why sentence should not be pronounced. The *Black Hills Journal* reported his dispirited comments, "I don't know that I have; Mr. Parker and Allen have said all that can be said in my behalf, at the present time, I suppose." The *Black Hills Daily Times* of October 18 continued:

> The judge addressed him, eloquently and feelingly, and at great length referring to his past life, and the position he was now placed in. . . . He also tried to get him to look forward towards a life of honesty and usefulness in the future, but for any impression it had upon him, he might have talked to a stone. He stood it all, as immovable as an Indian Fakir.

Only known photo of Clark Pelton. COURTESY
OF AMERICAN HERITAGE CENTER, UNIVERSITY
OF WYOMING, LARAMIE

*Detroit House of Corrections in 1881. Laughing Sam would spend a little over three years
behind its walls.* AUTHOR'S COLLECTION

Judge Moody gave Laughing Sam the maximum sentence that could be rendered under the law, nine years and eight months in the House of Corrections in Detroit, Michigan.[25]

The last laugh on Laughing Sam was this gibe in the *Omaha Daily Bee*, "'Laughing Sam' gets nine years and eight months for saying 'Hands up!' This is no laughing matter for Samuel but he will have to grin and bear it."[26]

There was a reason for the excessive sentence handed down by Judge Moody: frustration. This was the first conviction for highway robbery in a U.S. District Court in Dakota and Laughing Sam paid for this frustration. This type of crime was prevalent in the Territory, but other locales, such as Blackburn and Wall in Wyoming, had been more successful in making arrests and convictions. In two ways, however, Laughing Sam was lucky; if he had been tried in a territorial court for this robbery he undoubtedly would have received a much harsher sentence, and he got unexpected help from Hugh Campbell, the man who prosecuted him.

It is almost unheard-of for a district attorney to intercede on behalf of a man he had prosecuted, but Campbell was obviously an honorable man who realized the unjustness of Sam's sentence. In Sam's pardon petition in 1882, Campbell explained the government's rationale:

> It was the first conviction for Highway Robbery which had been rendered in the Black Hills, and the sentence was placed near the maximum, 10 years, under Section 5456. RS.
> The main part of the robbery consisted of other articles and money belonging to Homan.
> But as the penalty for such an offense under the defective laws of the U.S. was but one year. And as the party robbed happened to have a U.S. pistol among the articles taken, I indicted him under this section.[27]

Sam Hartman was delivered to the Detroit House of Corrections on October 30, 1878. After a few months in prison, Sam wrote to Judge Moody requesting aid in obtaining a pardon. In reply, Judge Moody stated that he would be willing to help after Sam had served three years with good conduct. By the fall of 1881, Hartman, having served the requisite three years as a model prisoner, obtained the services of attorney Issac E. West in Yankton and began his quest for a pardon.[28]

On October 17, Superintendent Joseph Nicholson of the Detroit House of Corrections wrote Judge Moody attesting to Sam's good conduct. On Christmas day, on the advice of District Attorney Campbell, Hartman wrote directly to Attorney General Benjamin Harris Brewster and outlined his case. By mid January 1882, supporting letters from District Attorney Campbell, Superintendent Nicholson, Judge Moody, Attorney West, and Judge Alex T. Gray, who was U.S. Clerk of Pardons, had been forwarded to the attorney general. On January 23, the attorney general wrote to President Chester A. Arthur, recommending the pardon.

On February 3, the president gave his approval and the pardon was

Dakota Territory

Yankton, Dakota, June 12 1882

The Honorable
The Attorney General

Sir

I have the honor to transmit the papers in the application of Samuel S. Hartman for pardon.

And to state that Hartman was indicted Octr 2/78 charged with robbery of a P. O. etc property of U.S. in Indian county from possession of one Henry A. Hartman. Verdict of guilty Octr 5/78. Sentence 8 years & 6 months, Penitentiary Octr 16/78.

It was the first conviction for Highway Robbery

which had been recorded in the Black Hills, and the Sentence was passed near the Minnesota, 10 years, under Section 5456, R.S.

The manufacturing the robbery consisted of other articles & money belonging to Hartman. But as the penalty for such an offence under the chapter from Laws of the U.S. was but one year, and as the jury so that happened among the U.S. pointed out the whole Ticket, indicted him under this section, I think that to be been frivolous & seriously enough. He made good promise. This conduct has been

good in confinement. The Judge who tried him acts strongly recommends the pardon. And I heartily concur, and earnestly recommend his pardon.

Respectfully yours
Hugh J. Campbell
U.S. Attorney

Letter in support of Laughing Sam Hartman's pardon from U.S. Attorney Hugh Campbell to the U.S. attorney general. RG 204, Records of the Pardon Attorney, case file H-739, Samuel Hartman. NATIONAL ARCHIVES, WASHINGTON, D.C.

In Re APPLICATION for PARDON of

Samuel S. Hartman   Dist. *Dak. T.*

(Judge I. E. West.)   *1st Jud. Dist*

Yankton D.T.

Offense: *Highway Robbery.*

Sentence: *Oct. 1879 9 yrs. & 8 mos. in*

W.H. (Illinois) H. of C.

Filed: *Dec. 30/81*   Record *H. 739*

Notice to amend sent to

Application amended: _____, 187 .

Referred to U. S. Attorney: *Jan. 3*, 188*2*.

Reported by U. S. Attorney: _____, 187 .

Report:

Recommended by Dist. Att'y

& Judge — See letter with Report.

Reported to the Attorney General *Jan. 23*, 188*2*

Who *administered*   "   "   "

Pardon Ordered,   *Feb. 3*   "

Rep. to Sec. State,   " . *4*   "

Pardon delivered to   "   "

Mr. W. H. Parker

of Deadwood

Application for pardon of Laughing Sam Hartman. Records of the Pardon Attorney, case file H-739, Samuel Hartman. NATIONAL ARCHIVES, WASHINGTON, D.C.

ordered. On the fourth, the paperwork was referred to the secretary of state, who sent it to W. H. Parker, the defense attorney in Sam's trial. It finally reached the Detroit House of Corrections on February 10, 1882, and Sam was released.[29]

In retrospect, Sam Hartman's Christmas letter to the attorney general is an exceptionally sincere letter, no crying on anyone's shoulder or shifting the blame elsewhere. It was straightforward, intelligently written, and concise. In his semi-literate spelling, Sam wrote, "I have tryed to prove to all through my conduct that I want to and will do what is right and I dont think that their is any that doubt my Sincerity."[30] No one did. Prison was a sobering experience and Sam seemingly cast aside his belligerent and wrathful attitude. Following his release maybe Sam Hartman finally deserved to be called "Laughing Sam."

VI. IDAHO

WYATT EARP

Stampede to Coeur d'Alene

As a legendary personage in America's frontier West, Wyatt Earp stands in the forefront; however, for some reason he seemingly triggers either admiration or contempt in those who study his life history. There appears to be no compromise when the pros and cons of this controversial individual are recorded or discussed, yet there is no clear reason for polemics. His detractors claim he was a horse thief, a pimp, a bunko artist, a tinhorn gambler, and a remorseless killer; his defenders state he was a first-class lawman who helped clean up the Kansas cow towns and eliminate the lawless elements of Tombstone. The truth? It undoubtedly lies somewhere in the middle.

A major problem is that Wyatt Earp's biographers and chroniclers have focused their studies and writings on Earp's escapades in Tombstone, Arizona and the gun battle at the OK Corral, and have overlooked his later career. Hopefully, someone in the near future will write a complete biography of Wyatt Earp. Presented here is the history of Wyatt's brief sojourn in the Coeur d'Alene gold fields of Idaho in 1884.[1]

For those who are not familiar with Wyatt Earp's career, a brief history is in order. By the time Wyatt Berry Stapp Earp was born on March 19, 1848 in Monmouth, Illinois, his parents, Nicholas and Victoria Ann Earp, were struck with wanderlust. Nicholas Earp had been previously married and widowed in Hartford, Ohio County, Kentucky. He had one living son, Newton Jasper, born October 7, 1837, when he married Victoria Ann Cooksley on July 30, 1840. The Earps had three children born in Kentucky, James Cooksley, June 28, 1841, Virgil

Walter, July 18, 1843, and Martha Elizabeth, September 25, 1845. From Kentucky the Earps moved to Monmouth, Illinois where Wyatt was born. In 1850 the Earps again pulled up roots and moved to Pella, Marion County, Iowa where two more sons were born, Morgan on April 24, 1851 and Warren Baxter on March 9, 1855. In 1856 the family moved back to Monmouth, Illinois where a daughter, Virginia Ann, was born February 26, 1858. In that same year Nicholas took his family back to Pella, Iowa where their last child, a daughter they named Adelia, was born June 16, 1861. In May, 1864, Nicholas Earp, as wagon master, led a wagon train of forty wagons west to San Bernardino, California. With Nicholas and his wife were children James, Wyatt, Morgan, Warren, and Adelia. In late 1868 the Earp family was in Barton County, Missouri, where Nicholas was appointed constable of the town of Lamar in the summer of 1869.

Wyatt's law career began on November 19, 1869 when his father resigned as constable of Lamar to become justice of the peace and Wyatt was appointed in his place. He served until mid March 1871. On April 1 Wyatt and two others were indicted for stealing two horses in late March. Wyatt was arrested on April 6 and was released on five hundred dollars bail. One of the defendants was acquitted but Wyatt's case was never tried, probably because it became lost in the shuffle when Federal Court was moved from Van Buren, Arkansas to Fort Smith, Arkansas in 1871.

Chronologically, Wyatt Earp's service as a lawman is as follows: April 25, 1875 to April 20, 1876, city policeman in Wichita, Kansas; April 17–24, 1876 to April 1, 1877 and May 12, 1878 to September 4, 1879, deputy city marshal, Dodge City, Kansas; July 27, 1880 to November 9, 1880, deputy sheriff, Pinal County, Arizona; December 29, 1881 to April 1882, United States deputy marshal, Arizona Territory.

Wyatt Earp was involved in some seven to nine killings, according to his chroniclers; following is a list of the killings credited to him: (1) July 25, 1878, cowboy George Hoy was shot in the arm in Dodge City, Kansas by Wyatt or fellow Deputy City Marshal Jim Masterson. Hoy died on August 21 as a result of his wound; (2) October 26, 1881, Wyatt, Virgil, and Morgan Earp and John H. "Doc" Holliday battled "cowboys" Ike and Billy Clanton and Frank and Tom McLaury in a lot near the OK Corral in Tombstone, Arizona. Virgil and Morgan Earp were wounded while both McLaury brothers and Billy Clanton were killed; (3) In retaliation for the deaths of the McLaurys and Clanton, Virgil Earp was shot in ambush and crippled on December 29, 1881 and Morgan Earp was assassinated on the night of March 18, 1882. Wyatt and Warren Earp and a posse of their friends shot and killed suspected assassin Frank Stillwell in Tucson on March 20; (4) The Earps and their associates killed another of the accused killers, Florintino Cruz, at South Pass in the Dragoon Mountains on March 22; (5) On March 24, the Earps and their posse battled a contingent of the cowboys at Mescal Springs, Arizona—cowboy Johnny Barnes reportedly was wounded and later died of his wounds and Wyatt presumably killed William "Curley Bill" Brocious; (6) Some writers claim that Wyatt returned to Arizona in July 1882 with Doc Holliday, met a party of his friends, and hunted down and killed cowboy Johnny Ringo in Turkey Creek Canyon on July 13; (7) Wyatt and Virgil reportedly avenged the killing of their younger brother, Warren, who was gunned down in a Wilcox, Arizona saloon in 1900 by John Boyett. Immediately heading for Wilcox, they were rumored to have secretly killed Boyett. Readers will have to do their own research to draw their conclusions regarding the character of Wyatt Earp and how many victims can be held to his account.

One last controversy needs to be summarily examined—that of Wyatt's affairs of the heart. On January 10, 1870, while constable in Lamar, Missouri, Wyatt married Urilla Sutherland, who reportedly died about a year later. At some point between the summer of 1877 and spring of 1878, Wyatt took up with twenty-seven-year-old Celia Ann "Mattie" Blaylock, a native of Johnson County, Iowa. Where Wyatt met her—or possibly married her—is unknown, but Mattie reportedly was with him when he returned to Dodge City, Kansas in May 1878 to again take up duties as a deputy city marshal. When Wyatt went to Tombstone in November, 1879, Mattie was with him, but it was not long before he deserted her for a beautiful brunette Jewish girl from San Francisco named Josephine "Josie" Sarah Marcus.

Josephine Marcus first came to Tombstone at age eighteen, in November 1879, to perform in a stage troupe production called *Pinafore on Wheels*. She returned the following May as the fiancée of John H. Behan, soon-to-be sheriff of newly formed Cochise County, Arizona and supporter of the cowboy contingent, who ultimately became a political and personal opponent of Wyatt Earp. During the summer of 1881, Josie dumped Behan for Wyatt. According to Josie, Wyatt went to Arizona and killed Johnny Ringo in July of 1882, and shortly afterward met her in San Francisco, where the two were married by a captain of a yacht beyond the three-mile limit. No record has been found of Wyatt's marriage to either Mattie Blaylock or Josephine Marcus; however, Josephine remained by his side as his wife until his death in 1929.

Following the bloodletting in retaliation for the shooting of Virgil Earp and murder of Morgan Earp, murder warrants were issued and the Earp faction fled Arizona for New Mexico. Separating from the others, Wyatt, brother Warren, and Doc Holliday headed for Trinidad, Colorado where friend Bat Masterson served as city marshal while maintaining a gambling room. Here Wyatt split with Holliday for the last time. Wyatt and Josephine spent the next year gambling and prospecting in the Colorado mining towns of Gunnison, Silverton, Ouray, and Aspen. In June 1883 Wyatt made a quick trip to Dodge City, Kansas as a member of the now famous "Dodge City Peace Commission" to support the rights of ousted fellow gambler Luke Short.

Upper left: Wyatt Earp in 1885. AUTHOR'S COLLECTION
Upper right: Josephine Marcus Earp in 1880. AUTHOR'S COLLECTION
Lower left: James Earp in 1881. AUTHOR'S COLLECTION
Lower right: Warren Earp in 1888. AUTHOR'S COLLECTION

Two more of the Earp brothers: Virgil (left) in 1885 and Morgan (right) in 1880.
AUTHOR'S COLLECTION

Returning to Colorado, Wyatt again heard the call of the wild, this time from the newly found gold fields of the Coeur d'Alenes in the panhandle of Idaho.

There had been rumors of gold in the Coeur d'Alene Mountains since 1867, when a team of gold seekers had prospected the area. In the fall of 1882 Andrew J. Prichard prospected the area and claimed there was gold in paying quantities, but his assertions were generally doubted. Prichard had been grubstaked by a rich widow and when he discovered gold near the forks of Prichard and Eagle Creeks the following fall he named his diggings the "Widow's Claim" after his benefactor.[2]

According to *The Ballyhoo Bonanza* by John Fahey, Prichard wanted to finance a religious colony in the mountains and wrote of his findings to "like minded 'Liberals.'" Fahey wrote:

> Most of the true believers were farmers from western territories who contented themselves with tacking location notices on trees and returning home to wait for spring and wealth. Prichard himself filed eighty-acre claims for his son, Jesse, and three friends. As they started for the Coeur D'Alenes, the Liberals had whispered "Gold!" Newspapers talked of it. Railroads promoted it. Swells of prospectors broke across the mountains, some dragging supplies on sleds behind them, others struggling under heavy packs.[3]

To illustrate the migration to the Coeur d'Alene gold fields, miner Eugene V. Smalley's graphically written firsthand account for an 1884 issue of *Century Magazine* is classic:

> Of all the stampedes in old times or in recent years, the great Coeur D'Alene stampede of the winter and spring of 1884 was probably the

most remarkable. The country it invaded was less known than any other part of the Rocky Mountain chain. No roads traversed it; there was not even a bridal trail. To make matters worse, the entire region was covered with a forest growth of cedar, pine, and fir, so dense as to resemble a Hindustan jungle. "Begorra, ye'll find the trees growin' as thick as a bunch of matches," said an old Irish miner, whom I encountered on my way to the region, and he did not exaggerate. To make matters still worse, the snowfalls are phenomenal, and the stampede began in the dead of winter, when the snow was twelve to twenty feet deep in the mountain passes. Yet, in spite of these obstacles, over five thousand made their way into the heart of the Coeur D'Alene Mountains during the months of January, February, and March. With them went women of certain class, dressed in men's clothes and hauling their feminine wardrobes on sleds.

The great rush did not occur, however, until February, when the toboggan period began. A toboggan is a low sled used in Canada, and until the snows melted in April last it was the only mode of transportation to the mines. The toboggan men, wearing snowshoes, and hauling from one to two hundred pounds on their rude sleds, could make from ten to twenty miles a day over the mountains, following the "blazing" on the trees that indicated the trail. When they camped at night they cut green saplings and laid them on the snow to support their fire. In the morning the smoldering embers would be down at the bottom of the well in the snow twelve or fifteen feet deep.[4]

When the news of Prichard's "Widow's Claim" first spread across both sides of the mountains, a few people made their way to the gold fields before the monumental rush began in February. Among these were the Earps. According to Josie Earp, "Naturally it wasn't long before we [Wyatt and Josie] left Colorado. We set out excitedly for Idaho in the late winter of 1883–1884, after hearing of the news of the silver-mining [actually gold] boom in the Coeur D'Alene. Wyatt's older brother Jim had preceded [sic] us there, coming over from Montana where he had been for some time the previous year."[5]

Apparently James, Wyatt, and Josie Earp were among the first gold seekers to the Coeur d'Alene, arriving sometime in late January. According to the Stuart Lake notes, they moved into a cabin "at the foot of the mountain." Warren Earp must have joined his brothers in the Coeur d'Alenes at some point during the summer, as a W. B. Earp registered to vote in Shoshone County, Idaho on September 26, 1884. This man was undoubtedly Warren, as the age (twenty-nine) and birthplace (Iowa) he listed correspond with Warren's.[6] Wyatt and James evidently made a quick entrance into the gold fields to test the legal waters of registering claims, for the first record of them was on February 1 when they jumped a claim belonging to Andrew J. Prichard. On June 9, Prichard brought suit against the Earps, but it took two years, until May 3, 1886, before a jury found in Prichard's favor and he recovered possession of his claim.[7]

As in Tombstone and other locations, the Earps were quick to align themselves with compatible allies. The names of J. E. "Jack" Enright,

Photo of the Coeur d'Alene mining district about the time the Earps were there in 1884.
AUTHOR'S COLLECTION

Alfred Holman or Holeman, and Daniel S. Ferguson can be found on almost all of the Earp's transactions. All three had been gamblers and mining speculators in the Wood River mining towns in south-central Idaho when the gold strike in the Coeur d'Alenes occurred, and headed north to join the rush. Ferguson and Enright moved into cabins near the Earps'. Others mentioned as Earp cohorts were John Hardy, Henry White, W. F. Stoll, L. F. Butler, William Chambers, F. S. Wickersham, William Payne, Habian Charles, R. Graham, W. Osborne, John Williams, John Cochrane, Charles "Red" Foley, D. T. Hayes, and the indomitable Charles Sweeney, who became a legend throughout

Another scene of the Coeur d'Alene mining area about the time the Earps were there in 1884. ACCESSION NO. 76–133.8, IDAHO STATE HISTORICAL SOCIETY, BOISE

the Idaho mining area.[8] An excerpt from the cover of Fahey's *The Ballyhoo Bonanzan* summarizes Sweeney's career:

> The years from 1885 to 1910 saw Idaho's Coeur d'Alene mines evolve from a scattered group of prospect holes to corporations that produced a third or more of the nation's lead. A major catalyst in this transformation was Charles Sweeny, a second-generation Irish immigrant who had ventured westward to seek his fortune after the Civil War and moved to the Coeur d'Alenes during the first wave of the gold rush in 1883–84. Sweeny bought up the district's first townsite and plunged immediately into the prospecting, speculation, and manipulation that were to characterize his whole career.[9]

On March 15, another suit was brought against the Earps and others, maintaining that the Earps entered the claim on March 15, 1884, taking forcible possession on May 20. They were sued on June 14, Wyatt was served with a notice on July 1, and the case came before the court on July 25, but this time the Earps obtained the judgment.[10]

By April Wyatt and company began buying up placer claims, and town lots in the newly formed town of Eagle City located in the forks of Eagle and Prichard Creeks. The tent and raw lumber city sprang up in early 1884, following the discovery of gold the previous fall, and was within walking distance of the streams where gold was being panned. Fahey noted, "Eagle City consisted of rude board and canvas structures strung for about two miles along its two streets, Eagle and Prichard, which met at right angles in the town's center." Up to eight hundred men working their claims would lodge overnight in Eagle City. The town occupied the area's only open flat space of a hundred acres, and lots with raw log buildings were selling for fifteen hundred dollars each. Area historian Judge Richard Magnuson of Wallace, Idaho, noted:

> Eagle City was the first to spring up, and it soon was a city of tents. When spring came, most of the population moved to Murrayville (now Murray) which was four miles upstream on Prichard Creek. Eagle City died shortly after its beginning. Murray became a large city and the county seat. . . . Travel in the winter to Eagle City was almost unbelievable at that time. Freight rates were as high as 25¢ per pound for short distances. Dog sleds were used. All in all it was quite colorful.

The rise and fall of Eagle City would cover a period of only about eight months.[11]

The first property transaction by the Earps occurred on April, 7, 1884, when Wyatt and James Earp, Enright, Holman, and Ferguson paid five hundred dollars to Florence McCarthy for ten acres of placer claim on Prichard Creek. On the same day the Earps and Holman paid Fay Buzard $2,250 for "One circular duck tent fifty feet in diameter and forty-five feet high. The pine flooring and sills in said tent contained. One wooden stope building 25 feet by 25 feet in the rear of said tent with all and singular the improvements and fixtures connected therewith." This tent was in Eagle City and according to a 1981 article in the *Evening News* from Kellogg, Idaho, it housed a dance hall the Earps ran until they opened the White Elephant saloon. On April 9, the three men paid Buzzard five hundred dollars for a town lot, undoubtedly the land containing the tent.

Continuing their land-buying spree, the Earps, Enright, Holman, and Ferguson bought a half interest in the Bloomfield placer claim on April 7 from Frank Crozier for five hundred dollars. On the fifteenth, Wyatt, Enright, Holman, and Ferguson bought a portion of Point of the Rocks placer claim on Eagle Creek and other valuable considerations for one dollar from W. H. Carroll, and, on April 30, William R. Vaughn sold the Earps, Enright, Holman, Ferguson, and John Hardy five acres in Dream Gulch for one thousand dollars.[12]

The Earps, with Holman and Enright, also invested in another lucrative enterprise in Eagle City, the saloon business. On April 26, tent saloon owners Sanford and Owens sold the two Earps, Enright, and Holman for $132 "One tent with poles door and floor situated on lot north of S. H. Hays store and immediately adjoining same The stove pipe chares [sic] tables benches bar and bar fixtures contained together with all stock in said building contained with all lamps schandelires [sic] and their fixtures" (spacing as in the original). Wyatt and James would operate the saloon until a lawsuit was filed for retention of the land that housed the tent saloon after the lease ran out. By mid July the Earps advertised their White Elephant Saloon, located in the New Theater Building, twice in the Weekly Eagle, claiming it was, "The Largest and Finest appointed Saloon in the Coeur d'Alenes."[13]

Like everyone else, the Earps wanted to strike it rich, and were listed as locators of several placer and lode mining claims during the spring of 1884. Wyatt was listed as locator of two placer claims: the Enola on March 15, and an unnamed claim on April 3. Wyatt was also the locator of several lode mining claims: the most promising was the Golden Gate on the east fork of Reeder Gulch and eight miles from Eagle City on May 1, followed by the Consolidated Grizzly Bear on May 10, the Dividend, two miles up Faney Gulch and five miles from Eagle City, on May 11, and the Dead Scratch on the slope of Bald Mountain on the north fork of Eagle Creek on May 18, of which the Spokane Falls Evening Review reported "assays $103.45 gold and $10.21 silver." James Earp was locator of only one lode mining claim, the Jesse Jay, on May 29, which was located on the west fork of Reeder Gulch, five miles from Eagle City.[14]

Lawsuits would continue to plague Wyatt, but they would come from an associate, William Payne. On April 30, Payne sued Wyatt over land in Eagle City, alleging that two men armed with revolvers made forcible entry on the land at gunpoint on April 26. Payne was awarded a jury verdict of twenty-five dollars on July 18, but the judge trebled the amount, and Wyatt paid off seventy-five dollars on August 4.[15]

On May 14, a more critical suit was brought against Wyatt by Payne, this time for the land that housed the White Elephant Saloon. Payne owned the land and had leased it to saloon keepers Sanford and

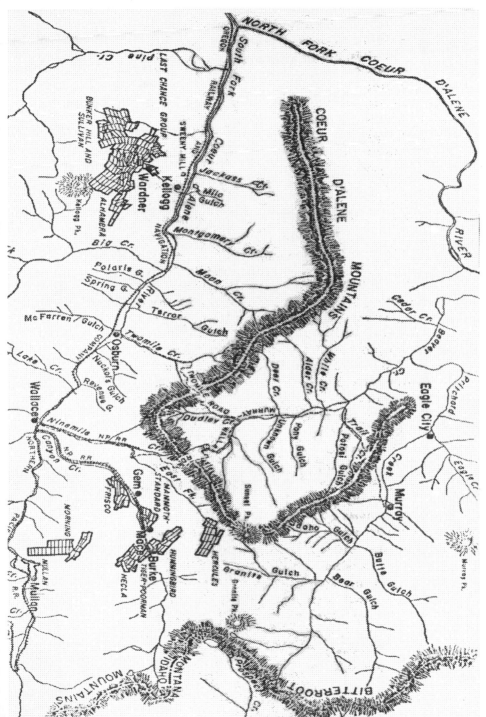

Map of the Coeur d'Alene mining district around 1910. AUTHOR'S COLLECTION

Owens, who in turn sold the tent saloon to the Earps. The Earps kept the saloon on the land after expiration of the lease and Payne wanted his land. Judge Magnuson made these historical notes, "It is interesting to note that [Wyatt] Earp contested this action on the basis that the court did not have jurisdiction for the reason that the land was in Kootenai County and not in Shoshone County. This was at a time when the sheriffs of both counties were battling over who had authority in the gold fields." Nevertheless, Wyatt's contention was fruitless and judgment was awarded to the plaintiff. Payne recovered his land and collected $33.61 from Wyatt on August 4.[16]

Whenever the subject of Wyatt Earp is raised the word gunfight is not far behind, so the question arises whether or not Wyatt had any shoot-outs in Idaho. To those fans of blazing gunfire, regretfully he did not. However, Wyatt was indirectly involved in two separate shootings, one of which was concerned with his friend and business partner, Daniel S. Ferguson. According to the *Spokane Falls Evening Review,* "Ferguson is 23 years of age, and is said to be respectably connected, his father being Adam Ferguson, of North Platte, Nebraska." That Ferguson was a reckless young man, and a hot-headed one, there can be no doubt, for in October 1881, he had a confrontation with a man well known to be dangerous.

At the early age of twenty or twenty-one, Ferguson was working the gambling halls in his hometown of North Platte. On October 10, 1881, he had a difference of opinion with notorious Bill Tucker, who ran the dissolute Cowboy's Rest Saloon and Dance Hall in Ogallala, Nebraska and was operating a saloon in North Platte during the off season. On June 26, 1880, Tucker had a disagreement over a prostitute in Ogallala that resulted in a shoot-out with William "Texas Billy" Thompson, the brash younger brother of the notorious Ben Thompson. Tucker lost three fingers of his left hand while filling Billy's body with buckshot; however, both men recovered.

Apparently Tucker's renown had made no impression on Ferguson, and he challenged the saloon man to fight. Ferguson quickly fired off four shots as Tucker reached in his pocket for his pistol. Tucker was lucky, for the day was cold and the thick clothing he wore absorbed the shots; he escaped with bruises and gashes on his abdomen and four holes in his clothing. Ferguson was arrested by Con Groner, sheriff of Lincoln County, on the charge of attempted murder and was held under one thousand dollars bond until his trial. On November 26, the jury found Ferguson not guilty, but convicted him of assault and battery, for which he was fined. The shooting in Eagle City, Idaho would be much more consequential.[17]

The gold strike stirred the interest in mining property throughout businesses in the Northwest. Thomas Steele, agent for the Northwestern Mining Company, had been sent to the Idaho gold fields from Sun River, Montana by James Steele of the Willamette Bank of Portland, Oregon. Thirty-year-old Thomas Steele was originally from Omaha,

Nebraska, the son of Dr. James R. Steele. On the afternoon of June 19, Steele started up Prichard Creek on business but had to return to Eagle City for some forgotten papers. Because of a severe rainstorm he decided to put off the trip until the following day. The *Spokane Falls Evening Review* stated, "Later in the afternoon, he met a fallen woman, with whom it is said, he was intimate, and in her company visited several saloons, he drinking but little and she drinking to intoxication."

While in one of the saloons around 1 A.M. Steele tried to get the woman to go home, but she would have none of it. Taking her by the arm, he got her out of the saloon and made it fifty yards before the woman balked, lay down in the street, and slurringly said she would stay there all night. Steele blew up and struck the woman several times until Hess, the keeper of the saloon they had just left, ran up and asked Steele not to hurt the woman. Following closely on the saloon man's heels was Dan Ferguson, who also asked Steele to desist. In answer, Steele hit the woman again, walked up to Ferguson and said, "Maybe you want some of this. Damn you, I'll fix you," and pulled out a pistol and struck Ferguson on the head, causing the pistol to discharge.

Ferguson quickly pulled his own revolver, and the two men exchanged gunfire, Steele shooting once and Ferguson twice. In its coverage of the ensuing events, the *Spokane Falls Evening Review* also indicated that Wyatt continued his career as a lawman in the Idaho gold fields: "Steele fell, mortally wounded, the ball entering just below the left ribs and coming out of the back, about two inches to the right of the spinal column. After the shooting Ferguson immediately sought Wyatt Earp, Deputy Sheriff of Kootenai county, whose headquarters are at this place."

Minutes later, Sheriff Dunwell and his deputy Frank McDonald arrived and, finding Steele dead, took the drunken woman to the jail. The verdict of the coroner's jury was that "Thomas Steele had come to his death by a gun-shot wound from a pistol in the hands of Dan Ferguson." An arrest warrant was immediately sworn out for Ferguson, and he was released under a three-thousand-dollar bond. At his preliminary hearing the next morning, Ferguson was reportedly acquitted on the grounds of self-defense.[18]

In the Stuart Lake notes, Wyatt recollects his participation reportedly in the words of Ferguson at the coroner's inquest:

> Determined not to be arrested—at the time, I walked away to'rd my cabin. Finding that I was short of cartridges I went to Jack Enright's cabin, but he too was short, so I passed through my own cabin, to that of Wyatt Earp, which was directly back of mine at the foot of the mountain. Wyatt was standing outside by the door and in his underclothes. As I approached he said, "Those pistol shots sounded like there was a fight up the street." "Yes I had one." I answered. "Did you win it?" "Yes." "Well wait until I get my clothes on and I'll go up and look over the battle ground." He returned shortly stating "The man was dead before the sheriff reached him. I told the sheriff that you would not surrender until the inquest in the morning," and he said, 'all right.' Now what do you in-

tend doing—ride or stay?" "Stick:" I answered,—and went to bed at my cabin. At the inquest the next morning I handed the sheriff one gun, was acquitted, and he returned it at once.[19]

However, there was more to the case. On July 15, a Shoshone County grand jury handed down an indictment for murder against Ferguson.[20] Ferguson reportedly took off for the Wood River country and did not know of the indictment, which was supposedly initiated by pressure from friends of Steele. McInnes writes, "Law enforcement officials simply waited for Ferguson to return to Eagle City, where they would arrest him. Steele's friends even bribed the telegraph operator at Eagle City to prevent any messages from reaching Ferguson, so that he would return unaware of the charges pending against him. . . . Many of Ferguson's friends feared he would be railroaded into the penitentiary, or even worse, lynched if he returned. One of those friends was Wyatt Earp. Earp went to the telegraph station and attempted to send a message to Al Holman, at Wood River. Holman could then warn Ferguson. The telegrapher, however, refused to send the message."[21]

Returning to Stuart Lake's notes on Wyatt Earp's remembrances, which are slightly dissimilar:

> Wyatt Earp's loyalty to a friend now enters into the story. The Grand Jury convened . . . and through the job of the foreman indicted Ferguson. Wyatt having knowledge of their intentions, went to the telegraph office and asked Toplitz, the operator, if anyone had sent Ferguson a message? "No, and if they do we will indict them." Wyatt grabbed at him, but ducking under Wyatt's arm, sprang outside the office with Wyatt at his heels. Realizing that he could not catch him, Wyatt grabbed up a big stone and slammed it after him just grazing his head and scaring him so badly that he tripped and fell. In a second Wyatt had him by the neck and kicking him a few times in the ribs dragged him to the office. "Now send this telegram or I'll beat you to death!" He sent it and Ferguson received it.[22]

Ferguson skipped the country and was never prosecuted for the killing of Thomas Steele.

Although there are no official records verifying Earp's position as a deputy in Kootenai County, the assertion is explained by historian Richard Magnuson:

> At about the time in question [killing of Thomas Steele], there was a dispute going on over the county the Murray gold fields were located in. For a short time, both Kootenai County and Shoshone County had peace officers in that area. I believe it was in July, 1884 that the District Court heard a case involving this dispute and ruled that the Murray gold fields were within the confines of Shoshone County and the problem was ended. The early confusion accounts for Wyatt Earp being a deputy sheriff in Kootenai County.[23]

At this time the reputation and fame of Wyatt were widespread, and undoubtedly preceded him to Idaho, which would justify his appointment as a deputy sheriff.

The other Idaho gun battle that involved Wyatt Earp actually occurred some two and a half months earlier, and this one drew a crowd. The affray resulted over a property dispute involving associates of Wyatt Earp. Around the first week in March Phillip Wyman sold a lot on the east side of Eagle Street, which he claimed to have located in 1883, to Enright, Holman, Payne, and Ferguson, who in turn erected a tent on the property. On the other side, Sam Black maintained that he located the same lot in 1883 and that he sold the lot in January 1884 to William Buzzard, who built a cabin at the rear of the property. Enright and party claimed Buzzard's cabin was built on the alley, not the lot.[24]

The man Bill Buzzard is quite an enigma. He has been reported as a hero in the 1868 Bear River, Wyoming conflict that brought fame to Thomas "Bear River Tom" Smith, who was later shot and killed while serving as marshal of Abilene, Kansas. Buzzard is also reported to have been leader of a band of villains in Bodie, California. No confirming evidence has been uncovered in either case. The man was doubtlessly Fay Buzzard, or Buzard as his name was sometimes listed, who was the only Buzzard or Buzard on the 1884 Shoshone County, Idaho Voter Registration, which recorded him as twenty-eight years old and from Kansas. This would make him an unlikely participant in the Bear River incident as he would have been only twelve years old.[25]

On the morning of March 28, 1884, the ground in Eagle City was covered with two to three feet of snow, and the town was thronged by people who could not mine their claims. Buzzard was hauling logs to the lot to build a boardinghouse and hotel when he was accosted by Enright, who protested the action. Buzzard leveled a Winchester rifle at his assailant and ordered him off the property. According to the *Spokane Falls Evening Review,* Enright stated he would be back and warned gathering spectators that "they might find some other portion of the town healthier." Within a short time Enright, with Payne, Holman, and Ferguson, returned armed with a Winchester rifle, shotguns, and revolvers and came up against Buzzard, his friend Charles Gable, and two unnamed men armed with Winchesters, shotguns, and Sharp's rifles. When warned to leave, the crowd hastily complied.

Buzzard then jumped up on a breastwork of hewn logs, fired one shot, and quickly dropped behind the barricade as he continued firing. Enright and his group took up position behind a snowbank and began to encircle their besieged opponents. Within ten minutes Buzzard and his crew were forced to retreat to his cabin. As Buzzard dashed toward safety, two bullets whipped through the crown of his hat and one grazed the rim. Buzzard and his friends made it safely inside his cabin, but the attacking party followed and the shooting continued until Deputy Sheriff W. E. Hunt arrived and disarmed both sides. A man from the Eagle City Theater named McDaniels appeared waving a white flag to prevent further hostilities.

Only one casualty was suffered; a carpenter named John Burdett was struck in the fleshy part of his thigh as he dove into an adjacent cabin for protection. As for Wyatt Earp's participation, the *Spokane Falls Evening Review* reported:

> The Earp brothers, James and Wyatt, took a prominent part as peacemakers. With characteristic coolness, they stood where the bullets from both parties flew about them, joked the participants upon their poor marksmanship, and although they pronounced the affair a fine picnic, used their best endeavors to stop the shooting. After Mr. Hunt had disarmed the parties in the cabin, the Earps announced the fact to those outside, and told them to put up their guns, as the fight must end.

All's well that ends well, and when the fight concluded Buzzard and Enright made up, giving each other compliments on having made a square fight. Then both men, along with Payne, visited the wounded Burdett, offering him both assistance and money. So ended the Battle of the Snowdrifts. To further show that no animosity remained, Fay Buzard (Buzzard) sold property located in Eagle City to the Earps and Holman ten days later.[26]

By late summer the Coeur d'Alene gold stampede was over, and the Earps salvaged what they could and moved on to greener pastures. There is no record of Wyatt after August 14. Warren remained in Idaho at least until September 26, but by the time the election took place on November 4, he too was gone. As an aside, Wyatt failed to pay taxes of $8.67 on "one tent and improvements on three lots in rear Harkins Bank Eagle City . . . at a valuation of $270.00," and the Shoshone County Commissioners took title on November 10, 1884.[27]

Warren Earp was the first of the remaining brothers to die. He at times followed Wyatt on his wanderings throughout the West, but in 1891 went to Arizona where he went to work for Henry C. Hooker on the Sierra Bonita Ranch. As the most irascible of the brothers, Warren got into one scrape after another until his death in 1900 in Wilcox, Arizona. Warren and one John Boyett had been on bad terms for several years, and in the early morning hours of July 6, the unarmed Warren was gunned down by Boyett in the Headquarters Saloon as he advanced on his adversary. Rumor was that Boyett had been paid to kill Warren. Wyatt and Virgil Earp immediately came to Wilcox and were reported to have secretly killed Boyett. True or not, the two Earps did go to Wilcox, Boyett did disappear, and no record of him has been found after he killed Warren.

James Earp's life was not as controversial. Returning to California after leaving the Coeur d'Alenes in 1884, he reportedly drove a hack in San Bernardino for many years, supplementing his income by a Civil War pension. James died on January 25, 1926 in Los Angeles, California. Virgil Earp died of pneumonia in Goldfield, Nevada on October 19, 1905 while serving as a special officer, and Newton Earp, the peaceful one of the family, died near Sacramento, California on December 18, 1928.

Wyatt Earp spent his latter years wandering throughout the west with his wife Josie. In 1885, with his brother Virgil, he opened two sa-

CERTIFICATE OF SALE.

TERRITORY OF IDAHO, }
COUNTY OF ~~NEZ PERCE~~, Shoshone } ss.

I, Frank Carle .... Assessor and Tax Collector for the County of ~~Nez Perce~~ Shoshone in the Territory of Idaho, do hereby certify that by virtue of an Act of the Legislature of Idaho Territory, entitled "an Act to regulate the manner of collecting Territorial and County Revenue in Idaho Territory," approved February 10th, A. D. 1881, did as said Tax Collector on the tenth .... day of November at 4 P.M. 1884 levy upon the following described property, to-wit:

one tent & improvements on three lots in rear Harkins Bank Eagle City in said County & Territory and assessed to Wyatt S. Earp at a valuation of $270.00

The said Levy being for taxes due to the Territory of Idaho and Shoshone County, with costs and charges due thereon. Said property was assessed for the fiscal year 1884, ~~and 18~~...., and to all owners and claimants known or unknown. The said tax was levied according to law, and no part thereof had been paid, and at the time of sale hereinafter spoken of were wholly unpaid. That publication of the intention to sell for the taxes, including said property for said tax, was made as provided by law, said publication being made by one insertion one time a week for three successive weeks in the Idaho Sun a newspaper published in said County of Shoshone That said publication designated the time and place of commencing said sale, which time was not less than twenty-one days, nor more than thirty five ....days from the first appearance of the publication. That the property assessed is described thus:.................

one tent & imh on lot in frt Harkins Bank Eagle City in $270.00 Personal property $20.00

situated within said County, on the 26th day of December .... A. D 1884 to which time the sale was duly postponed, in accordance with law, was offered at public auction in front of the Court House in said County. That at said auction the Clerk of the board of Co. Commission was the bidder, who was willing to take the least quantity of said property and pay the taxes due thereon, amounting, including $1 for this certificate, to $8.69/100 .... That the said smallest quantity of land described to-wit: all of the above described lots and improvements their on

was stricken off to said Clerk of the Board of County Commissioners .... who paid the said amount of taxes and costs, and therefore became the purchaser of said last described land. Said property was sold subject to redemption pursuant to the statute in such cases made and provided.

Given under my hand this 26th day of December .... A. D. 1884

FRANK Carle Shoshone
Assessor and Tax Collector, ~~Nez Perce~~ County, Idaho.

By ....
Deputy

Certificate of Sale, Territory of Idaho, County of Shoshone, levied November 10, 1884 on Wyatt Earp's property in Eagle City, Idaho, dated December 26, 1884.

loons and gambling houses in San Diego, California. He also was reported to have been kept busy running a string of thoroughbred racehorses. During the 1890s, Wyatt lived in San Francisco where he issued his controversial decision as referee in the Bob Fitzsimmons–Tom Sharkey prizefight. The debate continues today.

When the rush to the Alaska gold fields occurred in 1898, Wyatt was right there, opening a saloon in Nome. Selling out in 1901, he returned to the States financially well off. In 1902, he followed the mining boom to Tonopah and Goldfield, Nevada where he again opened a saloon, which he sold to his partner, Al Martin, in 1903. For the remainder of his days Wyatt prospected for ore, spending the winters in the California/Arizona desert and the summers in San Francisco and Los Angeles. In contrast with his stormy life, Wyatt died peacefully in his bed in Los Angeles on January 13, 1929. Josephine survived him by nearly seventeen years, passing away on December 19, 1944.[28]

So ends the saga of Wyatt Earp. There will always be contention, but maybe it is best that controversy surrounds him, for this will keep him forever alive in the minds of all of us who savor the aura of the Old West.

VII. OREGON

Z. G. HARSHMAN

Golden Eagles and Railroad Ties

MOST CRIMINALS, WHEN THEY ARE CAUGHT, have excuses for why they led a life of crime: alcohol abuse or compulsive gambling, poverty, hanging with the wrong crowd, and today, abusive treatment as a child or drug addiction. Z. G. Harshman became a criminal because of golden eagles and railroad ties. From the moment Harshman counterfeited his first gold coin he was hooked; he loved it, and, although he always got caught, as soon as he was free he would start again. As for the railroad ties, well, that will come later.

Z. G. Harshman was certainly not an outlaw with the notoriety of a Jesse James or a Billy the Kid, and would have been no more than a name and number in penitentiary records if not for one fact: Harshman and "Old Bill" Miner attempted a train robbery near Portland, Oregon in 1903, and blew it. As a result, for a short time, Harshman became headline news in Oregon. While researching data for *The Grey Fox*, a biography of Miner, a thorough search was made for information about Harshman, which disclosed that he lived a tragic but quite interesting and colorful life, deserving a story of his own.

He was born Zebulon Gay Harshman on April 21, 1860 in New Salem, Pike County, Illinois. He began working on his father's farm at an early age and attended twelve years of schooling. He stated that school was easy for him, claiming: "I was always way ahead of my class." At age seventeen, he started working for wages, but around 1880 he left home and headed west. For six months he herded cattle and horses on the plains of Wyoming, leaving to work in a stone quarry at Fort Collins, Colorado for another six months. He earned enough money to buy a span of mules, and worked for the Denver and Rio Grande Railroad for several more months.

In early 1882, Harshman came to Pendleton, Oregon and grew wheat in Cold Springs canyon for about a year.[1] Moving on, he obtained a homestead along the border of what is now Gilliam and Morrow Counties where he met and courted fourteen-year-old Nancy Dean, daughter of Hazel Dean, whose ranch was eight miles south of Morgan.[2]

On March 11, 1883, Z. G. Harshman and Nancy Dean were married at the house of Mr. T. Kendal, near the town of Morgan in Umatilla County (now Morrow County). The Harshmans' homestead was located in Gilliam County, fifteen miles south of Arlington and two miles west of the Morrow County Line.[3]

For four years the Harshmans farmed their homestead, and in 1884 their first child was born, a son they named Harvey. During this time Harshman had no trouble with the law, but he was known as a quarrelsome man who was always at odds with his neighbors, and prone to occasional bouts with the bottle. To his credit, he was regarded as industrious although unsuccessful in obtaining very much property. At the end of this four-year period, however, trouble came to Harshman in a roundabout way.[4]

Approximately one and a half miles northeast of Harshman's residence, a young single man named Thomas J. Golphene (pronounced Golfeenee) established a homestead of one hundred and sixty acres. Since Golphene had no water on his homestead, he was granted permission to obtain his water from the Harshmans. In this new pioneer country, female companionship was scarce, and Golphene started visiting the Harshman cabin while Harshman was away.

Nancy Harshman evidently was not adverse to Golphene's visits, nor his advances, and in time the two became lovers. What caused her infidelity is not known but several factors likely had their effect: her marriage at age fourteen, the nine-year difference in age between the two, and Harshman's quarrelsome nature and drinking. This state of affairs continued until the spring of 1887.

Harshman first became suspicious of his wife's infidelity in a somewhat humorous way. Returning home in the evenings, he soon noticed an ever-increasing amount of horse manure piling up where Golphene would hitch his horse. Whether or not Harshman confronted his wife with his suspicions mattered little, for Golphene had the gall to brag about his conquest to all of his neighbors. To be cuckolded was one thing, but to be humiliated by his wife's lover was more than Harshman could endure.

On the evening of Thursday, May 19, 1887, Harshman made his way to Golphene's cabin, arriving there after dusk. The cabin was dark and Golphene was asleep when Harshman crept up to the window. Lighting a wad of paper, Harshman smashed the window and tossed the torch inside. Immediately awakened by the noise and fire,

Golphene rose up in alarm and Harshman blasted him with both barrels of his shotgun, nearly decapitating him. Calmly crawling in through the window, Harshman laid the victim's shirt over the head and body, and left the cabin without disturbing anything.

On Sunday morning, May 22, Harshman went to the home of John L. Logan, located about a mile from Golphene's cabin, and told Logan, "Haven't seen Golphene around for quite a while. Maybe we better go and look." The two men proceeded to Golphene's house. Reluctant to enter the cabin, Harshman remained outside while Logan went inside. He found Golphene's body on the bed in a terrible state of decomposition. On May 23, the coroner, Dr. Bacon, held an inquest, with the verdict that the deceased was killed by an unknown party. In spite of the verdict, everyone knew about Golphene's affair with Harshman's wife and surmised that Harshman had killed him.[5]

A reporter from the *Morning Oregonian* accompanied a deputy sheriff to the area on May 26 to investigate the case. He reported the following particulars:

> We found a number of the neighbors gathered at the house of Andy Douglass, where the murdered man was last seen, who were determined to ferret the matter to the bottom if possible.
>
> Suspicion points to a neighbor of Golphenee [*sic*], with whose wife the latter is said to have been intimate. There is little doubt in the minds of those who are acquainted with the circumstances of the case that this was an act of desperation, committed by a man who believed he was vindicating his honor by slaying his wife's paramour.
>
> As soon as the above was learned and talked over it seemed the general opinion that, although the crime was committed in a cowardly manner, that the supposed murderer cannot be convicted, on account of Golphenee's rumored intimacy with his wife, and because the dead man was not content without boasting of the matter to neighbors.[6]

The consensus of his neighbors was correct. Harshman was never indicted as the evidence offered by the state was insufficient to bring about a conviction.[7] In spite of the shame and scandal, Harshman and his wife remained together and had two more sons, Oliver in 1888 and Floyd on March 22, 1891. The residents of the area grudgingly accepted Harshman's actions because of the circumstances surrounding the case, but the stigma of being a craven murderer followed him.

In 1892, Harshman lost his homestead to the Oregon Railway and Navigation Company, apparently for not improving his homestead to meet company standards. By April the family had moved to the state of Washington, near the town of Rochester in Thurston County, where Harshman began farming again.[8]

Marital problems also plagued Harshman during this period. According to the records of the Eastern Oregon State Hospital, "Patient states he was married at 23 and that domestic relations were happy for about a year, after which time his wife 'got stuck on another man.' However, he and his wife lived together for about 10 years, on and off,

Photograph of the Harshman family taken in Centralia, Washington, in late 1892 or early 1893. In back, left to right: Z. G., Floyd, and Nancy; seated in front, Oliver.
AUTHOR'S COLLECTION

at the end of which time he left her." Nancy Harshman and the children returned to Oregon where she obtained a divorce and later married a man named Matthews.[9]

Although industrious, Harshman was never successful at farming. His failure and his marital problems were the likely reasons he turned to counterfeiting. During the summer of 1893, Harshman, now thirty-three, joined a counterfeiting ring in Rochester consisting of Ross Hickey, a twenty-three-year-old engineer from Rochester; George Burley, a woodsman from Elma, age twenty-eight; and a twenty-six-year-old miner from Indiana named James M. Heath. The band began fraudulently producing five-dollar gold coins and one-dollar, half-dollar, and ten-cent silver pieces.

On September 1, Harshman passed some of the counterfeit coins in both Pierce and Thurston Counties. On October 8, he circulated more of the bogus coins in Lewis County. Returning to Thurston County, Harshman passed an additional quantity of the counterfeit coins on October 20 to an unsuspecting citizen named N. R. Harris.

By October, the U.S. Marshals' Office in Tacoma became aware of the gang's activities and, on October 10, arrested Burley in Rochester. From that point the U.S. authorities quickly rounded up the other members of the gang. On November 11, 1893 a U.S. warrant was issued for Harshman's arrest. Tracing Harshman to Thurston County, U.S. Deputy Marshal E. A. Minsch arrested him there on December 23. The next day U.S. Commissioner A. Reeves Ayers committed Harshman to the Pierce County jail at Tacoma in default of $1,400 bail. On January 10, 1894, Heath was arrested in Olympia, and on the thirteenth, the authorities caught up with Hickey in Rochester.

In Tacoma on February 10, 1894, Harshman was brought before the grand jury in U.S. Circuit Court and indicted two days later. On March 17, Harshman pled guilty to charges of counterfeiting and passing counterfeit coins. Judge Cornelius H. Hanford fined Harshman one dollar and sentenced him to serve ten months at hard labor at the U.S. Penitentiary at McNeil's Island, Washington. The three other defendants were each sentenced to one year's imprisonment at hard labor.

Harshman was delivered to McNeil's Island on March 17 and registered as Gay Harshman, Convict No. 111. The following information was recorded: Height-5' 7½", Weight-165 lbs., Hair-Brown, Eyes-Blue, Habits-Temperate, First Offense. He was released on December 28, 1894.[10]

Harshman's prison term apparently had no effect on him. Within a year he was back at the counterfeiting game, this time using the alias of W. T. "Billy" Montcalm. On December 20, 1895, Harshman passed several bogus gold and silver coins in Tacoma, Washington. On January 10, 1896, a warrant was issued for his arrest. For five months he evaded arrest, but on June 20, he passed more of the counterfeit gold coins at Kangley in King County, Washington. U.S. Deputy Marshal C. S.

Bridges tracked Harshman to Palmer, Washington and arrested him on June 26.

The next day, Harshman was brought before U.S. Commissioner M. L. Clifford at Tacoma and remanded to the Pierce County jail in default of $2,000 bail. Indicted by the grand jury in U.S. District Court at Seattle on December 8, 1896 Harshman entered a plea of not guilty. He was brought to trial on December 9 and found guilty by jury the next day. On December 21, Harshman again faced Judge Hanford. This second offense earned him eight years at hard labor at McNeil's Island. As Convict No. 86, Harshman began his second term on the day of his sentencing.[11]

Because this was Harshman's second conviction, a request to transfer him to another penitentiary was sent to the attorney general in Washington, D.C. On January 14, 1897, a new commitment was issued which ordered him to be transferred to the California State Prison at San Quentin. On February 6, U.S. Marshal James C. Drake took Harshman into custody, delivering him to San Quentin on February 8. He was registered as Gay Harshman, Convict No. 17175, Occupation-Gardener, Height-5' 6", Eyes-Blue, Hair-Chestnut.

While in San Quentin, Harshman met a man over fifty years of age who had served a term of nearly twenty years for stage robbery. He was William A. "Old Bill" Miner, and their association would alter the course of Harshman's life, vaulting him into the headlines of the major newspaper in Oregon. During his imprisonment Harshman was a model prisoner and, after serving a little over five years of his sentence, he was released on May 23, 1902.[12]

Following his discharge, Harshman returned to Oregon and worked in various logging camps around Astoria, Near City, and Goble. During this period, he reportedly contracted with the railroad to make railroad ties. After finishing the job, he was infuriated when the railroad refused to accept or pay for his work. Having also lost his homestead to the railroad, the enraged Harshman vowed to get even with them in some way. He got his chance during the summer of 1903 when Bill Miner appeared at a lumber camp where Harshman was working. Here the two men mapped out a scheme that would ultimately prove disastrous for Harshman.

Bill Miner had been released from San Quentin a year prior to Harshman's discharge. Through the influence of another San Quentin inmate, Jake "Cowboy Jake" Terry, Miner went to the northern section of Washington where he took a job in the oyster beds and at the same time joined Terry in his smuggling operations along the border of the United States and Canada.

During the summer of 1903, Miner made a trip south to Oregon. At the Farr Brother's lumber camp near Goble he ran across the forty-three-year-old Harshman. According to the *Oregon Journal*, Harshman, now using the alias of John Williams, had been contemplating holding up a train and was on the lookout for confederates he could trust.

Harshman, in his rage against the railroad, confronted Miner with his plans, to which the old bandit readily agreed.[13]

The major problem was that neither Miner nor Harshman knew the first thing about robbing trains, which later became humorously apparent. Nevertheless, the two men made their initial plans and after informing Harshman that he could get a third reliable man, Miner headed for Sagit County, Washington.

In Washington, Miner enlisted a naive seventeen-year-old named Charles Hoehn into the scheme and, on August 17, the two left for Oregon. At Goble, Miner and Hoehn met Harshman, who was still using the alias of John Williams. The three men worked for a short period at a lumber camp, piling wood while daily discussing the planned robbery. Spreading a story that they were going to the vicinity of Nehalem to open a coal mine, the trio went by wagon to an abandoned fisherman's cabin on Government Island, about sixteen miles below Goble. Returning the wagon to Goble, they spent several days at the cabin. Hoehn later stated that he first learned about the robbery plans while on Government Island, and claimed that he was forced to participate because he was under the complete control of Miner. Since Harshman's and Hoehn's stories conflict as to what transpired prior to the robbery, the most plausible chain of events will be presented.[14]

On the night of September 19, 1903, the three would-be bandits made their first attempt to rob the Oregon Railway and Navigation Express train. Miner picked the town of Clarnie, less than ten miles outside Portland, to stage the holdup. He reasoned that, after the robbery, they would be close enough to Portland to return quickly to the city and disappear into its populace.

Arriving in Clarnie, Hoehn was sent down to the tracks with a set of red stop signals to await the approaching train, while Miner and Harshman stationed themselves on a high bank ready to fire upon the train after it stopped. Hoehn, not familiar with train signals, was on the wrong side of the track when the train approached. Naturally, the engineer ignored the waving red lights and sped on.

The robbers had brought along twenty pounds of dynamite, probably stolen from the lumber camp where they had worked, for the purpose of blowing open the express car door. Miner, seeing that the train was not going to stop, ordered Harshman to light a stick of dynamite and toss it on the express car as it passed. Harshman refused because he was afraid that the explosion might injure the passengers. Miner and Harshman commenced quarreling on top of the embankment as the train roared past, carrying away their booty, with Hoehn below waving the red signals in vain.[15]

Patching up their differences, Miner and Harshman soon formalized a new plan. Hoehn was sent to Goble to purchase a boat, which he bought from a fisherman named McIntire for twenty dollars. Hoehn floated the boat down the Columbia River to Corbett, twenty-one miles east of Portland, where he cached it and caught a train back to Goble. On the twentieth, Miner bought whiskey, sugar, coffee, and other provisions. The three men left the fisherman's cabin on September 23 and walked to Troutdale. As soon as they arrived, Hoehn was sent three miles up the track to Corbett with instructions to flag the train.[16]

At 8:15 on the night of September 23, the Oregon Railway and Navigation Fast Express Number 6 left Portland heading east. When the train paused at Troutdale, Miner and Harshman, who were masked with black cloth and were carrying several sticks of dynamite, climbed into the blind baggage car just behind the engine tender. Finding a tramp named Robert Bryden in the car, Miner and Harshman searched him for weapons and then ordered him into the coal box with a warning to stay put or they would kill him. As the train left the station, the two bandits climbed over the tender to the engine where they covered engineer Ollie Barrett and fireman H. F. Stevenson with revolvers and ordered them to stop the train at the twenty-one-mile post at Corbett.

Bringing the train to a halt, the two trainmen were ordered off the train by Miner and Harshman, and were told to lead the way to the express car. One of the bandits called out to Hoehn, who emerged from the side of the tracks carrying a rifle. Reaching the express car, they forced Barrett to order express messenger Fred Korner to open the door. Suspecting a robbery, Korner put out the lights and made no reply. For several minutes Miner and Harshman discussed the situation and decided to dynamite the door.

Lighting the dynamite fuses, which were tied to poles, the bandits placed them against the express car door. The door was completely shattered by the explosion, and Korner, who was hiding in the dark interior of the car, immediately fired his shotgun at the bandits. Harshman, who was in front of the others, was hit in the right side of his head and fell headlong into a ditch along the track siding. A stray slug also caught engineer Barrett in the shoulder. With this turn of events, Hoehn immediately fled over the bank to where the boat was cached on the Columbia River. Miner, after checking on the condition of Harshman, saw the game was over and took off after Hoehn, leaving Harshman behind.[17]

News of the attempted robbery was sent immediately to Portland and a special train was ordered to bring a posse to the area. The train was delayed for two hours until Multnomah County Sheriff William Storey could be located. The train reached the robbery scene about 12:30 P.M. with Sheriff Storey, his posse, and Captain James Nevins, superintendent of the Pinkerton's Detective Agency, and his men. They found Harshman still lying facedown in the ditch. Harshman and engineer Barrett were placed under medical care on the train, which immediately returned to Portland.

Meanwhile, the posse dispersed in groups between Bridal Veil and Portland in search of the fugitives. Near Bridal Veil, one group picked up the tramp, Robert Bryden, who said he had stayed hidden in the coal box until arriving in Bridal Veil. Bryden was held pending identification of the robbers. Word was sent to Sheriff Biedecker on the Washington State side of the river and a search was begun there. No trace of the robbers could be found and rewards were issued in the amount of $1,300 for each of the fugitives.

Harshman was taken to the Good Samaritan Hospital in Portland. On examination, it was found that the side of his skull was fractured where the shotgun blast hit him, five centimeters above the right ear. The hospital reported that they expected him to die at any time. He gave his name as Jim Conners but would give no other information. He had to be force-fed as he refused all food and drink, and was sullen and morose in manner, refusing to speak to anyone.[18]

When Miner left the scene of the robbery and reached the cached boat, he told Hoehn that Harshman was dead, and they immediately crossed the river to the Washington State side. From there, they went to Government Island and burned their cabin. The two then split up, both returning to the bay area of Washington, where Hoehn, using the name of Charles Morgan, took a job in a shingle mill near Bow, while Miner again went to work on the oyster beds. There were no leads to the identities or destination of Miner and Hoehn.[19]

While Harshman remained in the hospital under care and guard, officials sent his description statewide for identification. Finally, on October 6, the Tacoma police identified him as Jeplan [sic] Gay Harshman. Upon receiving this information, Sheriff Storey, who had been hunting the fugitives in Oregon and Washington since the holdup, returned immediately to Portland and confronted Harshman in the hospital.

With his identity now known, Harshman broke down and related the details of the robbery, naming his confederates. His story was partially fabricated as he stated that there were five men involved in the robbery: himself, Bill Morgan [Miner], Morgan's nephew Charles Morgan [Hoehn], George Underwood, and Jim James, a supposed relation of Jesse James. The rest of his confession was accurate, including the information that the Morgans could be found at Samish Flats in Washington.[20]

About ten days prior to Harshman's confession, Pinkerton's Captain James Nevins obtained a lead on Hoehn from a young boy in Portland who knew him. The boy was enlisted by Pinkerton's, taken to Bow, and assigned to work alongside of Hoehn. The object was to watch Hoehn to see if he would lead them to Bill Morgan (Miner). After Harshman's confession and the identities of the other robbers became known, Captain Nevins promptly ordered Hoehn's arrest via Sagit County Sheriff Risbell. On October 7, Sheriff Risbell rode the fifteen miles of railroad track to Bow on a velocipede and made the arrest. Hoehn was taken to Mount Vernon, Washington and jailed. Two days later, Hoehn broke down and confessed to the attempted robbery, stating, like Harshman, that there were five men involved. Sheriff Risbell and a posse began searching the Samish Bay area for Morgan (Miner).[21]

On October 1, Miner left his job on the oyster beds and headed for Whatcom, Washington to see his sister. While there, he evidently learned of Harshman's confession and/or the arrest of Hoehn. Fearing his own arrest, Miner told his sister that he was going to Anacortes, Washington, and on October 9 he disappeared, leaving behind his overcoat which was stained with Harshman's blood.[22]

On October 10, Sheriff Storey arrived at Whatcom. Obtaining the information via Hoehn or the Pinkertons that Morgan (Miner) had a sister in Whatcom, Storey obtained a warrant and went to her home, where he discovered the bloody overcoat and Miner's true name.

From Whatcom, Sheriff Storey proceeded to Mount Vernon to pick up Hoehn. On October 11, Storey and Captain Nevins took Hoehn into custody and left for Portland. The next morning Hoehn was locked up in the Multnomah County jail. On the same day, Harshman was released from the hospital and placed in jail with Hoehn. Both would-be train robbers finally admitted that there were only three men involved in the robbery attempt. Harshman added that Miner was known as Jim James as well as Morgan.[23]

During the week of October 12, a vagrant named James Fenning was arrested in Everett, Washington as Bill Morgan, the third member of the train robbing crew. When the news reached Portland, the *Oregon Journal* picked up the story and reported:

> In the first place the detectives say Feeney [*sic*] does not correspond with the description of the fugitive robber given by Harshman or Hoehn. . . .
> Furthermore it is stated that Feeney was in jail at Everett, serving a term for vagrancy at the time the attempted robbery took place. . . .
> Harshman, the other bandit under arrest, is too ill to make the trip to the Washington town for the purpose of identifying Feeney. But from a description of the latter, Harshman does not hesitate to say that he does not believe the prisoner is Morgan.

Sheriff Storey was so desperate to arrest the third bandit that he had Fenning held in jail at Everett until requisition papers were drawn up. On the nineteenth, Storey picked up Fenning, brought him back to Portland, and locked him up in the Multnomah County jail. The whole episode was a farce from the beginning, and Fenning was released on November 10 by order of the district attorney. Sheriff Storey, in trying to explain the whole thing away, stated that Harshman, when brought face to face with Fenning, said the man was definitely not the third bandit.[24]

Harshman and Hoehn were kept in jail without bond until brought into Multnomah County Court on November 13, 1903. As the statutes of Oregon did not cover the charge of train robbery, Harshman pled guilty to two charges: assault with a deadly weapon and

/25, $1,300.00 REWARD

The following rewards are offered for the ar=rest and conviction of A. E. MINER, alias WM. A. MINER, alias WM. MORGAN, alias OLD BILL MINER, who in company with GAY HARSHMAN and CHAS. HOEHN (the two latter are now in custody), held up O. R. & N. Co. Passenger train No. 6 at mile post No. 21, near Corbett, Oregon, on the night of September 23rd, 1903.

$500.00 by the Oregon Railroad and Navigation Co.
$500.00 by the Pacific Express Co.
$300.00 by the State of Oregon

Above is a photograph of A. E. MINER alias WM. MORGAN, and the following is his description:

RESIDENCE—Sammish Flats, Wash.

NATIVITY—Canadian.   COLOR—White.

OCCUPATION—Shoemaker.

CRIMINAL OCCUPATION—Stage and Train Robber

AGE—50 years; looks to be 55.

HEIGHT—5 ft. 9½ in.

WEIGHT—About 145 pounds.   Slim build.

COMPLEXION—Medium Dark.

COLOR OF HAIR—Quite Grey.   Original color, brown and brushes it back from temples.

EYES—Brown.   NOSE—Long.

STYLE AND COLOR OF BEARD—When last seen (October 1, 1903), was smooth shaven.

PECULIARITIES AND MARKS—Slight squint in right eye.   India ink marks at base of left thumb.   Projecting ears   Dancing girl in India ink on right forearm.   Face somewhat pitted; badly wrinkled at base of nose and on cheeks about eyes.   High cheek bones.   Flesh mole on left shoulder blade.   Mole on breast near point of right shoulder.   Walks erect.   Is said to be a sodomist and may have a boy with him.

Miner was liberated from prison at San Quentin, Calif., June 17th, 1901, where he had served a sentence of 25 years for stage robbery, less his good time allowance.

Miner's usual system of working is to locate himself in a cabin in a secluded place near a stage line, on a pretense of prospecting or following some lawful occupation.   He then selects a time and place for robbery, and after committing a crime leaves the country by avoiding the highways, and does not appear again in the vicinity where the robbery was committed.

HIS VICTIMS ARE ALMOST INVARIABLY STAGE LINES, although he may again participate in a train or other robbery.   He is likely carrying a Winchester rifle and a Colts revolver.

We have sufficient evidence to convict Miner of the O. R. & N. Co. train robbery.

If located, arrest and notify by wire at our expense the undersigned at the nearest office listed above, when arrangements will be immediately made to have the authorities of Multnomah County, Oregon, request his detention and send an agent for him, with necessary requisition papers.

PINKERTON'S NATIONAL DETECTIVE AGENCY,

303 Marquam Building,

PORTLAND, OREGON.

Or   JAMES NEVINS,
      Res. Gen'l Supt.

PORTLAND, OREGON, October 27th, 1908.

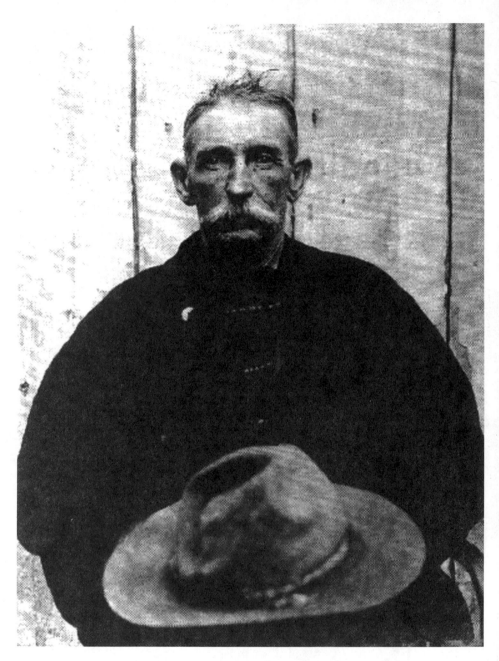

Bill Miner at the time of his capture for train robbery in British Columbia, Canada in May 1906. COURTESY OF PROVINCIAL ARCHIVES OF BRITISH COLUMBIA, VICTORIA

attempted robbery. Still suffering from his wound, Harshman had to be assisted to and from the courtroom.

Charles Hoehn pled not guilty to the charge of attempted robbery even though he had confessed his guilt earlier. Nevertheless, on the thirteenth, Hoehn was found guilty by Judge Cleland and sentenced to ten years' imprisonment. On November 24, Harshman was returned to court, found guilty, and sentenced to a total of twelve years' imprisonment by Judge Cleland, five years on one charge and seven years on the other.[25]

Hoehn was delivered to the Oregon State Penitentiary at Salem on November 16 and was registered as convict number 4792. Because of petitions submitted by residents of Washington State citing his youth and gullibility at the time of the attempted robbery, Governor George E. Chamberlain commuted Hoehn's sentence and he was released on November 14, 1907.[26]

Harshman entered the Oregon State Penitentiary on November 28 as convict number 4796. Contrary to earlier predictions, Harshman survived his wound, although he was paralyzed on his left side for three years and suffered dizzy spells for five years. In 1906, Harshman received a severe blow when news reached him that his youngest son, Floyd, had died of typhoid fever on November 22. Harshman followed the prison rules and never gave the officials any trouble. After serving a little over eight years of his sentence, he was discharged with time off for good behavior on March 28, 1912.[27]

If train robbery was not Harshman's forte, counterfeiting certainly was. In less than three years following his discharge he was at it again, with the same results: getting caught. Between December 1, 1914 and February 13, 1915, Harshman, now using the alias of Stark, made molds and counterfeited silver half-dollars and five-dollar gold pieces in Marshfield, Coos County, Oregon. Apparently word leaked out and he was arrested on February 14, 1915 in Marshfield.

Harshman was taken to Portland, where he was indicted by grand jury in U.S. District Court on February 27 and remanded to jail in default of $2,500 bail. On March 20, he pled guilty and was sentenced by Judge Robert S. Bean to seven years' imprisonment at McNeil's Island. In custody of U.S. Deputy Marshal D. B. Fuller, Harshman was delivered to McNeil's Island on March 21 and was registered as Convict No. 2574. A little over five years later, on May 14, 1920, the sixty-year-old Harshman was released from prison.[28]

After his discharge, Harshman returned to Oregon and herded sheep near Prineville for about a year and then headed south to mine in California and Arizona. In 1923 he took a job as watchman for the Humbolt Lumber Company at Crescent City on the northern coast of California.

Z. G. Harshman was perceivably more adept at building stills and making moonshine liquor than he had been at counterfeiting, and now that prohibition was in effect, he began bootlegging whiskey to local

Oregon State Prison photograph of Charles Hoehn taken in November 1903.
COURTESY OF OREGON STATE PENITENTIARY, SALEM

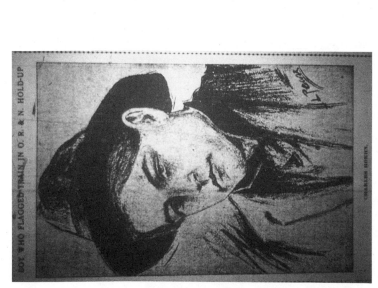

Artist's drawing of seventeen-year-old Charles Hoehn after his arrest for the train robbery near Portland, Oregon in October 1903.
AUTHOR'S COLLECTION

Oregon State Prison photograph of Z. G. Harshman taken in November 1903. COURTESY OF OREGON STATE PENITENTIARY, SALEM

Z. G. Harshman after his arrest for train robbery near Portland, Oregon in September 1903.
AUTHOR'S COLLECTION

Photograph of Z. G. Harshman taken around 1913 when he was logging between trips to the penitentiary.

COURTESY OF EVERETT HARSHMAN OF HERRNER, OREGON

doctors around Crescent City—strictly for medical use, of course. He reportedly spent time in prison for bootlegging; however, there are no prison records to substantiate the charge. Harshman might have been jailed locally, but it was of minor consequence since the unpopularity of prohibition had caused a large majority of people to make bathtub gin or bootleg whiskey, or to purchase illegal booze.

Throughout his sordid career Harshman deeply regretted the abandonment of his family and attempted to make amends in the only way he could. While working for the Humbolt Lumber Company he frugally saved several thousand dollars which he split equally between his two sons, Harvey and Oliver. From the autumn of 1928 until 1931, Harshman gave his son Harvey a total of $2,150, which was used to build up his sheep ranching business in Eightmile, Oregon, around fourteen miles southwest of Heppner.

In 1929 Harshman retired from the lumber company and returned to Oregon to live with his son Harvey and assist him with the ranch work. For five years Harshman worked with his son as a partner in the business but, because of the Depression, prices dropped and the ranch showed no profit.

To his family, Harshman often related the story of the Portland train robbery, claiming that it would have succeeded if the others had not run off. He also instructed those around the ranch how to build stills and produce moonshine whiskey. His grandson, Everett Harshman, related that at one point they had fourteen fifty-gallon barrels of mash which were hidden in dugouts covered with sagebrush and dirt.

By the mid 1930s, Z. G. Harshman began showing signs of senility and dementia. The ranch hands thought it great fun to tell the old man that they heard someone in the chicken house and watch him grab his revolver and rush out to shoot a chicken thief. Around 1937, Harshman's condition worsened and he became paranoid, blaming his son Harvey for the failing financial conditions of the ranch. According to Harshman's statements in the records of the Eastern Oregon State Hospital:

> Two years ago [1937] his son [Harvey] repudiated his contract with patient, tried to drive patient off his place, but patient refused to go until he received one-third of the money he had put up for the sheep originally. They quarreled, and patient states his son called him all sorts of names and abused him.

Old Z. G. Harshman's paranoia mounted and he threatened to kill his son Harvey. The old man had a vintage single-action Colt six-shooter which he placed under his pillow at night. Fearing his father's actions, Harvey had the revolver taken away and sold. Harshman then threatened to blow up his son with dynamite. In the spring of 1939 the situation became so perilous that Harvey decided to commit his father to a mental institution.[29]

On April 27, 1939, on the recommendation of Dr. Archie D. Mc-

Murdo, Morrow County Judge Bert Johnson ordered Z. G. Harshman committed to the Eastern Oregon State Hospital at Pendleton. Morrow County Sheriff C. J. D. Bauman took Harshman to the hospital the same day. Harshman clearly displayed his anger when he gave the following information to the hospital staff regarding his commitment:

> States that his son had him sent here to get rid of him so that his son could keep all the money they made with their sheep. . . . He also states that his son put the judge up to committing him, and that his son gambles and drinks constantly, and that his son is "sore" at the patient because of the patient's complaining about the excessive amount of drinking and gambling the son did. . . . Patient states he drinks very rarely, but his two sons are both drunkards.

Harshman proved to be a model patient, according to the following observations by the medical staff:

> Patient is neat and clean. Since admission has caused no trouble on the ward; is quiet and agreeable, of a jovial disposition and quite cooperative. He spends most of his time sitting in the day room and playing chess or sitting on the porch. . . . Patient answers questions relevantly

Z. G. Harshman at age 79 when he entered the Eastern Oregon State Hospital for dementia. COURTESY OF EASTERN OREGON PSYCHIATRIC CENTER, PENDLETON

and coherently except when on the subject of his son in Heppner, at which time he manifests a fixity of thought.

When Oliver Harshman was asked by the medical staff what the symptoms of his father's illness were, he stated: "To kill his son, Harvey, seemed to be about the only thing. He talked about that all the time."[30]

It seemed predestined that Z. G. Harshman end his life behind bars in some manner. At 7:45 P.M. on July 4, 1942, in Ward 7 of the Eastern Oregon State Hospital, the eighty-two-year-old Harshman died of a cerebral hemorrhage due to generalized arteriosclerosis.[31] His two sons paid for his funeral, which was held at the Bomboy Funeral Home in Pendleton on July 6, and he was buried in the Olney City Cemetery.[32] His tombstone reads:

FATHER

Z. G. HARSHMAN

1860–1942

To characterize Z. G. Harshman as a desperado would be a mistake. Describing him as a good guy would also be inaccurate. Harshman falls somewhere in the middle: a cantankerous, ornery, and fractious man who could not stay out of trouble, yet one who sincerely loved his family, furnishing his son the means to start his own business.

Harshman will not go down in history as a famous outlaw, but he holds the dubious distinction of being the man who launched Bill Miner's career as a train robber. So, no matter if a man's name is only a footnote in any given account, there is always a story behind that man, as the case of Zebulon Gay Harshman proves.

VIII. NEBRASKA

THE HERRON BROTHERS

Bandits' Burlesque

On MONDAY EVENING, July 28, 1890, a humorously inept train robbery took place one mile west of Arabia, Nebraska. As a comedy of errors, this holdup committed by the Herron brothers is classic in the annals of old west outlawry. The train robbery, however, was not the only peculiarity in the story of the Herron brothers. Neither state nor county officials in Nebraska knew the first names of the outlaw brothers, only their initials, J. A. and V. Existing records clarify this unaccountable point.

The Herrons were originally from Burr Oak, Noble County, Indiana. They were sons of Ohio natives Richard and Sarah J. Herron, who were aged fifty and forty respectively in 1880. John A. Herron, the first son, was born in Noble County in 1862 and was listed as "crippled." The fifth child, V. Herron, whose full name was Charles Velson, was born in 1870. Between J. A. and V., there were three additional children born: Mark W. in 1864, William E. in 1865, and Ella May in 1867.

Both John A. and Charles Velson Herron apparently were known by their initials. In the case of V., there were possibly other relatives named Charles so, not wanting to be called Velson, he chose to be known as Vee, which the officials in Nebraska took to be the initial V. As far as can be determined, the brothers, after migrating to Nebraska, were known in the area as J. A. and V., or Vee, Herron.[1]

In 1884, J. A. left Indiana for Nebraska, settling at Emerick in Madison County where he began farming. In January of 1889, his younger brother V. joined him. At the time the Herrons committed the train robbery, they were respected small farmers in Madison County.[2]

Left: Nebraska State Prison photo of J. A. (John A.) Herron.
Right: Nebraska State Prison photo of V. (Charles Velson) Herron.
NEBRASKA STATE HISTORICAL SOCIETY, LINCOLN

What possessed the two brothers to rob a train is not known. The hardscrabble life of a frontier farmer earned little cash in the 1880s, and the severe blizzards and droughts of 1887 and 1888 were economically disastrous. J. A. Herron was not exempt, and likely found himself in financial straits along with thousands of other shoestring farmers. After his brother arrived, the two evidently devised the train robbery scheme to put some much-needed cash in their pockets.

Neither man had a previous criminal record, so regardless of how ludicrous their plan was, it took a little internal fortitude for the two brothers to carry it out. From the start, the scheme was doomed to failure and their inexperience was blatantly evident throughout the entire proceeding.

On the morning of July 28, 1890, the Herrons bought tickets for Long Pine at the Fremont, Elkhorn, and Missouri Valley Railroad station at Meadow Grove, seventeen miles west of Norfolk, Nebraska. Intending to rob the passengers en route, the Herrons failed to muster enough courage to pull it off during the one-hundred-mile ride.

Arriving at Long Pine, the Herrons disembarked; however, the minute they got off the train, their courage miraculously returned and they decided to make another try. Purchasing tickets for Arabia, twelve miles east of Valentine, the brothers headed back to the train. Making their first mistake, they gave the agent a counterfeit dollar for the tickets. Before the train left the station the agent discovered the fraud, found the Herrons, and forced them to give him a good dollar for the counterfeit one. From this point, things would go from bad to worse.

The distance from Long Pine to Arabia was approximately fifty miles and during the trip the Herrons once again lost their nerve. When the train stopped they immediately got off. As soon as the train started to leave, the two brothers again regained their fleeting temerity, jumped back on board, and hid in a closet in the rear passenger car.

For the Herrons it was now or never, so they donned their false beards, bolstered their faltering nerves, and stepped out of the closet. Entering the passageway, they came face to face with the conductor, Michael Nealon. Shoving a revolver in his face, one of the Herrons commanded him to throw up his hands and give up his cash. Immediately complying with the order, the hapless conductor was relieved of two dollars and thirty-five cents.

Marching the conductor ahead of them, the bandits passed through two coaches, robbing the passengers on their way. If the Herrons thought their efforts would be amply rewarded, they were sadly disappointed. Their dreams of big money quickly vanished, for their take was only two dollars from Milton Vandorn, three dollars and eighty cents from Edward Stucker, three dollars from W. H. Albright, and four dollars and fifty cents from Charles Womeldorf. All told, their plunder added up to a dismal fifteen dollars and sixty-five cents.[3]

The robbery came to an abrupt halt when the brakeman, S. C. Moorman, attempted to enter the day car from the sleeper. With his adrenalin pumping and his frazzled nerves close to the breaking point, one of the Herrons impulsively fired a pistol shot at the unsuspecting brakeman. Fortunately, the shot went wild, plowing harmlessly through the glass doors into the sleeper. Too unnerved to continue the robbery, the bandits pulled the bell rope and jumped off as the train slowed. In the darkness, the two brothers ran south into the Sand Hills of Cherry County.

The Sand Hills area of western Nebraska is a cowman's paradise: a sea of grass flowing over hillocks like waves as far as one can see. Trees are virtually nonexistent except along the meandering Niobrara River. Into this vast grassland the Herrons fled and were fortunate the next morning to stumble onto a ranch house several miles from the railroad. Realizing that they had no hope of finding their way out of the area alone, the brothers persuaded the rancher to take them to Wood Lake, twenty-four miles southeast of Valentine, where they planned to head east on the same railroad they had robbed.

In their anxiety, the two brothers foolishly neglected to discard their false beards or hide their revolvers and plunder, which the ranchman could not help but notice. Unobserved by the Herrons, the rancher managed to pass the information to another man before leaving with the bandits in his buckboard. As soon as the buckboard was out of sight, the man mounted a fast horse and carried the news into Wood Lake.

Inevitably, on Wednesday, July 30, 1890, the Herrons were captured three miles south of Wood Lake by C. A. Johnson, Billy Day, Louis Meyers, and other men from Wood Lake. The news was immediately telegraphed to Deputy Sheriff Will Johnson at Valentine. Accompanied by County Attorney Ed Clarke, the deputy headed for Wood Lake to pick up the prisoners. The Herrons were brought to Valentine that evening on the nine o'clock train. A throng of over one hundred people had gathered at the depot to look at the bandits and followed them all the way to the jail. The two admitted they were brothers, but gave only their initials and last name.[4]

On August 2, a complaint was filed by County Attorney Clarke, charging the Herrons with both robbery and assault with intent to kill. An official warrant was issued from the Cherry County Courthouse the same day. The defendants pled not guilty and, on a motion by the state, Judge F. M. Walcott ordered the case continued until August 12. Bail was set at one thousand dollars each, which the Herrons could not raise, and they were locked up in the Cherry County jail.[5]

Realizing that they had little chance of beating the indictment at their preliminary hearing, the Herrons attempted to escape jail during the first part of the week of August 4. They were discovered by Deputy Sheriff Johnson, who quickly spoiled their plans. This prompted *The Republican* in Valentine to remark: "Does such actions assist in confirming their guilt or not?"[6]

Failing in their escape attempt, the Herrons consequently faced their preliminary hearing on August 12 in District Court in Valentine. The hearing, which was conducted in greater detail and was far more interesting than the actual trial, was thoroughly covered by *The Republican*:

> Tuesday afternoon quite a large audience gathered at the court house to hear the preliminary trial of J. A. and V. Herron, charged in Judge Walcott's court with train robbery on July 28, 1890. County Attorney Clark [*sic*], assisted by B. T. White appeared for the prosecution in an able manner; W. V. Allen, of Madison, and Burnham & Keaston appeared for the defendants. The examination of three state witnesses, Mrs Wixon [*sic*: Mrs. Mary C. Mason], Mr. Cleveland, and Conductor Nealon, who swore to the identity of the men, engaged the attention of the court during the entire afternoon. [Mary Mason and L. M. Cleveland were passengers on the train.] The testimony did not seem to disturb the prisoners much, but when the revolvers, belt, sack, false beard and gripsack were introduced as testimony it created considerable uneasiness upon the part of the prisoners and caused them to color up in the face to such an extent that their actions were noticeable by nearly every person in the court room. At the hour of six o'clock court adjourned to 8 o'clock Wednesday. Court was convened Wednesday morning at the appointed hour and the work of examining witnesses was resumed and lasted until 11:30 o'clock. From the evidence introduced a man of fair judgement would be convinced beyond all reasonable doubt that the men who were charged with the crime were guilty. The most binding testimony was that of Mr. Albright who swore positively that the prisoners are the men who did the robbing. The testimony of Mr. Overmire

[train passenger C. R. Overmeyer] was also very binding. The defense did not introduce any testimony but strived very hard to destroy the testimony introduced by the prosecuting attorney. The prisoners were bound over in the sum of $12,000 to appear at the district court, and not being able to give the required amount of bail they were again sent back to the county jail.

The newspaper erroneously reported the amount of bail, which was one thousand dollars each, and failed to state that the charge of robbing M. F. Nealon be substituted for the evidence in the three additional complaints.[7]

The brothers knew they had a good chance of being convicted when their trial came up on October 14 in District Court at Valentine. What they did not know was how stiff a sentence they would receive, and this uncertainty made them more desperate than ever. At dusk on October 11, three days before their scheduled trial, they successfully broke out of the Cherry County jail. The newspaper failed to reveal how they accomplished their escape, but reported that it was not a difficult task to execute. Cherry County Sheriff David Hanna offered a reward of one hundred and fifty dollars for their capture.

The two brothers had learned their lesson about the Sand Hills region, and headed east along the Niobrara River on foot. Although the terrain was extremely rugged, they knew they would not become lost if they followed the river; however, it did slow them down. By Thursday, October 16, they had traveled only sixty miles when they reached Carns, a post office stop located along the river about fifteen miles northeast of Bassett. The two fugitives were soon spotted and captured by Dave Johnson and Fred Weise. The two men brought their captives back to Valentine the next day and received the reward offered by Sheriff Hanna. It was reported that the two men went off rejoicing.[8]

Following their recapture, the Herrons' attorney, William V. Allen of Madison, immediately telegraphed District Judge Moses P. Kinkaid requesting permission to allow the Herrons to plead guilty in his chambers at O'Neill. The request was granted and the Herrons were scheduled to face Judge Kinkaid the next week.[9]

Just in case the Herrons decided to pull another disappearing act, they were taken to O'Neill by four Cherry County officials, prompting this quip in *The Republican*:

> County Clerk [B. T.] White, County Attorney Clarke, Sheriff Hanna, and Judge Walcott attended court at O'Neill last week to see that the train robbers would be properly looked after.[10]

On the twenty-fifth, Judge Kinkaid handed down a sentence of nine years at hard labor to J. A. and seven years at hard labor to his brother V. They were also ordered to pay the cost of the prosecution.[11]

Not taking any chances, Sheriff Hanna delivered the two train robbers to the Nebraska State Penitentiary at Lincoln on the day they were sentenced. J. A. was registered as Convict No. 1837 and his

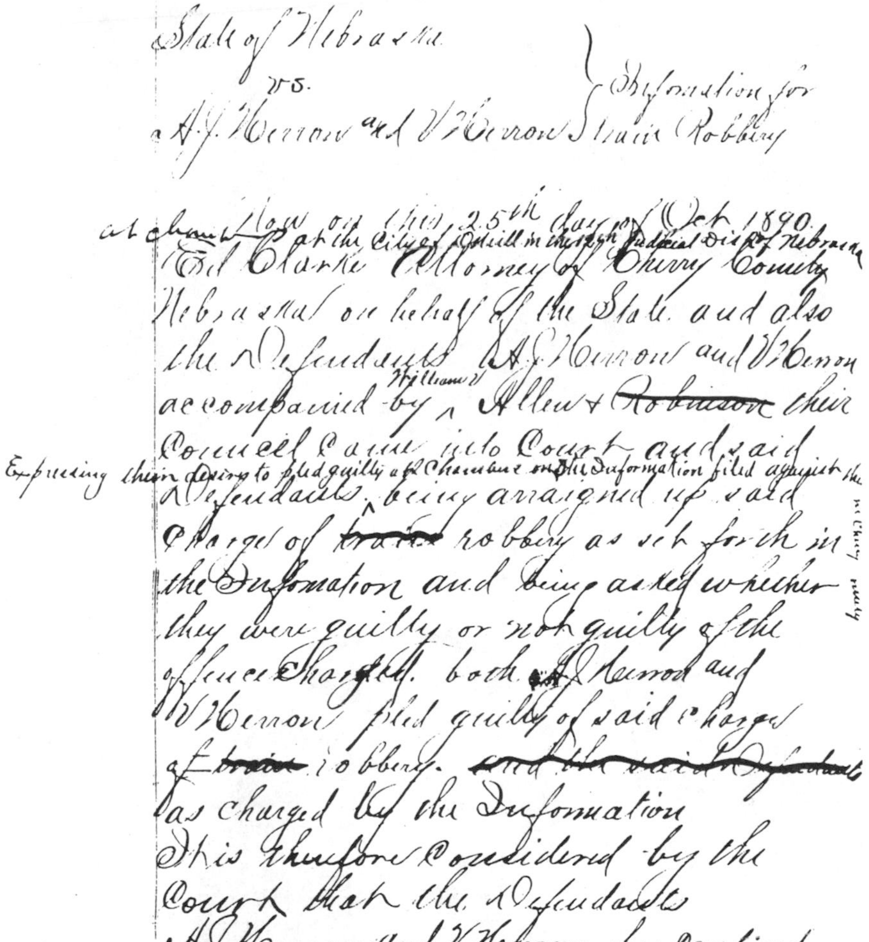

State of Nebraska

vs.   } Information for

A. J. Herron and V. Herron Train Robbery

Now on this 25th day of Oct. 1890 at Chambers at the City of O'Neill in the 9th Judicial Dist. of Nebraska E. L. Clarke Attorney of Cherry County Nebraska on behalf of the State and also the Defendants A. J. Herron and V. Herron accompanied by William Allen & ~~Robinson~~ their Council came into Court and said Defendants, Expressing their desire to plead guilty at Chambers on the Information filed against the being arraigned up said Charge of ~~train~~ robbery as set forth in the Information and being asked whether they were guilty or not guilty of the offence Charged, both A. J. Herron and V. Herron plead guilty of said charge of ~~train~~ robbery. ~~and the said Defendants~~ as charged by the Information It is therefore Considered by the Court that the Defendants A. J. Herron and V. Herron be Confined In the State Penitentiary of the State of Nebraska at hard labor Sundays excepted the said V. Herron for the term of Seven years and the said A. J. Herron for the term of Nine years and each be Kept at hard labor Sundays excepted and that they pay the cost of this Prosecution.

in Cherry County

Bill of Information for train robbery charges against the Herron brothers.
State of Nebraska v J. A. and V. Herron, Cherry County District Court
Records, Case no. 342. CHERY COUNTY DISTRICT COURT, VALENTINE,
NEBRASKA

Revolver, holster, and false whiskers used by the Herron brothers during their train robbery near Arabia, Nebraska in 1890. COURTESY OF CHERRY COUNTY, NEBRASKA HISTORICAL SOCIETY, VALENTINE

Sheriff David Hanna in his later years. COURTESY OF CHERRY COUNTY, NEBRASKA HISTORICAL SOCIETY, VALENTINE

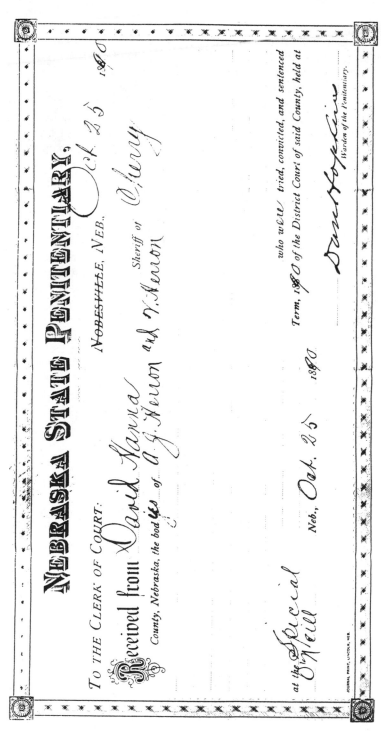

Receipt from the Nebraska State Penitentiary to Sheriff David Hanna for delivery of A. J. [sic] and V. Herron. Cherry County District Court Case no. 342. CHERRY COUNTY DISTRICT COURT, VALENTINE, NEBRASKA

brother as No. 1836. Both brothers were listed as being five foot seven inches in height with dark complexion and dark hair; however, J. A. had light blue eyes while his brother's were reported as grey.

The Herrons were not considered dangerous criminals in their home county of Madison, Nebraska, and the residents there undoubtedly shared the dim view of the railroads held by most small farmers and laboring people at the time. In 1894, these citizens of Madison expressed their feelings when they made an appeal to Governor Lorenzo Crounse on behalf of the brothers. As a result, J. A. Herron was paroled and released into the custody of Burt Lyons of Madison on March 27, 1894. In January 1895, J. A. applied for a pardon which was denied; however, he was officially discharged with good time on March 25, 1897. On January 2, 1895, Governor Crounse ordered V. Herron to be paroled and released on January 18 to W. L. Bickley of Madison. He was officially discharged on November 25, 1895, with good time.[12]

In spite of their rash acts of robbing a train and escaping from the Cherry County jail, the Herron brothers were not hardened criminals. Their paroles to upstanding citizens of Madison, Nebraska attest to this. They learned their lesson the hard way and, as far as can be determined, were never again charged with a criminal offense in Nebraska. The Herrons learned that it was better to live the life of a poor farmer than that of a poor convict and most likely followed this course to the end of their days.

IX. INDIANA

THE WHITE CAPS

Matters of Moral Regulation

UNTIL THE EMERGENCE IN 1940 of Walter Van Tilberg Clark's anti-vigilante novel, *The Ox-Bow Incident*, vigilantism or regulation was accepted, if not sanctioned, in the United States. Hollywood's adaptation of the novel helped turn the tide to condemnation. The portrayal of vigilantes as self-righteous and pharisaical is pretty much on target, and when we think of vigilantes we usually imagine a scene somewhere on America's western frontier, where a band of men is hanging one or more desperadoes from a cottonwood tree. However, the eastern portion of America had its vigilantes too; the Regulators of South Carolina in the mid 1700s, the Bald Knobbers of southern Missouri in the 1880s—and the White Caps of Indiana.

The lynching, or rather whipping, of James N. Keen was the first known exploit of the White Caps, a body of moral regulators operating in Indiana during the latter half of the nineteenth century. Although Keen was not hanged, there was strong evidence that he would have been had he remained in Harrison County. The word lynch was used during these early years to describe any act of punishment. Author Richard Maxwell Brown, an authority on violence in America, offers an overall view of the White Caps:

> White capping first broke out in southern Indiana in 1887, spread into Ohio the next year, and by 1889, had surfaced in New York, New Jersey, West Virginia, Arkansas, Iowa, and Texas. From 1887 through 1900 at least 239 cases of white capping occurred throughout America. Whereas organized vigilantism was largely a Western occurrence in this period and the mob lynching of Negroes mainly a Southern phenome-

non, white capping had a great impact on the North and East as well as elsewhere.

White capping in its origin and thrust was a movement of violent moral regulation by local masked bands. . . . White Caps thus operated in the realm of human behavior where the authority of the law was either not clear or non-existent. In this sense, white capping fell into the vigilantes' tradition, but, in its use of masks, it was probably influenced by the Ku Klux Klan of the Reconstruction era.[1]

Brown's account is accurate except for the date of the inception of White capping. According to Madeleine M. Noble in her doctoral dissertation on the White Caps of Harrison County and Crawford County, Indiana, the organization came into existence in 1872 "from a desire to keep a tighter reign locally on evil-doers and moral offenders." However, the whipping of Keen predates Noble's claim by one year, and is documented by a newspaper article written at the time the act was committed.[2]

The White Caps, previously referred to by the press or known by the people as regulators, whip-ups, Ku Klux, and Knights of the Switch, were fundamentally concerned with moral offenders such as wife beaters, drunkards, immoral couples, slackers and shiftless men who were poor family providers, and petty neighborhood thieves. Although White capping became widespread, the major concentration of their actions took place in the southern part of Indiana, which reflected the puritan legacy of the Southern back country. Harrison and Crawford Counties suffered the heaviest intensity of White Cap vigilance, recording eighty incidents of chastisement from 1873 through 1893. Whipping was the main form of punishment meted out by the night-riding White Caps, who were likely known at this time as regulators, and in 1871 James Keen would become their first victim.[3]

The following is quoted from the *Corydon Republican*, the only source of reference to the flogging of James N. Keen:

> On last Saturday night [July 8, 1871], about twelve o'clock, James N. Keen, a young man aged about thirty years, who resides in Scott township, seven miles west of Corydon, was aroused from his bed, and forcibly taken from the house, by a band of twenty men, disguised with blackened faces; stripped of all his clothing, tied to a tree, and severely whipped across the shoulders, back and legs, with large hickory switches, inflicting several cuts and gashes across those parts of his person, causing the blood to trickle down the legs of Keen to the ground. After the infliction of this severe punishment, Mr. K. was released, and ordered to get his movable effects ready and leave the country. He thinks he recognized about four of the lynchers, the others being so disguised that he was unable to recognize them in the dark.
>
> The lynchers stated that there had been considerable petty stealing in the neighborhood, and charged Mr. Keen with being guilty of the depredations, but he affirms his innocence, and says they have this only as an excuse for their conduct, and he believes they took this method to get him out of the community because he is an intense Republican, the entire neighborhood, with the exception of his family, being composed

of Democrats of the strictest Bourbon persuasion. Mr. K. owns several acres of land in the vicinity, all of which he will have to sell at a sacrifice, as he is afraid his life will be taken if he remains in the neighborhood.[4]

An undated article in the same newspaper, published around 1919, outlined the crux of the problem with clear understanding:

It will be noted that the regulators did not call themselves White Caps at that time but it was some years later that they became known as such. They were doubtless following the example of the Klux [sic] Klux of the South that had come into existence following the Civil War.

Scott Township had its disloyal Knights of the Golden Circle during the Civil War and Mr. Keen may have told the truth when he said that it was his politics that prompted the flogging. He left the country declaring that he had not been guilty of the things charged against him and no proof to the contrary was ever submitted.[5]

The White Caps continued their moral regulation in the form of whippings and floggings, becoming bolder with every act of violence until 1889, when they committed their first and only act of murder: the lynching of James Deavin and Charles Tennyson in Corydon, Harrison County.

Lying approximately ten miles west of Louisville, Kentucky, Harrison County, Indiana is bordered on the east by Crawford County, on the west by Floyd County, and on the south by the meandering Ohio River. On the night of June 7 James Deavin and Charles Tennyson, representing themselves as stock buyers but intent on robbery, requested food and lodging at the home of well-to-do farmer James LeMay, four miles northeast of Corydon, the county seat of Harrison County.[6]

The two men were well-known robbers and counterfeiters from Floyd County, both having served time in the penitentiary. The *Courier-Journal* gave these stats on the two men:

Deavin was born near the place he was captured [New Albany], and reared at the "Oakland grocery" on the pike between Lanesville and Edwardsville. He was thirty-five years of age, five feet six inches in height, weighed one hundred and sixty pounds, and had light brown hair. Tennyson was twenty-four years of age, six feet and one inch tall, of slender build, dark hair and moustache, and was rather handsome.

As a young man, James Deavin drove a peddler wagon through Floyd and Harrison Counties and did part time work as a deck hand on the Ohio River. Around 1882 he married a Corydon girl named Emma and subsequently had two children. Following the lynching, Deavin's widow stated to a *Courier-Journal* reporter, "I hadn't lived with him two years I began to find out he was a very bad man. The first wrong I learned of him was finding out he was doing little mean things and small stealing. I quarreled with him about this and told him I could not live with him."

By 1885 Deavin was locally known as a born crook who reveled in depravity, and had deserted his wife and two children to take up with several prostitutes in New Albany. Both Deavin and Tennyson had recently swindled one Louis Bottorff of Charleston, Indiana out of two thousand dollars.[7]

With the unsuspecting LeMay were his wife, two nieces, Lucy and Matilda LeMay, and his hired man, Elkana Fellmy. During supper the actions of the two men caused LeMay to become suspicious and he armed himself with a revolver. Following the meal, as Deavin and Tennyson were told their room was ready, one of the pair suddenly drew his revolver, ordered the family into a bedroom, and closed the door. LeMay immediately pulled out his revolver, but was fired on by the robber nearest him. In the fusillade LeMay got off three shots and was wounded five times, while his niece Lucy was shot in the arm. After emptying his revolver, Deavin ran out the door while Tennyson dove headfirst out a window. Matilda followed the robbers out the door and began ringing the farm bell for help, but both men escaped.[8]

Their freedom was short lived; they were apprehended the next day in New Albany, Indiana by the Floyd County Sheriff and returned to Corydon and jailed pending trial. The press was soon at work with the helpful incentive from the *New Albany Evening Tribune* that a lynching was imminent.[9]

Just at midnight on June 12, the White Caps, one hundred and fifty strong, rode into Corydon for what the *New Albany Evening Tribune* later referred to as the "expected Harrison County neck tie party." The night riders were very efficient, the whole operation taking only around forty minutes. First they obtained a steel rail from the railroad depot to batter down the jail door, took blacksmith tools from the shop of Amiel Bulliet, and then marched on the jail. After throwing guards around the building they broke into the jail and overcame token resistance from Sheriff Clabe Shuck and Prosecuting Attorney Thomas J. Wilson.

Dragging Deavin and Tennyson from their cells, the mob headed for the bridge over Big Indian Creek west of town. Deavin coolly met his fate with rancorous disdain but Tennyson was described as carrying on like "a jibbing lunatic." The pair was hanged from projections on either side of the bridge, their bodies not removed until the following morning. The White Caps disbanded in an orderly manner, most of them taking the roads heading north and west.[10]

There is one unusual aspect to this narrative. While conducting her doctoral research, Madeleine Noble unearthed the name of one of the White Cap leaders. She reported that after the lynching, part of the mob, "led by John Rainboldt of Potato Run, a Civil War veteran, headed westward back home to Scott township."[11]

As in most vigilante cases, no one was ever charged, arrested, or tried for the lynchings, and this only bolstered the supercilious conduct and reckless acts of the White Caps. Four years later this would all come to an explosive ending.

Two miles east of the town of Laconia in the remote wilds of Mosquito Creek Bottom in Boone Township, bordering the Ohio River at

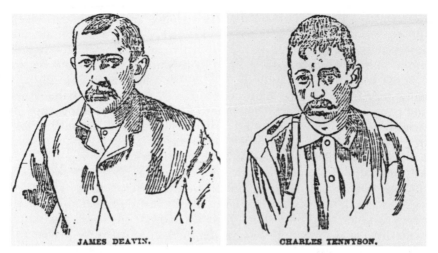

James Deavin (left) and Charles Tennyson (right), lynch victims of the White Caps in Harrison County, Indiana. AUTHOR'S COLLECTION

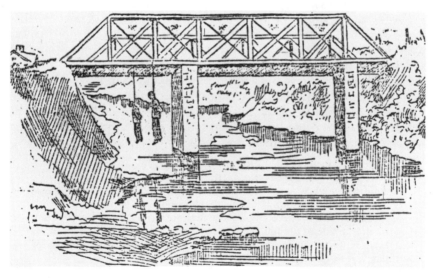

Scene of the lynching on June 12, 1889, of Deavin and Tennyson from the bridge over Big Indian Creek in Corydon, Indiana. AUTHOR'S COLLECTION

the southern tip of Harrison County, stood a crude cabin in a deep hollow serviced by a nearly impassable road, v-shaped so that anyone approaching could be seen. In the cabin lived a family named Conrad, pronounced Coonrad by the natives, consisting of Edward and Betsey Conrad, their two sons, William, aged 35, and Sam, aged 25, and their daughter Fannie. The reputation of the family was not good; the father and sons were reported to be somewhat shiftless, just doing enough work to get by. It was rumored the two boys were dull-witted and frequently fought with each other, and that their sister Fannie bore a child that was fathered by one of her brothers. It was also reported that Edward Conrad was an ineffective man who was physically abused by his sons, which came from statements by the father to his neighbors.

On March 6, 1893, Edward Conrad was found murdered in woods near his home. A ghastly wound on the side of his head, apparently made by a stave, was the cause of death. A coroner's jury placed the murder at the sons' door. William and Sam Conrad were arrested shortly after their father's funeral, and were reportedly ill-treated. However, during a preliminary trial, their mother gave testimony as to their innocence, and the two brothers were released because of insufficient evidence to indict. The consensus of the residents of the community was that the Conrads were guilty, and shortly after William and Sam returned to their home they began receiving warnings from the White Caps to leave the county, which they adamantly refused to do.[12]

After their father's death, William and Sam Conrad tried to find work as farm laborers but no one would hire them. During the last week in July the Conrads were accused of burning a barn belonging to a neighbor named Fakes, and the White Caps sent them a much stronger warning, threatening to whip them and then hang them. Realizing that a raid was imminent, the two brothers immediately went to the town of Elizabeth and bought a large store of buckshot. The *Courier-Journal* reported that William Conrad made these statements to a friend following the White Cap raid:

> Rumors in the neighborhood had caused me and Sam to believe that we would be made victims of the White Caps. When we awoke one morning [August 5] and found our dogs poisoned we, of course, knew that an attack would soon be made, and began sleeping in the corn patch near the house. About 2 o'clock Sunday morning [August 6] we heard a noise up the side of the hill. We had not been asleep during the night. In a few minutes about forty men walked through the garden path about fifteen feet from where we lay.[13]

Other sources, including Mrs. Betsey Conrad, reported that the two brothers bored auger holes for their shotgun barrels in the flooring of their front porch, and were hiding there when they heard the White Caps arrive. Mrs. Conrad stated that her sons climbed out from under the porch and ran into the corn field before raiders rode up.[14]

On Saturday, August 5, 1893, a picnic and dance were held at Laconia, two miles from the Conrad home, offering complete cover for

Artist's sketch of William Conrad.
AUTHOR'S COLLECTION

Artist's sketch of Sam Conrad.
AUTHOR'S COLLECTION

Artist's sketch of their mother, Betsey Conrad.
AUTHOR'S COLLECTION

the White Caps. Late that evening the forty-some raiders met in the woods east of Old Goshen Church near Laconia, and just past midnight rode to the Conrad home wearing white muslin masks. After riding into the yard and dismounting, one of the raiders jerked a rail out of the fence and joined the others in breaking down the cabin door. Charging through the door, the mob proceeded to break up the furniture, tear up the beds, and literally wreck the interior of the cabin.

Demanding to know the whereabouts of Bill and Sam, the raiders put pistols to the women's heads and dragged them out of the house. When the women refused to tell, the mob threatened to throw Mrs. Conrad in the cistern. At this juncture one of the night-riders brought up a lantern, which allowed the two Conrad brothers, who were armed with two shotguns apiece, a clear view of the proceedings. When another of the raiders started to put a rope around their sister's neck, the Conrad brothers opened fire on the men on the porch. Two men fell at first fire. Although the Conrads were careful not to shoot their mother and sister, Mrs. Conrad was superficially wounded in the forehead with two buckshot.

A few of the vigilantes returned fire, but the Conrads changed positions, continuing to rain buckshot into the ranks of their adversaries, and three more men fell. Bedlam ensued and the attackers fled down the hollow, dragging their two comrades off the porch and then abandoning them in the yard when the Conrads fired a final volley.[15]

At daylight, Mrs. Conrad ventured outside and found a large bundle of hickory switches and a sixty-foot rope that the mob had dropped in their hasty retreat. She also found Edward Houston and William May on the ground, some distance from the house. Both men had buckshot in the stomach, breast, and face, but Houston was dead while May, who also had one eye shot out, was still alive. Further on she discovered Albert N. Howe dead and Louis Wiseman still alive, both with wounds in the back of their heads. Further on Mrs. Conrad found John Timberlake dead, his abdomen ripped open with buckshot. Upon being shot, Timberlake had run into the Conrad house, leaped through a rear window, and fallen dead two hundred yards from the house. Wiseman died shortly after being found, but May lived for several hours. The five dead men were well-respected farmers in the community.

The *Courier-Journal* reported that William Conrad stated "I am sure that more men were wounded then were killed. I don't see how each shot could fail to hit five or six men." Conrad was probably right, for three farmers of Heth Township, William Fisher, John Tindell, and William Huddell, were reported missing, and their horses were later found running loose in the Ohio River hills near the Conrad cabin.[16]

At her sons' urging, Betsey Conrad hurried to the house of Lizzie Jones, a relative living close by, and reported what had taken place and asked that the bodies be taken away. Neighbors arrived at the Conrad cabin just past six o'clock Sunday morning and removed the bodies.

ED HOUSTON.

WILLIAM MAY

ALFRED HOWE.

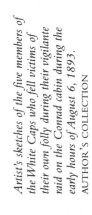

Artist's sketches of the five members of the White Caps who fell victims of their own folly during their vigilante raid on the Conrad cabin during the early hours of August 6, 1893.
AUTHOR'S COLLECTION

LOUIS WISEMAN.

JOHN TIMBERLAKE.

William and Sam Conrad reportedly watched the proceedings from a hill, and then were ferried across the Ohio River to Kentucky by ferryman William Noe. On Monday night Noe brought them back for their mother and sister. On Tuesday morning, the four Conrads boarded the skiff at West Point, and as they were crossing the river to Kentucky, Mrs. Conrad related the tragic events of that morning to Noe, stating that she and her daughter raised the masks of the two men who held them and recognized them as Noah Elbert and McHester "Mack" Harbaugh. The brothers said that they did not kill the two men for fear of hitting their mother and sister, and stated that they blamed their troubles on Elbert, Harbaugh, Thomas Crozier, Fred Radamaker, Dr. B. F. Forbes, who sent them the White Cap message, and Constable Adam F. Anderson, who had arrested them for the murder of their father, and threatened to come back and kill them. Before reaching the shoreline, Mrs. Conrad fainted from exhaustion and grief and had to be revived by her sons and the ferryman. After landing, the Conrad brothers carried their mother up the riverbank.[17]

Reacting to the threats by the Conrads, Elbert and Harbaugh filed complaints for surety of the peace against the brothers. On August 9 City Marshal James Hudson of Corydon went to the Conrad home to serve the writs but found the place deserted. Regardless of threats and revenge, the Conrads had gone. According to the *Indianapolis Journal*, Betsey Conrad and her daughter Fannie "came over from Kentucky last Saturday [August 12], and this morning [August 14] they started back in a wagon, carrying their household goods with them. They said the boys would never return to Indiana." The family reportedly settled in Hardin County, Kentucky.[18]

Rumors abounded about the Conrads; one on August 8 that the Conrad house had burned to the ground, and another on the fifteenth that William Conrad had been shot and killed trying to take household goods across the Ohio River into Kentucky. Both rumors proved false; however, this tragic event became headline news at the same time as the World's Fair was being held in Chicago. On August 15, James Yeager, an aspiring entrepreneur from Corydon, went to the Conrad home in Hardin County to hire the boys to give exhibitions at the World's Fair in Chicago. Mrs. Conrad would not let him see her sons, but told him to leave a written proposition and come back for his answer that evening. Nothing came of Yeager's scheme, and he later claimed that the Conrads did not understand that kind of business.[19] Regardless, the raid on the Conrad home created its own attraction, and effect, throughout middle America.

Newspaper editorials started to appear from all over, universally in support of the Conrads. On August 8, the *Indianapolis Journal* lambasted the White Caps, ending the article with, ". . . the Journal hopes they [the Conrads] will live to learn that it congratulates them on having given so hot a welcome to the White-cappers." The *New Albany Daily Ledger* stated, "The sympathy of the Kentuckians is with them [the

Conrad brothers], and any attempt to arrest them or any White cap visitation from Indiana will be resisted to the death." The *Indianapolis Journal* on the tenth and sixteenth of August printed a series of condemnations from newspapers in Louisville, Kentucky, Cincinnati, Ohio, and Chicago, Illinois, and as far away as Richmond, Virginia and Washington, D.C. Even satire was exhibited in this *Chicago Dispatch* commentary: "It is a terrible disappointment to an Indiana mob whenever it is obliged to postpone a lynching, and the Conrad boys, of Corydon, have got themselves thoroughly disliked by their ungentlemanly rudeness in objecting to being lynched." One Chicago man reportedly wrote to White Capper Mack Harbaugh that one hundred men were ready to come and help the Conrads finish up the gang, while Marshall Hudson in Corydon received a letter from Louisville that twenty-five "stayers" could be gotten on short notice and that if the Conrads were not left alone there would be "hell to pay."[20]

The desired effect was obtained, and some good resulted from the adversity; never again would the White Caps ride in the counties of Harrison and Crawford in southern Indiana. Ironically, a little more than thirty years later the Conrad brothers were exonerated of the murder of their father. Soon after the raid on the Conrad cabin, a neighbor of the Conrads named Robert Brown left Indiana and settled somewhere in the west. On his death bed, around 1925, Brown confessed that he had killed Edward Conrad in a fit of rage.[21]

X. WYOMING

THE POWELLS

A Legacy of Malice

*I*T SEEMS THAT SOME FAMILIES are destined to live in a world of hate, discord, strife, retribution, and malice. One such family was the Powells of Albany County, Wyoming.* The members of this family were totally unable to function in an atmosphere of normalcy, and their lives were marked with dissension. When they were not feuding with their neighbors they were squabbling among themselves. If they were not stealing their neighbors' livestock and goods they were burning their property in retaliation for some offense, real or imagined. When they should have been tending their livestock they were in court facing criminal charges. This malevolent lifestyle was passed from generation to generation until the crescendo of family bloodshed reached its climax, and the Powell lineage ceased to exist.

The Powell name would likely have remained in obscurity if not for one definitive incident: Fred Powell was shot and killed by an assassin, allegedly the notorious Tom Horn. This assumption arose from the ambush killing of Fred Powell's friend, rustler William Lewis, a little

---

*In *Tales Never Told around the Campfire: True Stories of Frontier America* (Ohio University Press/Swallow Press, 1992), I have told the story of the murders of cattle rustler William Lewis and of his only friend, Fred Powell (in chapter 10: "Wyoming: Cattle Barons Versus Rustlers," parts 3 and 4). In the course of researching these incidents, it became obvious to me that the turbulent Powell family story deserved a chapter of its own, and so I wrote "The Powells: A Legacy of Malice." Some of the source materials cited here are inevitably the same, but as the entire family gets entangled in the story it becomes all the more compelling.

over one month before Powell's death. The manner in which the two men met their deaths was identical, and the consensus theory is that Horn was paid by the big Wyoming cattle corporations to kill both men in retaliation for their rustling activities. In Lewis' case it was likely fact; Powell's death was another matter entirely.[1]

Fred Powell was a scourge to all of his neighbors; his wife Mary and later their son Bill followed in his footsteps. To those he liked, Powell was undoubtedly friendly and pleasant; but he had a mean streak, and the unfortunate individuals who incurred his wrath would suffer from petty reprisals such as destruction of property, arson, and general harassment. He also rustled their stock. The golden rule for Powell meant do unto others before they do it unto you.

Born in Virginia, Frederick U. Powell was thirty-seven years old at the time of his death in September 1895. He came to Wyoming around the late 1870s, and took a job with the Union Pacific Railroad in Cheyenne. Having lost an arm while in service, he was given a job as night watchman by the railroad. The company later fired him when it was discovered that he had taken twenty dollars from a man who was hopping freight trains across the country. Powell then moved to the Sybille country.

In about 1881 Powell settled on 160 acres on Horse Creek in Albany County, located six miles from the Laramie County line and seven miles southwest of the ranch of his friend William Lewis. On December 23, 1882, he married twenty-three-year-old Mary (Keane) Wanless in Laramie County. Their only child, William Edwin, was born in 1884. The Powell family's lifestyle was chaotic from the start. Despite the loss of his arm, Fred Powell was described as a tough and husky man who was regarded as a rustler from the moment he located on Horse Creek.[2]

On July 24, 1889, Powell reportedly stole four head of cattle in Albany County—one from Hugh McPhee, two from a man named Hayward, and another from a man named Lannon. On September 7, a criminal warrant was issued and Powell was arrested. Unable to post a six-hundred-dollar bond, he was remanded to jail. At a preliminary hearing held September 10, the court ordered him to appear before a grand jury on October 16. His bond was reduced to three hundred dollars, which was furnished by his father-in-law, John Keane. Oddly enough, Powell's brothers-in-law, William E. and Charles Keane, were prosecution witnesses. Apparently either the grand jury did not find enough evidence to indict him or else the plaintiffs dropped their charges, for Powell never stood trial.[3]

On August 16 of the following year, S. L. Moyer charged Powell with grand larceny in Justice of the Peace Court in Cheyenne and a warrant was issued. Constable B. S. Smith arrested Powell the same day. On the evening of the eighteenth, Powell appeared in court with his attorney, J. C. Baird. After the prosecution had presented its evidence, the defense made a motion to dismiss on the grounds that "the evi-

Tom Horn in jail in Cheyenne in 1903. AUTHOR'S COLLECTION

Frederick U. Powell

TO

Miss Mary Wanless

MARRIAGE LICENSE.

TERRITORY OF WYOMING, COUNTY OF LARAMIE, SS.

The People of the Territory of Wyoming to any Person authorized to Solemnize Marriage, Greeting:

You are hereby authorized to join in the **Holy Bonds of Matrimony** and to celebrate within this County the Rites and Ceremonies of Marriage between

Mr. *Frederick U. Powell* of *Laramie* County *Wyoming* and

Miss *Mary Wanless* of *Laramie* County *Wyoming* and this shall be your good and sufficient Warrant; and you are required to return this License to me, within three months from the celebration of such Marriage, with a Certificate of the same appended hereto, and signed by you, under a penalty of Five Hundred Dollars.

IN WITNESS WHEREOF, I have hereunto set my hand and the seal of said County, this *2d* day of *Dec* 18*82*

John K. Jeffrey County Clerk.

by *Wm W. Jeffrey* Deputy

CERTIFICATE OF MARRIAGE.

I, *C. M. Sanders* a *pastor* officiating in the County of Laramie, and Territory of Wyoming, do hereby certify that I did, on the *23* day of *Dec* A. D. 185*2*, unite in marriage Mr. *F. U. Powell* of *Laramie*, aged *24* years, and Miss *Mary Wanless* of *Laramie* county, aged *23* years, the parties named in the within License, at the house of *Congl. Parsonage* in said County and Territory, according to the rites of *Wyoming*.

Given under my hand at _____ in said County and Territory, this _____ day

Name *Mrs. C. M. Sanders* Residence *Cheyenne*

Name *Mary H. Sanders* Residence *Cheyenne*

Witness to the Ceremony.

C. M. Sanders

TERRITORY OF WYOMING, ⎫
COUNTY OF LARAMIE, ⎬ ss.
⎭

Received and filed for Record *16* day of *Dec* A. D. 188*2*, and recorded in Book *2* of Marriages, page *218*

John K. Jeffrey

Laramie County Marriage License for Fred and Mary Powell, dated December 23, 1882.
WYOMING STATE ARCHIVES, MUSEUMS, AND HISTORICAL DEPARTMENT, CHEYENNE

dence did not show that any crime had been committed by the defendant." Justice W. P. Carroll sustained the motion and ordered "that the complaint in this case is hereby dismissed and the defendant is discharged from custody."[4]

Fred Powell's troubles took a different turn early in 1892, when his wife sued him for divorce. On January 4, in Laramie County District Court in Cheyenne, Mary Powell filed her petition claiming that for seven years her husband had failed to provide for her or their seven-year-old son. She also stated that Powell had threatened to shoot her with a revolver the previous November 30, chased and struck her with a knife on December 19, and abducted their child on December 30. On January 4, a summons to appear in court on February 6 was issued and served on Powell. He failed to show up in court, but the divorce was granted on February 19, and Mary was given custody of their child. Following the divorce, Mary lived in Laramie. But strange as it may seem, it appears that she and son Bill lived at the ranch with Powell periodically until his death.[5]

Five months after the divorce, Fred Powell again ran afoul of the law. This pattern would repeat every year until his death. On July 15, 1892, he was arrested by Albany County Sheriff C. C. Yund for stealing a horse on July 11 that belonged to Josiah Fisher. The preliminary hearing in Laramie began on the sixteenth and Powell pled not guilty. For four days both sides presented their evidence and Powell was bound over for trial during the next court term. He was released on two hundred dollars bond. The trial began September 19 with Justice J. H. Hayford presiding, and ended the same day, with the jury's verdict of not guilty.[6]

Less than a year later, on July 23, 1893, Powell for reasons unknown began a vendetta against his Albany County neighbors. He was charged that day with malicious trespass and destroying fences belonging to Etherton P. Baker. Apparently wanting to avoid another encounter with Justice Hayford, on July 29 Powell requested and received a change of venue to Justice M. A. Hance's court. He was tried on the thirty-first, found guilty, and fined fifty dollars plus thirty-nine dollars in court costs. Powell immediately filed an appeal, which was granted on September 12, and he was released on a two-hundred-dollar appearance bond. His luck held; four days later the jury again turned in a verdict of not guilty.[7]

Thus encouraged, Powell evidently figured he could get away with anything; his luck, however, was running out. On April 24, 1894, he continued his reprisal against his neighbors by setting fire to clothing, bedding, and food products belonging to Joseph Trugillo and Etherton P. Baker. Three days later Sheriff C. C. Frazer arrested him on the charge of incendiarism and hauled him into court. The case was continued until the thirtieth. Still apprehensive of a ruling under Justice Hayford, Powell requested and was granted a change of venue to Justice Hance's court, and the case was tried that day. Both Mary and young Bill Powell appeared as defense witnesses. In spite of this, the jury had had quite enough of Powell and found him guilty. He was fined fifty dollars or, if in default, a jail sentence at one dollar per day until the fine was paid. Naturally he appealed, and was released on a bond of one hundred dollars.[8]

It seemed that Powell was incapable of staying out of trouble. On July 8, 1894, he trespassed on the property of Harry P. Richardson and rode off on one of Richardson's horses without the owner's consent. He was arrested on the tenth on the charge of malicious trespass, and, on the thirteenth, again received a change of venue from Justice Hayford's court to Justice Hance's. Trial was held the same day and Justice Hance, tired of Powell's antics, quickly found him guilty and fined him forty-five dollars. Powell appealed for retrial and was released on one hundred dollars bond.[9]

Fred Powell's appeal of his conviction for incendiarism came to court on September 12 under Judge J. W. Blake. By this time everyone was fed up with Powell and the jury found him guilty the next day. On the eighteenth, Judge Blake sentenced him to four months in the county jail, retroactive to September 14. Because of his conviction, prosecuting attorney William H. Bramel entered a *nolle prosequi* (unwilling to prosecute) on September 15 in the Richardson case.[10]

Following his release from jail, Powell began to receive anonymous letters warning him to stop stealing stock and leave the country, or face the consequences. At first, he probably dismissed them as idle threats. The situation changed drastically after William Lewis was killed. The *Daily Sun-Leader* gave a stark summary of the circumstances:

> The statement was repeatedly heard after the Lewis killing that "One Armed" Powell would be the next to go, and Sheriff [Ira] Fredendall told Powell at the sale of the Lewis stock that he, Powell, was a fool to stay on Horse Creek and run the risk of losing his life at any moment. Powell appeared to be considerably frightened after the murder of Lewis became known, and it is understood that he was selling out preparatory to leaving the country.
>
> Not long ago Mrs. Powell was in this city [Cheyenne] and called at the Sun-Leader office. She stated that their cattle had all been sold and that they intended going away.

On September 3 Fred Powell reportedly received this last letter:

> Laramie, Wyo., September 2, 1895
> Mr. Powell—This is your third and last warning. There are three things for you to do—quit killing other people's cattle or be killed yourself, or leave the country yourself at once.

The letter, written in a disguised hand by a good penman, was of course unsigned.[11]

Whatever his intentions, Powell did not move fast enough. At 7:30 on the morning of September 10, Fred Powell died. The following account is the statement of Andrew Ross, Powell's hired man:

> I have worked for Fred U. Powell one month. We were alone on the ranch. Mr. Powell and I, we got up about 4 a.m. this morning. We started

STATE

T~~ERRITORY~~ OF WYOMING, } ss:

COUNTY OF ALBANY.

JAMES M. FENWICK.
I, ~~J. W. MELDRUM,~~ Clerk of the District Court, within and for said
county, in the ~~Territory~~ aforesaid, do hereby certify the foregoing to be a true
and correct transcript of the judgment entered in the journal of said court in
the above entitled action.

Witness, my hand and the seal of said Court this *18th* day of
September A. D. 1894

James M. Fenwick
Clerk District Court.

By Robt. Gale, Dep.

STATE
The People of the ~~Territory~~ of Wyoming:

To the Sheriff of Albany County, ~~and the Warden and Officers~~ in
charge of the *Jail* at *Albany County*
in the State of *Wyoming* **Greeting:**

Whereas, *Frederick W. Powell* has been duly
convicted in the District Court of said County and Territory, of the crime
of *Malicious Mischief*
and judgment has been pronounced against him that he be punished by imprisonment in the *County Jail*
at *Albany County, State of Wyoming*
for the term of *four months*
all of which appears of record as is shown by the certified transcript of the
judgment endorsed hereon and made a part hereof:

Now this is to Command You, the said Sheriff of Albany County, to
take and keep ~~and safely deliver the said~~ *the said Frederick*
W. Powell ~~into the custody of the said Warden or~~
~~other Officer in charge of said prison, at your earliest convenience.~~
And this is to Command You, the said ~~Warden~~ *Sheriff* and other Officers in charge
of said *jail* ~~prison~~, to receive ~~of and from said Sheriff~~ the said *Frederick*
W. Powell convicted and sentenced as
aforesaid, and him the said *Frederick W. Powell*
keep and imprison in the said *jail* ~~prison~~ for the term of *four months*
And these presents shall be your authority for the same
Herein fail not.

Witness, Hon. *J. W. Blake* Judge
of said District Court, this *18th* day of *September* A. D. 1894
Attest my hand and the seal of Court, the day and year last above
written.

James M. Fenwick,
Clerk District Court for said District.

By Robt. Gale, Dep.

Judgment in Criminal Case no. 598 against Fred Powell for Malicious Mischief
(incendiarism) in 1894. WYOMING STATE ARCHIVES, MUSEUMS, AND
HISTORICAL DEPARTMENT, CHEYENNE

to haul hay, hauled one load and started for another. We got to a place about _ mile from the ranch down the creek, stopped wagon, got off. Mr. Powell told me to cut some willows so we could fix the rack. [To replace a stick that was missing from a hay rack.] As I was cutting the second willow I heard a shot fired. I looked around and saw Mr. Powell with his hand on his breast. I ran toward him. He exclaimed "Oh! My God!," then fell. I went to him. Examined him and found he was dead. I then went to the ranch of Mr. [Benjamin] Fay and notified Mr. Fay.

I examined the surrounding vicinity and from what I could ascertain the shot was fired from a ledge of rocks about 250 feet [yards?] distant. I examined the body and found a gunshot wound entering the breast near the center and came out at right of spine near 4th rib. I couldn't see any person when I heard the shot or afterward.[12]

Arriving at the Fay ranch, the badly frightened Ross encountered Beulah Richardson, who carried the mail between Laramie and Summit. She immediately took the news to Sheriff Grant in Laramie. Ironically, she was the wife of Harry P. Richardson, who had brought charges against Powell for malicious trespass.

At the time of the killing, Mary Powell was in Laramie, and when she received the news she left for the ranch with the sheriff and Coroner Andrew Miller. The inquest was held later that day, and the verdict read, "A gun shot wound inflicted with feloneous [sic] intent by a party or parties to the jury unknown."[13]

After Sheriff Grant had made his investigation the *Daily Sun-Leader* gave a more detailed report:

It was supposed that the parties who shot Lewis also killed Powell. . . . Powell was shot but once and killed instantly. A rifle ball entered the left side, near the heart, and came out over the right hip. The range was downward. The assassin was concealed behind a ledge of rocks on the opposite side of the creek, and was over 200 yards distant when the fatal shot was fired.

After Ross ran away, the killer walked down to the body, viewed his work and returned to the hill, where he mounted his horse and rode away. His footprints were clearly discernible and careful measurements show he wore a No. 8 boot, and was a man of considerable weight. The officers suspect who the assassin was but have no tangible evidence.[14]

On the eleventh of September, Mary Powell brought Fred's body to Laramie, where at 4 P.M. the next day he was buried. She adamantly denied that he had received any warning letters to leave the country.[15] The questions remain: Who killed Fred Powell and why?

Tom Horn was suspected of Powell's murder, and he was brought before a grand jury for questioning. Because of insufficient evidence he was not indicted, and no one was ever arrested for the killing of Fred Powell.[16]

Following Powell's death, his brother-in-law, Charles Keane, moved to the Powell ranch where he helped take care of the stock and did whatever work needed to be done. On the evening of January 21, he picked up the following letter from the Laramie Post Office, which was printed in the *Boomerang*:

VERDICT OF CORONER'S JURY.

STATE OF WYOMING, } ss.
COUNTY OF ALBANY.

In the Matter of the Inquest upon the Body of _Fred N Powell_ Deceased.

Before _Andrew Miller_, Coroner.

We, the undersigned, jurors summoned to appear before _Andrew Miller_, Coroner of the County of Albany, in the State of Wyoming, at _ranch of deceased at Albany County_ on the _10th_ day of _September_, A. D. 189_5_, to enquire into the cause of the death of _Fred N Powell_

having been duly sworn according to law, and having made such inquiry, and having inspected the body, and having heard the testimony adduced, upon our oaths, each and all, do say that we find the name of the deceased was _Fred N Powell_; that __he was a native of _the State of Virginia_ aged about _27_ years, and that __he came to h_is_ death on or about the _10"_ day of _September_, A. D. 189_5_ _at 7 30 o'clock a.m._ in this County by _a gun shot wound inflicted with felonious intent by a party or parties to the Jury unknown_

All of which we duly certify by this verdict of our inquest, in writing, and by us signed, this _10th_ day of _September_, A. D. 189_5_.

W J Hills
Benj C Fay.
Charles H Phillips

Coroner's Jury verdict in the death of Fred Powell. WYOMING STATE ARCHIVES, MUSEUMS, AND HISTORICAL DEPARTMENT, CHEYENNE

Charles Keane:
If you don't leave this country within three days your life will be taken the same as Powell's was.

Unlike Powell, Charles Keane's character was never in question, so this death threat was likely a ruse meant to muddy the waters concerning Powell's death. According to the article in the *Boomerang*, the threat worked:

He [Charles Keane] was seen by a *Boomerang* representative this morning to whom he said that he would comply with the warning . . . and he did not think it would be wise for him to court death in this instance. The services of James Stirling were secured to accompany him back to the ranch to make the necessary preparations for abandoning the property.

Mrs. [Mary] Powell stated this morning that it now looked to her as though someone wanted the property, and that if this were the case she would gladly sell it instead of having the system of assassination carried out.[17]

Unlike Lewis' killing, the evidence shows that there was no connection between the big cattlemen and Powell or Charles Keane, and they had no reason to eliminate either one of them. All of Powell's court cases and litigations were with his neighbors, who were small ranchers. What grounds would the prominent cattlemen have to kill Powell—because he was a known rustler? This is highly unlikely, and would have been a foolish move since loose talk had already linked the cattlemen with Tom Horn in the killing of William Lewis. The plausible solution to the question of who killed Powell was provided by his wife Mary.

Mary Powell, though she led a willful life of dubious integrity, still had her good side, as attested to by a reliable source provided to the author through the Wyoming Archives. It is also revealed that Mary stated with absolute certainty that she knew who killed her husband, which is conceivably the truth. Here is a firsthand account of Mary Powell's views and convictions; however, the names of those involved are withheld by request:

Mrs. Powell [Mary] was very alert and recalled many incidents concerning the murder of her husband Fred. She again told us that Tom Horn did not kill Fred Powell. She said that legend had been established and try as she might she would never be able to change the story. And she said, she could not prove the murderer's guilt.

The Powells were feuding with a neighboring rancher. The rancher was not a very pleasant man. Perhaps his disposition could be attributed to his childhood. He was a "Street Orphan" picked up by the authorities in some city to save expense of caring for him he was then shipped with others to a point in Iowa where they were chosen by people in the west. He was chosen by a Wyoming rancher, probably for cheap labor.

After the murder of Powell, Mary made life miserable for the rancher. He did not drink and Mary was noted for her alcohol intake. If she had liquor with her when she crossed the rancher's path she insisted he drink with her. Out came her trusty gun and quirt.

She told us one time she accosted him at the Leslie Mine in the hills near her home. She insisted he drink with her. She threatened him with bodily harm and used the quirt on him.

The rancher ran down into the mine to avoid her attack. Mary rolled stones into the mine. The rancher knew he wasn't going to escape so he came up. Mary forced him to drink until he collapsed.

Mary Powell was quite a character but she was not a liar.[18]

Fred Powell's history of criminal activity guaranteed him many enemies among his neighbors; there were probably others he had provoked who never took him to court. If this rancher did in fact kill Powell, he timed his act well. Only six weeks had passed since the death of Lewis, and rumors that the cattlemen's hired killer Tom Horn had done the deed were rampant. The rancher could pull off a copycat killing in hopes that the suspicion would fall on Horn and the big cattlemen. That is in any case what happened. Whoever was in fact responsible for the shooting, public opinion credited Tom Horn.

Mary Powell, however, followed her own instincts. Although the evidence is circumstantial, Mary Powell was likely correct in her assumption. After Fred Powell's assassination, Mary began her vendetta against the rancher. If he had known that she would take this course of retaliation, he might well have reconsidered his actions.

Mary Powell's life was as turbulent as her husband's. A strong-willed and outspoken woman, she had a character to match Fred Powell's. Born Mary Nora Keane on August 7, 1859, the firstborn child of Irish Catholic immigrants John and Mary Keane, she is recorded as the first white child born in Golden, Colorado. The Keanes had three more children in Colorado: William E. in 1861, Alice in 1863, and Katie in 1865.[19]

In the spring of 1868, Laramie was spawned in the southeastern portion of Wyoming with the arrival of the Union Pacific Railroad. With it came thirty-five-year-old John Keane, his wife Mary, thirty-one, and their three children. Keane immediately obtained a plat of land one mile east of town and built a farmhouse. He also began building a saloon in Laramie between C and D Streets and Second and Third. Unfortunately, it was Keane's unfinished building that became the gallows for desperadoes Big Ned Wilson, Con Wagner, and Asa Moore, who were lynched by Laramie vigilantes on the night of October 18, 1868. Perhaps John Keane was part of the group.[20]

By 1870, the Keane family had grown. On June 21, 1868, a son, Patrick "Patsy" Sarsfield Keane, was born. He was recorded as the first white child to be born in Laramie; however, his short life ended on December 28, 1878, from the effects of a severe cold. In February 1870 twins Rosy and Charles were the last children born into the Keane family. During the years 1883 and 1884, John Keane was listed as farming east and south of Laramie's city limits.[21]

In 1951, Wyoming historian Mary Lou Pence wrote that John Keane wanted the best for his firstborn, and sent Mary east for schooling in a convent. If this was true, Mary was back by the time she was sixteen, for at that time she left home. Mary Lou Pence also quoted the following statement about Mary Powell from an old-time resident: "Before that [the killing of Fred Powell] she was about the softest-spoken lady hereabouts. Never any pretending about Mary. When Fred'd brag how he intended the Powells to be big cattle kings one day, Mary'd say, quiet-like, 'I like our home here. Only thing I'd change, maybe, is the south window—make it bigger so I could pot some meadow violets.'" This is a nice way to think of Mary; however, documentation will show that this was just a bit of romanticism.

Mary Nora Keane's life took a tempestuous course on January 30, 1875, when, at sixteen, she married John G. Garrett in Laramie. The wedding was officiated by Eugene Cusson, Catholic pastor, and was witnessed by Mary's parents. Judging by subsequent events, marriage held no satisfaction for Mary, for by 1878, she was no longer living with Garrett. It is probable that the marriage had been annulled. At this point, Mary was working, presumably as a waitress, at the New York House Restaurant, opposite the Laramie railroad depot. On August 30, Mary attempted suicide, according to this report in the *Laramie Daily Sentinel*:

> Miss Mary Kane [*sic*], a young lady employed at the New York House, took a dose of morphine and sugar of lead last evening, for the purpose of ending her life. Shortly after taking the dose she notified a young man of her acquaintance that she wished to take a walk with him and tell him something. Strolling out towards the eastern limits of the city, she imparted to the young man the information that she had swallowed the poisonous decoction, when he at once summoned a physician, who administered an emetic, with good results.
>
> The only cause for the rash act is that the young lady's character had been assailed by various parties, which, coming to her ears, rendered life to her no longer desirable.
>
> Miss Kane is an industrious girl, and as her recovery is almost certain, it is to be hoped that she will in future so conduct herself as to be above all aspersions of slanderers.[22]

One wonders who the young man in question was; perhaps he was Charles F. Wanless, who became Mary's second husband. Wanless, son of Canadian-born A. D. and Marie Wanless, was a fur trapper who led an exciting and romantic life that likely appealed to twenty-one-year-old Mary. For whatever reason, the two were married on September 29, 1880. This marriage was also short-lived, ending in the spring of 1881. In 1883 and 1884, Charles Wanless was living in Laramie with his brother Frank at 401 South B., and was working as a trapper. The end of this marriage also marked the first time Mary ran afoul of the law.

Following their wedding, the Wanlesses took room and board in Laramie at the home of C. R. Lawrence, and in April they skipped out without paying their bill. On April 21, Lawrence filed a writ of attachment charging the pair of intent to defraud. Wanless was apparently working for the Union Pacific Railroad, but since he could not be found, his wages were garnished on the twenty-seventh and the action was dismissed at the cost of the plaintiff. At this point Mary was no longer living with Wanless, and, on April 28, she filed a writ of replevin against him for "One Dolman (a woman's cloak with cape-like arm pieces) wrongfully detained by defendant."[23]

Mary's unconventional behavior and willful conduct alienated her from her parents, a fact that the *Laramie Weekly Sentinel* inadvertently pointed out in a notice of probate concerning her mother's will. On May 17, 1889, Mary Keane died of dropsy. On the twenty-third, in Albany County Probate Court, her will was proved and a date was set for a probate hearing. All the children, except Mary, were listed as heirs.[24]

As for Mary's father, in January of 1891 he bought the Humbolt House on Front Street near the Laramie depot, and reopened it as the Gem City Hotel. The *Weekly Sentinel* listed it as a first-class hotel. Two and a half years later, on August 26, Keane's house east of town burned; however, the newspaper stated that most of the furniture was saved and the house was fully insured. John Keane died on or about March 19, 1900.[25]

It was shortly after the break with Wanless that Mary met Fred Powell. She married him in December of 1882, and subsequently divorced him in 1892. As previously mentioned, Mary continued to live off and on at Powell's ranch following the divorce, likely because she figured this would be the only way she could keep control of her interest in the ranch. This was the way things stood until the assassination of Fred Powell.

In 1951, Mary Lou Pence wrote a story about Mary Powell, from which these lines are taken:

> The next years [following Powell's death] were a struggle, and the once wistful and contented girl became a gaunt, raw-boned woman with sharp crow-footed wrinkles around her eyes. She kept her rifle close at hand. She gathered her stock (and the neighbor's too, some said), and she stacked the wild hay from her fields for the work animals.
>
> "Fight back," she would tell her son Bill. "That's the only way they'll let us live."
>
> "Your horses are over in my corral," she informed one man. "They broke through my fences. If you want them you'd better come after them."
>
> When the rancher arrived to pick up his stock, she said: "Pay me $50, I'm charging board."
>
> But occasionally a cowboy would tell how Mary fixed the cow chip poultice that took the rattler fang's poison out of his leg.[26]

At least a portion of what Pence wrote is based on fact; for the next twenty years Mary Powell would be in and out of court fighting various and sundry charges.

Two years after Powell's death, Mary found herself in real trouble with the law. On May 25, 1897, she and one Richard Colford were charged with committing a burglary of the house and outbuilding of Laramie resident Joseph Becker the day before. Several household tools valued at around five dollars were stolen and Becker filed a complaint on the twenty-fifth. Only Mary was scheduled to be tried the following September 11; however, since the court file shows no further action, the case was apparently settled out of court and charges were dismissed.[27]

Following in her husband's footsteps, Mary, with her son Bill, was indicted in two cases for stealing livestock in 1905. On March 10, they were charged with stealing seven head of cattle, valued at $105, and two cows and two calves valued at ninety dollars, all belonging to Henry L. Stevens. The theft took place on March 1, and Mary and Bill were arrested on the twelfth. The preliminary hearing in Justice Court was held on the eighteenth and the Powells pled not guilty. Through their attorney, H. V. Grosbeck, they demanded a jury trial, which was denied, and they were bound over for trial in District Court in Laramie and were released on bonds of one thousand dollars each.

On April 24, their attorney made a plea to the jurisdiction of the court that the cases be dismissed on grounds that the defendants were denied a jury trial by the Justice Court. The plea was overruled and trial began the next day. On the thirtieth, Bill got off with a not guilty verdict but Mary was found guilty in one case. The second case was dismissed on May 4 because of the previous verdict. Mary appealed for a new trial on the thirty-first, and was released on one thousand dollars bond. A year later, on May 16, Mary withdrew her not guilty plea and substituted a plea of *nolo contendere* (do not wish to contend). Judge Charles E. Carpenter sentenced her to three months in the Albany County jail, and jail time at one dollar per day for a four-dollar cost of action.[28]

For the next four years, Mary stayed out of trouble, but on October 1, 1910, she allegedly stole three horses valued at $150 from Daniel T. Davis. On the eleventh a warrant was issued and Mary was arrested and brought to Laramie for a preliminary hearing in Justice Court the same day. Trial was set for the spring term of District Court, and she was released on $150 bail. Trial was held on April 18, 1911, and on the twenty-second the jury brought in a verdict of not guilty. One witness for the prosecution was Joe Tietze, who would experience the wrath of Mary Powell. It came on the evening of the same day he had testified against Mary at her preliminary hearing.[29]

A rash of fires spread across the Sybille country for three successive nights in October 1910, and Mary Powell was the prime suspect. On the night of the eleventh, Joe Tietze's barn burned to the ground. The following night, outbuildings and haystacks on the Swigart ranch and two haystacks at the Tillotson ranch went up in smoke. On the night of the thirteenth, Elizabeth Richardson found her haystack ablaze. The

STATE OF WYOMING, } ss:
COUNTY OF ALBANY.

IN JUSTICE'S COURT.
Before *R. E. Fitch* J. P.

THE STATE OF WYOMING,
vs.
Mary Powell and Richard Colford
Defendant

INFORMATION.

The said *Mary Powell and Richard Colfor*

Defendant S, *are* accused of the offence of *Burglary*

for that the said Defendant, on the *24th* day of *May*, A. D. 1897

at the ____ County of Albany, in the State of Wyoming

did break and enter into a dwelling house situate No 90, Block 128, City of Laramie occupied by Joseph Becker and did then and there steal from said premises one oil stove of the value of $2.00 The property of said John Becker and the said Mary Powell and Richard Colford further accuses of breaking and entering into an out ho situate on said premises No 90 Block 128 in the City of Laramie County of Alb and State of Wyoming on the 24th da of May 1897 and therefrom to steal an carry away 1 Drill of the value of $2.00 1 Carpenters chisel of the value of 80 cents, 3 M. Wrenches of the value of one dollar and fifty ce and one Blacksmiths Punch of the value 50 cents, the Property of Joseph Becker

contrary to the form of the statute in such case made and provided, and against the peace and dignity of the
State of Wyoming *Mons C Jahnen*
County and Prosecuting Attorney
of Albany County, Wyoming

Charges of Burglary against Mary Powell in 1897. WYOMING STATE ARCHIVES, MUSEUMS, AND HISTORICAL DEPARTMENT, CHEYENNE

law worked swiftly; Sheriff W. W. Bower arrested Mary on October 14, and hauled her into Justice Court in Laramie, charged with arson for the Richardson fire. A preliminary hearing was set for October 25, and Mary was jailed in default of $2,500 bond. On the twenty-second, bail was reduced to $750, which was paid, and Mary was released. Mary pled not guilty and the trial began on the twenty-seventh. Probable cause was found and trial was set for the next term in District Court.

On March 22, 1911, before the start of her trial, Mary filed an affidavit for change of venue in District Court. She claimed that she could not receive a fair trial "because of the excitement and prejudice in the County against me . . . that I have in the past been frequently accused of crimes of which I was absolutely innocent but that such charges were scattered broad cast thru the County." She also stated that her son Bill had been arrested for theft of several horses and this would also damage her chances for a fair trial. Countering Mary's appeal, prosecuting attorney Frank E. Anderson stated, "that said defendant has been convicted of a misdemeanor in this county, but of no other crime or crimes; that there is no excitement or prejudice against said defendant in this county . . . that said Mary Powell can obtain a fair and impartial trial in this county of Albany." Judge Charles E. Carpenter agreed and denied her motion on April 13, opening day of Mary's trial.

Mary was a very busy woman during April 1911, shuttling between two court trials. Her trial for arson resulted in a hung jury on the twenty-first, and Judge Carpenter discharged the jury. Mary would have to face a retrial in the next term of court. On September 16, Mary, through her attorney M. C. Brown, made a motion for continuance on the grounds that, "if she can secure the presence of certain witnesses . . . she can make her innocence clearly appear." The trial transcript reads:

> . . . that there was a certain sheep herder working for the Richardsons, saw her [Mary Powell] when she was out on the range, hunting her stock, that he was camped not far from the place that the hay was said to be burned, that he must have been the first to see the fire, being nearer to it than any other person; that he knew this affiant road [sic] to her cart on the night of the fire, is said to occurred, and knew of her leaving the hill for her home in town. As soon as she arrived there from the north, and could get her horse harnessed into [sic] the cart, that she did not go to the haystack, said to have been burned after she had returned to her cart, that she tried repeatedly to find this witness, but has been unable to do so, that she is informed that this man was discharged by the Richardsons who had him employed, shortly after the burning of said hay.

A "John Doe" subpoena had been issued in Justice Court on October 26, 1910, but the missing sheepherder was never found. On November 10, 1911, Judge Carpenter ordered a continuance in her second trial until the next term of court, and released Mary on a $750 bond.

THE STATE OF WYOMING,
  COUNTY OF ALBANY.   } ss.

IN THE DISTRICT COURT FOR SAID COUNTY.

THE STATE OF WYOMING,
                           PLAINTIFF,
                VS.

    Mary Powell

                    DEFENDANT .

INFORMATION.

Comes Now Frank E. Anderson *County and Prosecuting Attorney of the County of Albany, in the State of Wyoming, and in the name and by the authority of the State of Wyoming, informs the Court and gives the Court to understand that* Mary Powell

late of the county aforesaid, on the 13th *day of* October *, A. D. 19 10,* *at the County of Albany and State of Wyoming, did* then and there wilfully, maliciously, and feloniously, set fire to a stack of hay, then and there situated, the property of another person, to-wit: Mrs. Elizabeth Richardson, of the value of one hundred dollars, and the said Mary Powell did then and there and thereby, and with the intent aforesaid, burn and destroy said stack of hay, to the damage of said Mrs. Elizabeth Richardson, in the sum of $100.00

Information in the 1910 case against Mary Powell for arson. WYOMING STATE ARCHIVES, MUSEUMS, AND HISTORICAL DEPARTMENT, CHEYENNE

Mary's second trial for arson commenced the following March 26, and her luck held again. By March 29, this jury also could not reach a verdict and, on May 6, Judge Carpenter ordered the case be retired until the September court term. On September 17, 1912, prosecuting attorney Anderson made a motion that the case be dismissed because there was insufficient evidence to secure a conviction. Judge Carpenter complied and dismissed the case.[30]

In her last three trials, Mary got a break and escaped conviction, but she did not learn her lesson, and it took her only eight months to find herself in trouble again. On May 29, 1913, one Katherine Martin brought charges against Mary for assault and battery. She was brought into Justice Court in Laramie and was released on a fifty-dollar bond, pending trial on the thirty-first. Mary acted as her own attorney, and the jury returned a verdict of not guilty. The following November, she was back in court.[31]

John Daly charged Mary with malicious mischief on November 7, 1913, a warrant was issued on the thirteenth and she was arrested by Sheriff S. W. Frazer and brought into Justice Court. A motion to quash the indictment was overruled and the jury found her guilty. She was fined ten dollars and $24.80 in court costs. One of the witnesses against her was George Baccus, who would pay several times over for his testimony. Mary began her vendetta the following February.[32]

Baccus filed charges against Mary on February 10, 1914, for trespass on his property at Thirteenth and Grand in Laramie. A warrant was issued the following day, and Mary was hauled into Justice Court again. Mary entered a plea of not guilty, but the case was dismissed on the understanding that she keep away from Baccus. Mary readily agreed and she was discharged. Nevertheless, she could not control her temper and took revenge on Baccus a few months later.[33]

At nearly fifty-five years of age, Mary Powell was fit and tough. At 9 P.M. on June 15, Mary punched Baccus out, slugging him in the face three times, causing him to seek aid from Laramie policeman Steve Miller. The confrontation took place in front of a Chinese restaurant on Front Street, between Grand Avenue and Thornburg Street. A complaint of disturbance and breach of the peace was filed on June 17 by officer Miller, and Mary was arrested and brought into Justice Court again, found guilty by Justice of the Peace Carl Jackson, and fined ten dollars and $8.50 in court costs. Mary appealed the decision the same day and the case went to a jury trial under Judge V. J. Tidball the following November 20.

Mary again acted as her own attorney, and went at loggerheads with prosecuting attorney Will McMurray. Uncharacteristic as it sounds, the *Boomerang* described Mary Powell as "a soft-voiced woman" who spoke "in an even, low tone." The newspaper remarked that the trial drew a large crowd and that Mary's questions were cleverly worded. Mary stated that she had met Baccus by appointment at the restaurant at 5 P.M., and that "he was cordial in the afternoon, but very indifferent in the evening," adding, "One day he was nice as he can be. The next day he is like a snake."

Baccus claimed that Mary blooded his nose and he asked Officer Miller to arrest her "while he got away on his horse." Baccus also remarked that the police were afraid to arrest Mary for some reason. The *Boomerang* also gave an interesting account of Mary's cross-examination of Baccus and her wrangling with McMurray:

> "Did you strike me," she asked Baccus.
> McMurray objected.
> Baccus was ordered to reply, however, and he denied it.
> "Where do you suppose I got two black eyes and a bruised chin," Mrs. Powell asked the witness.
> "Objected to on the ground that she is asking opinion of the witness," said McMurray.
> "Objection sustained," said Judge Tidball.
> Mrs. Powell remained silent for a moment, then said sharply:
> "Isn't it a fact that you are trying to drive me out of town?"
> McMurray put in an objection to this question, too.
> "What language did you use when you struck me?" asked Mrs. Powell. McMurray contended that she was commenting and inferring in her queries.

Mary's eloquence did her little good, for the jury found her guilty that afternoon and she was fined ten dollars and $18.55 in court costs. It seems that nothing could deter Mary, and her wrath overcame her reasoning, for she beat up Baccus again the following spring.[34]

On April 16, 1915, Mary accosted Baccus in Laramie and, according to the court docket, "did then in a rude, insolent, and angry manner, unlawfully touch, beat, strike, and wound the person of George Baccus." A warrant was issued the same day and Mary was arrested and brought into Justice Court by Carl Jackson, who was now sheriff. She was charged with assault and battery, and her trial was called the next day. Through her attorney, C. M. Eby, Mary had the case continued until the twentieth. Mary pled not guilty, but Justice Hugh Hinds was well aware of her past behavior and found her guilty. She was again fined ten dollars, and ordered to pay $7.50 in court costs. Finally, Mary called off her vendetta against Baccus; however, she still had enough ill will left for one last caper.[35]

From Mary Powell's past actions it is very clear that she, like her husband, was an irritation and a bane to her neighbors. In many cases, Mary's acts were retaliatory, but in one case there seems to have been no apparent reason for her wrathful behavior.

Dr. Florence Patrick was a neighbor who lived in the valley near Mary's ranch on Horse Creek. It was said that Mary would periodically push rocks down on Dr. Patrick's house to scare her out. Having suffered enough from this harassment, Dr. Patrick decided to move to Laramie around the early part of 1917, and Mary gladly helped her pack her belongings. She also packed up Dr. Patrick's silver and hauled it to her own home.

In early spring, Mary invited Dr. Patrick for dinner, and had the gall to serve her with her own silver. Dr. Patrick immediately recognized her silver, which had a P engraved on each piece. On April 9, Dr. Patrick filed an affidavit in Justice Court for a warrant to search Mary's premises for her personal property. The justice docket reads, "Warrant issued April 9, 1917, and delivered to sheriff of Albany County. Return: Nothing found." Apparently, Mary anticipated Dr. Patrick's actions and hid the silver.[36]

For twenty years, Mary Powell had created havoc among her neighbors, incurred their animosity, and been in and out of court numerous times. Fred Powell would have been proud of her; however, this was her last hurrah. Now it was son Bill's turn.

Bill Powell was a chip off the old block. In December 1910, along with William H. Frazee, he was indicted in Albany County for stealing livestock. The court records maintained that the two stole a total of fourteen horses from John Biddick on November 28, and came back the next day and stole twenty-two more horses. On December 12, Biddick filed charges against both men for the November 28th theft. Warrants were issued the same day, and the two were arrested by Sheriff W. W. Bower. In Justice Court, Powell and Frazee pled not guilty. On the thirteenth, the case was continued until the twenty-second, and both men were released on December 15, under bonds of $1,500 each.

On December 22, when Powell and Frazee were to appear for trial, Biddick filed the second charge. Both defendants again pled not guilty and trial was set for January 3. By the time the first trial commenced on the twenty-second, Frazee had skipped out and his bond was forfeited. Bill appeared in court with his attorney, M. C. Brown, and obtained a continuance until January 3, 1911, the date set for the second trial. When Justice Court convened on the third, Powell was bound over for trial in both cases during the next term of District Court. He was unable to put up a bond of $2,500 and was remanded to jail. On March 9, a bench warrant was issued for Frazee. He was never brought to trial.

Bill's arrest and trial occurred while his mother was facing charges of arson, and she used his case in a motion for a change of venue on the grounds that "the arrest of certain young men for the larceny of horses and among them the son of this affiant has created widespread excitement and prejudice against this affiant." Mary's motion was denied following her son's trial on April 10. Like his mother, Bill got a break and was found not guilty on the eleventh.[37]

By 1920, horse theft was passé, but, in answer to Prohibition, bootlegging was in, and Bill was into it from the start. The temperance crusade in America began over one hundred years before Prohibition. In 1810, there were some fourteen thousand distilleries producing twenty-five million gallons of liquor each year. Not counting wine, beer, and hard cider, this was well over three gallons for every man, woman, and child in America. In 1819, an English reformer stated that

TRANSCRIPT.
JUSTICE DOCKET.

STATE OF WYOMING, } ss.
COUNTY OF ALBANY.

IN JUSTICE'S COURT,

Before John Reid, Justice of the Peace.

THE STATE OF WYOMING
vs.
.... William E. Powell ....
.... And ....
.... William H. Frazee ....
Defendant. s.

December 22nd. A.D. 1910.

Stealing Live Stock.

Information Sworn to by John Riddick. December 22nd. A.D. 1910. And Filed. Charging the Defendants With the Offence of Stealing Live Stock. For that the Said Defendants on the 29th. day of November A.D. 1910. at the County of Albany in the State of Wyoming. Twenty two Horses. Each of the Value of One Hundred Dollars. And of the total and aggregate Value of Two Thousand Two Hundred Dollars of the Personal goods. Chattels. And Personal Property of John Riddick then And there being found. Unlawfully And Feloniously did then and there Steal. take. Carry Away. lead Away. & Drive Away. Contrary to the form, of the Statute in Such Case Made And provided. And Against the Peace And Dignity of the State of Wyoming. Criminal Warrant Issued And Delivered to Sheriff W.W. Borven for Service. Returned By said Sheriff And Served as follows. Served the Within by taken the Within Named Defendants into Court. Information Read to the Defendants. Who after a Plea of Not Guilty. And Preliminary Examination Set for January 3rd 1911. 10. A.M. 1911. January 3rd 1911. Case Called the Defendant William E. Powell in Court With his Attorney. M.C. Brown the following Witnesses Were Sworn on the part of the State. William Wallis. Harve Jones. Leon Frazee. Frank Murray. James Fitzgerald. William Rowe. the following Witnesses Were Sworn And Testified on part of the Defendant. Frank Carter And James Fitzgerald. After Hearing all the evidence there appearing to the Court that the Offence of Stealing live Stock Had been Committed as Charged in the Information. And that there being Probable Cause the Defendant William E. Powell is Bound over to Appear at the Next term of the District Court Within And for the Said County of Albany State of Wyoming Bond for his Appearance as Aforesaid is fixed at $2500.00 Said Bond Not being furnished. he Was Remanded to the Custody of the Sheriff of the Aforesaid County to be Held by him in the County Jail Subject to the Above Conditions And Untill disposed of According to Law.

Witnesses for the State.

Witnesses for the State		
William Wallis.	Paid $	2.00
Harve Jones.	"	2.00
Leon Frazee.	"	2.00
Frank Murray.	"	2.00
James Fitzgerald.	"	6.00
William Rowe.	"	23.40
Witnesses for Defendant.		
Frank Carter.	Paid $	1.00
James Fitzgerald.		

John Reid
Justice of the Peace.

Transcript of the justice docket in the 1910 case against William Powell and William Frazee for stealing livestock. WYOMING STATE ARCHIVES, MUSEUMS, AND HISTORICAL DEPARTMENT, CHEYENNE

one could go into almost anyone's house and be asked to drink wine or spirits, even in the morning. America was known as the alcoholic republic. The biggest reform movement, promoted by press campaigns and lecturers, began in the 1830s, and by 1860 per-capita alcohol consumption had been drastically reduced.

Around the turn of the century, the temperance movement changed its tactics and began a campaign for Prohibition. Supported by the Protestant churches and the election of a Prohibition majority in Congress, the Eighteenth Amendment, which banned the manufacture, sale, or transport of intoxicating liquors, was passed on December 18, 1917. It was ratified on January 16, 1919, and went into effect exactly one year later. Prohibition was highly unpopular with the general public, and Bill Powell immediately jumped on the bandwagon, giving the people what they deemed it was their right to have regardless of the law.

In late fall of 1920, word reached U.S. Prohibition agents in Cheyenne that Bill and others were making bootleg whiskey on his ranch on Horse Creek. On November 20 U.S. Commissioner David W. Gill issued a search warrant to agent John Burns, who raided Powell's ranch the same day. Burns found a copper still, one hundred gallons of sugar mash, a hydrometer stem, and one gallon of white whiskey. He also found William Sharp, William T. Knowles, and Bill Powell, and they were charged with three counts of violating the National Prohibition Act: unlawful possession of equipment, manufacturing intoxicating whiskey, and possession of whiskey for the purpose of being sold.

Trial was held on May 31, 1921 in U.S. District Court at Cheyenne. Defense attorney Hugo Donzelman pulled a surprise on the prosecution by issuing a subpoena for U.S. Commissioner Gill to appear as a witness for the defense and to bring both the affidavit and the search warrant into court. The jury apparently had little regard for the charges and found the defendants not guilty.[38]

Like his father and mother before him, Bill Powell was a vexation to his neighbors. On July 21, 1923, he trespassed on the land of Neil Clark in Albany County, after being warned to stay off the land by Clark and occupant Charles Byers. Charges were filed and an arrest warrant issued on the twenty-third. Two days later, Bill was arrested and brought into Justice Court. Through his attorney, J. R. Sullivan, Bill entered a plea of not guilty and was released on his own recognizance until his trial on July 30.

Bill, now represented by attorney G. R. McConnell, demanded a jury trial, which Justice Harry J. Hunt granted. Following prosecuting attorney George W. Patterson's presentation of his case, the defense counsel made a motion to dismiss on grounds that the state had not proven that Bill trespassed on the land described in the presentation. The motion was overruled. Following the testimony of the defense and closing arguments between counsel, the jury retired to reach a verdict. While the jury was deliberating, Bill blew his top and slugged prosecutor Patterson. He was sentenced to serve three days in jail for contempt of court. At 9 P.M., the jury returned with its verdict—guilty, with a plea for leniency. Bill was fined $25 and court costs of $71.80, which he immediately paid. The court then suspended his three-day jail sentence.[39]

A year and a half later, Bill was back in the bootlegging game. On the night of January 27, 1925, in rural Albany County, Prohibition agents James Capen and Hugh B. Curry, with Assistant Prohibition Director Charles F. Peterson, were scouting the area for possible liquor violations and noticed a light not far from them. Proceeding toward the light, they saw a dugout and detected the scent of mash. Entering the dugout, they found a seventy-five-gallon still with water heating, a ten-gallon pressure tank, one gallon of white whiskey, and Bill Powell and Hazel E. O'Reilley cleaning moonshine equipment. Needless to say, the two moonshiners were indicted on the identical counts that Bill had been charged with in 1920.

On February 18, U.S. Attorney A. D. Walter presented the information in U.S. District Court at Cheyenne for "the consideration of the Court . . . and that due process of law be awarded against William Powell and Hazel E. O'Reilley." The evidence was sufficient and a trial was scheduled for April 15.

This time Bill knew he could not beat a conviction, and both he and Hazel O'Reilley entered a guilty plea on the fifteenth in U.S. District Court in Cheyenne. The judgment was a fine of $150 for O'Reilley and $250 for Bill, or incarceration in the Albany County jail until either paid their fine. They most likely had made that much from their whiskey sales, and both gladly paid their fines the same day.[40]

Between 1925 and 1931, likely in Cheyenne, Bill Powell met Sarah May "Billie" Phelps. The two were kindred spirits; Bill was a bootlegger while Billie was into prostitution. There is no record of their marriage in Albany or Laramie Counties;[41] however, Billie took the Powell name and they lived as man and wife, off and on, until Bill's death. Billie's son Alonzo, born in 1919, lived with them but kept the Phelps name. Bill and Billie avoided conflict with the law until 1931, when they ran into trouble with the F.B.I.

By 1931, everyone knew that Prohibition was on the way out; however, the Depression had hit full force. Bill and Billie needed to make money, so Bill got involved in Billie's trade. In November, the two went to Denver, Colorado, and checked into the Edelweiss Hotel on the twenty-second. Here they met Ernest Booth and his wife Pauline Jackson Booth, and worked out a deal to bring Pauline back to Laramie to work as a prostitute. They headed back to Wyoming on December 12. On the thirty-first, they got a room at the New Mecca Hotel in Laramie, where Billie and Pauline apparently practiced their profession. By the end of January 1932, the Booths left for Fort Collins, Colorado.

Somehow, F.B.I. agents A. H. Gere and John L. Geraghty, and Laramie Police Sergeant Phil Kuntz, got wind of the operation, and made a full investigation. On May 9, 1932, the Powells and Ernest Booth were indicted by a grand jury in U.S. District Court in Cheyenne on three counts of interstate transportation of a woman for immoral purposes. Trial was set for May 26. A bench warrant was issued for Booth on May 13, and he posted a bond of two thousand dollars before U.S. Commissioner Robert E. Foot in Denver, Colorado. Subpoenas for witnesses were issued throughout the month of May and the trial did not begin until July 11. Pauline Booth was brought back from Fort Collins as a witness for the prosecution, and all three defendants pled guilty.

On July 18, District Judge T. Blake Kennedy sentenced Bill Powell to thirty days in Albany County jail. U.S. Marshal R. John Allen took Powell to Laramie to begin his sentence the next day. As ringleaders, it was Booth and Billie Powell who got the stiffer sentences. On July 26, Booth got four months in the Laramie County jail at Cheyenne, and Billie was sentenced on August 1 to three months in the Albany County jail. Marshal Allen delivered her to jail the same day.

Billie Powell didn't fare so well behind bars. In mid August, Dr. Josiah P. Markley was summoned to the jail and found her suffering from nervousness, hysteria, insomnia, and an irregular appetite. He treated her for two weeks and Dr. D. Harold Finch was called in for consultation. On September 2, both doctors wrote letters that reached U.S. District Clerk Charles J. Ohnhaus in Cheyenne, recommending that Billie be released. The letters got results; on the same day, September 2, Billie was paroled to attorney S. C. Downey, who served as probation officer. On November 2, Downey wrote Ohnhaus that "the defendant . . . has carried herself all right and no complaints have been filed." Judge Kennedy discharged her from parole on November 4.[42]

Three years later, tragedy hit the Powell family; for Mary it was twofold, for Bill, it was the end of the line. In January 1935, Bill was shot to death by his fifteen-year-old stepson, Alonzo Phelps, whose background seemed to follow the Powell tradition.

Previously, on March 8, 1934, Brigham Young University's basketball team had come to Laramie to play in a championship series at the Wyoming University gym. While they were shooting the hoops, fourteen-year-old Alonzo Phelps and two other juveniles were ripping off the teams' personal belongings from the locker room. They gained entrance by pulling out pieces of a cracked window, unlocking the window catch, and climbing into the locker room. The three were soon caught, according to the March 10 issue of the *Republican-Boomerang:*

> No charges had been preferred this afternoon against three High school youths arrested last night. . . .
> Alonzo Phelps, 14, Thurman Chase, 15, and James Orell, 15, are being held in the county jail, pending an investigation. . . . Phelps, authorities said today, has confessed his part as the ringleader, and Chase has admitted that he helped, police reported. Orell is believed to have re-

ceived a part of the loot, but he is not thought to have taken any other part in the theft. He is accused of having kept the lookout outside the gym.

Police recovered four basketball uniforms owned by the team, a leather bag belonging to Jay Whitman, and a part of a small amount of cash [$10.20] taken from the effects of Earl Giles, another B.Y.U. player.

On the thirteenth, Judge V. J. Tidball released the three youths on parole. Orell was given a severe reprimand by the judge, Chase was turned over to his mother, and Phelps was paroled to a Mary Baillie of Laramie.[43]

The following November 30, Alonzo Phelps was arrested by the Laramie police for drunkenness and placed in the juvenile ward. The next day Bill Powell came to the youngster's rescue and made a plea for his release. The police discharged Phelps into Powell's custody the same day.[44]

Within a few weeks the Powell ranch on Horse Creek was to witness another killing, occurring almost forty years after the murder of Fred Powell. On the night of January 5, 1935, there were three people at the Powell ranch besides Bill Powell and Alonzo Phelps: Mary Powell, her brother Charles Keane, who now lived at the ranch, and Bill's so-called wife Billie who was visiting but actually lived in Cheyenne.

At 9 P.M., Bill told Alonzo to take a bath, but the boy begged off, claiming he had a cold and did not want to aggravate it. An argument ensued and Bill violently beat Phelps, who ran into a bedroom, grabbed a .22 caliber automatic pistol from a holster on the floor, and cried, "I've got a gun, and if you don't stand back, I'll kill you." Powell leaped at the boy and knocked him across the bed. Young Phelps fired at Powell from a prone position, sending a slug through his abdomen. At the same time Phelps pulled the trigger Mary Powell came through the doorway to see what was going on, and was superficially wounded in the left arm by the bullet that had hit her son.

Phelps and his mother put Powell in a truck and rushed him to the Ivinson Hospital in Laramie. On the way, the two agreed to explain that the shooting was accidental. Powell died following an operation the next morning; however, before he died he told the authorities that the shooting was an accident. That afternoon, Phelps told prosecuting attorney Glenn Parker what actually happened, stating he couldn't stand the strain of questioning. The boy said he shot Powell because he was afraid, but when questioned further, said, "No, I wasn't afraid, not as long as I had the gun in my hand." This statement got Phelps arrested on a charge of second-degree murder.

On January 7, 1935, headlines in the *Tribune-Leader* screamed, "SON OF TOM HORN VICTIM KILLED BY HIS STEP-SON." On the ninth, Alonzo Phelps was arraigned in Justice Court in Laramie, and bound over for trial at the next term of District Court. On default of $2,500 bond, the boy was remanded into the custody of the sheriff. The trial began on April 4, before Judge V. J. Tidball. Prosecutor Glenn Parker and defense attorney Frank E. Anderson hammered away at each other, Parker claiming the killing was deliberate and malicious while Anderson asserted that the boy acted out of fear, and shot in self-defense. The fate of Alonzo Phelps went to the jury around 2:30 P.M. on April 5.

The jury returned with its verdict at five minutes before ten o'-clock the next morning—not guilty. That afternoon, the *Republican-Boomerang* reported that when the verdict was read, Phelps gave a sigh of relief and momentarily slumped forward. The newspaper continued, "His mother, Mrs. Billie Phelps, stationed herself at the courtroom exit and thanked each juror individually as the men filed out." Apparently, Bill Powell's death didn't pull too hard at her heartstrings.[45]

Following the death of Bill Powell, Mary reportedly sold the ranch on Horse Creek. Mary Lou Pence wrote, "Down the old trail she rode, and in the town of her youth she banked her last fires. There in Laramie, the school children who knew her loved her. She spent the final years peacefully."[46]

Nevertheless, there was one final misfortune in the life of Mary Powell. On October 23, 1940, her brother, Charles Keane, who had stuck by Mary throughout her life, was struck and killed by a freight train at the Union Pacific yards in Laramie. It was reported that Keane had been suffering from infirmities of old age, which is probably the reason the accident occurred.[47]

Mary Powell's turbulent and wayward life ended at age eighty-one in Cheyenne on January 13, 1941. On the previous December 29, Mary went to visit her daughter-in-law, Billie Phelps Powell, in Cheyenne. It is reported that Billie was working as a prostitute at the Tivoli Rooms on Cary Avenue. It was here, on January 5, that Mary suffered a severe heart attack. She was rushed to the hospital, but it was too late, for Mary died eight days later. Was it predestination that the last place Mary would visit was a house of ill repute?

Mary remained a Catholic throughout her life, and a rosary service was held for her on the evening of January 15 at the Shannon Funeral Home. Reverend John McDevitt officiated at her funeral service in the St. Lawrence O'Toole Catholic Church in Laramie the next day. It was in the Green Hill Cemetery that Mary Powell finally found the peace she never had in life.[48]

Not much of this narrative has been favorable to Mary Keane Powell, so it is only fair to conclude with these positive words, which graced her obituary in the *Republican-Boomerang*:

> Stories that Mrs. Powell rode the range and handled the heavier work of cattle ranching with the efficiency and dexterity of regular cowhands were more than fiction. She was one of those early pioneer women who fought and worked right along side their men to tame the western frontier.[49]

In retrospect, the lives of the more infamous women of the West, such as Belle Starr and Cattle Kate Watson, pale when compared to the

WYOMING S'

THE STATE ITS FIELD

Cheyen

Cheyenne, Wyoming's largest city, a prosperous, progressive, healthful community of 21,000 people, is the land and air gateway to the West.

TRIBUNE VOL. 41; NO. 6
LEADER VOL. 68; NO. 95

Price 5 Cents

Cheyenne,

SON OF TOM HORN VICTIM KILLED BY HIS STEP-SON

Chief Ex Democr

GOVE

STATE OFFI

BILLY POWELL SHOT AT RANCH SUNDAY DURING QUARREL WITH FIFTEEN-YEAR-OLD LON PHELPS

Charge of Second Degree Murder to Be Lodged Against Slayer of Former Famous Frontier Days Performer

William Powell, 45, Horse Creek rancher whose father died by Tom Horn's gun toward the end of the last century, himself died by the gun in a Laramie hospital Sunday.

His stepson, Alonzo Phelps, 15, is being held in Albany County jail and Prosecuting Attorney Glenn Parker has said a second degree murder charge will be filed against him in connection with the shooting.

Phelps admitted to officers, they said Monday, that he shot Powell in the abdomen with a .22 caliber automatic pistol at their ranch home Saturday night during a quarrel.

During the quarrel, the officers quoted Phelps as saying, he ran into a bedroom and drew the gun from a holster lying on the floor.

He warned Powell to stay away but his stepfather leaped at him and struck him, knocking him across the bed, the officers said.

Lying across the bed he fired twice, one of the bullets striking Powell's mother, Mrs. Mary Powell, when she ran into the room and inflicting a superficial wound in the left arm, officers said Phelps admitted.

Phelps told the officers he took Powell to Laramie in a truck and that on the way he and his mother agreed to explain the shooting as accidental but that he couldn't stand the strain of questioning and told the true story, officers said.

CURTAILMENT OIL WELLS IS HELD INVALID

Supreme Court Says NRA Has Cut Flow Without Authority

WASHINGTON, Jan. 7.—(AP)— In its first decision on federal new deal legislation, the supreme court today held invalid the clause of the National Industrial Recovery Act under which the government is attempting to curtail oil production.

MORNING PAPER ISSUED SUNDAY DELIGHTS CITY

Staff Called for Emergency Duty Gets Out New Tribune Edition

THE TRIBUNE-LEADER'S Sunday morning "welcome" issue was the talk of the town. It was a pleasant surprise to new state officers and members of the legislature.

It may interest readers of this paper to know that all preparation for the Sunday morning issue was made after 3 o'clock Saturday afternoon.

At that hour, while the Saturday evening issue was still in process of publication, the publisher of the TRIBUNE-LEADER consulted with various departmental heads.

John Charles Thompson, editor and managing editor, replied, "Although I have been on duty for the evening issue, it will not be the first time in my newspaper experience I have been called upon in an emergency. To make a long story short, I am ready to go, if you say the word."

The word was said.

W. I. N. Cox, business manager, responded in a similar strain, and indicated that, in his judgment, a most creditable Sunday morning issue could be produced, notwithstanding the brief notice.

Clarence M. Lee, foreman, who had been off duty Saturday, replied, "You know, good printers never ask any questions. There are a number of the boys available

---

Headlines in the January 7th issue of the Wyoming State Tribune–Cheyenne State Leader *regarding the killing of Bill Powell.* WYOMING STATE ARCHIVES, MUSEUMS, AND HISTORICAL DEPARTMENT, CHEYENNE

Mary Powell in the late 1930s. WYOMING STATE ARCHIVES, MUSEUMS, AND HISTORICAL DEPARTMENT, CHEYENNE

life of Mary Powell, an indisputably rugged, tough, and notorious woman. But this is not surprising to anyone who has examined the lives of many well-known folk heroes of the western frontier; those genuinely deserving fame or notoriety are more often than not left behind in the dust.

XI. MONTANA

THE WHITNEY BROTHERS

The Ones Who Got Away

On December 1, 1951, a man in Glasgow, Montana wrote a letter to Wyoming Governor Frank Barrett. It was not an ordinary letter, but he was not an ordinary man. His letter was a confession to a bank robbery that had haunted him for forty years. The writer was Charley Whitney who, with his brother Hugh, had robbed the State Bank of Cokeville, Wyoming in September 1911. The letter was conscientiously and legibly written by a man who was truly repentant and had lived an honest and productive life since his mistake.

Bank robbers were lucky if they escaped after a robbery; however, the Whitneys not only escaped, but completely disappeared. But the brothers were not run-of-the-mill outlaws. In a sense, they were not really outlaws at all, at least not the habitual kind.

Although the bank robbery took place in Wyoming, the reasons that led to the crime can be traced to Idaho, where the Whitneys spent much of their early life. Hugh Whitney was born on March 4, 1889, and his brother Charley Spraig Whitney on April 19, 1890. Their birthplace was Anatone, Washington, in the southeastern corner of the state near the border of Oregon and Idaho.[1] Their parents were Fred H. and Charlotte "Lottie" Lathrop Whitney. Fred Whitney, one of eight children of Timothy and Avis Douglas Whitney, was born in Hudson, Maine in 1851; from the 1860s until the 1880s, the family moved continually westward, finally settling at Indian Valley near Weiser, Idaho. Fred and Lottie Whitney moved to Anatone, Washington following their marriage, and reportedly moved back to the Weiser area after Hugh and Charley were born. There were four other Whitney children: Florence, born in 1886; Helen, in 1892; Bruce, in 1896; and Ethel, in 1898.[2]

Hugh and Charley Whitney's early life was not a bed of roses, as Charley revealed in his 1951 letter to Governor Barrett:

> . . . our childhood was blighted—almost from the infancy by the way our father treated us.
>
> Every child will love and respect their parents if given a chance.
>
> We had a wonderful mother that we dearly loved. Not one man in a million in this age of the world was like our father, for he was the lord and master and he treated mother and us children as chattel slaves. Father never gave us a penny, and he bought us only the barest necessities of life, and about everything our childhood hearts yearned for we never had. It was all work and no play, we were beaten and cowed so we trembled at the sound of his footsteps.
>
> When he went away he always left Hugh and me a stint to do, and on returning he would horsewhip us if he was not satisfied with the work we did. Several times he beat us so hard with a green willow or buggy whip that the whipping put black and blue streaks all over our backs from our necks to our ankles, and I can produce men still living that can substantiate this statement.

Enough was enough, so on February 22, 1904, the Whitney boys left home and took a job herding sheep at forty dollars a month. That summer, the brothers, now fifteen and sixteen years old, were proficient enough to find a sheepherding job at men's wages. Charley stated, "I still think I was the youngest boy that ever herded a large band of sheep in those Mountains."[3]

The Whitneys were able to escape their father's wrath but not his control. Fred Whitney told his sons that they had to pay him for all the food and clothing he had provided and continue to pay him until they turned twenty-one. For three years the boys worked in eastern Oregon and western Idaho, sending back almost every dollar they earned to their father. At one outfit, the Higgins Brothers Sheep Company near Council, Idaho, they were remembered as spending money only on guns and ammunition. The two brothers liked to hunt and practice shooting, especially Hugh, who became an expert sharpshooter.[4]

On March 5, 1907, the brothers, now older and somewhat wiser, decided to free themselves from their father's domination. Obtaining a job in eastern Oregon, they worked for one month, collected their wages, and headed for Cokeville in the southwestern part of Wyoming where their aunt, Mary Ella Whitney Stoner, was living with her two children, Clarence and Grayce.

Neither of the Whitneys fit the image of the stereotypical cowboy, tall and rawboned. Hugh was five foot eight inches tall, of stocky build, with dark complexion and dark curly hair that fell forward over his forehead. Charley Whitney was taller at five foot nine and a half inches, with grey or grey-blue eyes, medium complexion, and brown hair. Both were rather handsome young men. The Whitneys had no trouble finding jobs around Cokeville, and were considered honest, amiable,

Hugh and Charley Whitney, c. 1909–1910. COURTESY OF ARTHUR AND BERNICE
ROBINSON, COKEVILLE, WYOMING

and adept at handling cattle and sheep. However, Hugh's obsession with marksmanship practice would later cause both brothers problems with an employer.[5]

In 1908, Fred Whitney and his family moved to a farm on Cottonwood Creek, two miles south of Council, Idaho. Their home was located on the west side of the railroad tracks and one of the Whitney brothers, who was about ten years of age, supposedly tried to hold up the P.I.N. railroad near his home. Stopping the train after sighting the young boy armed with a shotgun, the engineer got off the engine and booted the youngster's britches all the way to his home. If this was true, the boy had to have been twelve-year-old Bruce Whitney.

Fred Whitney worked at several jobs around Council, and at one point was road commissioner for that part of the country. Hugh and Charley's mother, Lottie Whitney, was highly respected in Council as one who always had time to help others in need. According to Charley, she was a wonderful mother but was treated like a slave by their father.

It is interesting that on July 30, 1892, in Lander, Wyoming, one Fred Whitney helped furnish a four-hundred-dollar bond for Butch Cassidy, who had been charged with horse theft. Two years later, after several continuances, Cassidy was sentenced to two years' imprisonment at the Wyoming State Penitentiary. It is not known if this Fred Whitney was the father of the Whitney brothers.[6]

Hugh and Charley's initial problems can be traced to Cokeville. According to Charley Whitney, "That nefarious crook in Cokeville, Charley Manning was the cause of my brothers downfall. We were green, ignorant, and gullible at the time and an easy prey for every confidence man that came along, and any one who knew our background knows the reason why."[7] Charlie Manning apparently was a combination of both Robert Louis Stevenson's Dr. Jekyll and Mr. Hyde and Charles Dickens' Fagin. Born on December 25, 1881, in Pass Christian, Mississippi, Manning came to Cokeville as a young man and worked on several ranches and in a cement plant. In 1905, he married Louella Stoffer, a daughter of a prominent sheepman. Manning, a handsome, baby-faced man, is remembered around Cokeville as a good family man with no bad habits who was kind and loving to his wife and children.

The other side of the coin portrays Charlie Manning as a shady character, a gambler and blackmailer who carried out his unlawful enterprises outside of Cokeville and worked only as a gambler after 1910. He reportedly ran a gang known as the Boxcar Bandits in Cokeville. It was a small band, consisting of Manning, Tex Taylor, and Tex Long, and they raided merchandise from boxcars at the Cokeville siding. Just what influence Manning had over the Whitneys is not known, but Hugh supposedly became involved with the gang in 1910 and committed several small robberies, none of which have been documented. Regardless, Manning would play an important role in the lives and future of both brothers.[8]

Charlie Manning, c. early 1900s. MARY E. STONER COLLECTION

Bad luck spiraled for the Whitneys while they were working for a prominent Cokeville sheep rancher named Pete W. Olsen. They went to work for Olsen about 1907, and remained in his employ for two years. Olsen stated that Charley Whitney was quiet and efficient but Hugh, although a good worker, was a sullen loner who was hard to get along with. Olsen also said that he bought Hugh more ammunition than he did clothing and food, and that Whitney spent most of his earnings on cartons or cases of ammunition. A problem arose from Hugh's constant practice with his pistol and rifle, which Olsen claimed kept the animals jumpy and nervous.

There are other accounts of what caused the enmity between Olsen and the Whitneys. One states that both parties were involved in a sheep rustling deal, and Olsen reneged, leaving the Whitneys without work or pay and Hugh under the threat of being charged with sheep stealing if he implicated Olsen. Whether this account is true or not, Olsen remained prominent in the sheep business for years, although he was described by Errol Jack Lloyd in his master's thesis, "The History of Cokeville, Wyoming," as "shrewd, unscrupulous, with the heart of a coyote and the confident, substantial exterior of respectability."

A probable scenario is that Olsen's foreman, Ezra Christiansen, fired the two brothers because Hugh constantly used firearms when herding the sheep and killed a prize ram. Both brothers were hoping to get their jobs back and waited at the ranch until Olsen returned from Evanston two days later. After gathering the facts, Olsen refused to reinstate the Whitneys and docked their wages to pay for the damage. A violent argument ensued but, upon the arrival of the other ranch hands, no gunplay occurred. The two brothers left with Hugh angrily vowing to shoot Olsen on sight.

Running into Christiansen when they returned to the range to pick up their belongings, Hugh Whitney reportedly beat him unmercifully with brass knuckles and left him on the range. Christiansen supposedly died from the beating and Hugh was arrested but escaped before he could be transported to the county jail. This story is certainly untrue, for there are no records to substantiate a murder charge. The ensuing account, which is more realistic, was unearthed by writers Jim Dullenty and Mary Stoner Hadley.

Following his discharge from the Olsen ranch, Hugh went to work for the Green River Livestock Company in Rock Springs. Hugh returned to Cokeville in short order claiming Christiansen had sent word to the Green River Company to discharge him. He then found employment with the Beckwith-Quinn Company with the same results. Hugh got word to Christiansen to stop bad-mouthing him or he would trounce him the next time they met. This occurred in June 1910, and when Hugh knocked Christiansen down, his head hit a rail and he remained unconscious for eighteen hours. Hugh fled to Green River but was tracked by Deputy Dan Hanson, who brought him back to face charges of assault. Since there was no jail in Cokeville, he was confined in Frank Mau's saloon. Although Hugh managed to escape, he was convicted in his absence, fined fifty dollars, and sentenced to sixty days in jail. Hugh later returned and had the charges dropped by paying a fine of thirty-five dollars. Whatever the problem, Olsen did blackball the brothers from working at any of the area ranches. As a result, the Whitneys and Olsen became bitter enemies.[9]

According to author Robert R. Rose, one of the Whitneys, presumably Hugh, attempted to hold up Tommie Holland's saloon in Cokeville. Whitney entered the saloon masked with a handkerchief and pointed his revolver at a half a dozen men who were playing poker. A young cowboy reached over and pulled down Whitney's mask. The would-be robber pretended it was all a joke, bought everyone a round of drinks, and sat down to play poker. When the game broke up at dawn, Whitney had won all the money and rode out of town.

With no work around Cokeville, Hugh Whitney headed for Oregon and was joined by Charley. Following their return to Cokeville in April 1911, Hugh found employment on the ranges in Idaho and southern Montana. Charley remained in Wyoming, where he apparently found a job, not having the violent reputation of his brother.[10]

In mid June 1911, Hugh Whitney was in desperate need of money and turned to Charlie Manning for help. According to the June 20 edition of the *Herald-Republican:* "Last week at Lima, Mont. he [Hugh Whitney] pawned his gun at a store and used some of the money to wire to Jack [sic] Manning, care of Bob Bowman, at Cokeville, asking him that fifteen dollars be telegraphed him. The money arrived and Whitney redeemed his gun." Later in the week, Hugh and a friend from Rigby, Idaho named Albert F. Sesler, also known as Albert Ross, went to Monida, Montana for a night on the town. The events that followed would put Hugh Whitney's name high on the list of the most notorious outlaws of Montana, Idaho, and Wyoming.

On the evening of June 16, 1911, Whitney and Ross went to a combination saloon and pool hall in Monida, supposedly with four hundred dollars between them. What occurred is not known, but they likely drank and gambled too much and upon waking the next morning they found themselves broke. Believing they had been fleeced, they returned to the saloon that morning, held up the bartender, and retrieved at least two hundred dollars of what they had lost. They no doubt figured they were in the right, for instead of quickly fleeing town, they casually walked to the railroad station, bought tickets for Pocatello, Idaho, on the Oregon Shortline Railroad, and boarded the train.

In the meantime, the bartender sent a telegram requesting that a law officer board the train at Spencer, Idaho, and arrest Whitney and Ross. Upon boarding the train, Deputy Sheriff Sam Milton of Fremont County enlisted the aid of conductor William Kidd. They entered the car where Whitney and Ross were playing cards with two traveling men, and quickly arrested both men. Laying his revolver in a vacant seat across the aisle, the deputy started to put handcuffs on Whitney, calling his prisoner a "dirty, yellow, cowardly son of a bitch."

Whitney's volcanic temper erupted under this verbal abuse, and he jumped across the aisle, grabbed the weapon, and shot Milton in the shoulder and stomach. Conductor Kidd, attempting to grapple with Whitney, was shot in the stomach and lungs. As both men fell to the floor, Whitney pulled the emergency cord. As the train slowed down, he and Ross jumped off at milepost 245, between China Point and Highbridge. Several shots were fired at Whitney from the baggage, mail, and express cars, but none hit him as he quickly took cover in a brushy draw and made his escape into the rough sagebrush of the hill country. Conductor Kidd died that evening in a Pocatello hospital but Milton recovered, although he was handicapped the rest of his life. Albert Ross managed to escape and was never caught. Several accounts written about this incident erroneously reported that Whitney and Ross robbed the train.[11]

Word was sent across the country to be on the lookout for Hugh Whitney and numerous posses assembled throughout the area. One of the first to take the trail was Warden Conley of the Montana State Prison at Deer Lodge, who set out by automobile with a pack of bloodhounds. At Silver Bow, Conley was joined by Under Sheriff

Erwin of Dillon and Sheriff O'Rourke and Under Sheriff Murray of Silver Bow. On June 18, the Oregon Short Line Railroad offered a reward of a thousand dollars for Whitney. The next day, Governor James H. Hawley of Idaho upped the amount by five hundred dollars.[12]

Hugh Whitney was determined to avoid capture, and this gritty, hunted man proved this by his remarkable effort to remain free. The pursuit of Hugh Whitney became one of the most concentrated manhunts in the history of Idaho.

A posse that formed at Hamer, reluctant to head into the brush after Whitney, began patrolling between mileposts 245 and 218 at Hamer. The fugitive dodged the posse, and on the morning of the eighteenth he stopped at the McGill ranch near Hamer for food. Mrs. McGill noticed that he seemed nervous and furtive throughout the meal, and bolted his food. After packing sandwiches for him, she called her husband as Whitney was leaving. McGill sent several of his farm hands and his sixteen-year-old son, Edgar McGill, after the fugitive. Joined by Deputy Sheriff G. W. Bailey, the men gave chase on foot, yelling at Whitney to stop. Whitney shouted back, "I don't have to stop for you."

Realizing the fugitive was outdistancing the men, young McGill returned to the ranch where he picked up a rifle, mounted a horse belonging to a man named Spoon Savage, and set out alone after the outlaw. It was the boy's bad luck to run across Whitney as he disappeared over a hill. As McGill crested the hill, he was shot in the leg and knocked off his horse. When the game youngster attempted to shoot back, Whitney shot him in the breast, warning him not to follow or he would have to kill him. Whitney took the boy's horse and rifle and rode eastward.[13]

The Snake River was at high-water stage and guards were posted at all the bridges and ferries. Just before dawn on the nineteenth, Whitney rode onto the bridge near Menan guarded by Rube Scott. Sighting the wanted man, Scott shouted, "Get down off that horse you dirty yellow coward," and fired his shotgun at him. Whitney quickly pulled his weapon, spurred his horse into a run, and shot Scott's weapon from his hand, taking off the right trigger finger. Scott immediately rolled off the bridge as the gunman rode off unscathed.

By the nineteenth, several posses had set out after Whitney. Chief Agent Joe Jones and detectives Edgley and Keyes of the Oregon Short Line Railroad joined Bonneville County Sheriff Bucklin at Idaho Falls. They headed for Just's ranch, twelve miles east of the city, hoping to head off the outlaw. Sheriff Fisher of Fremont County arrived at Rigby at 5 A.M. and set out toward the southeast with a posse of ten men in two automobiles, plus the bloodhounds from Deer Lake. Shortly after leaving Rigby, Sheriff Fisher's group was joined by a posse from Market Lake.

Around 9:30 A.M., Sheriff Fisher's posse caught sight of Whitney, but by doubling back and crossing streams, the fugitive threw them off the track. One of the posse, Deputy Sheriff Robert O'Ley, reportedly

WANTED FOR MURDER

HUGH WHITNEY

HUGH WHITNEY

Who shot and fatally wounded Conductor William Kidd, on O. S. L. Train No. 4, June 17th, between Spencer and Dubois, Idaho, while resisting arrest by Deputy Sheriff. Also wounded three other persons in making his escape.

DESCRIPTION

Age, about 23 years; height, 5 feet, 8 inches; weight, 165 lbs.; stocky build; very dark complexion; smooth shaven; dark curley hair which comes down over forehead.

He is a sheephearder and cowboy and dresses as such always wears a handkerchief around his neck; he is an expert marksman; does not drink but smokes cigarettes; wears high heel boots with nails in end of heels.

In company with Whitney was a man supposed to be Albert F. Sesler, whose description as near as we have it is as follows:

Age, 25 years; height, 5 feet, 11 inches; weight, 150 or 155 lbs.; light complexion; thin face; inclined to be round shouldered; supposed to be ex-railroad man, but has been traveling and working with Whitney for some time near Cokeville, Wyoming.

REWARD

W. H. Bancroft, Vice-President & General Manager of the Oregon Short Line Railroad Company, issues following bulletin, dated June 18th, 1911.

"THE OREGON SHORT LINE RAILROAD COMPANY WILL PAY A REWARD OF ONE THOUSAND DOLLARS FOR THE ARREST AND CONVICTION OF THE HOLDUPS WHO YESTERDAY SHOT AND PROBABLY FATALLY WOUNDED CONDUCTOR KIDD."

(Signed) W. H. BANCROFT.

Governor of Idaho issues following reward:

"A reward of five hundred dollars each is hereby offered by the State of Idaho for the bodies, dead or alive, of the persons who wounded and killed Conductor William Kidd, in Fremont County, Idaho, on the 17th day of June, 1911. Said reward will be paid out of the Treasury of the State of Idaho.

(Signed) JAMES H. HAWLEY, Governor.

Attest: W. L. GIFFORD, Secretary of State.
Dated Boise, Idaho June 19th, 1911, at 10 o'clock a.m.

Officers keep a close watch for parties. Arrest and notify J. F. Fisher, Sheriff, Fremont County, St. Anthony, Idaho, who holds warrant charging murder for these parties, or Joseph Jones, Chief Special Agent, O. S. L. R. R., Deseret News Building, Salt Lake City.

Wanted poster offering rewards for Hugh Whitney, issued two days after he shot and killed Conductor William Kidd on June 17, 1911. AUTHOR'S COLLECTION

ran across Whitney but was shot before he could draw his weapon. The outlaw then spurred his horse as fast as it would go up Willow Creek toward Soda Springs. A news dispatch the next day stated that O'Ley was not wounded and had returned to Idaho Falls.

Three posses under Deputy Sheriff Kistner left Blackfoot for Grey's Lake and another group headed north from Soda Springs to intercept Whitney. At 7 P.M., a band of twenty Blackfoot Indians from Fort Hall took to the trail. Every crossing of the Blackfoot and Snake Rivers was guarded by armed men. Reports circulated that the lawmen had the outlaw cornered between Willow Creek and Idaho Falls, and that Whitney would be captured before morning. In total, there were about two hundred men now searching for Hugh Whitney.[14]

Later in the day, a posse from the Willow Creek area near Rigby picked up Whitney's trail. The slippery fugitive managed to elude them and rode to the Fall Creek Ranch in Swan Valley, owned by Ed Daniels and Joe Jones. The ranchers knew nothing of Whitney's escapades and gave him a late dinner. Two hours after he left, the Willow Creek posse arrived at the ranch. Upon being told that Whitney had ridden out on the west side of the river, they borrowed more suitable clothing and started in pursuit.

Outguessing the posse, Whitney changed directions and went up the south side of the river to the Edwards ranch, where he was taken across on the Edwards' ferry. He then rode to the ranch of a personal friend, Ed Janes, and told the rancher he was headed for Cokeville to try to find work. At the time he talked to Janes, Hugh Whitney did not know he had killed anyone, stating he only meant to stop those who were following him.[15]

He was next spotted near Iona, north of the Fort Hall Indian Reservation, and the Indian police were ordered to shoot to kill. Again the crafty fugitive outwitted the lawmen by turning eastward toward the forbidding Caribou Mountains. On the morning of the twentieth, he rode up to the ranch of Cal Pelot, sixteen miles east of Idaho Falls, and obtained a meal. While eating, Whitney appeared nervous and kept his revolver out, however, he let Pelot's young son use his rifle to shoot at a circling eagle. Two hours after Whitney left, Pelot joined a posse of cowboys under rancher Jim Buck, who had ridden to his ranch and informed him of Whitney's crimes.

Several posses trailed Whitney into the foothills of the Caribou Mountains. Sheriff Bucklin's posse, Deputy Sheriff Kistner's posse, and the group of cowboys from the Jim Buck ranch tracked him to the Willow Creek Canyon, near Grey's Lake, approximately twenty miles west of the Wyoming border. Around 3 A.M. on the twenty-first, the now desperate fugitive boldly attempted to steal a fresh mount from the posse while they were camped near the Brinson mine, but the barking of the hounds frightened him off. The next morning the posse found tracks of his unshod horse, but the hounds lost the scent when it began raining.

After trailing Whitney for forty-eight straight hours, Sheriff Bucklin gave up the chase. Deputy Sheriff Kistner and the cowboys continued in pursuit until they reached the Yellow Creek country, one of the wildest areas in Idaho, located about ten miles east of Grey's Lake. Here Kistner abandoned the hunt.

The cowboys were a different breed and came close to capturing Whitney. They nearly had him boxed in as evening approached on June 22. Spotting him on a high ridge with binoculars, the cowboys immediately gave chase. Just before they reached the ridge, darkness fell and they lost their quarry. Jim Buck's cowboys were the last ones to see Hugh Whitney in Idaho.[16]

Whether right or wrong, it was an extraordinary feat for one lone man, with only three meals and no sleep for five days, to escape the clutches of so many who were in pursuit of him. The resolute fugitive had one advantage; he knew the area as well as or better than most of his pursuers, a fact he adroitly proved.

After crossing the Wyoming line, Hugh headed for the Cokeville area where he contacted his brother Charley. For the next three months, he hid out in the hills around Cokeville, although he was reportedly seen several times in the Jackson Hole country. In early September, Charley disappeared from Cokeville and joined his brother.

Hugh Whitney was between a rock and a hard place. He realized that he could not remain in the area much longer and avoid capture. And he had to have funds to leave. He was also deep in debt to Charlie Manning, who, by threatening to expose him, pressured him to raise cash. The two brothers reportedly robbed the Tom Taylor sheep camp at Salt Canyon near Montpelier, Idaho on the night of September 5. Tying up sheepherder Felix Romero, the brothers helped themselves to his dinner and rode away on two valuable horses belonging to Taylor and his wife.

The next day the brothers were seen purchasing a jug of whiskey, ammunition, and some food items in the Steward Grocery in Montpelier and were spotted in front of the Capitol Saloon. Local freighter Marion Perkins claimed he saw the two outlaws with the stolen horses resting in Montpelier Canyon the same day. For the next five days the Whitneys completely disappeared, surfacing only to hold up the bank at Cokeville, Wyoming.[17]

It was two o'clock in the afternoon of Monday, September 11, 1911, when Hugh and Charley Whitney entered the front door of the State Bank of Cokeville. Cashier Asa D. Noblitt, who was working on the books, thought Charley Whitney was there on banking business. Both brothers then pulled out their revolvers and told Noblitt to open the safe or they would crack his head. He informed the bandits that the timelock on the safe would not open until 3 P.M., so the two helped themselves to about one hundred dollars from the cashiers' drawers. Hugh, with wry humor, told Noblitt that he would write a check for the full amount when he came that way again.

The Whitneys had planned the robbery to correspond with the time when depositors would bring in their daily receipts. Within the next hour the pair relieved ten customers of their money, jewelry, and watches, with Charley holding up the victims while Hugh collected the loot. Each victim was then herded into the vault. According to the *Kemmerer Camera:*

> Emil Nelson was the first to enter and he was held up, relieved of what he had, and deposited in the large vault. He was followed by Ernest Jackson and others in order, a stranger by the name of McCharles, Gilligan the druggist, George Hewitt, Al Porter, Contractor Graham, John H. Stoner, Earl Haggerty and Ed Marks, each of whom was relieved of his money and valuables and then deposited in the vault.

Haggerty was the biggest loser, contributing $137 in cash and a number of checks. He was allowed to keep his diamond ring after he told the bandits it was given to him by his mother. Neither bandit was masked and conversed genially with all of the victims who knew them. The robbery was so brazen that several people thought it was a joke, and laughed when first told to throw their money and valuables into the sack. The total amount of the Whitneys' plunder was just over four hundred dollars. Local legend has it that Charlie Manning was in the bank during the robbery but the detailed article from the *Camera* dispels this myth.

Around 2:55 P.M., Miss Imogene Collett of the Cokeville Mercantile Company entered the bank with a deposit, saw what was happening, and dropped a handful of checks on the floor. One version has Hugh motioning for her bag and Charley countermanding his brother, stating they were not robbing women. Hugh then reportedly took a cigar out of Earl Haggerty's pocket and shoved it into Miss Collett's mouth, telling her that this would keep her mouth shut. She then proceeded back to her firm with the money. However, the newspapers that covered the story state that Hugh Whitney ordered Noblitt to tell her to come back later, which she did, after she had spread the alarm. When the distraught woman left the bank, the bandits quickly herded Noblitt into the vault with the others, closed and barricaded the vault, and fled through the back door.

As soon as Noblitt broke out of the vault, he telegraphed Kemmerer, Wyoming to send law officers. At 3:11 P.M., Deputy Sheriff Carl Rogers and Constable Sam W. Potter left Kemmerer by train for Cokeville.[18]

Prior to the robbery, the Whitneys staked their three horses at the mouth of a canyon at Smith's Fork, and followed a stream to a spot just north of the bank. Here they hid their rifles in a haystack before crossing a narrow field to the bank. The captives broke out of the vault and sounded the alarm just as the Whitneys were darting back across the field. Reaching the haystack, they retrieved their rifles and disappeared over the bank of a stream. Deputy Sheriff Daniel C. Hanson, Christus Marino, and Earl Haggerty were the first to pursue the robbers.

State Bank of Cokeville, Wyoming, robbed by Hugh and Charley Whitney on September 11, 1911. WYOMING STATE ARCHIVES, MUSEUMS, AND HISTORICAL DEPARTMENT, CHEYENNE

The Whitneys had nearly reached their horses when they were spotted by Marino, the only one of the pursuers who was mounted. Riding after the bandits, he was quickly discouraged by a rifle shot through his hat and took cover in a half-filled irrigation ditch. The other pursuers returned to town to form a posse. Marshal Ulysses Twiss attempted to follow the robbers, but the Whitneys' mounts hurdled fenced areas that the marshal's horse could not jump.

The delay gave the Whitneys breathing room and they fled toward the mountains on Smith's Fork Road, heading north through Homer to Collett Flat where they stole food, another horse, and a complete camp outfit from Tim Kinney's sheep camp. The two bandits then headed for Lake Alice, an area they knew well. The country was up in arms and several posses were formed in the surrounding areas. One posse started in pursuit from as far away as Montpelier, Idaho.

A somewhat disorganized posse of a half-dozen riders finally assembled in Cokeville. Shortly after leaving town, they met a rider who informed them that the Whitneys were seventeen miles from Cokeville and were riding hard. The posse admitted defeat and returned to town.

The following day, Uinta County Deputy Sheriffs Scruggs and Rich McMinn trailed the bandits with bloodhounds to Lake Alice, but lost the trail where the two fugitives had ridden their horses into a stream. The trail would remain cold for the next forty years.

On the evening of the twelfth, The Oregon Short Line Railroad offered an additional reward of $1,500 for the arrest of Hugh Whitney. Three weeks after the bank robbery, Governor Robert M. Carey of Wyoming offered a reward of five hundred dollars each for the two brothers, but it was too late to have any effect. By this time everyone involved in the search was positive the Whitneys had left Wyoming.[19]

The Whitneys became so notorious that, for a year, they were blamed for any robbery that was committed, even as far away as California. Hugh's name has also been loosely linked with Butch Cassidy and the Hole-in-the-Wall gang. This is pure fiction, for the gang's last holdup was a train robbery at Wagner, Montana on July 3, 1901, when Hugh Whitney was thirteen years old.[20]

The two brothers had ridden hard toward the east, crossed the mountains, and covered fifty-five miles before they stopped to rest the next morning. They headed for Cody, Wyoming, where they sold the horses and changed their names. Continuing eastward, they reached Wisconsin, likely the town of Wautoma, where the Whitney family had lived in the 1860s and 1870s. They obtained work in a saddlery shop under their new names. The Whitneys successfully escaped retribution from the law but not from their old nemesis, Charlie Manning.[21]

In 1952, Charley Whitney related the following story to a *Wyoming State Tribune* reporter:

> Neither the deed nor a past acquaintance left them alone. That acquaintance was Charlie Manning.
>
> The nefarious badman . . . found out where the brothers were located thru a letter Hugh had written to a mutual friend [Whitney's cousin, Clarence Stoner].
>
> Manning paid them a visit at the expense of Uinta County on the pretense he could get the boys to return and give themselves up. But his real purpose was blackmail. He tried to get the Whitney brothers, now wanted by the law, to write threatening letters to their former friends back in Wyoming for a "shakedown."
>
> Hugh and Charley stalled him off, making a promise they would return voluntarily to Cokeville that fall. Meanwhile, they changed their names again, gave Manning the slip at Minneapolis where they feared a double-cross.[22]

Manning's chicanery ultimately brought more infamy to the Whitneys. After the brothers gave him the slip in Minneapolis in the spring of 1912, Manning returned to Cokeville with a new set of plans. Later evidence indicates that Manning did induce the Whitneys to write an extortion letter to their old enemy, Pete Olsen. Even though the Whitneys were no longer around for Manning to blackmail, he had the letter. On the successive nights of June 18 and 19, 1912, he put his plan in motion, first enlisting the aid of twenty-eight-year-old Albert "Bert" Dalton, a teamster-sheepherder-drifter from Missouri who had been in Wyoming for only three months.[23]

On Wednesday, June 20, Pete Olsen found a letter on his gate ordering him to deliver $1,500 that night at the Bear River bridge or harm would come to him and his family. The letter was signed Hugh and Charley Whitney. Olsen immediately notified Cokeville City Marshal Dan Hanson, who telephoned Uinta County Sheriff John H. Ward at Evanston for assistance. Hanson suspected that Bert Dalton was connected with the scheme and deputized Will and Roy Collett to watch him, telling the Colletts that he would intercept the Whitneys that night.

Shortly before 10 P.M., Hanson mounted his horse and rode to the Bear River bridge. Approaching the site, he spotted a man in the darkness and ordered him to halt. Ignoring the command, the man fired his rifle at the marshal, striking him in the left side just below the heart. A second shot missed Hanson but killed his horse. A short time later, Sheriff Ward arrived by automobile and noticed an object by the roadside near the bridge but did not stop. Upon reaching town, Ward found out where Hanson had gone and returned to the bridge. Finding the mortally wounded marshal around 12:30 A.M., Ward rushed him to the Wyman Hotel. Hanson remained alive for several hours and, in front of four witnesses, identified Bert Dalton and not one of the Whitneys as his assailant.[24]

Wyoming State Penitentiary photograph of Albert "Bert" Dalton. WYOMING STATE ARCHIVES, MUSEUMS, AND HISTORICAL DEPARTMENT, CHEYENNE

Both Will and Roy Collett heard the shots about 10:10 P.M., but did not investigate. At 10:35 P.M., Roy Collett observed Dalton entering the Fuller saloon, where he began playing a guitar. Upon the statement of the dying lawman, Sheriff Ward arrested Bert Dalton at 4 A.M., June 21, at George Hewitt's place. Later in the day, Dalton gave this testimony, which had been cooked up between Dalton and Manning:

> My name is Bert Dalton. Wednesday night of the 19th, I saw Hugh Whitney and the night previous I saw both Hugh and Charlie Whitney back of the schoolhouse. They approached me by saying "hello there." I said hello. They walked up to me and Hugh said, "Do you know me?" Well I didn't know him at first. He had a flash light and turned it on me, and after he had turned the flash light on I recognized him as Hugh Whitney. Whitney said, "We have got a little scheme here to get some money and we will need a little help with the horses." I said, "Well I haven't got anything to do with that, I am not working any scheme to get money."
>
> Whitney said, "You won't be doing anything wrong or harming anybody; we are going to have the money anyway and if we have help we will get away alright and nobody will get hurt but if we don't have help somebody is liable to get tangled up and get hurt. We are going to get $1500 and we will divide that if you help with the horses."
>
> I was to meet them east of town at a given signal with light between 9:30 and 10:30. I was at the appointed place but received no signal and came back to my room. I had not been feeling well the last couple of days and was up against it. I figured on taking part of the money. I was arrested this morning about 4 o'clock while in bed at Hewett's.
>
> Question by Sheriff Rich [from Montpelier, Idaho]—How did you come to meet the Whitney brothers back of the schoolhouse?
>
> Answer—Just by chance.
>
> Question—Are you telling the absolute truth when you say you saw the Whitney boys?
>
> Answer—Yes, I am telling nothing but the truth. I realize that I am somewhat up against it. Hugh had on a dark shirt and an ordinary hat. Charlie had on a dark suit. I saw Hugh Whitney on the night of the 19th, back of Wyman's saloon.
>
> Question—Did you tell anyone in Cokeville that you had seen and talked with the Whitney boys?
>
> Answer—I told Charlie Manning and he replied, "Well they are getting damned bold."[25]

Beginning on July 22, Dalton's four-day preliminary hearing for murder was held in Cokeville under Justice E. J. Tuckett. He entered a plea of not guilty, but the court found probable cause and Dalton was bound over for trial in the fall term of District Court and was denied bail. Charlie Manning was one of the witnesses and claimed he was at one of the meetings between Dalton and the Whitneys. Dalton began to realize that he was a scapegoat and emphatically denied that Manning was there.

At the conclusion of the hearing, Dalton was taken to Evanston and jailed by Uinta County Deputy Sheriff Rich McMinn. While en route, Dalton changed his tune and told McMinn that the Whitneys had nothing to do with the extortion and murder, confessing that Manning planned the whole scheme and shot Hanson. Dalton explained that he was now telling the truth to get even with Manning for lying.[26]

In the frenzy caused by Hanson's murder and Dalton's confession, several reports of phantom sightings of Hugh and Charley Whitney filtered into Cokeville. On June 21, a rumor circulated that the brothers had organized a large band of outlaws that was going to swoop down on the town and rescue Dalton. Six of the best "gun-fighters" in Cokeville took charge of the jail while groups of armed men patrolled the town. On the twenty-sixth, Pete Olsen received a telegram from a friend in Kemmerer that the Whitneys had been seen near his sheep-shearing camp.

Although failing in his initial effort, Charlie Manning had no intention of giving up his scheme. He sent Olsen new demands for money, increasing the amount because of the trouble it had caused "the Whitney gang." By July 20, Olsen was in a panic and went to Cheyenne to appeal to the attorney general and the governor for protection.[27]

The inflated notoriety of the Whitneys inspired author Frank Calkins to write:

> Though not widely known outside western Wyoming and eastern Idaho, the Whitney Brothers had deservedly bad reputations. It was said one of them [Hugh] could ride his horse at a good clip down the main street of a small town and hit every telegraph pole he passed with a slug from his revolver. One of my neighbors still vividly remembers the whipping he got when he forgot his parents' instructions and left the safety of his back-country cabin on a day when the Whitneys were supposed to be riding through.[28]

On August 8, 1912, Dalton again made news when he escaped from jail at Evanston with two other inmates, Ernest Crutcher and Walter Van Fossen. Deputy Sheriff Rich McMinn and Winn S. Trombley, night marshal at Evanston, immediately started in pursuit but lost Dalton's trail at Parley's Canyon. The officers doggedly continued the hunt and picked up his trail again, tracking the fugitive across the Wyoming line and halfway through Utah.

On August 14, Salt Lake County Sheriff Joseph Sharp received information that Dalton was working on a ranch five miles south of Sandy, Utah. Sharp summoned his deputy, C. L. Schettler, and F. E. Hanson, brother of the slain Cokeville marshal. At 5 P.M., the three lawmen caught the fugitive off guard. Dalton, who was pitching hay from the top of a haystack, meekly surrendered. The prisoner was taken to Salt Lake City and jailed. He was turned over to the Wyoming officers and brought back to Evanston to face trial for Hanson's murder.[29]

The trial commenced on Wednesday, September 3, 1912, in District Court at Evanston under Judge D. H. Craig. The prosecution was conducted by attorney John R. Arnold and the defense by attorney

Abraham Crawford. The extortion letter was presented as evidence and positively identified by several witnesses as being written by one of the Whitneys. On Friday, the case was argued by both sides and went to the jury at 6:15 P.M. Apparently Dalton's attorney presented a good argument. At 10 P.M., the jury returned a verdict of manslaughter.[30]

On September 14, Bert Dalton was sentenced to fifteen to twenty years' imprisonment in the Wyoming State Penitentiary, and was delivered to the prison the next day by Sheriff Ward. Dalton, Inmate No. 1829, was one of nineteen convicts who escaped from the penitentiary at 3 P.M., October 12, 1912, an event which initiated an outbreak of mutiny and killing, and the escape of nine other prisoners the next day. Dalton made his way to Big Piney, approximately sixty miles northeast of Cokeville, where he took a job cutting timber. Again, the tenacious Deputy Sheriff Rich McMinn took to the trail. It took the deputy just over two months to find his quarry.

On December 24, McMinn located Dalton in the logging camp and wired Sheriff Ward, who immediately left for Big Piney. At 2 P.M. on the twenty-sixth, the two lawmen took off for the logging camp, arriving there at seven that evening. Hearing the buggy tires crunching through the snow, Dalton slipped under the tent flap and disappeared without a coat, hat, or gloves. McMinn took off after Dalton alone and tracked him for fifteen grueling hours. He finally located the nearly frozen fugitive holed up in a mountain cabin.

Entering the cabin, McMinn was greeted by Dalton, who shook his hand and told him to come in and get warm. Dalton told the officer that he left his rifle at the camp so he would not commit murder. He stuck to his story regarding Manning, stoutly denying that he killed Hanson. McMinn seemingly accepted Dalton's story, and did not handcuff or shackle his prisoner. On December 30, Sheriff Ward returned Dalton to the penitentiary.[31]

In 1914, Dalton signed a confession, implicating only Manning in the extortion scheme and the murder of Hanson. His statements completely exonerated the Whitneys. The prison officials apparently believed Dalton's confession for, on July 21, 1915, he was paroled by Governor John B. Kendrick and was officially discharged on March 21, 1923.[32]

Two years after the murder of Daniel C. Hanson, Charlie Manning would pay the ultimate price for his crimes. Following his failure to gain any monetary return from the Olsen extortion scheme, he continued gambling around Cokeville until he was arrested and fined five hundred dollars on July 25, 1913 for "unlawfully, feloniously, open, deal, play and carry on a certain game of poker, in such case against the peace and dignity of the State of Wyoming." Manning came up with new plan, spinning his malevolent web around Albert Meadors and Clarence Stoner, a cousin of the Whitney brothers who had been laid off from his job and needed money.

Late in the evening of July 2, 1914, the three men robbed the Oregon Short Line fast mail train No. 5 near Kamela, Oregon. Finding only a small amount of money in the express car safe, Manning and Meadors went into the coach to rob the passengers, leaving Stoner to guard the crew. Deputy Sheriff George McDuffie of Heppner, Oregon was on board and quickly reacted, drawing his weapon. Spotting the deputy, Manning fired at him, striking him near the heart. McDuffie was lucky; the bullet only glanced off a deck of cards and brass pencil holder in his coat pocket. McDuffie quickly returned fire and put two slugs into the bandit's heart and one into his head. Manning was dead before he hit the floor. With his leader dead and the robbery gone sour, Meadors fled from the coach, found Stoner, and the two escaped into the darkness.

The dead bandit was first identified as Hugh Whitney because of a watch found on him inscribed with Whitney's name. On July 4, 1914, the dead robber was positively identified as Charlie Manning. It was reported that Whitney had lost the watch to Manning in a poker game. The next day, Manning's brother-in-law, Fred Stoffer, claimed the body and brought it back to Cokeville for burial. Stoner and Meadors were caught on July 4, and were tried and sentenced in September to thirteen years in the Oregon State Penitentiary. Stoner was pardoned on October 15, 1917, and was a law-abiding citizen the remainder of his life.[33]

The Pete Olsen affair was just one of many tales that circulated about the Whitneys for years to come, and they became a legend. Many believed them guilty of every crime committed in the area and dubbed them the Bear River Bandits. In September 1926, Denver Police Chief Robert F. Reed wired Sheriff H. W. Henderson in Pocatello, Idaho that Hugh Whitney had been located in the Colorado capital. It proved to be a false lead. In 1942, between Mud Lake and Dubois, Idaho, a skeleton was found with a rusted rifle beside it. Area law officers claimed it was Hugh Whitney. Even in the 1960s Hugh's name resurfaced. Utah deer hunters said a grizzled old mountain man was living in the old outlaw's refuge of Browns Park and would shoot at them if they got too close. They claimed he was Hugh Whitney. What actually happened to the two brothers was less sensational, yet more dramatic than the reports that circulated about them.[34]

After giving Manning the slip in Minneapolis, the brothers cautiously made their way to eastern Montana to start a new life. It was unlikely that they ever knew they had been implicated in the Olsen blackmail scheme.

In the fall of 1912, two young men arrived in Glasgow, Valley County, Montana. The oldest gave his name as George Walter Brown and the younger as Frank S. Taylor. The two men formed a business partnership as ranchers and stockmen. Time proved them responsible citizens, and they earned the respect of their neighbors and residents of the community. No one ever knew or suspected they were the wanted outlaws, Hugh and Charley Whitney.[35]

*Left to right: Hugh Whitney,
Charley Whitney, and their
cousin, Clarence Stoner, c. 1909.*
MARY E. STONER COLLECTION

Newspaper photo of Hugh Whitney, c. 1911.
WYOMING STATE ARCHIVES, MUSEUMS, AND
HISTORICAL DEPARTMENT, CHEYENNE

HUGH WHITNEY.
His death led to confession.

After the United States entered the First World War, Hugh Whitney enlisted as George W. Brown in the 23rd Engineers, Wagon Company No. 3, in November, 1917. He saw action in France and was mustered out June 17, 1919 at Fort D. A. Russell in Cheyenne, Wyoming.[36]

On April 13, 1918, Charley Whitney, under the alias of Frank S. Taylor, followed his brother into service, enlisting at Glasgow, Montana as a private in Company H, 363rd Infantry, 91st Division. He saw combat at Meuse-Argonne from September 26 through October 4, 1918, and Lys Scheldt Andencarde in Belgium from October 31 until Armistice Day, November 11, 1918. Charley was never wounded and was mustered out on May 19, 1919 at Fort D. A. Russell.[37]

Following the war, the two brothers resumed ranching near Glasgow and, with service money they had saved, bought additional livestock and land. Between 1934 and 1935, Hugh sold his interest in the ranch to Charley and migrated to Lake Ootsa, British Columbia, approximately one hundred miles southeast of Smithers. Still retaining the name George W. Brown, Hugh remained single and worked as a laborer in British Columbia and Saskatchewan.[38]

Through the years, Charley Whitney became involved in church activities and took an active part in community affairs. He served several years on the Glasgow school board and on the board of directors of the Glasgow State Bank. However, he felt his life was a sham. The stigma of being a wanted man hung over him like a dark cloud, but for his brother's sake he remained silent about his past.[39]

About the second week of September, 1950, Hugh Whitney suffered a heart attack and was hospitalized in the City Hospital in Saskatoon, Saskatchewan. On October 24, 1950, Hugh Whitney died of a coronary occlusion. His funeral expenses of twenty-five dollars were paid for by the city of Saskatoon and the funeral was conducted on October 27, by Reverend G. D. Wilkie at the Park Funeral Chapel. He was buried under the name George W. Brown in the Woodlawn Cemetery in Saskatoon, but no stone marks his grave. Like his brother Charley, Hugh Whitney lived an honest life after committing the bank robbery in 1911.[40]

During the same month his brother died, Charley Whitney went into business with another man, with the under sheriff financing the project. When Charley received the news in January, 1951, that his brother Hugh was dead he was heartbroken. But it was a mixed blessing, for now he was free to rectify the mistake he had made nearly forty years ago, deciding to turn himself in to the authorities and not "continue this life of shame any longer." First, he settled all his accounts, paid off the loan to the under sheriff and sold his ranch. By late fall Charley was debt free.[41]

Charley requested advice from Montana Governor John W. Bonner, disclosing his true identity and his desire to turn himself in to the Wyoming authorities. After investigation, Governor Bonner wrote

Wyoming Governor Frank A. Barrett, attesting to Whitney's exemplary life in Montana since 1912:

> I enclose herewith correspondence pertaining to a matter, which in my experience as governor, has no parallel. It reveals a story of a man, who, for four decades, has enjoyed the finest reputation as a citizen of Montana and who is respected and admired by all who know him. Throughout the nearly 40 years he has resided in Montana, however, he has lived under an assumed name. . . .
>
> Whitney has led a model life as a rancher, farmer, and stockman of eastern Montana. His entire residence in this state has never been marked by a citation for even a minor legal offense. He enjoys the trust, confidence of all persons who have known him . . . Charley Whitney is deserving of utmost consideration and clemency.[42]

On the evening of June 18, 1952, Whitney walked into Governor Barrett's office with his confession, entitled "Forty Years a Fugitive," and more than a dozen character references written by prominent Montana citizens. Shortly before noon the next day, Whitney voluntarily appeared before Judge Robert Christmas in District Court at Kemmerer and pled guilty to the charge of armed bank robbery. There were legal complications that faced the court: the 1911 bank robbery had been committed in Uinta County, but the county had divided and Cokeville was now in Lincoln County. Secondly, the State Bank of Cokeville was now defunct. So, in essence, Wyoming had a rather complex case.

For these reasons, plus the recommendations from Governors Bonner and Barrett, the numerous affidavits from the citizens of Montana, and Whitney's excellent record, Judge Christmas ordered Charley paroled on his own recognizance on the condition that he submit a written report to the court the first day of each term of court. Upon issuing the parole, Judge Christmas remarked: "I see no use or purpose in sending you to the penitentiary." Leaving the courtroom, Whitney quietly remarked: "That's a big load off my shoulders. The judge showed more fairness then I expected."[43]

Charley Whitney was true to his word. He returned to Montana where, on June 26, he went to work taking care of livestock on the Matador Ranch, thirty miles south of Malta. From here, he sent his first letter to Judge Christmas on October 23, 1952. Charley wrote that he had been working on a new design for a semi-automatic rifle for several years, and that he had finished his invention but was swindled by some patent attorneys who altered his design and took him for over three hundred dollars. Whitney called it "legalized larceny."

Over the next two years, Charley faithfully wrote to Judge Christmas. In April 1954, he went to visit cousins in Idaho and Oregon, whom he had not seen for fifty years. Whitney's last letter was written on November 4, 1954, informing Judge Christmas that he planned to leave the Matador Ranch on January 1, 1955, to visit his brother and sister in San Francisco, whom he had not seen since 1911. On Decem-

Left to right: Wyoming Governor Frank A. Barrett and Charley Whitney at Whitney's voluntary surrender on June 18, 1952. WYOMING STATE ARCHIVES, MUSEUMS, AND HISTORICAL DEPARTMENT, CHEYENNE

ber 6, 1954, Judge Christmas terminated Charley Whitney's parole and officially discharged him.[44]

Charley had never married, but in 1950 he had become engaged to a woman in New Jersey through a mail-order romance magazine. After he was officially discharged, the pair were married but it proved to be a very unhappy union and ended in divorce.[45]

Charley Whitney remained in Montana the rest of his life. In 1955, he moved to Eureka and farmed until he retired in 1966. At that point he moved to 113 Lupfer Avenue in Whitefish, Flathead County. In 1968, Charley went to live at the Oldenberg Rest Home in Whitefish.

Since 1943, when he suffered his first stroke, Charley had been in poor health and had been hospitalized several times, including three times in the Veterans Hospital at Fort Harrison. On November 8, 1968, hardening of the arteries caused him to suffer another stroke and he was taken to the Hot Springs Manor at Hot Springs, Montana. For five days Whitney was attended by Dr. H. A. Fandrich but his condition steadily deteriorated. At 7:15 A.M. on November 13, seventy-eight-year-old Charley Whitney died.

His funeral service was conducted on November 16 in the Austin Chapel in Whitefish. Reverend Dennis Hanson, pastor of the Christ Lutheran Church, officiated at the service, which was attended by several veterans of World War I. Charley was buried with full military honors in the veterans section of Whitefish Cemetery.[46]

Hugh and Charley Whitney were never bona fide outlaws. Forty years of fear, guilt, and remorse outlined in this statement by Charley in 1952 attest to that: "If we are not punished for our mistakes we certainly are punished by them and Hugh and I have paid a mighty sum for our mistakes in the form of bitter remorse—tears and regret."[47]

Tombstone of Charley Whitney in the Whitefish Cemetery. COURTESY OF AUSTIN FUNERAL HOME, WHITEFISH, MONTANA

NOTES

INTRODUCTION

1. George Brown Tindall, *America: A Narrative History* (New York, London: W. W. Norton & Company, 1988), pp. 730–731, 782–784, 876–881, 885–894; Roger Butterfield, *The American Past* (New York: Simon and Schuster, 1947), pp. 224–225, 226–227, 234–235, 244–245, 254, 258–259, 266–267.

2. Mark Dugan and John Boessenecker, *The Grey Fox: The True Story of Bill Miner, Last of the Old-Time Bandits* (Norman: University of Oklahoma Press, 1992), p. 130.

3. There are several reliable books covering the warfare between Missouri and Kansas before and during the Civil War; the following is a partial list: A. T. Andreas, *History of the State of Kansas*, 2 vols. (Chicago, 1883); Wiley Britton, *The Civil War on the Border*, 2 vols. (New York: G. P. Putnam's Sons, The Knickerbocker Press, 1899); Richard S. Brownlee, *Grey Ghosts of the Confederacy* (Baton Rouge: Louisiana State University Press, 1958); John N. Edwards, *Noted Guerrillas* (St. Louis, Mo.: H. W. Brand & Company, 1879); Thomas Goodrich, *Bloody Dawn* (Kent, Ohio: Kent State University Press, 1991); Jay Monaghan, *Civil War on the Western Border, 1854–1865* (Boston and Toronto: Little, Brown and Company, 1955); Alice Nichols, *Bleeding Kansas* (New York: Oxford University Press, 1954).

4. Darrell Garwood, *Crossroads of America* (New York: W. W. Norton & Company, Inc., 1948), pp. 46–47. The following quote provides evidence of western Missouri's significant southern population and the enmity between factions: "Missouri from the beginning was an outpost state for the south. . . . [Kansas City's] own population had remained largely southern in origin. Of its five or six thousand residents in 1860, only seventy-two voted for Abraham Lincoln; and the names of these voters were prominently posted as a blacklist on the courthouse door in Independence."

5. The following is only a fraction of the multitude of publications depicting the career of Jesse James: James William Buel, *The Border Bandits* (Chicago: Thompson and Thomas, n.d.); James D. Horan, *Desperate Men* (New York: G. P. Putnam's Sons, 1949); Robertus Love, *The Rise and Fall of Jesse James* (New York: G. P. Putnam's Sons, 1926); William A. Settle, Jr., *Jesse James Was His Name* (Columbia: University of Missouri Press, 1966).

6. Notable among the multitudes of publications depicting the life of Billy the Kid are the following: Walter Noble Burns, *The Saga of Billy the Kid* (New York: Grosset and Dunlap, 1926); Donald Cline, *Alias Billy the Kid: The Man Behind the Legend* (Santa Fe, New Mexico: Sunstone Press, 1986); Maurice G. Fulton, *History of the Lincoln County War*, ed. Robert N. Mullen (Tucson: University of Arizona Press, 1968); Pat F. Garrett, *The Authentic Life of Billy the Kid* (1882; reprint, Norman: University of Oklahoma Press, 1954); Frederick Nolan, *The Lincoln County War* (Norman: University of Oklahoma Press, 1992); C. L. Sonnichsen and William V. Morrison, *Alias Billy the Kid* (Albuquerque: University of New Mexico

Press, 1955); Robert M. Utley, *Billy the Kid, A Short and Violent Life* (Lincoln: University of Nebraska Press, 1989).

7. Pearl Baker, *Wild Bunch at Robbers Roost* (New York: Abelard-Schuman, 1971); Lula Betenson, as told to Dora Flack, *Butch Cassidy, My Brother* (Provo, Utah: Brigham Young University Press, 1975); Charles Kelley, *The Outlaw Trail* (New York: Bonanza, 1959); James D. Horan, *Desperate Men* (New York: G. P. Putnam's Sons, 1949); James D. Horan, *The Gunfighters, The Authentic Wild West* (New York: Crown, 1976); James D. Horan, *The Wild Bunch* (New York: Signet, 1958); James D. Horan and Paul Sann, *Pictorial History of the Wild West* (New York: Crown, 1954); Alan Swallow, ed., *The Wild Bunch* (Denver, Colo.: Sage Books, 1966).

8. Edward M. Kirby, *The Rise and Fall of the Sundance Kid* (Iola, Wisconsin: Western Publications, 1983); Larry Pointer, *In Search of Butch Cassidy* (Norman: University of Oklahoma Press, 1977).

9. Anne Meadows, *Digging Up Butch and Sundance* (New York: St. Martin's Press, 1994).

10. Donna B. Ernst, *Sundance, My Uncle* (College Station, Texas: Creative Publishing Company, 1992); Anne Meadows, *Digging Up Butch and Sundance*; Larry Pointer, *In Search of Butch Cassidy*.

CHAPTER I

NOTE: Much of the material cited in these notes can be credited to three major sources: (1) Douglas Macneal, "Introducing David Lewis," "Settling the Confession's Hash," "A Brief Chronology of Firm Dates in David Lewis' Life," "Uttering, Publishing and Passing—Counterfeiting in 1816," "A Suspicious Camp, an Arrest in Bedford, and a Showdown on the Sinnemahoning," *Centre County Heritage* 24, no. 2 (Fall 1987), pp. 1–44; (2) Douglas Macneal, "Amplification: David Lewis in Centre County in 1813," *Centre County Heritage* 26, no. 1 (Spring 1989), pp. 27–33; (3) Mac E. Barrick, "Who Was Lewis the Robber," *Cumberland County History* 6, no. 2 (Winter 1989), pp. 55–72. When possible the original sources will be cited from the articles above; otherwise the article will be cited. The holdings of these sources will not be cited as they can be found at the Centre Library in Bellefonte, Pennsylvania.

PART ONE:
1. James Q. Wilson, "Crime and American Culture," *The Public Interest* 70 (Winter 1983), pp. 24, 25.

2. Wilson, p. 31; George Brown Tindall, *America, A Narrative History* (New York, London: W. W. Norton & Company, 1988), pp. 517, 518; *The Wall Street Journal*, May 4, 1983.

3. Tindall, pp. 379–381, 390–391; Ray Dupont Smith, "Currency and Banking in Pennsylvania Prior to 1837" (master's thesis, Pennsylvania State College, 1934), pp. 118–148; Roger Butterfield, *The American Past* (New York: Simon and Schuster, 1947), pp. 62–63, 70; William H. Dillistin, *Bank Note Reporters and Counterfeit Detectors 1826–1866* (New York, 1949), p. 7.

4. C. D. Rishel, *The Life and Adventures of David Lewis, Robber and Counterfeiter, The Terror of the Cumberland Valley* (Newville, Cumberland County, Pa., 1890), pp. 66–67. This book contains the purported confession of David Lewis.

PART TWO:
5. John Blair Linn, *History of Centre and Clinton Counties, Pennsylvania* (Philadelphia, 1883), p. 255; Rishel, p. 34; Adelia Fink Spangler Genealogical Collection, Notebook 103–104, p. 39; *Carlisle (Pennsylvania) American Volunteer*, Sep-

tember 28, 1820; City of Philadelphia, Department of Records, Record Series 38.36, Convict Sentence Docket E (Walnut Street Prison, Philadelphia), 1815–1819. The actual year of Lewis' birth is controversial. Macneal claims 1788 is the correct year, but the confession states he was born in 1790. Since David's father reportedly died in 1790, 1788 is the most probable year of his birth. Further confirmation is contained in the Walnut Street Prison Sentence Docket: when David Lewis entered the prison on June 8, 1816, he stated his age as 28; *The Elk Horn* (Elk County, Pennsylvania Historical Society) 27, no. 2 (Summer 1991), pp. 1, 3.

6. Adelia Fink Spangler Genealogical Collection, Notebook 103–104, p. 39, and Notebook 158; Bureau of the Census, *U.S. Census, 1790, Pennsylvania*, p. 153. Jane Lewis is listed as head of household, indicating that Lewis Lewis had died; "Lonesome Grave," unpublished article furnished to author by Gladys Murray, Centre County Library, Bellefonte, Pennsylvania; *The Elk Horn* 27, no. 2 (Summer 1991), pp. 1, 3.

7. Rishel, pp. 34–39; Butterfield, p. 48; *Bedford Gazette*, April 27, 1991. Editor Ned Frear has extensively researched Lewis' actions in Bedford, Pennsylvania, and wrote a series of articles for his newspaper in 1991. Letter from Bill Lind of the National Archives, Washington, D.C., to author, January 14, 1992. A search of the court-martial cases failed to unearth Lewis' case; however, the files are not complete before 1809; *United States v Philander Noble,* Bellefonte Court of Common Pleas (April 4, 5, 6, 1813).

8. Rishel, pp. 39–41. Daniel Tompkins was reelected for a second term as governor of New York on April 23, 1810.

9. Rishel, pp. 41–57.

10. Rishel, pp. 58–59; *American Volunteer*, September 21, 1820; *United States v Philander Noble.*

11. *American Volunteer*, May 9, 1816; *United States v Philander Noble.*

12. Rishel, pp. 55–56; *United States v Philander Noble*; Tindall, p. 366.

13. *United States v Philander Noble.*

14. Rishel, pp. 59–61; Barrick, p. 58; *Bedford Gazette*, June 1, August 10, 1991.

15. *American Volunteer*, May 9, 1816.

16. Ned Frear, *Davey Lewis* (Bedford, Pa.: Published by the *Bedford Gazette*, 1976), no page numbers; *Bedford Gazette*, March 9, 23, 1991; *American Volunteer*, May 9, 1816; *Centre County Heritage* 24, no. 2 (Fall 1987), pp. 3, 29–30; William M. Hall, *Reminiscences and Sketches, Historical and Biographical* (Harrisburg, Pa.: Meyers, 1890), p. 249. According to Judge William Hall, writing many years later, David Lewis' mother was a sister of William Drenning. This is in error, as David's mother's maiden name was Dill. It is probable that Lewis' mother and Drenning's wife were sisters.

17. *Centre County Heritage* 24, no. 2 (Fall 1987), pp. 36–38.

18. Rishel, pp. 62–63; *Centre County Heritage* 24, no. 2 (Fall 1987), pp. 23–24; *Commonwealth v David Lewis,* nos. 2, 3, 4, Docket of the 4th District, Court of Oyer and Terminer, Bedford County, Pennsylvania (January and February Terms, 1816); Frear, *Davey Lewis.*

19. *American Volunteer*, January 16, 1816; *Bedford Gazette*, March 9, 1991.

20. *Centre County Heritage* 24, no. 2 (Fall 1987), pp. 39–40; *Bedford Gazette*, March 9, 16, 1991; Frear, *Davey Lewis.* (Statements and quotes in sources cited in notes 20, 21, and 22 were taken from *Commonwealth v David Lewis.*)

21. *Centre County Heritage* 24, no. 2 (Fall 1987), p. 40.

22. *Centre County Heritage* 24, no. 2 (Fall 1987), pp. 40–41; *Bedford Gazette*, March 16, 23, April 27, June 1, 1991; *American Volunteer*, January 18, May 9, 1816; Frear, *Davey Lewis.*

23. *Commonwealth v David Lewis*; *Centre County Heritage* 24, no. 2 (Fall 1987), pp. 3–5, 24, 34–35, 40–41; Hall, p. 261; Frear, "Davey Lewis."

24. *Bedford Gazette*, March 23, June 1, 1991; Rishel, p. 63; *American Volunteer*, May 9, 1816.

25. *Bedford Gazette*, March 18, 1816, June 1, 1991.

26. Barrick, p. 58; Frear, *Davey Lewis*.

27. Record Series 38.36, Convict Sentence Docket E (Walnut Street Prison, Philadelphia), 1815–1819.

28. *American Volunteer*, May 9, 1816; Record Series 38.36, Convict Sentence Docket E (Walnut Street Prison, Philadelphia), 1815–1819.

29. *Commonwealth v David Lewis;* Barrick, pp. 58–60; *American Volunteer*, July 6, 1820; Record Series 38.36, Convict Sentence Docket E (Walnut Street Prison, Philadelphia), 1815–1819; *Pennsylvania Archives*, 9th ser., vol. 7, p. 5162.

PART THREE:

30. Rishel, pp. 63–64; Barrick, p. 62; *American Volunteer*, December 30, 1819; Hall, p. 264; Frear, *Davey Lewis*.

31. *American Volunteer*, October 14, 1819; Barrick, pp. 60–61; Rishel, p. 64; Frear, *Davey Lewis*.

32. *American Volunteer*, October 14, 1819; *Oracle of Dauphin* (Harrisburg), October 23, 1819; Barrick, pp. 61–62; Frear, *Davey Lewis*; William Henry Egle, ed., *Notes and Queries, Historical and Genealogical Chiefly Relating to Interior Pennsylvania* (Harrisburg, Pa.: Harrisburg Publishing Company, 1895), vol. 1, p. 337; *Pennsylvania Archives*, 9th ser., vol. 7, p. 5295.

33. *American Volunteer*, November 11, 1819; *Harrisburg Chronicle,* November 22, 1819; Barrick, p. 62; Frear, *Davey Lewis*.

34. *American Volunteer*, December 30, 1819; Barrick, p. 62; Frear, *Davey Lewis*.

35. *Carlisle Republican*, January 18, 1820; Barrick, pp. 62–63.

36. *American Volunteer*, January 27, 1820; Barrick, p. 63.

37. *Centre County Heritage* 24, no. 2 (Fall 1987), p. 8.

38. *Carlisle Republican*, April 25, 1820.

39. Frear, *Davey Lewis*; Rishel, pp. 64–65; *Carlisle Republican*, April 25, 1820.

40. *American Volunteer*, April 27, 1820; Barrick, p. 64; Rishel, p. 65; Frear, *Davey Lewis*.

41. Barrick, p. 64; *Carlisle Republican*, May 9, 1820.

42. Barrick, pp. 65–66; *Harrisburg Chronicle,* May 8, 1820; Rishel, p. 68; Frear, *Davey Lewis*; *Pennsylvania Archives*, 9th ser., vol. 7, pp. 5313–5314; *American Volunteer*, June 1, 1820; *Carlisle Republican*, July 4, 1820.

43. Barrick, pp. 66–67; Rishel, p. 69; Frear, "Davey Lewis"; *Franklin Repository*, June 27, 1820.

44. Rishel, pp. 70–73; *Harrisburg Chronicle,* June 24, 1820; Frear, *Davey Lewis*; Barrick, p. 67; *Franklin Repository*, June 27, 1820; John Blair Linn, *History of Centre and Clinton Counties, Pennsylvania* (Philadelphia: L. H. Everts, 1883), p. 62; Egle, vol. 1, p. 337.

45. Linn, p. 61.

46. Linn, p. 61; *American Volunteer*, July 20, 1820; Barrick, p. 70.

47. "Lonesome Grave," unpublished article furnished to author by Gladys Murray, Centre County Library, Bellefonte, Pennsylvania; *The Elk Horn* 27, no. 2 (Summer 1991), pp. 1, 3; Lewis Cass Aldrich, ed., *History of Clearfield County, Pennsylvania* (Syracuse, N.Y.: D. Mason & Company, Publishers, 1887), pp. 69–70; S. L. McCracken papers, "Granny Leathers—Her Ancestry And Descendants," Cameron County Historical Society, Emporium, Pennsylvania. This paper, which contains considerable research on Jane Dill Lewis, states that she moved in 1812 from Clearfield back to near Milesburg to settle the estates of her two former husbands. She remained in this area until 1820 when she married Reese Stevens and moved to Bennett's Branch in Clearfield County (now Elk County).

48. *American Volunteer,* July 20, 1820; *Patriot* (Bellefonte), July 8, 1820; Linn, pp. 61–63; Barrick, pp. 68–69; *Centre County Heritage* 24, no. 2 (Fall 1987), pp. 42–44; Michael A. Leeson, comp., *History of the Counties of McKean, Elk, Cameron and Potter, Pennsylvania, with Biographical Selections* (Chicago: J. H. Beers & Co., Publishers, 1890), vol. 2, pp. 384–385.

49. *York Recorder,* July 26, 1820; Barrick, pp. 69–70; Linn, pp. 62–63; *American Volunteer,* July 27, September 21, 1820; S. L. McCracken papers, "Granny Leathers—Her Ancestry And Descendants." This paper states that David Lewis' father, Lewis Lewis, and his sister, Sarah Passmore, are also buried in the Milesburg Cemetery.

PART FOUR:

50. *Centre County Heritage* 24, no. 2 (Fall 1987), p. 7.

51. Hall, p. 256; Linn, p. 63.

52. Rishel, pp. 4, 63; *Centre County Heritage* 24, no. 2 (Fall 1987), p. 15.

53. *American Volunteer,* September 21, 1820.

54. *Centre County Heritage* 24, no. 2 (Fall 1987), pp. 17, 19; Linn, p. 63. The 1817 vote tallied Findlay, 66,420, Hiester, 59,415; the 1820 vote tallied Findlay, 66,308, Hiester, 67,905.

55. *American Volunteer,* January 27, 1820.

56. Mac E. Barrick, "Lewis the Robber in Life and Legend," *Pennsylvania Folklore* 17, no. 8 (1967), pp. 10–13.

57. Egle, vol. 1, p. 337.

CHAPTER II

NOTE: All North Carolina Court Records cited are in the holdings of the Division of Archives and History, North Carolina Department of Cultural Resources, Raleigh. Many of these records give little or no information as to the type of crime committed, date the crime was committed, or actual trial dates.

1. David Leroy Corbitt, *The Formation of the North Carolina Counties, 1663–1943* (Raleigh: Division of Archives and History, North Carolina Department of Cultural Resources, 1950), pp. 17, 42, 51, 149–152, 239–242.

2. Keith Blaylock file, Lees-McRae College Library, Banner Elk, North Carolina; Marrion W. Ward, "Legendary Bushwacker Keith Blaylock" (unpublished, 1987), p. 1; Waymouth T. Jordan, Jr., comp., *North Carolina Troops, 1861–1865: A Roster,* vol. 7, *Infantry, 22nd–26th Regiments* (Raleigh, N.C.: Division of Archives and History, 1979), p. 535; Gravestone of Keith Blaylock in the Montezuma Cemetery, Montezuma, North Carolina; Bureau of the Census, *U.S. Census, 1850, Caldwell County, North Carolina,* family no. 87, p. 9. The census shows Keith born in Yancey County; *Record of Funeral,* Columbus Filmore Blalock [*sic*], October 6, 1925, Bend, Deschutes, Oregon, as compiled by F. J. Feineman, of St. Louis, Missouri, in the year 1928. This funeral record of Keith's son Columbus "Lum" Blaylock states that Keith was born in Burnsville, Yancey County, North Carolina.

3. Records of the Blaylock Family Association, Colleen Blaylock Green, Ripley, Oklahoma; John Preston Arthur, *A History of Watauga County, North Carolina* (Richmond, Va.: Everett Waddy Co., 1915), p. 160; Interview on July 18, 1990, with Mabel Blaylock Smith of Pineola, North Carolina, granddaughter of Keith Blaylock; Bureau of the Census, *U.S. Census, 1850, Yancey County, North Carolina,* family no. 158 (Alfred Keith); *1850 Yancey County, North Carolina Mortality Schedule,* Emaline R. Keith; Tombstone of Emaline R. Keith in the Garland Cemetery near Forbes, Mitchell County, North Carolina; Articles from newspapers, 1840–1900: *Highland Messenger,* February 25, 1847, *Asheville News,* November 3,

1859, furnished to author by Yancey County historian Paul Kardulis of Burnsville, North Carolina.

4. Bureau of the Census, *U.S. Census, 1850, Caldwell County, North Carolina,* family no. 87, p. 9; Coffey Family Records, furnished to author by Margaret Farley of Blowing Rock, North Carolina; Interview on March 8, 1995, with Jack Williams of Johnson City, Tennessee, great-grandson of Austin Coffey; Interview on March 8, 1995, with Sally Collins of Blowing Rock, North Carolina, great-granddaughter of Austin Coffey.

5. Caldwell County, North Carolina Deed Book 1, p. 396, Caldwell County, North Carolina Register of Deeds Office, Lenoir.

6. John Preston Arthur, *Western North Carolina: A History* (Raleigh, N.C.: Edwards and Broughton Printing Company, 1914), p. 333; *The Heritage of the Toe River Valley* (Charlotte, N.C.: Delmar Publishing Company, 1994), vol. 1, article no. 180; *U.S. Census, 1850, Caldwell County, North Carolina,* dwelling no. 769.

7. Caldwell County, North Carolina Deed Book 17, p. 351; Caldwell County, North Carolina Deed Book 18, p. 334; Bureau of the Census, *U.S. Census, 1860, Watauga County, North Carolina,* family no. 581.

8. Caldwell County, North Carolina Deed Book 17, p. 350.

9. *War of the Rebellion: A Compilation of the Official Records of the Union and Confederate Armies,* series 3, vol. 5 (Washington: Government Printing Office, 1893), p. 693; George Brown Tindall, *America: A Narrative History* (New York, London: W. W. Norton & Company, 1988), pp. 656–657; William R. Trotter, *Bushwhackers: The Civil War in North Carolina,* vol. 2, *The Mountains* (Greensboro, N.C.: Signal Research, Inc., 1988), pp. 39–41.

10. Jordan, *North Carolina Troops,* vol. 7, p. 535.

11. Walter Clark, ed., *Histories of the Several Regiments and Battalions from North Carolina in the Great War 1861–'65* (Goldsboro, N.C.: Nash Brothers, 1901), vol. 2, p. 330.

12. Samuel A'Court Ashe, *History of North Carolina,* vol. 2, *From 1783 to 1925* (Raleigh, N.C.: Edwards and Broughton Printing Company, 1925), p. 693; Arthur, *Western North Carolina: A History,* p. 333; *The Confederate Veteran* 6, no. 6 (June 1898), p. 263; Rupert Gillett, "Old Timers Love to Tell of Watauga Bushwhacking Hero," *Charlotte Observer,* September 18, 1927 (held by Belk Library, Appalachian State University, Boone, North Carolina); Clark, p. 330.

13. Clark, pp. 330–331; Jordan, *North Carolina Troops,* vol. 7, p. 535; Gillett; John W. Moore, *Roster of North Carolina Troops in the War Between the States* (Raleigh, N.C.: Ashe and Gatling, 1882), p. 386.

14. Arthur, *A History of Watauga County,* p. 161.

15. *Record of Funeral,* Columbus Filmore Blalock [*sic*], October 6, 1925. He died in Bend, Oregon on that date.

16. Gillett; Ward, p. 2; Arthur, *A History of Watauga County,* pp. 162–163.

17. National Archives, Adjutant Generals Office, RG 15, War of the Rebellion Pension Certificate no. 58976, William Blalock; National Archives, Military Records Branch, RG 94, Compiled Military Service Records (C.M.S.R.), William Blaylock, Company D, 10th Regiment, Michigan Cavalry; Bureau of the Census, *U.S. Census, 1890, Mitchell County, North Carolina,* Linville Township, Special Schedule, Surviving Soldiers, Sailors, and Marines, and Widows, Etc., p. 1; Arthur, *A History of Watauga County,* pp. 161, 163.

18. George W. Kirk file, Lees-McRae College Library; National Archives, Military Records Branch, RG 94, C.M.S.R., George W. Kirk, Company I, 4th Regiment, Tennessee Infantry and Company A, 3rd North Carolina Mounted Infantry; National Archives, Adjutant Generals Office, RG 15, War of the Rebellion Pension Certificate no. 929.318, George W. Kirk; Manley Wade Wellman, *Kingdom of Madison* (Chapel Hill: University of North Carolina Press, 1973), p. 86.

19. George W. Kirk File, Lees-McRae College Library; Joe Patton, "Kirk's Raid," *The Wake Forest Student*, March 25, 1955; Arthur, *A History of Watauga County*, pp. 164–165.

20. Arthur, *A History of Watauga County*, pp. 165–166; Keith Blaylock File, Lees-McRae College.

21. Adjutant Generals Office, RG 15, War of the Rebellion Pension Certificate no. 58976, William Blalock; Keith Blaylock File, Statement of Blaine Coffey, n.d., Lees-McRae College Library; Arthur, *A History of Watauga County*, p. 161.

22. Arthur, *A History of Watauga County*, pp. 161–162, 165–166, 169; *State v William Blaylock, Murder,* Caldwell County, North Carolina Minute Docket, Superior Court 1867–1868, C.R. 017.311.2 (Spring Term 1867), pp. 7, 8.

23. George W. Kirk file, Lees-McRae College Library; National Archives, Military Records Branch, RG 94, C.M.S.R., George W. Kirk, Company A, 3rd North Carolina Mounted Infantry; Adjutant Generals Office, RG 15, War of the Rebellion Pension Certificate no. 929.318, George W. Kirk; Wellman, p. 87; Phillip Shaw Paludan, *Victims, A True Story of the Civil War* (Knoxville: University of Tennessee Press, 1981), p. 102.

24. Adjutant Generals Office, RG 15, War of the Rebellion Pension Certificate no. 176.751, Nancy Franklin; U.S. House, Nancy Franklin (H.Rpt.49-1793) (Washington: Government Printing Office, 1886) (Y1.1/8:49-1793); Bureau of the Census, *U.S. Census, 1860, Madison County, North Carolina,* family no. 784; William R. Trotter, pp. 135–136; Paludan, p. 22; Wellman, pp. 88–89. Wellman's book is an undocumented history of Madison County, North Carolina, while Paludan's *Victims* is an excellent history of a brutal Civil War killing in which the Franklin incident is a side issue; Paludan did enough research, however, to report that there was evidence that Nancy Franklin was not a Confederate sympathizer. Trotter's book, which is supposed to be an end-noted, reliable history of the Civil War, is disappointing. Not only is the Franklin story inaccurate but another chapter devoted to Keith and Malinda Blaylock is erroneous. No primary research is noted, and the entire book is based on secondary sources.

25. *State v William Blaylock, William Estes, Joseph White, et. al., Affray,* Caldwell County, North Carolina Minute Docket, Superior Court 1843–1866, C.R. 017.311.1 (Fall Term 1866), pp. 5, 6, 7.

26. Arthur, *A History of Watauga County,* p. 167.

27. Ward, pp. 3,4; *State v Wm. Blaylock, Malinda Blaylock, J. D. English, Forcible Trespass,* Mitchell County, North Carolina Minutes, Superior Court, 1861–1876, C.066.30002 (Fall Term 1868), p. 97.

28. *State v William Blaylock, William Estes, Joseph White, et. al., Affray,* pp. 5–7; Ward, pp. 3,4; Arthur, *A History of Watauga County,* p. 166.

29. Gillett.

30. Arthur, *A History of Watauga County,* pp. 167, 168; *State v William Blaylock, Milton Webb, Taylor Green, Sampson Calloway,* Caldwell County, North Carolina Minute Docket, Superior Court 1867–1868, C.R. 017.311.2 (Fall Term 1867), p. 3.

31. Gillett; Ward, pp. 5, 6; Arthur, *A History of Watauga County,* pp. 166, 167; Keith Blaylock file, Lees-McRae College Library.

32. George W. Kirk file, Lees-McRae College Library; *State v William Blaylock, William Estes, Joseph White, et. al., Affray,* pp. 5, 6, 7; Arthur, *A History of Watauga County,* pp. 177–179.

33. *State v William Blaylock, William Estes, David Moore, J. R. Pritchard, Forcible Trespass,* Caldwell County, North Carolina Minute Docket, Superior Court 1843–1866, C.R. 017.311.1 (Fall Term 1866), p. 4.

34. *The Correspondence of Jonathan Worth,* ed. by J. G. deRoulhac Hamilton (Raleigh: Edwards and Broughton, 1909), vol. 2, pp. 726–727.

35. Adjutant Generals Office, RG 15, War of the Rebellion Pension Certificate no. 58976, William Blalock; C.M.S.R., William Blaylock, Company D, 10th Regiment, Michigan Cavalry.

36. Arthur, *A History of Watauga County*, pp. 184–185; Gillett; Letter: Finley Patterson Moore to J. M. Bernhardt, September 23, 1927, Keith Blaylock file, Lees–McRae College Library; *State v William Blaylock, Murder,* Caldwell County, North Carolina Minute Docket, Superior Court 1867–1868, C.R. 017.311.2, (Spring Term 1867), pp. 8, 9.

37. *The Correspondence of Jonathan Worth*, vol. 2, p. 726.

38. *State v William Blaylock, Murder,* pp. 7, 8.

39. Caldwell County Estate Records, C.R. 017.508.8, Division of Archives and History, North Carolina Department of Cultural Resources, Raleigh.

40. *State v William Blaylock,* Caldwell County, North Carolina Minute Docket, Superior Court 1843–1866, C.R. 017.311.1 (Fall Term 1866), p. 3.

41. *State v William Blaylock, William Estes, David Moore, J. R. Pritchard, Forcible Trespass,* p. 4.

42. *State v William Blaylock, William Estes, Joseph White, et. al., Affray,* pp. 5–7.

43. *State v William Blaylock, William Estes, Lampton Estes, Jr., Assault and Battery,* Caldwell County, North Carolina Minute Docket, Superior Court 1867–1868, C.R. 017.311.2 (Spring Term 1867), p. 3.

44. *State v William Blaylock, Forcible Trespass,* Caldwell County, North Carolina Minute Docket, Superior Court 1867–1868, C.R. 017.311.2 (Spring Term 1867), p. 3.

45. *State v William Blaylock, William Estes, David Moore, J. R. Pritchard, Assault and Battery,* Caldwell County, North Carolina Minute Docket, Superior Court 1867–1868, C.R. 017.311.2 (Spring Term 1867), p. 6.

46. *State v William Blaylock, Forcible Trespass,* p. 10.

47. *State v William Blaylock, William Estes, Lampton Estes, Jr., Forcible Trespass,* Caldwell County, North Carolina Minute Docket, Superior Court 1867–1868, C.R. 017.311.2 (Spring Term 1867), p. 10.

48. *State v William Blaylock, William Estes, David Moore, J. R. Pritchard, Assault and Battery,* pp. 11 and 13.

49. *State v William Blaylock, Milton Webb, Taylor Green, Sampson Calloway,* Caldwell County, North Carolina Minute Docket, Superior Court 1867–1868, C.R. 017.311.2 (Fall Term, 1867), p. 3.

50. *State v William Blaylock, Assault and Battery,* Caldwell County, North Carolina Minute Docket, Superior Court 1867–1868, C.R. 017.311.2 (Fall Term 1867), p. 4.

51. *State v William Blaylock, Murder: Executive Clemency,* Caldwell County, North Carolina Minute Docket, Superior Court 1867–1868, C.R. 017.311.2 (Fall Term 1867), p. 7.

52. *State v William Blaylock, J. R. Pritchard, Forcible Trespass,* Caldwell County, North Carolina Minute Docket, Superior Court 1867–1868, C.R. 017.311.2 (Spring Term 1868), p. 2.

53. *State v Wm. Blaylock, Malinda Blaylock, J. D. English, Forcible Trespass,* Mitchell County, North Carolina Minutes, Superior Court, 1861–1876, C.066.30002 (Fall Term 1868), p. 97.

54. *The Heritage of the Toe River Valley*, vol. 1 (1994), article no. 180; 1867 Mitchell County Tax List, Cranberry and Linville Districts, p. 100, Division of Archives and History, North Carolina Department of Cultural Resources, Raleigh; *U.S. Census, 1870, Mitchell County, North Carolina,* p. 8; Avery County Historical Society, Newland, North Carolina, *Avery County Heritage*, vol. 4, *Historical Sites* (1986), p. 106. Jack Blaylock went to the State of Washington after 1903 and nothing more is known of him.

55. *The Heritage of the Toe River Valley*, article no. 180. Sam Blaylock died in Elizabethton, Tennessee, on October 31, 1953, and was buried in Newland, North Carolina; *Avery Journal* (Newland, North Carolina), November 1, 1953 (held by the Belk Library, Appalachian State University, Boone, North Carolina); *U.S. Census, 1890, Mitchell County, North Carolina*, dwelling no. 91, p. 67.

56. National Archives, Records of the Department of Treasury, RG 56, Register of Claim Cases Heard By the Commissioners, 1871–1880 (Entry 331), vol. 19, claim nos. 9578 and 9579.

57. Adjutant Generals Office, RG 15, War of the Rebellion Pension Certificate no. 58976, William Blalock; *The Mountain Voice* (Bakersville, North Carolina), November 5, 1880 (held by the Division of Archives and History, North Carolina Department of Cultural Resources, Raleigh); Clark, vol. 2, p. 331; Ward, p. 8; Interview with Mabel Blaylock Smith (granddaughter of Keith Blaylock), July 18, 1990; Interview with Avery County historian John Hayes, of Montezuma, North Carolina, on April 12, 1995.

58. *State v Wm. Blaylock,* Mitchell County, North Carolina Minutes, Superior Court, 1861–1876, C.066.30002 (Fall Term 1874), pp. 389, 410.

59. *State v. Columbus Blaylock, et al.,* Mitchell County, North Carolina Minutes, Superior Court, 1876–1884, C.066.30003 (Spring Term 1881), p. 31; (Fall Term 1881), p. 91.

60. Grantee Index to Real Estate Conveyances, Mitchell County, North Carolina, pp. 112–114 and Grantor Index to Real Estate Conveyances, Mitchell County, North Carolina, pp. 123–125; Mitchell County, North Carolina Deed Book 28, p. 83–84, Mitchell County, North Carolina Register of Deeds Office, Bakersville.

61. *Avery County Heritage*, vol. 4, *Historical Sites,* pp. 104–108; William S. Powell, *The North Carolina Gazeteer* (Chapel Hill: University of North Carolina Press, 1968), p. 331.

62. Interview with Mabel Blaylock Smith (granddaughter of Keith Blaylock), July 18, 1990.

63. *Hickory Times-Mercury*, March 11, 1903 (held by the Division of Archives and History, North Carolina Department of Cultural Resources, Raleigh); Gravestone of Malinda Blaylock in the Montezuma Cemetery, Montezuma, North Carolina.

64. Certificate of Death, Martha Jane Blaylock, Avery County Death Records, vol. 34, p. 500, Avery County Register of Deeds Office, Newland, North Carolina. This record shows Martha Blaylock was born December 15, 1878.

65. Certificate of Death, Aaron Paul Blaylock, Avery County Death Records, vol. 41, p. 8. Paul's death record (died April 9, 1982) reports his date of birth and that his father was Keith Blaylock; *Avery Journal,* April 15, 1982.

66. Burke County Marriage Book 8, p. 370, Burke County Register of Deeds, Morganton, North Carolina.

67. *Avery Journal,* February 27, 1964. Martha Blaylock's obituary reports she was survived by two sons, E. J. and Paul; Certificate of Death, Martha Jane Blaylock. Martha died of pneumonia at age 85 on February 22, 1964 and was buried in Boone's Fork Cemetery near Blowing Rock; *U.S. Census, 1920, Avery County, North Carolina*, Linville Township, dwelling no. 10, p. 225. The census lists Martha J. Holifield [*sic*], age 41, son Ed. J. Holifield, age 19, and fourteen-year-old son Aaron P. Blaylock as Holifield.

68. The death date of Mary Blaylock Coffey is taken from her gravestone in the White Springs Cemetery in Coffey's Gap, North Carolina.

69. *The Lenoir (North Carolina) Weekly News,* May 12, 1905; Inverview with John Hayes, April 12, 1995; Certificate of Death, John Bunyon Ledford, Avery County, North Carolina Death Records, book 19, p. 100.

70. Interview with John Hayes, April 12, 1995; Mitchell County, North Carolina Minutes, Superior Court, 1892–1896, 1902–1906, C.066.30006 (May Term 1905), pp. 342, 344, 345; *The Lenoir (North Carolina) Weekly News*, May 26, June 9, 1905; Certificate of Death, John Bunyon Ledford, Avery County, North Carolina Death Records, book 19, p. 100.

71. Ward, pp. 9–10.

72. Gillett.

73. Interview with Mabel Blaylock Smith (granddaughter of Keith Blaylock), July 18, 1990; *Morganton Herald*, June 19, 1913.

74. Keith Blaylock file, Lees-McRae College Library; Ward, pp. 9–10; Interview with John Hayes, April 12, 1995; Interview with Mabel Blaylock Smith (granddaughter of Keith Blaylock), July 18, 1990; Interview with Retired Judge J. Ray Braswell of Newland, North Carolina on February 1, 1991; Adjutant Generals Office, RG 15, War of the Rebellion Pension Certificate no. 58976, William Blalock. A declaration from Martha Blaylock in the pension file states the date of Keith's death was August 11, 1913.

CHAPTER III

NOTE: A portion of the material in this chapter was previously published in slightly different form in the author's biography of Ham White, *Knight of the Road* (Athens, Ohio: University of Ohio Press/Swallow Press, 1990).

1. "The Ancestors and Descendants of Hamilton White and His Wife Tabitha Hutchings Who Came to Bastrop County, Texas in 1836," furnished to author by Laura G. Cunningham of Austin, Texas, great-niece of Ham White; "Family Recollections—Hamilton White," furnished to author by Laura G. Cunningham.

2. "The Ancestors and Descendants of Hamilton White and His Wife Tabitha Hutchings"; Kenneth Kesselus, *Bastrop County Before Statehood* (Austin, Texas: Jenkins Publishing Company, 1986), pp. 151–178, 181, 216, 242, 250, 296.

3. "The Ancestors and Descendants of Hamilton White and His Wife Tabitha Hutchings"; Bastrop County Deed Indexes, listed under the names Hamilton, Ham, H., Tabitha W., and T. W. White. Bastrop County Clerk's Office, Bastrop, Texas; Bureau of the Census, *U.S. Census, 1860, Bastrop County, Texas,* p. 86 (consulted in the Texas State Archives, Austin); *1860 Bastrop County, Texas Agricultural Census,* schedule 4, Ham White, no. 15, Texas State Archives, Austin. The *Agricultural Census* listed the following livestock as belonging to White: 10 horses; 110 cattle; 4 oxen; 30 hogs; valued at $1,600.

4. "The Ancestors and Descendants of Hamilton White and His Wife Tabitha Hutchings"; Bureau of the Census, *U.S. Census, 1850, Bastrop County, Texas,* p. 183 and *U.S. Census, 1860, Bastrop County, Texas,* p. 86, Texas State Archives, Austin.

5. Walter Prescott Webb, ed., *The Handbook of Texas* (Austin, Texas: Texas State Historical Commission, 1952), vol. 1, pp. 121–122; vol. 2, p. 83.

6. Diary of Mary Ann McDowell, entry for Saturday, 15 June, 1867, Texas State Archives, Austin; Agent Bryon Porter to Lieut. J. T. Kirkman, Bureau of R. F. and A. L., Galveston, Texas, July 5, 1867, Freedman's Bureau Records, Bastrop County, Texas, Texas State Archives, Austin; *The Handbook of Texas,* vol. 1, p. 644.

7. *True Issue* (LaGrange, Texas), June 11, 1859 (held by Texas State Archives, Austin).

8. Bastrop County District Court Minutes (BCDCM), Book C, pp. 614, 616, 632; Book D, p. 42, Bastrop County Clerk's Office, Bastrop, Texas.

9. The State of Texas Federal Population Schedules, *Seventh Census of the United States, 1860,* vol. 4, p. 1873; "Family Recollections—Hamilton White";

National Archives, RG 204, Application for Clemency, Ham White, Record H, File H–46 (1879).

10. BCDCM, Book C, p. 653.

11. BCDCM, Book D, pp. 272, 334, 363.

12. *Houston Daily Telegraph,* June 21, 1867 (held by the Eugene C. Barker Texas History Center, University of Texas, Austin).

13. Freedman's Bureau Records, Bastrop County, Texas, July 5, 1867.

14. BCDCM, Book D, p. 384.

15. *The Handbook of Texas,* vol. 1, pp. 370, 469, 470.

16. RG 204, Application for Clemency, Ham White. Included in these records is an article titled "Stand and Deliver" from the *Wheeling (West Virginia) Evening Standard,* June 2, 1877, a four-column interview and autobiography of Ham White.

17. *Austin Daily Democratic Statesman,* March 29, 1877 (held by the Eugene C. Barker Texas History Center).

18. RG 204, Application for Clemency, Ham White.

19. *Bastrop Advertiser,* October 9, 1875 (Eugene C. Barker Texas History Center); *Austin Daily Democratic Statesman,* October 9, 1875.

20. *Austin Daily Democratic Statesman,* March 31, 1877.

21. Executive Record Book, Governor Richard Coke, Records of the Secretary of State, Texas, p. 91, Texas State Archives, Austin. The *Bastrop Advertiser* ran the reward weekly from October 16 until November 13, 1875.

CHAPTER IV

1. The list of California stage robberies was furnished to the author by Robert Olson of Pico Rivera, California: 1) Cloverdale, November 4, 1870; 2) Cloverdale, February 16, 1871; 3) Cloverdale, July 12, 1871; 4) Cloverdale, August 10, 1871; 5) Healdsburg, August 16, 1871; 6) Sebastopol, September 12, 1871; 7) Cloverdale, October 10, 1871.

2. John Boessenecker, *Badge and Buckshot* (Norman: University of Oklahoma Press, 1988), pp. 46–53; *San Francisco Examiner,* December 29, 1889 (held by California State Library, Sacramento); *Russian River Flag* (Healdsburg, California), January 4, 1872 (held by California State Library, Sacramento). "Rattling Jack" Brown was not related to Lodi and Johnny Brown; however, his brother Tom Brown became one of California's most notorious stage robbers in the late 1870s.

3. *Russian River Flag,* January 4, 1872; San Quentin Prison Register, inmate nos. 5096, Henry [*sic*] B. Mitchell; 7444, Matt Lynch Bully; 8306, Matt Lynch Bully, California State Archives, Sacramento; Erwin G. Gudde, *Place Names* (Berkeley: University of California Press, 1969), p. 283; A. L. Kroeber, *Handbook of the Indians of California* (New York: Dover Publications, 1976), pp. 222–235.

4. *State of California v Harvey Bell Mitchell, Robbery,* Sonoma County Court Case 627, California State Archives, Sacramento; *Russian River Flag,* January 4, 1872.

5. *Russian River Flag,* December 28, 1871.

6. *San Francisco Examiner,* December 29, 1889.

7. *Russian River Flag,* December 28, 1871; January 4, 1872.

8. *San Francisco Examiner,* December 29, 1889.

9. *Daily Territorial Enterprise* (Virginia City, Nevada), January 3, 1872 (held by Nevada State Library, Carson City).

10. *Russian River Flag,* January 4, 1872; *Daily Territorial Enterprise,* January 3, 1872.

11. *San Francisco Alta California,* January 12, 1872 (held by California State Library, Sacramento); *Russian River Flag,* January 18, 1872; *State of California v Harvey Bell Mitchell, Robbery,* Sonoma County Court Case 627; San Quentin Prison Register, inmate number 5096, Henry [*sic*] B. Mitchell.

12. San Quentin Prison Register, inmate no. 5096, Henry [*sic*] B. Mitchell; Mark Dugan and John Boessenecker, *The Grey Fox: The True Story of Bill Miner, Last of the Old-Time Bandits* (Norman: University of Oklahoma Press, 1992), pp. 21–22.

13. San Quentin Prison Register, inmate number 5096, Henry [*sic*] B. Mitchell; *Daily Territorial Enterprise,* January 3, 1872.

14. San Quentin Punishment Book, entry February 29, 1872, California State Archives, Sacramento; *Daily Territorial Enterprise,* October 27, 1872.

15. San Quentin Prison Register, inmate no. 5096, Henry [*sic*] B. Mitchell; *Gold Hill (Nevada) Evening News,* December 3, 1872 (held by Nevada State Library, Carson City).

16. Register of Actions and Fee Book, Mendocino County Court, Year 1877, p. 100. Mendocino County Clerks Office, Ukiah, California; *The People of California v Mat* [sic] *Lynch Bully, Burglary in the 2nd Degree,* Mendocino County Court Case 1237, California State Archives, Sacramento; San Quentin Prison Register, inmate no. 7444, Matt Lynch Bully.

17. Register of Actions and Fee Book, Mendocino County Court, Year 1878, p. 156; *The People of California v Mat* [sic] *Lynch Bully, Burglary in the 1st Degree,* Mendocino County Court Case 1554.

18. San Quentin Prison Register, inmate no. 8306, Matt Lynch Bully; San Quentin Log Book, entry July 27, 1878. California State Archives, Sacramento; James B. Hume and Jno. N. Thacker, *Wells Fargo & Co's. Robbers Record* (San Francisco, California: H. S. Crocker & Co., 1884), p. 55.

CHAPTER V

1. General Register of Prisons at Detroit House of Corrections, October 1, 1877–December 26, 1883, Samuel S. Hartman, p. 71, Burton Historical Collections, Detroit Public Library, Detroit, Michigan; *Black Hills Daily Times,* October 8, 1878 (held by Hearst Free Library, Lead, South Dakota); Bureau of the Census, *U.S. Census, 1850, Davis County, Iowa,* p. 294; *U.S. Census, 1860, Atchison County, Kansas,* p. 53.

2. *U.S. Census, 1850, Davis County, Iowa,* p. 294; *U.S. Census, 1860, Atchison County, Kansas,* p. 53; General Register of Prisons at Detroit House of Corrections, October 1, 1877–December 26, 1883, Samuel S. Hartman, p. 71.

3. Mercer County, Illinois Deed Book A, transaction no. 4057, Mercer County Register of Deeds Office, Aledo, Illinois.

4. Bureau of the Census, *U.S. Census, 1850, Mercer County, Illinois,* family dwelling no. 701; *The History of the Reorganized Church of Jesus Christ of Latter Day Saints,* vol. 2, *1836–1844* (Independence, Missouri: Herald House, 1967), pp. 255–263; Harold Schindler, *Orrin Porter Rockwell, Man of God, Son of Thunder,* 2d ed. (Salt Lake City: University of Utah Press, 1983), pp. 31, 44, 52; *History of Mercer and Henderson Counties* (Chicago: H. H. Hill & Company, 1882), p. 220.

5. Bureau of the Census, *U.S. Census, 1860, Atchison County, Kansas,* p. 53; *History of Mercer and Henderson Counties,* p. 503; Mercer County, Illinois Deed Book A, transaction no. 5170.

6. National Archives, Military Records Branch, RG 94, Compiled Military Service Records (C.M.S.R.), Samuel Hartman, Company I, 7th Cavalry, Kansas Volunteers. Sam Hartman's name was never entered on the muster roll; Simeon

M. Fox, "The Story of the Seventh Kansas," *Kansas State Historical Society Transactions* 8 (1903–1904), pp. 25–26; Kansas State Militia Card Index, S. Hartman, vol. 1, p. 82, Kansas State Historical Society, Topeka.

7. *Atchison Freedom's Champion,* April 26, 1862 (held by Kansas University Library, Lawrence); Sheffield Ingalls, *History of Atchison County* (Standard Publishing Company, 1916), pp. 142–143.

8. Kansas State Militia Card Index, S. Hartman, vol. 1, p. 82.

9. *Black Hills Daily Times,* October 8, 1878.

10. Glenn Chesney Quiett, *Pay Dirt* (Lincoln, Nebraska: Johnsen Publishing Company, 1971), pp. 236–254; Watson Parker, *Gold in the Black Hills* (Norman: University of Oklahoma Press, 1966), pp. 10–38.

11. *Black Hills Daily Times,* October 8, 1878; *Omaha Daily Bee,* October 6, 1877 (held by Nebraska State Historical Society, Lincoln).

12. For the complete history of the life and death of Wild Bill Hickok, see Joseph G. Rosa, *They Called Him Wild Bill* (Norman: University of Oklahoma Press, 1969).

13. *Black Hills Weekly Times,* August 26, 1876 (Hearst Free Library, Lead, South Dakota); Kenneth C. Keller, *Seth Bullock, Frontier Marshal* (Aberdeen, South Dakota: North Plains Press, 1972), pp. 61–63.

14. Harry (Sam) Young, *Hard Knocks* (Portland, Oregon: Wells & Company, 1915), p. 198.

15. *Omaha Daily Bee,* September 24, October 16, and November 19, 1877. A search of every issue of the *Sidney Telegraph* from early fall 1876 through late spring 1877 failed to reveal the details of the Sidney shoot-out; however, this newspaper was not inclined to report the seamy side of Sidney's development.

16. *Black Hills Daily Times,* April 19 and June 13, 1877.

17. *Black Hills Daily Times,* August 20, September 27, 29, 1877; Doug Engebretson, *Empty Saddles, Forgotten Names* (Aberdeen, South Dakota: North Plains Press, 1982), pp. 53–75; Agnes Wright Spring, *The Cheyenne and Black Hills Stage and Express Routes* (Glendale, California: Arthur H. Clark Company, 1949), pp. 210–212, 220–240; Jesse Brown and A. M. Williard, *The Black Hills Trails* (Rapid City, South Dakota: Rapid City Journal Company, 1924), pp. 258–261; *Description and History of Convicts in United States Penitentiary, at Laramie City, Wyoming Territory,* no. 57—James Wall, no. 58—Duncan Blackburn, no. 87—Clark Pelton alias William Webster (held by Wyoming State Archives, Museums, and Historical Department, Cheyenne).

18. *Omaha Daily Bee,* September 24, 1877; *Black Hills Daily Times,* October 8, 1878; Brown and Williard, pp. 258–259; Engebretson, pp. 96–97.

19. *Omaha Daily Bee,* September 24, 1877.

20. *Omaha Daily Bee,* October 3, 6, 1877; *Cheyenne Daily Leader,* October 9, 1877. Wyoming State Archives, Museums, and Historical Department, Cheyenne; *Black Hills Weekly Times,* January 20, 1878; Spring, pp. 220–221.

21. *Cheyenne Daily Leader,* October 4, 1877, July 3, 1879; *Black Hills Daily Times,* January 20, 1878, July 3, 1879; Engebretson, p. 97.

22. *Omaha Daily Bee,* November 19, 1877; Spring, p. 221; *The State v William Webster,* Laramie County District Court Criminal Case File no. 2–14, Wyoming State Archives, Museums, and Historical Department, Cheyenne; *Description and History of Convicts in United States Penitentiary, at Laramie City, Wyoming Territory,* no. 87—Clark Pelton alias William Webster; Elnora L. Frye, *Atlas of Wyoming Outlaws at the Territorial Penitentiary* (Laramie, Wy.: Jelm Mountain Publications, 1990), pp. 75–76; Murray L. Carroll, "Clark Pelton, The Stage-Robbing Kid," *True West,* August 1990, pp. 16–21.

23. *Omaha Daily Bee,* October 16, November 28, 1877.

24. National Archives, Records of the District Court for the District of

North Dakota, 1861–1962, Unit 6NCN; *Omaha Daily Bee,* January 5, 1878; *Omaha Daily Herald,* January 6, 1878 (held by Nebraska State Historical Society, Lincoln); *Black Hills Daily Times,* January 11, 1878; *Black Hills Weekly Times,* January 20, 1878; *Yankton Press and Dakotaian,* January 10, 1878 (held by South Dakota Historical Society, Pierre).

25. *Black Hills Daily Times,* October 3, 5, 7, 8, 9, 10, 11, 14, 16, 1878; *Black Hills Journal,* October 19, 1878 (South Dakota Historical Society, Pierre).

26. *Omaha Daily Bee,* October 24, 1878.

27. National Archives, RG 204, Records of the Pardon Attorney, Case File H–739, Samuel Hartman.

28. General Register of Prisons at Detroit House of Corrections, October 1, 1877–December 26, 1883, p. 71; RG 204, Records of the Pardon Attorney, Case File H–739, Samuel Hartman.

29. RG 204, Records of the Pardon Attorney, Case File H–739, Samuel Hartman; General Register of Prisons at Detroit House of Corrections, October 1, 1877–December 26, 1883, p. 71; National Archives, Department of Justice Administration Jail Reports, RG 60, Monthly Report of U.S. Prisoners in the Detroit House of Corrections at Wayne County, State of Michigan, on the 28th day of February, 1882, p. 1.

30. RG 204, Records of the Pardon Attorney, Case File H–739, Samuel Hartman.

Chapter VI

NOTE: The research of the Coeur d'Alene gold strike and Wyatt Earp's actions there in 1884 is credited to retired District Court Judge Richard Magnuson of Wallace, Idaho. Judge Magnuson, foremost historian of the area, has collected data on the gold strike and its denizens since the 1950s, and has graciously provided the author with his findings. All citations of official records are from Judge Magnuson's holdings.

1. There are numerous books dealing with the life and times of Wyatt Earp, mainly concentrating on his law career in Kansas and, especially, Tombstone, Arizona. The following is a partial list: Ed Bartholomew, *Wyatt Earp, the Untold Story* (Toyahvale, Texas: Frontier Book Company, 1963); Ed Bartholomew, *Wyatt Earp, the Man and the Myth* (Toyahvale, Texas: Frontier Book Company, 1964); Glenn G. Boyer, ed., *I Married Wyatt Earp: The Recollections of Josephine Sarah Marcus Earp* (Tucson, Arizona: University of Arizona Press, 1976); Don Chaput, *The Earp Papers: In a Brother's Image* (Encampment, Wyoming: Affiliated Writers Of America, 1994); Don Chaput, *Virgil Earp, Western Peace Officer* (Encampment, Wyoming: Affiliated Writers Of America, 1994); Richard E. Erwin, *The Truth About Wyatt Earp* (Carpinteria, California: The O.K. Press, 1992); Stuart N. Lake, *Wyatt Earp, Frontier Marshal* (Boston, Mass.: Houghton Mifflin Company, 1931); Paula Mitchell Marks, *And Die in the West* (New York: William Morrow and Company, Inc., 1989); Nyle H. Miller and Joseph W. Snell, *Why the West Was Wild* (Topeka: Kansas State Historical Society, 1963); Alford E. Turner, *The Earps Talk* (College Station, Texas: Creative Publishing Company, 1980); Alford E. Turner, *The OK Corral Inquest* (College Station, Texas: Creative Publishing Company, 1981); Frank Waters, *The Earp Brothers of Tombstone* (New York: Clarkson N. Potter, 1960).

The following are publications that deal with Wyatt Earp's career after Tombstone: Richard E. Churchill, *Doc Holliday, Bat Masterson and Wyatt Earp, Their Colorado Careers* (Leadville, Colo.: Timberline Books, 1974); Jack DeMattos, *The Earp Decision* (College Station, Texas: Creative Publishing Company, 1989); Jeffery M. Kintop and Guy Louis Rocha, *The Earps' Last Frontier* (Reno, Nevada: Great Basin Press, 1989).

2. Eugene G. Smalley, "The Coeur D'Alene Stampede," *Century Magazine* 28, no. 6 (October 1884), p. 841.

3. John Fahey, *The Ballyhoo Bonanza, Charles Sweeney and the Idaho Mines* (Seattle and London: University of Washington Press, 1971), pp. 15–18.

4. Smalley, p. 841.

5. Smalley, p. 841; Boyer, p. 121.

6. Shoshone County, Idaho Voter Registration, October 3, 1884; Untitled and undated article, Stuart Lake Notes, Lake Collection, Huntington Library, San Marino, California.

7. *A. J. Prichard, et al., v W. and James Earp,* Records of the First Judicial District Court for the District of the Territory of Idaho, 1884, case no. 24 (June 3, 1884).

8. Richard Magnuson notes; Roscoe G. Wilson, "Wyatt Earp Was Unlucky in Idaho Gun Battle," *Arizona Days and Ways,* January 17, 1959; Elmer D. McInnes, "Wyatt Earp's Coeur D'Alene Comrade," *Old West* (Spring 1996), pp. 51, 52; *Kellogg (Idaho) Evening News,* December 24, 1981; Untitled and undated article, Stuart Lake Notes, Lake Collection.

9. Fahey, jacket cover.

10. Records of the First Judicial District Court for the District of the Territory of Idaho, 1884, case no. 13, June 14, 1884.

11. Fahey, p. 19; Smalley, p. 841; Richard Magnuson notes.

12. Shoshone County, Idaho Deed Book F, pp. 466, 468, 470, 472, 476, 520; *Kellogg (Idaho) Evening News,* December 24, 1981.

13. *W. Payne v W. Earp,* Records of the First Judicial District Court for the District of the Territory of Idaho, 1884, case no. 8 (May 14, 1884); Bill of Sale, Sanford and Owens to Wyatt S. Earp, James C. Earp, J. E. Enright and A. Holman, dated April 26, 1884. Original in Richard Magnuson holdings; *Eagle (Idaho) Weekly Eagle,* July 11 and 18, 1884.

14. Lode Location Claim Records, 1884, and Placer Claim Location Records, 1884. Richard Magnuson holdings; *Spokane Falls Evening Review,* June 11, 1884.

15. *W. Payne v W. Earp,* Records of the First Judicial District Court for the District of the Territory of Idaho, 1884, case no. 3 (April 30, 1884).

16. *W. Payne v W. Earp,* Records of the First Judicial District Court for the District of the Territory of Idaho, 1884, case no. 8 (May 14, 1884); Bill of Sale, Sanford and Owens to Wyatt S. Earp, James C. Earp, J. E. Enright and A. Holman, dated April 26, 1884; Richard Magnuson notes.

17. *Spokane Falls Evening Review,* June 21, 1884; Untitled and undated article, Stuart Lake Notes, Lake Collection; McInnes, p. 51; Robert DeArment, *Bat Masterson* (Norman: University of Oklahoma Press, 1979), p. 186.

18. *Spokane Falls Evening Review,* June 21, 1884; McInnes, p. 51.

19. Untitled and undated article, Stuart Lake Notes, Lake Collection.

20. *People of the United States in Idaho Territory v Daniel S. Ferguson,* Records of the First Judicial District Court for the District of the Territory of Idaho, July Term 1884 (July 15, 1884).

21. McInnes, p. 51.

22. Untitled and undated article, Stuart Lake Notes, Lake Collection.

23. Richard Magnuson notes.

24. *Spokane Falls Evening Review,* April 5, 1884.

25. *Kellogg (Idaho) Evening News,* December 24, 1981; Shoshone County, Idaho Voter Registration, October 3, 1884.

26. *Coeur d'Alene Miner,* April 1, 1893; *Spokane Falls Evening Review,* April 5, 1884; Shoshone County, Idaho Deed Book F, p. 468.

27. Shoshone County, Idaho Voter Registration, October 3, 1884; Richard Magnuson notes; Certificate of Sale, Territory of Idaho, County of Shoshone,

levied November 10, 1884, on property of Wyat [sic] S. Earp, dated December 26, 1884.

28. See note 1 for publications regarding the Earps.

CHAPTER VII

1. Eastern Oregon State Hospital (E.O.S.H.) Records, patient no. 3601, Zebulin [sic] Gay Harshman. Eastern Oregon Psychiatric Center, Pendleton; Standard Certificate of Death, state file no. 208, Z. G. Harshman. Oregon State Health Division, Vital Statistics Section, Salem; RG 129, McNeil Island Penitentiary Log Book no. 2 (July, 1909–February, 1923), p. 61. Federal Archives and Records Center, Seattle, Washington.

2. *Portland Morning Oregonian,* October 7, 1903 (held by Multnomah County Library, Portland Oregon); The tombstone of Nancy Dean (Harshman) Matthews, in the Dean Cemetery in Gilliam County, gives her date of birth as February 10, 1869. Photo and information furnished to author by Chris Childs, Gilliam County Clerk, Condon, Oregon; Morrow County Historical Society; *The History of Morrow County Oregon* (Portland, Oregon: Taylor Publishing Company, 1983), p. 173.

3. Marriage Certificate, Nancy Dean and Z. G. Harshman, Umatilla County Marriage Book D, p. 212, Umatilla County Clerks Office, Pendleton, Oregon; Location of the Harshman homestead furnished to author by Marion Weatherford of Arlington, Oregon.

4. Bureau of the Census, *U.S. Census, 1892, Thurston County, Washington,* names beginning with the letter H, Archives and Records Management Division, Olympia, Washington. The census shows that Harvey Harshman was age seven when the census was enumerated in April of 1892; *Portland Morning Oregonian,* October 7, 1903.

5. Interviews with Marion Weatherford of Arlington, Oregon, November 6 and 10, 1987. Mr. Weatherford researched the story of Golphene's killing for the author, and obtained the details from a decendant of John L. Logan. This account agrees in almost every detail with the newspaper report; *Portland Morning Oregonian,* May 24, 27, 1887.

6. *Portland Morning Oregonian,* May 27, 1887.

7. *Portland Morning Oregonian,* October 7, 1903; Letter: Gilliam County Trial Court Clerk Sue Miller to author, dated November 19, 1987, stating that there are no records of indictment or trial of Harshman for the murder of Thomas Golphene.

8. *U.S. Census, 1892, Thurston County, Washington.* The census erroneously lists the child as a female, although the name reported is Oliver. Both Oliver and Floyd are listed as being born in Oregon; Interview with Lloyd Harshman of Milton-Freewater, Oregon, grandson of Z. G. Harshman, January 21, 1988. Mr. Harshman stated that Z. G. Harshman had two sons who survived, Oliver and his father, Harvey, but had no daughter; The tombstone of Floyd Harshman in the Dean Cemetery in Gilliam County, Oregon gives his birthdate as March 22, 1891. Photo and information furnished to author by Chris Childs, Gilliam County Clerk, Condon, Oregon; E.O.S.H. Records.

9. E.O.S.H. Records; *Oregon Daily Journal,* October 16, 1903 (Multnomah County Library, Portland, Oregon).

10. *U.S. v Gay Harshman,* RG 21, U.S. Circuit Court, Tacoma, Washington, case no. 270, Federal Archives and Records Center, Seattle, Washington; RG 129, McNeil Island Penitentiary Log Book no. 1 (1892–1909), p. 10, Federal Archives and Records Center, Seattle, Washington.

11. *U.S. v Gay Harshman,* RG 21, U.S. District Court, Seattle, Washington, case no. 1035, Federal Archives and Records Center, Seattle, Washington; RG 129, McNeil Island Penitentiary Log Book no. 1 (1892–1909), p.44.

12. San Quentin Prison Register, convict no. 17175, Gay Harshman, F 3653-9 (VB 113), California State Archives, Sacramento; For the life of Bill Miner see Mark Dugan and John Boessenecker, *The Grey Fox.*

13. *Oregon Daily Journal,* October 16, 1903; Interview with Everett Harshman of Heppner, Oregon, grandson of Z. G. Harshman, March 30, 1987. Mr. Harshman stated that, on being asked the reason he became involved in the train robbery, his grandfather, Z. G., related this story of the railroad refusing to pay for his work making railroad ties; For the life of Jake Terry see Mark Dugan, *Tales Never Told around the Campfire* (Athens: Ohio University Press/Swallow Press, 1992).

14. *Portland Morning Oregonian,* October 13, 1903; *Oregon Daily Journal,* October 16, 1903.

15. *Portland Morning Oregonian,* October 14, 1903.

16. *Portland Morning Oregonian,* October 12, 13, 1903; *Oregon Daily Journal,* October 16, 1903; *Bellingham Herald,* September 24, 1903.

17. *Bellingham Reveille,* September 24, 1903 (held by Bellingham Public Library, Bellingham, Washington); *Oregon Daily Journal,* September 24, 25, 26, and October 12, 1903; *Portland Morning Oregonian,* October 12, 1903; *Mount Vernon Argus,* October 16, 1903 (held by Skagit County Historical Museum, LaConner, Washington).

18. *Oregon Daily Journal,* September 25, 26, 1903; E.O.S.H. Records.

19. *Portland Morning Oregonian,* October 9, 12, 1903; *Oregon Daily Journal,* October 12, 1903.

20. *Portland Morning Oregonian,* October 7, 9, 1903.

21. *Portland Morning Oregonian,* October 11, 12, and 13, 1903; *Oregon Daily Journal,* October 12, 1903; *Bellingham Herald,* October 12, 1903; *Mount Vernon Argus,* October 16, 1903.

22. *Portland Morning Oregonian,* October 11, 12, 1903; *Bellingham Herald,* October 12, 1903.

23. *Portland Morning Oregonian,* October 11, 12, 13, 1903; *Oregon Daily Journal,* October 12, 1903; *Bellingham Herald,* October 12, 1903.

24. *Oregon Journal,* October 17, 1903; *Portland Morning Oregonian,* November 11, 1903.

25. *Portland Morning Oregonian,* November 14, 25, 1903; Oregon State Penitentiary Great Register, vol. 5 (1894–1910), pp. 168, 169, Oregon State Archives, Salem.

26. Oregon State Penitentiary Great Register, vol. 5 (1894–1910), pp. 168, 169; Case Files, convict no. 4792, Charles Hoehn, Oregon State Penitentiary, Salem; Secretary of State, Record of Pardons, Remissions and Commutations, vol. 1 (1904–1911), Charles Hoehn, p. 229, Oregon State Archives, Salem.

27. Oregon State Penitentiary Great Register, vol. 5 (1894–1910), pp. 168, 169; Case Files, convict no. 4796, Gay Harshman. Oregon State Penitentiary, Salem; Tombstone of Floyd Harshman in the Dean Cemetery, Gilliam County, Oregon. Photo furnished to author by Chris Childs, County Clerk of Gilliam County; Lloyd Harshman interview, January 21, 1988; E.O.S.H. Records.

28. *U.S. v Gay Harshman,* RG 21, U.S. District Court, Portland, Oregon, case no. 6291, Federal Archives and Records Center, Seattle, Washington; RG 129, McNeil Island Penitentiary Log Book no. 2 (July 1909–February 1923), p. 61.

29. E.O.S.H. Records; Lloyd Harshman interview, January 21, 1988; Everett Harshman interview, March 30, 1987; Taped interview with Noel G. Harshman of Eightmile, Oregon, great-grandson of Z. G. Harshman, November 10, 1987.

30. E.O.S.H. Records.

31. E.O.S.H. Records; Standard Certificate of Death, State File no. 208, Z. G. Harshman.

32. Lloyd Harshman interview, January 21, 1988; Everett Harshman interview, March 30, 1987; Letter: Ms. Patricia L. Graham, Parks, Recreation and Cemetery Department, Pendleton, Oregon, dated January 15, 1988. Ms. Graham furnished the author with Harshman's interment record and photograph of his grave.

CHAPTER VIII

1. Nebraska State Penitentiary Records, inmate no. 1836, V. Herron, inmate no. 1837, J. A. Herron, State of Nebraska Board of Paroles, Lincoln; *U.S. Census, 1880, Noble County, Indiana,* p. 12.

2. Nebraska State Penitentiary Records, inmate no. 1836, V. Herron, inmate no. 1837, J. A. Herron; *The Republican* (Valentine, Nebraska), August 1, 1890 (held by Nebraska State Historical Society, Lincoln).

3. *The Republican,* August 1, 1890; *The Western Outlook,* October, 1970 (held by Cherry County Historical Society, Valentine, Nebraska); *State of Nebraska v J. A. and V. Herron,* Cherry County District Court Records, Information, case nos. 341, 342, 343, 345, Cherry County District Court, Valentine, Nebraska; Undated article on the train robbery in the Cherry County Historical Museum, Valentine, Nebraska.

4. *The Western Outlook,* October 1970; *The Republican,* August 1, 1890; Undated article on the train robbery in the Cherry County Historical Museum.

5. *State of Nebraska v J. A. Herron, V. Herron,* Cherry County Criminal Court Docket, pp. 180 and 182, Cherry County District Court, Valentine, Nebraska.

6. *The Republican,* August 8, 1890.

7. *The Republican,* August 15, 1890; Cherry County Criminal Court Docket, p. 184; Cherry County District Court Records, Information, case no. 342.

8. *The Republican,* October 17, 24, 1890; *The Western Outlook,* October 1970; Cherry County District Court Records, Information, case no. 342.

9. *The Republican,* October 24, 1890; Cherry County District Court Records, Information, case no. 342.

10. *The Republican,* October 31, 1890.

11. Cherry County District Court Records, Information, case no. 342; *The Republican,* October 31, 1890.

12. Nebraska State Penitentiary Records, inmate no. 1837, A. J. [*sic*] Herron, inmate no. 1836, V. Herron.

CHAPTER IX

1. Richard Maxwell Brown, *Strain of Violence* (New York: Oxford University Press, 1975), pp. 150–151.

2. Madeleine M. Noble, "The White Caps of Harrison and Crawford County, Indiana: A Study in the Violent Enforcement of Morality" (Ph.D. diss., University of Michigan, 1973), p. 96; White Cap File: *Corydon Republican,* July 13, 1871, quoted in an undated *Corydon Republican* newspaper article published around 1919 (held by Corydon Public Library, Corydon, Indiana).

3. Noble, pp. 1–11; Brown, p. 150.

4. *Corydon Republican,* July 13, 1871.

5. White Cap File: Undated *Corydon Republican* newspaper article published around 1919.

6. *An Atlas of Harrison County, Indiana* (Philadelphia: D. J. Lake & Co., 1882; repr. Evansville, In.: Unigraphic, Inc., 1977), p. 48; Arville L. Funk, *Historical Al-*

manac of Harrison County [Indiana] (Corydon, In.: Alfco Publications, 1974), p. 17; *Indianapolis Journal*, June 10, 1889 (held by Indiana State Library, Indianapolis, Indiana).

7. *Louisville Courier-Journal*, June 14, 1889 (held by Louisville Public Library, Louisville, Kentucky).

8. *An Atlas of Harrison County, Indiana*, p. 48; *Indiana's Birthplace, A History of Harrison County, Indiana*, originally compiled by William A. Roose (1911), revised in 1966 by Arville L. Funk (Corydon, In.: Adams Press, 1966), pp. 61–62; *Indianapolis Journal*, June 10, 1889; Noble, p. 120.

9. *Indianapolis Journal*, June 10, 1889; *New Albany Evening Tribune*, June 10, 1889 (held by New Albany/Floyd County Public Library, New Albany, Indiana).

10. *Corydon Republican*, June 13, 1889; *Louisville Courier-Journal*, June 14, 1889; *New Albany Evening Tribune*, June 13, 1889; Noble, pp. 121–122.

11. Noble, p. 122.

12. *New Albany Daily Ledger*, August 7, 8, 1893 (held by New Albany/Floyd County Public Library, New Albany, Indiana and Corydon Public Library, Corydon, Indiana); *New Albany Public Press*, August 9, 1893 (held by New Albany/Floyd County Public Library); White Cap File: *Louisville Courier-Journal*, August 14, 1893; Noble, pp. 128–129.

13. *New Albany Daily Ledger*, August 7, 1893; *New Albany Public Press*, August 9, 1893; Noble, pp. 129–130; *Louisville Courier-Journal*, August 14, 1893.

14. *New Albany Daily Ledger*, August 7, 8, 1893; *New Albany Public Press*, August 9, 1893.

15. *Indianapolis Journal*, August 7, 8, 10, 1893; *New Albany Daily Ledger*, August 7, 11, 1893; Noble, pp. 130–132; *New Albany Public Press*, August 9, 1893.

16. *New Albany Daily Ledger*, August 7, 9, 1893; Noble, p. 132; *New Albany Public Press*, August 9, 1893, *Louisville Courier-Journal*, August 14, 1893.

17. *New Albany Daily Ledger*, August 7, 9, 10, 11, 1893; Noble, pp. 132, 134; *Indianapolis Journal*, August 9, 1893.

18. *New Albany Daily Ledger*, August 10, 11, 16, 1893; *Indianapolis Journal*, August 15, 1893.

19. *New Albany Daily Ledger*, August 16, 1893; Noble, p. 135.

20. *New Albany Daily Ledger*, August 10, 1893; *Indianapolis Journal*, August 10, 11, 1893; Noble, pp. 134–135.

21. *An Atlas of Harrison County, Indiana*, p. 49; *Corydon Republican*, August 11, 1938, Noble, pp. 135–136.

CHAPTER X

NOTE: Much of this story is contained in the author's article, "Family Traditions," *Annals of Wyoming* 64, no. 2 (Spring 1992).

1. William Lewis' life and death is chronicled in the author's book, *Tales Never Told around the Campfire* (Athens: Ohio University Press/Swallow Press, 1992), pp. 202–208.

2. *Cheyenne Daily Sun-Leader,* September 11, 1895 (held by Wyoming State Archives, Museums, and Historical Department, Cheyenne); Laramie County Marriage Records, vol. 2, bk. 2, p. 218, Wyoming State Archives, Museums, and Historical Department, Cheyenne; Dean F. Krakel, *The Saga of Tom Horn* (Lincoln: University of Nebraska Press), pp. 7, 8; Verdict of Coroners Jury, no. 133, Albany County, Wyoming, September 12, 1895, Fred U. Powell, Wyoming State Archives, Museums, and Historical Department, Cheyenne.

3. *Territory of Wyoming v Fredrick U. Powell, Stealing and Killing Neat Cattle*, Albany County Criminal Case no. 447, Wyoming State Archives, Museums, and His-

torical Department, Cheyenne. (All subsequent criminal and civil cases, unless otherwise indicated, are cited from the holdings of Wyoming State Archives, Museums, and Historical Department, Cheyenne.)

4. *State of Wyoming v Fred Powell, Grand Larceny,* Cheyenne Justice of the Peace Criminal Docket, pp. 185, 359.

5. *Mary N. Powell v Fredrick U. Powell, Divorce,* Laramie County District Court Civil Appearance Docket no. 5, p. 231, and Petition; Laramie County District Court Journal, vol. 12, pp. 618, 619.

6. *State of Wyoming v Fredrick U. Powell, Stealing Live Stock,* Albany County Criminal Case no. 560.

7. *State of Wyoming v Fredrick U. Powell, Malicious Trespass and Destruction of Property,* Albany County Criminal Case no. 584.

8. *State of Wyoming v Fredrick U. Powell, Incendiarism and Malicious Trespass,* Albany County Criminal Case no. 598.

9. *State of Wyoming v Fredrick U. Powell, Criminal Trespass,* Albany County Criminal Case no. 601.

10. *State of Wyoming v Fredrick U. Powell,* Albany County Criminal Case nos. 601 and 598.

11. *Cheyenne Daily Sun-Leader,* September 11, 1895.

12. Coroner's Inquest and Verdict of Coroner's Jury in death of Fredrick U. Powell, September 10, 1895, Wyoming State Archives, Museums, and Historical Department, Cheyenne.

13. *Cheyenne Daily Sun-Leader,* September 11, 1895; Coroner's Inquest and Verdict of Coroner's Jury in death of Fredrick U. Powell, September 10, 1895.

14. *Cheyenne Daily Sun-Leader,* September 11, 1895.

15. *Cheyenne Daily Sun-Leader,* September 12, 1895.

16. T. A. Larson, *History of Wyoming* (Lincoln: University of Nebraska Press, 1965), p. 373; *Laramie Republican-Boomerang,* January 13, 1941 (held by Wyoming State Archives, Museums, and Historical Department, Cheyenne).

17. *Laramie Republican-Boomerang,* January 27, 1896.

18. Letter dated August 23, 1990 to the author from a reliable source provided through the services of the Wyoming State Archives, Museums, and Historical Department, Cheyenne.

19. *Laramie Republican-Boomerang,* January 13, 1941; Bureau of the Census, *U.S. Census, 1870, Albany County, Wyoming Territory,* p. 19; Official Verification of Death: Mary Powell. State of Wyoming, Division of Health and Medical Services, Vital Records Services, Cheyenne. The Keane name is often erroneously listed as Kane in various documents and newspapers.

20. *U.S. Census, 1870, Albany County, Wyoming Territory,* p. 19; Mary Lou Pence, *The Laramie Story* (Casper, Wyoming: Prairie Publishing Co., 1987), pp. 5, 12; C. Exerta Brown, *Brown's Gazetteer of the Chicago and Northwestern Railroad and Branches of the Union Pacific Railroad (Cheyenne and Laramie section)* (Chicago: Bassett Brothers' Steam Printing House, 1868), p. 315.

21. *Laramie Daily Sentinel,* December 28, 1878 (held by Wyoming State Archives, Museums, and Historical Department, Cheyenne); Pence, *The Laramie Story,* p. 10; *U.S. Census, 1870, Albany County, Wyoming Territory,* p. 19; *Laramie City Directory, 1883–1884,* p. 70, Wyoming State Archives, Museums, and Historical Department, Cheyenne.

22. Mary Lou Pence, "The Woman Who Wouldn't Quit," *Denver Post-Empire Magazine,* February 25, 1951: Vertical File Collection, Mary Powell, Wyoming State Archives, Museums, and Historical Department, Cheyenne; Albany County, Wyoming Marriage Record, vol. B, p. 47, Wyoming State Archives, Museums, and Historical Department, Cheyenne; *Laramie Daily Sentinel,* August 1, 31, 1878.

23. Albany County, Wyoming Marriage License and Certificate Record, vol. B, p. 4, Wyoming State Archives, Museums, and Historical Department, Cheyenne; *U.S. Census, 1880, Albany County, Wyoming Territory*, p. 10; *Laramie City Directory, 1883–1884*, p. 90; Laramie Justice of the Peace, Civil and Criminal Docket, vol. 9, pp. 63 and 69.

24. *Laramie Weekly Sentinel*, May 25, 1889 (held by Wyoming State Archives, Museums, and Historical Department, Cheyenne).

25. *Laramie Weekly Sentinel*, January 24, 1891 and September 2, 1893; *Laramie Daily Boomerang*, March 19, 1900. Although there are no copies of this newspaper, there does exist a notation that John Keane's obituary is in this issue.

26. Mary Lou Pence, "The Woman Who Wouldn't Quit."

27. *State of Wyoming v Mary Powell, Burglary*, Albany County Criminal Case no. 653.

28. *State of Wyoming v Mary N. and Willie Powell, Stealing Livestock*, Albany County Criminal Case nos. 891 and 892.

29. *State of Wyoming v Mary Powell, Stealing Horses*, Albany County Criminal Case no. 1067.

30. *State of Wyoming v Mary Powell, Arson*, Albany County Criminal Case no. 1068.

31. *State of Wyoming v Mary Powell, Assault and Battery*, Laramie Justice of the Peace Criminal Docket, vol. C, p. 26.

32. *State of Wyoming v Mary Powell, Malicious Mischief*, Laramie Justice of the Peace Criminal Docket, vol. C, p. 49.

33. *State of Wyoming v Mary Powell, Trespass*, Laramie Justice of the Peace Criminal Docket, vol. C, p. 60; *Laramie Daily Boomerang*, February 11, 1914 (held by Wyoming State Archives, Museums, and Historical Department, Cheyenne).

34. *City of Laramie v Mary Powell, Disturbance and Breach of Peace*, Albany County Criminal Case no. 1183; *Laramie Daily Boomerang*, November 20, 1914.

35. *State of Wyoming v Mary Powell, Assault and Battery*, Laramie Justice of the Peace Criminal Docket, vol. C, p. 114.

36. Interview with historian and researcher Ellen Mueller of Cheyenne, Wyoming, November 5, 1990; Laramie Justice of the Peace Criminal Docket, vol. C, p. 224, Affidavit for Search Warrant.

37. *State of Wyoming v William Powell and William H. Frazee, Stealing Live Stock*, Albany County Criminal Case no. 1073; *State of Wyoming v Mary Powell, Arson*, Albany County Criminal Case no. 1068.

38. *U.S. v William Sharp, William T. Knowles, and William Powell*, National Archives, RG 21, Records of U.S. District Court, District of Wyoming, Criminal Case Files 1890–1925, box no. 41, entry 9, case no. 1263, National Archives and Records Center, Denver, Colorado.

39. *State of Wyoming v William E. Powell, Trespass*, Laramie Justice of the Peace Criminal Docket, vol. 1, pp. 83, 84.

40. *U.S. v William Powell and Hazel E. O'Reilley*, RG 21, Records of U.S. District Court, District of Wyoming, Criminal Case Files 1890–1925, box no. 76, entry 9, case no. 2386, National Archives and Records Center, Denver, Colorado.

41. Letter: Cindy Brown, Wyoming State Archives, Museums, and Historical Department, Cheyenne, to author, January 1991, stating that no marriage record exists for William Powell and Sarah May "Billie" Phelps in Albany or Laramie Counties, Wyoming.

42. *U.S. v William Powell, Sarah May Phelps, and William E. Booth*, RG 21, Records of U.S. District Court, District of Wyoming, Criminal Case Files 1890–1932, box no. 109, entry 9, case no. 3479, National Archives and Records Center, Denver, Colorado.

43. *Laramie Republican-Boomerang*, March 9, 10, 13, 1934.

44. *Wyoming State Tribune-Cheyenne State Leader*, January 7, 1935 (held by Wyoming State Archives, Museums, and Historical Department, Cheyenne); *Laramie Republican-Boomerang*, April 5, 1935.

45. *The Wyoming State Tribune-Cheyenne State Leader*, January 7, 1935; *Laramie Republican-Boomerang*, April 4, 5, 6, 1935; *State of Wyoming v Alonzo Phelps, Murder in the Second Degree*, Albany County Criminal Case no. 2166.

46. Mary Lou Pence, "The Woman Who Wouldn't Quit."

47. *Laramie Republican-Boomerang*, January 13, 1941.

48. *Laramie Republican-Boomerang*, January 13, 1941; Official Verification of Death: Mary Powell, State of Wyoming, Division of Health and Medical Services, Vital Records Services, Cheyenne; Interview with historian and researcher Ellen Mueller of Cheyenne, Wyoming, November 5, 1990; *Cheyenne City Directory, 1939–1940*, p. 266, Wyoming State Archives, Museums, and Historical Department, Cheyenne.

49. *Laramie Republican-Boomerang*, January 13, 1941.

CHAPTER XI

1. Certificate of Death, no. 68 6285, Charley Spraig Whitney, Department of Health and Environmental Sciences, Helena, Montana; Funeral Record of Charley Spraig Whitney, Austin Funeral Home, Whitefish, Montana; Registration of Death, no. 005607/50, George Brown [Hugh Whitney], Department of Public Health—Division of Vital Stastics, Regina, Saskatchewan; *State of Wyoming v Charley S. Whitney*, Lincoln County, Wyoming District Court Criminal Case File no. 856, Wyoming State Archives, Museums, and Historical Department, Cheyenne. One letter in the file written by Charley Whitney stated, "There was only thirteen months and fourteen days difference in our [Hugh's and Charley's] age."

2. Lincoln County, Wyoming District Court Criminal Case File no. 856; Mary E. Stoner, "My Father Was a Train Robber," *True West*, August 1983, p. 16. Mrs. Stoner, who graciously has shared her findings with the author, is a second cousin of the Whitney Brothers. Her father, Clarence Stoner, was the son of Mary Ella Whitney Stoner, sister of Fred Whitney. The following is a summary of the Whitney history. Sometime in the 1860s, Timothy and Avis Douglas Whitney moved to Wautoma, Wisconsin, where Timothy died in 1873. The family then moved to Indian Territory (Oklahoma) and, by 1882, had headed north via Canon City, Colorado, Evanston, Wyoming, and on to Indian Valley near Weiser, Idaho where Avis Whitney died in 1898; Jim Dullenty and Mary Stoner Hadley, "Wyoming's Outlaw Brothers," *Annals of Wyoming* 60, no. 2 (Fall 1988), p. 15.

3. Lincoln County, Wyoming District Court Criminal Case File no. 856; Letter from Charley S. Whitney to Wyoming Governor Frank F. Barrett, December 1, 1951.

4. Lincoln County, Wyoming District Court Criminal Case File no. 856; Lewis H. Daniels, "Hugh Whitney—Outlaw," *Snake River Echoes* (Rexburg, Idaho: Upper Snake River Valley Historical Society, 1977), p. 53; J. Patrick Wilde, "The Whitney Brothers," *Snake River Echoes* (1977), pp. 58–59.

5. Lincoln County, Wyoming District Court Criminal Case File no. 856; Stoner, p. 16; Daniels, pp. 53 and 55.

6. Daniels, p. 53; Marguerite Moore Diffendaffer, *Council Valley, Here They Labored* (Worthwhile Club of Council, Idaho with assistance from the Idaho State Historical Society, Boise, Idaho, 1977), p. 307; Larry Pointer, *In Search of Butch Cassidy* (Norman: University of Oklahoma Press, 1977), pp. 74–80; Lincoln County, Wyoming District Court Criminal Case File no. 856.

7. Lincoln County, Wyoming District Court Criminal Case File no. 856.

8. Stoner, pp. 16–19; Robert R. Rose, *Advocates and Adversaries* (Chicago: The Lakeside Press, 1977), p. 233; *Cheyenne Wyoming State Tribune,* June 19, 1952 (held by Wyoming State Archives, Museums, and Historical Department, Cheyenne); Dullenty and Hadley, pp. 16, 17.

9. Errol Jack Lloyd, "The History of Cokeville, Wyoming" (master's thesis, Utah State University, 1970), pp. 138–139; Wilde, p. 57; Dullenty and Hadley, p. 16.

10. Rose, pp. 235–236; Dullenty and Hadley, p. 17.

11. Daniels, p. 53; George A. Thompson, "How Come They Never Caught Hugh Whitney," *True West,* September–October 1979, pp. 25 and 59; *Salt Lake City Herald-Republican,* June 18, 19, 20, 1911 (held by Merriott Library, University of Utah, Salt Lake City).

12. *Herald-Republican,* June 18, 1911; Daniels, pp. 53–55.

13. *Salt Lake Tribune,* June 19, 1911 (held by Utah State Historical Society, Salt Lake City); *Herald-Republican,* June 19, 1911; Daniels, p. 53; Samuel Westlake Lundholm, "Best I Can Remember," *Snake River Echoes* (Rexburg, Idaho, 1977), p. 56.

14. *Salt Lake Tribune,* June 20, 1911; *Herald-Republican,* June 20, 1911.

15. Daniels, p. 54.

16. *Salt Lake Tribune,* June 21, 1911; *Herald-Republican,* June 21, 1911; Thompson, p. 60.

17. Daniels, p. 54; *Kemmerer Gazette,* June 20, 1952 (held by Wyoming State Archives, Museums, and Historical Department, Cheyenne); *Cheyenne Wyoming State Tribune,* June 19, 1952; Wilde, p. 58; Dullenty and Hadley, p. 18.

18. *Evanston Wyoming Times,* September 14, 1911 (held by Wyoming State Archives, Museums, and Historical Department, Cheyenne); *Kemmerer Camera,* September 13, 1911. News article furnished to author by Arthur and Bernice Robinson of Cokeville, Wyoming; *Herald-Republican,* September 12, 1911; *Denver Post,* June 19, 1952; *Kemmerer Gazette,* June 20, 1952; *Cheyenne Wyoming State Tribune,* June 19, 1952; Wilde, p. 58; Dullenty and Hadley, pp. 12, 13.

19. Wilde, p. 59; *Kemmerer Gazette,* June 20, 1952; *Cheyenne Wyoming State Tribune,* June 19, 1952; *Denver Post,* June 19, 1952; *Kemmerer Camera,* September 13, 20, October 4, 1911. News articles furnished to author by Arthur and Bernice Robinson of Cokeville, Wyoming.

20. Daniels, p. 54; Wilde, p. 59.

21. *Cheyenne Wyoming State Tribune,* June 19, 1952; Wilde, p. 60; Stoner, p. 17.

22. *Cheyenne Wyoming State Tribune,* June 19, 1952.

23. Wilde, p. 59; Wyoming State Penitentiary Records, inmate no. 1829, Bert Dalton, Wyoming State Archives, Museums, and Historical Department, Cheyenne.

24. *Wyoming Press,* June 22, September 7, 1912.

25. *Wyoming Press,* July 6, 1912.

26. *State of Wyoming, Uinta County v Bert Dalton for Murder,* case no. 289-3, Wyoming State Archives, Museums, and Historical Department, Cheyenne; *Wyoming Press,* July 6, 1912; Wilde, p. 59.

27. *Wyoming Press,* June 22, July 6, 27, 1912 (held by Wyoming State Archives, Museums, and Historical Department, Cheyenne).

28. Frank Calkins, *Jackson Hole* (New York: Alfred A. Knopf, 1973), pp. 125–126.

29. *Wyoming Press,* August 17, 1912.

30. *State of Wyoming, Uinta County vs. Bert Dalton for Murder,* case no. 289-3; *Wyoming Press,* September 7, 1912.

31. *Wyoming Press,* October 17, 1912, January 4, 1913; *Crook County Monitor* (Sundance), January 10, 1913 (held by Wyoming State Archives, Museums, and Historical Department, Cheyenne).

32. Wyoming State Penitentiary Records, inmate no. 1829, Bert Dalton; Wilde, p. 61.

33. Stoner, pp. 18–21; Rose, pp. 228, 229, and 233.

34. *Kemmerer Gazette*, September 22, 1926; Wilde, p. 60; Thompson, p. 60.

35. Lincoln County, Wyoming District Court Criminal Case File no. 856; Letter from Charley S. Whitney to Wyoming Governor Frank F. Barrett, December 1, 1951; *Kemmerer Gazette*, June 20, 1952.

36. Lincoln County, Wyoming District Court Criminal Case File no. 856; Letter from Charley S. Whitney to Wyoming Governor Frank F. Barrett, December 1, 1951.

37. Lincoln County, Wyoming District Court Criminal Case File no. 856; Document no. 170199, Honorable Discharge and Enlistment Record, Frank S. Taylor.

38. Registration of Death, no. 005607/50, George Brown [Hugh Whitney]; *Wyoming State Tribune*, June 19, 1952; Letter: Patricia Yates, Information Services, Saskatoon Public Library, Saskatoon, Saskatchewan to author dated February 17, 1988; Wilde, p. 60.

39. Lincoln County, Wyoming District Court Criminal Case File no. 856.

40. Registration of Death, no. 005607/50, George Brown [Hugh Whitney]; Interment Order no. 15154, George W. Brown, City of Saskatoon. Woodlawn Cemetery, City of Saskatoon, Parks and Recreation Section, Saskatoon, Saskatchewan; *Saskatoon Star-Phoenix*, October 26, 1950 (held by Saskatoon Public Library, Saskatoon, Saskatchewan).

41. Lincoln County, Wyoming District Court Criminal Case File no. 856; Letter from Charley S. Whitney to Wyoming Governor Frank F. Barrett, December 1, 1951.

42. *Kemmerer Gazette*, June 20, 1952.

43. Lincoln County, Wyoming District Court Criminal Case File no. 856; *Kemmerer Gazette*, June 20, 1952; *Wyoming State Tribune*, June 19, 1952; *Denver Post*, June 19, 1952.

44. Lincoln County, Wyoming District Court Criminal Case File no. 856.

45. Lincoln County, Wyoming District Court Criminal Case File no. 856; Stoner, p. 17.

46. Funeral Record of Charles Spraig Whitney; Certificate of Death, no. 68 6285, Charley Spraig Whitney; *Daily Interlake*, November 14, 1968 (held by Montana Historical Society, Helena).

47. Lincoln County, Wyoming District Court Criminal Case File no. 856.

INDEX

Aaron, N.C. *see* Montezuma, N.C.
Abilene, Ks., 141
Albany County, Wyo., 184–185, 197, 205–207
Albright, W. H., 166–167
Alexander, Mr., 94
Alexander, William, 49, 54
Alkali Stage Station (Wyo.), 117
Allegheny Mountain (Penn.), 26
Allen (Attorney), 121
Allen, J. J., 98
Allen, R. John (U.S. Marshal), 207
Allen, William V., 167–168
Allison, Robert, 26
Anacortes, Wash., 154
Anatone, Wash., 213
Anderson, Adam F. (Constable), 182
Anderson, Frank E. (District Attorney), 199, 201, 208–209
Anderson, John (Dr.), 33
Anderson, William (Bloody Bill), 6, 65
Andrus, Elisha William ("Bigfoot"), 102–103
Antofagasta, Chile, 14
Antrim, Catherine McCarty, 10
Antrim, William, 10
Aplwan, Llywd, 15
Arabia, Neb., 164–166
Arlington, Ore., 146
Armor, William, 49
Armstrong, William, 46
Arnold, John R., 229
Arroyo Pescado, Argentina, 15
Arthur, Chester A. (U.S. President), 123
Arthur, John Preston, 60, 64–67, 70, 72–73, 75–76
Ashe, Samuel A'Court, 64
Asheville, N.C., 66
Ashman, Richard, 37
Aspen, Co., 129
Astor, John Jacob, 22
Astoria, Ore., 150
Atchison, Ks., 109–110
Austin, Stephen F., 92
Austin, Tx., 90
Avery, Waightstill W. (Colonel), 67, 73
Ayers, A. Reeves (U.S. Commissioner), 149
Baccus, George, 201–202

Bacon, (Dr.), 147
Bahney (Major), 73
Bailey, G. W. (Deputy Sheriff), 220
Baillie, Mary, 208
Baird, J. C. (District Attorney), 185
Baker, Etherton P., 188
Bakersville, N.C., 79, 82, 85
Bald Eagle Creek (Penn.), 20, 48, 54
Bald Knobbers, 173
Ballew (Capt.), 63
Baltimore, Md., 25
Banner, C. C., 82
Barber, Thomas H., 78
Barker (Counterfeiter), 26, 30
Barnes, Johnny, 128
Barnett, Charles, 94
Barrett, Frank A. (Wyo. Governor), 213–214, 234
Barrett, Ollie, 152
Barrick, Mac E., 24, 57
Bass, Sam, 116
Bassett, Neb., 168
Bastrop, Tx., 90, 97
Baum, Meyer, 114
Bauman, C. J. D. (Sheriff), 162
Bean, Robert. S. (Judge), 157
Bear River, Wyo., 141
Beck, Israel, 67
Becker, Joseph, 197
Bedford, Penn., 26, 29–33, 36–40
Behan, John H. (Sheriff), 129
Bellefonte, Penn., 20–22, 24, 49, 53–55
Bellot, Cleto (Corregidor), 15–16
Benezette, Penn., 49
Benfield, Powell, 67
Bennett's Branch (Penn.), 48, 50
Berlin, Penn., 26
Berry, Sam "One-armed", 65
Beshore, Mr. and Mrs., 41–42
Bevans, Bill, 116
Bickley, W. L., 172
Biddick, John, 203

Biedecker (Sheriff), 153
Big Piney, Wyo., 230
Big River, Calif., 103, 105
Billingsley, Carroll, 93
Billy the Kid (Henry McCarty), 4, 10–12, 16, 89, 145
Blackburn, Duncan, 116–117
Blackfoot, Id., 222
Blackwell, William, 68
Blair, William T., 75
Blake, J. W. (Judge), 189
Blanchard, John, 54
Blaylock, Aaron Paul, 84
Blaylock, Celia Ann "Mattie", 129
Blaylock, Columbus Filmore "Lum", 64, 82, 84, 87
Blaylock, Isaac William "Willie", 79, 85
Blaylock, John, 60
Blaylock, John H. "Jack", 79
Blaylock, Malinda see Sarah Malinda Blaylock
Blaylock, Martha Jane née Hollifield, 84
Blaylock, Mary, 61
Blaylock, Mary A. see Mary A. Coffey
Blaylock, Mary E. "Polly" née Dorman, 60
Blaylock, Sam (alias of Sarah Malinda Blaylock), 63–64
Blaylock, Samuel Washington, 79, 82
Blaylock, Sarah Malinda née Pritchard, 61–65, 71, 79–87
Blaylock, Tilman, 60
Blaylock, William McKesson "Keith", 59–88
Blaylock, William R., 61
Bloody Run (Everett), Penn., 28
Blowing Rock, N.C., 61, 68, 72–73, 84
Blue Ridge Township, N.C., 63
Bodie, Cal., 141
Bond, Thomas B. (Judge), 107
Bonner, John W. (Mont. Governor), 233–234
Bonnet, Thomas, 39
Boone, N.C., 73
Booth, Ernest, 206–207
Booth, Newton (Calif. Governor), 105
Booth, Pauline Jackson, 206–207
Bottorff, Louis, 176
Bow, Wash., 153
Bower, W. W. (Sheriff), 199, 203
Bowles, B. A., 67
Bowman, Bob, 219
Boyd, John B., 73, 75–76
Boyer, Michael, 46
Boyett, John, 129, 142
Bradley, Lame, 117–120
Brady, William (Sheriff), 10
Bramel, William H., 189
Braswell, J. Ray (Judge), 87, 88
Braswell, Warsaw, 88
Braught, James, 109
Breathed, Raney, 27–30

Brewster, Benjamin Harris (U.S. Attorney General), 123
Bridal Veil, Ore., 152–153
Bridenthal, J. H., 28
Bridges, C. S. (U.S. Marshal), 150
Brocious, William "Curley Bill", 129
Brock, Isaac (General), 23–24
Brooks, Benjamin, 51
Brooks, David, 50
Brooks, John, 49, 54
Brown, 24
Brown, Charles, 103–104
Brown, Egbert (Colonel), 6
Brown, George Walter see Hugh Whitney
Brown, Jack ("Rattling Jack"), 103, 105
Brown, Johnny, 103–104
Brown, Lodi, 103–104
Brown, M. C., 199, 203
Brown, Richard Maxwell, 173–174
Brown, Robert, 183
Bryden, Robert, 152–153
Buck, Dan, 12
Buck, Jim, 222–223
Bucklin (Sheriff), 220, 222–223
Buffalo Gap, Wyo., 117
Buffington, Isaac, 23–24
Bull Scrape, N.C. see Montezuma, N.C.
Bullock, Seth (Sheriff), 120
Bulls Gap, Tenn., 66
Bully, Matt Lynch see Harvey Bell Mitchell
Burd, George, 30
Burdett, John, 141
Burley, George, 149
Burlington, Vt., 21
Burns, John (U.S. Prohibition Agent), 205
Burns, Walter Noble, 12
Burnside, Thomas, 54
Burnsville, N.C., 59, 61
Burr Oak, Ind., 164
Butler (Marshal), 119–120
Butler, Joseph, 49
Butler, L. F., 133
Buzard, Fay (Bill), 135–136, 141–142
Byers, Charles, 205
Calkins, Frank, 229
Calloway, Larkin, 72
Calloway, Sampson, 72, 78
Calloway, W. H. (Reverend), 84
Cambridge, Patrick, 54
Camp Vance (N.C.), 65–67
Campbell, Hugh J. (District Attorney), 121, 123
Capen, James (U.S. Prohibition Agent), 206
Carey, Joseph M. (Wyo. Governor), 226
Carlisle, Penn., 19–21, 25, 42, 56
Carnel, Samuel, 49
Carns, Neb., 168
Carothers, Andrew, 21
Carpenter, Charles E. (Judge), 197, 199, 201

262

Carroll, W. H., 136
Carroll, W. P. (Justice), 188
Casasola, Bonifacio, 15
Casey (Counterfeiter), 26, 30
Cassidy, Butch (Robert Leroy Parker), 4,
    12–16, 216, 226
Cedar Creek, Tx., 90–91, 93, 98
Challiss, George T., 110
Chamberlain, George E. (Ore. Governor),
    157
Chambers, William, 133
Chambersburg, Penn., 42–43
Chandler, Phillip, 67
Charles, Habian, 133
Charleston, S.C., 25
Chase, Thurman, 207–208
Cheyenne, Wyo., 116, 185, 188, 205–209,
    229, 233
Chicago, Ill., 3, 182–183
Childsville, N.C., 79
China Point, Id., 219
Chincleclamousche Township (Clearfield),
    Penn., 48–49
Cholila, Argentina, 12
Christiansen, Ezra, 217–218
Christmas, Robert (Judge), 234–235
Cincinnati, Oh., 183
Clanton, Billy, 128
Clanton, Ike, 128
Clark, Neil, 205
Clark, Noah, 70, 77
Clark, Walter, 82
Clark, Walter Van Tilberg, 173
Clarke, Ed (District Attorney), 167–168
Clarke, Jerome (Sue Mundy), 65
Clarnie, Ore., 151
Cleland (Judge), 157
Cleveland, Grover (U.S. President), 2–3
Cleveland, L. M., 167
Cleveland, Oh., 116
Clifford, M. L. (U.S. Commissioner), 150
Cloverdale, Calif., 103–104
Coal, Cela, 26
Cochrane, John, 133
Cody, Wyo., 226
Coffey, Austin, 61, 68, 72–73, 76
Coffey, David, 61, 72–73, 87
Coffey, Elisha, 71
Coffey, Enoch, 78
Coffey, Jesse Filmore, 61
Coffey, Levi, 71–72
Coffey, Margaret Ann, 61
Coffey, Mary A. (nee Blaylock), 60–61, 76,
    78, 85
Coffey, McCaleb, 68, 73
Coffey, Ruben, 68
Coffey, Thomas Austin, 61
Coffey, William, 68, 76
Coffey, Zachariah, 72

Coffey's Gap, N.C., 61
Coke, Richard (Tx. Governor), 97, 101
Cokeville, Wyo., 214, 216, 218–219,
    222–231, 234
Colfax, Schuyler (U.S. Vice President), 1, 6
Colford, Richard, 197
Collett Flat, Wyo., 225
Collett, Imogene, 224
Collett, Roy, 227–228
Collett, Will, 227–228
Collins, Joel, 116
Concha, Justo P. (Police Captain), 15
Confederate Conscription Act, 63
Conley (Prison Warden), 219
Connelly, John M., 36–53
Conners, Jim (alias of Z. G. Harshman), 153
Conrad, Betsey, 178–182
Conrad, Edward, 178, 183
Conrad, Fannie, 178–182
Conrad, Sam, 178–183
Conrad, William, 178–183
Cook, Jacob, 24
Cooke, Ed, 117
Cooke, Jay, 1
Corbett, Ore., 151–152
Corydon, In., 174, 176, 182–183
Council Bluffs, Ia., 8
Council, Id., 214, 216
Councill, J. D., 73
Councill, W. B. (Judge), 85
Covert (Counterfeiter), 26, 30
Covington, Neb., 111
Cowden, James (Captain), 38
Cox, Thomas, 107
Crab Orchard, Tenn., 66
Craft, M. A., 93
Craig, D. H. (Judge), 229
Crall, Jesse C., 110
Cranberry, N.C., 66
Crawford, Abraham, 230
Crawford, Thomas (Deputy Sheriff), 104
Credit Mobilier Company (Union Pacific
    Railroad), 1
Creigh, John (Judge), 20
Crescent City, Calif., 157
Crittenden, Thomas T. (Mo. Governor), 10
Cromwell, Thomas T., 37
Crook City, Wyo., 118
Crosby, Rufus, 24, 26
Crounse, Lorenzo (Neb. Governor), 172
Crozier, Frank, 136
Crozier, Thomas, 182
Crutcher, Ernest, 229
Cruz, Florintino, 128
Cumberland, Penn., 46
Cuny, Adolph, 117, 120
Curry, Hugh B. (U.S. Prohibition Agent),
    206
Curtin, C. (Dr.), 53

Curtis, Billy, 102
Curtis, J. D. ("Dock"), 103
Cusson, Eugene (Reverend), 195
Custer, Gen. George A., 111
Custer, S.D., 116
Dalton, Albert ("Bert"), 226–230
Daly, John, 201
Daniels, Ed, 222
Danites, The, 109
Darling, F. M., 116
Davis (Major), 70
Davis, Daniel T., 197
Davis, Edmund Jackson (Tx. Governor), 97
Davis, Martine née Pritchard, 88
Davis, Scott, 117
Day, Billy, 167
Deadwood, S.D., 111, 114, 116–118, 120
Dean, Hazel, 146
Dearborn, Henry (General), 23
Deavin, Emma, 175
Deavin, James, 175–176
Deep Gap, N.C., 73
Deer Lodge, Mont., 219
Deisal, Peter, 49, 51
Denisen, Hugh, 27
Denver, Co., 206–207, 231
Detroit, Mich., 23, 123
Dillistin, William H., 18
Dillon, Mont., 220
Dixon, W. H., 93
Dodge City, Ks., 128–129
Donahue, Cornelius ("Lame Johnny"), 118, 120
Donzelmann, Hugo, 205
Doubling Gap, Penn., 41, 43–44–46
Douglass (shooting victim), 93
Downey, S. C. (Probation Officer), 207
Drake, James C. (U.S. Marshal), 150
Draper, George (Sheriff), 120
Drenning, Lewis, 26, 30
Drenning, Samuel, 26
Drenning, William, 26, 29–30
Drenning, William, Jr., 26, 30
Driftwood Branch (Penn.), 50
Dubois, Id., 231
Dubs, John, 26
Dull, David, 24
Dullenty, Jim, 218
Duncan, James, 21, 55–57
Duncan Township, Ill., 109
Dundass, James, 54
Dunwell (Sheriff), 139
Eagle City, Id., 135–136, 138–142
Eagle Creek (Id.), 135–136
Eagles Nest, Wyo., 117
Earp, Adelia, 128
Earp, James Cooksley, 127, 132, 135–136, 142
Earp, Josephine "Josie" Sarah née Marcus, 129, 132, 142, 144

Earp, Martha Elizabeth, 128
Earp, Morgan, 128
Earp, Newton Jasper, 127, 142
Earp, Nicholas, 127
Earp, Urilla née Sutherland, 129
Earp, Victoria Ann née Cooksley, 127
Earp, Virgil Walter, 127–129, 142–143
Earp, Virginia Ann, 128
Earp, Warren Baxter, 128–129, 132, 142
Earp, Wyatt Berry Stapp, 127–144
East Berlin, Penn., 24
East Pennsborough, Penn., 41, 46
Eberly, 46
Eby, C. M., 202
Edgley (Railroad Detective), 220
Edwards, John Newman, 8
Eightmile, Ore., 161
Elbert, Noah, 182
Elizabeth, In., 178
Ellis, Aaron, 22, 24
Ellis, David, 67
Emerick, Neb., 164
Emmittsburg, Md., 25
English, J. D., 71, 79
Enright, J. E. "Jack", 132, 135–136, 141–142
Enser, Ephraim, 37–38
Ernst, Donna B., 14
Erwin (Under Sheriff), 220
Estes, Elijah, 70, 77
Estes, Joseph P., 78
Estes, Lampton, 78
Estes, Lampton, Jr., 71, 78
Estes, Madison, 78
Estes, Rebecca née Moore, 71
Estes, William, 75–78
Eucaliptus, Bolivia, 15
Eureka, Mont., 235
Evans, Jesse, 10
Evans, Robert, 14–15
Evanston, Wyo., 227–229
Everett, Wash., 154
Everly, Mr.,
Ewing, Thomas (General), 4–5
Fahey, John, 131, 135
Fakes (farmer), 178
Fandrich, H. A. (Dr.), 235
Far West, Mo., 109
Fay, Benjamin, 191
Fellmy, Elkana, 176
Fenning, James, 154
Ferguson, Adam, 138
Ferguson, Champ, 65
Ferguson, Daniel S., 133, 135–136, 138–141
Finch, D. Harold (Dr.), 207
Findlay, William (Penn. Governor), 35–36, 38, 40–46, 55–57
Fisher (Sheriff), 220
Fisher, Josiah, 188
Fisher, William, 180

Fitzsimmons, Bob, 144
Foley, Charles "Red", 133
Foot, Robert E. (U.S. Commissioner), 207
Forbes, B. F. (Dr.), 182
Ford, Bob, 8
Ford, Charley, 8
Forsyth, Benjamin (Major), 24
Fort Collins, Co., 145
Fort Collins, Co., 206–207
Fort D. A. Russell (Wyo.), 233
Fort George, Ont., 23–4
Fort Grant, Az., 10
Fort Hall (Id.), 222
Fort Harrison, Mont., 235
Fort Laramie, Wyo., 111, 117
Fort Niagara, N.Y., 23–24
Fort Pierre, S.D., 117
Fort Smith, Ark., 128
Foscoe, N.C., 71
Franklin, George, 69
Franklin, Joseph V., 66
Frazee, William H., 203
Frazer, C. C. (Sheriff), 188
Frazer, S. W. (Sheriff), 201
Frear, Ned, 31, 44
Fredendall, Ira (Sheriff), 189
Frederickstown, Md., 30
Fuller, D. B. (U.S. Marshal), 157
Gable, Charles, 141
Gallatin, Mo., 10
Gaona (General), 90
Gardner (bushwhacker), 72
Garrett, John G., 195
Garrett, Pat (Sheriff), 10–12
Geraghty, John L. (F.B.I. Agent), 206
Gere, A. H. (F.B.I. Agent), 206
Gettysburg, Penn., 26
Geyserville, Calif., 103
Gibbs (Counterfeiter), 26
Giles, Earl, 208
Gill, David W. (U.S. Commissioner), 205
Gillette, Rupert, 64
Gilligan (Bank robbery victim), 224
Glasgow, Mont., 231, 233
Glass, Robert (alias Anders), 73
Globe, The (N.C.), 61, 68, 73, 85
Goble, Ore., 150–152
Golden, Co., 194
Goldfield, Nev., 144
Goldsby (Counterfeiter), 26
Golphene, Thomas J., 146–147
González, Gil, 15–16
Good Hope Mills, Penn., 41
Government Island, Wash., 151–153
Gragg, Howard, 85
Gragg, James, 68, 85
Graham (Bank robbery victim), 224
Graham, R., 133
Grandfather Mountain (N.C.), 64
Grant (Sheriff), 191

Grant, Ulysses S. (U.S. President), 1
Gray, Alex T. (Judge), 123
Great Island (Lock Haven), Penn., 48–51
Green, Amos, 72
Green, Benjamin, 71
Green, Joseph, 72
Green, L. L., 72
Green, Lott, 72, 78
Green River, Wyo., 117
Green, Robert, 68
Green, Taylor, 72, 78–79
Greeneville, Tenn., 66
Green's Creek (Tx.), 94
Gregg, Andrew, 54
Grey's Lake, Id., 222
Groner, Con (Sheriff), 138
Grosbeck, H.V., 197
Gunnison, Co., 129
Hadley, Mary Stoner, 218
Hagerstown, Md., 38
Haggerty, Earl, 224
Halfman, 58
Halifax, Nova Scotia, 116
Hall, William M. (Judge), 30, 36, 56
Hamer, Id., 220
Hamilton, James (Judge), 21
Hammond, John, 49
Hance, M. A. (Justice), 188–189
Hanford, Cornelius H. (Judge), 149–150
Hanna, David (Sheriff), 168
Hannah, William, 49
Hanson, Daniel C. (Deputy Sheriff), 218,
    224, 227–230
Hanson, Dennis (Reverend), 235
Hanson, F. E., 229
Hanson, James, 36–40
Harbaugh, McHester "Mack", 182–183
Harbolt, Joseph, 39
Hardin County, Ky., 182
Hardy, John, 133, 136
Harlan, Ia., 119
Harmin, Larry, 33
Harris, N. R., 149
Harrisburg, Penn., 38, 41, 46–47, 58
Harshman, Everett, 161
Harshman, Floyd, 147, 157
Harshman, Harvey, 146, 161–163
Harshman, Nancy Dean, 146–149
Harshman, Oliver, 147, 161, 163
Harshman, Zebulon Gay, 145–163
Hartford, Ky., 127
Hartley, James (Lieutenant), 71
Hartman, Elizabeth, 108
Hartman, Idaletta, 109
Hartman, James B., 108–110
Hartman, Lenorah, 109
Hartman, Martha Ann, 108
Hartman, Mary F., 109
Hartman, Samuel S. ("Laughing Sam"),
    108–126

Hartman, Sarah J., 108
Hartman, William, 109
Hastings, Thomas, Jr., 54
Hawley, James H. (Id. Governor), 220
Hayes, D. T., 133
Hayford, J. H. (Justice), 188–189
Hays, Charles (Deputy Sheriff), 117
Hays, S. H., 136
Hayward (Rustling victim), 185
Healdsburg, Calif., 102–104
Heath, James M., 149
Hefflefinger, 38
Heister, Joseph (Penn. Governor), 57
Henderson, H. W. (Sheriff), 231
Henley, Barclay (District Attorney), 105,
Henley, Henry, 72
Heppner, Ore., 161, 231
Herron, Charles Velson "V.", 164
Herron, Ella May, 164
Herron, John A. "J. A.", 164
Herron, Mark W., 164
Herron, Richard, 164
Herron, Sarah J., 164
Herron, William E., 164
Hewitt, George, 224, 228
Hickey, Ross, 149
Hickok, Wild Bill, 111
Hickory, N.C., 84
Highbridge, Id., 219
Hinds, Hugh, 202
Hinkle, George M., 109
Hinkle, Mary, 109
Hipple, William, 27, 30
Hoehn, Charles, 151–154, 157
Holland, Tommy, 218
Holliday, John H. "Doc", 128–129
Hollifield, Edward Jerome, 85
Hollifield, Martha Jane see Martha Jane
    Blaylock
Holman, Alfred, 133, 135–136, 140–141
Holman, J. H., 105
Homan, Henry A., 118–119
Homer, Wyo., 225
Hooker, Henry C., 142
Horn, Tom, 184, 193–194
Hot Springs, Mont., 235
Houck, Calvin (Colonel), 67
Houston, Edward, 180
Houx, John L., 102–103
Howard, Nicholas, 44
Howe, Albert N., 180
Hoy, George, 128
Hoyt, John W. (Wyo. Governor), 120
Huddell, William, 180
Hudson, James (Marshal), 182–183
Hudson, Me., 213
Hume, James B., 107
Hunt, Harry J. (Justice), 205
Hunt, W. E. (Deputy Sheriff), 141–142
Huntingdon, Penn., 45

Huston, Charles, 30–32
Idaho Falls, Id., 220, 222
Ingalls, N.C., 79
Ingersoll, Jared (Penn. Attorney General), 30
Iona, Id., 222
Irvine (Justice), 53
Irvine, Capt. William N., 20
Irwin, John, Jr., 54
Ivy, Edmund, 72
Jackson, Carl (Justice and Sheriff), 201–202
Jackson, Ernest, 224
James, Alexander Franklin "Frank", 6–10, 89
James, Jesse Woodson, 4–10, 16, 31, 57, 89,
    145
Janes, Ed, 222
Jefferson, Thomas (U.S. President), 20
Johnson, Bert (Judge), 161
Johnson, C. A., 167
Johnson, Dave, 168
Johnson, Will (Deputy Sheriff), 167–168
John's River (N.C.), 61, 63, 67, 71
Jonas Ridge, N.C., 79
Jones, Albert A., 118–119
Jones, Bastian, 24
Jones, Daniel, 26
Jones, Joe, (Railroad Chief Agent), 220
Jones, Joe, 222
Jones, Lizzie, 180
Jones, Tom, 103
Juniata Crossings, Penn., 26, 36
Kamela, Ore., 231
Kangley, Wash., 149
Kansas City, Mo., 4–6
Kansas–Nebraska Bill, 4
Karthaus, Penn., 49
Keane, Alice, 194
Keane, Charles, 185, 191, 193–194, 208–209
Keane, John, 185, 194, 196
Keane, Katie, 194
Keane, Mary, 194, 196
Keane, Mary Nora, see Mary Powell,
Keane, Patrick "Patsy" Sarsfield, 194
Keane, Rosy, 194
Keane, William E., 185, 194
Kearney, Mo., 8
Keen, James N., 173–175
Keith, Alfred F., 60–61
Keith, Emaline R., 61
Keith, James A. (Colonel), 69
Kellogg, Id., 135
Kemmerer, Wyo., 224
Kendal, T., 146
Kendrick, John B. (Wyo. Governor), 230
Kennedy, T. Blake (U.S. District Judge), 207
Kerns, Abraham, 39
Kerr, John, 47
Keyes (Railroad Detective), 220
Kidd, William, 219
Kinkaid, Moses P. (Judge), 168
Kinney, Tim, 225

Kinston, N.C., 63
Kirk, George Washington (Colonel), 65–69, 73
Kirk, Mariah Louesa *née* Jones, 66
Kistner, (Deputy Sheriff), 222–223
Knights of the Golden Circle, 175
Knights of the Switch, 174
Knowles, William T., 205
Knoxville, Tenn., 67, 75
Kootenai County, Id., 138, 140
Korner, Fred, 152
Ku Klux Klan, 174
Kuhns, John, 45, 49
Kuntz, Phil (Police Sergeant), 206
La Grange, Tx., 92
Laconia, In., 176, 178
Lake Alice (Wyo.), 225
Lake Ootsa, B.C., 233
Lamar, Mo., 128
Lander, Wyo., 116, 216
Landers, Tillman, 69
Landisburg, Penn., 27
Lane, James H., 4
Langdon, C. W., 105
Lannon, (Rustling victim), 185
Laramie County, Wyo., 185
Laramie, Wyo., 117, 120, 188–191, 194–195, 197, 199, 201–202, 206–209
Lawrence, C. R., 195
Lawrence, Ks., 109
Lawrence, Ks., 4–5
Lawrence Raid (Ks.), 4–5
Leader (Jailer), 43
Leathers, Fredrick, 48–49
Lebo, Paul, 47, 49
Ledford, John Bunyon "Bun", 85
Ledford, Marion, 85
Ledford, Ruth *née* Clark, 85
Lee, Maj. Albert L., 110
Leeson, Michael A., 49
LeMay, James, 175
LeMay, Lucy, 176
LeMay, Matilda, 176
Lenoir, N.C., 67, 76
Lewis, Caleb, 20
Lewis, David, 17, 19–58
Lewis, Guian, 20
Lewis, Henry, 20
Lewis, Jacob, 20
Lewis, Jane Dill, 20, 22, 24, 48–50
Lewis, Jerry, 111
Lewis, Lewis, 20, 49
Lewis, Lewis, Jr, 20, 49
Lewis, Margarate, 22–24, 47
Lewis, Mary Ann, 47, 58
Lewis, Melinda, 22
Lewis, Sarah, 20
Lewis, Thomas, 20, 22–24, 27, 49
Lewis, William, 184–185, 189, 193–194
Lewistown, Penn., 38, 41

Liberty, Mo., 6
Lima, Mont., 219
Lincoln County War (N.M.), 10
Lincoln, N.M., 10
Lincoln, Neb., 117, 168
Lincolnton, N.C., 75
Linglestown, Penn., 37
Linn (Reverand), 53
Linn, John Blair, 46–47, 49–50, 56
Linsey, W. Reid, 70, 76–79
Linville River (N.C.), 67, 85, 87
Lloyd, Errol Jack, 217
Lockart, James, 37
Logan, John L., 147
Long, John (Sheriff), 119
Long Pine, Neb., 165–166
Long, Tex, 216
Los Angeles, Cal., 144
Louisville, Ky., 175, 183
Lyons, Burt, 172
Lytle, John, 27–28, 30–31
Madison, Neb., 172
Magnuson, Richard (Judge), 135, 138, 140
Malta, Mont., 234
Mann, Carl, 111, 114
Manning, Charley, 216, 219, 223–224, 226, 228–231
Manning, Louella Stoffer, 216
Marcus, Daniel, 70, 77
Marino, Christus, 224–225
Market Lake, Id., 220
Markley, Josiah P. (Dr.), 207
Marks, Ed, 224
Marlow, James (Captain), 72
Marshall, N.C., 66
Marshfield, Ore., 157
Martin, Al, 144
Martin, Katherine, 201
Martins (Breezewood), Penn., 27
Martinsburg, Penn., 27
Mason, Mary C., 167
Masterson, Bat (City Marshal), 129
Masterson, Jim (Deputy City Marshal), 128
Mau, Frank, 218
Maxwell, Pete, 10
May, William, 180
Mayhaw Creek (Tx.), 90
McCall, Jack, 111
McCall, R. R. (Sheriff), 76
McCarey, Patrick, 37
McCarthy, Florence, 135
McCharles (Bank robbery victim), 224
McClelland, John, 36, 40
McClellen, Thomas, 27
McConnell, G. R., 205
McConnelsburg, Penn., 27
McCurdy, 40
McDaniels, 141
McDevitt, John (Reverend), 209
McDonald, Frank (Deputy Sheriff), 139

McDowell. Mary Ann "Molly", 92
McDuffie, George (Deputy Sheriff), 231
McEwan, James, 110
McFarland, John, 41–43, 55–57
McGhee, James (Coroner), 49, 54
McGibbons, 39
McGill, Edgar, 220
McGolrick (Counterfeiter), 26
McGuire, Felix, 43–48
McInnes, Elmer D., 140
McIntire (fisherman), 151
McKibben (Colonel), 48
McKimie, Robert ("Reddy"), 116
McLaury, Frank, 128
McLaury, Tom, 128
McMinn, Rich (Deputy Sheriff), 225, 228–230
McMurdo, Archie D. (Dr.), 161
McMurray, Will (District Attorney), 201–202
McNeils Island, Wash., 149–150, 157
McPhee, Hugh, 185
Meadors, Albert, 230–231
Meadow Grove, Neb., 165
Meadows, Anne, 12
Meat Camp, N.C., 68
Medix Run, Penn., 49
Memphis, Tenn., 75
Menan, Id., 220
Mercer County, Ill., 108–110
Mescal Springs, Az., 128
Metzgar (Attorney), 20
Meyers, John, 43
Meyers, Louis, 167
Middlebury, Vt., 23–24
Miles, Evan, 54
Miles, Joseph, 54
Miles, Richard, 54
Milesburg, Penn., 20, 47, 54
Mill Hall, Penn., 53
Miller (Counterfeiter), 26
Miller, Andrew (Coroner), 191
Miller, Ed, 8
Miller, Michael, 26–27
Miller, Samuel, 42
Miller, Steve (Policeman), 201–202
Millersburg Township, Ill., 109
Milton, Sam (Deputy Sheriff), 219
Minch, E. A. (U.S. Marshal), 149
Miner, William ("Old Bill"), 3, 145, 150–154, 163
Minihan, James (Captain), 65
Minneapolis, Minn., 226, 231
Minneapolis, N.C., 66
Missouri Compromise, 4
Mitchell (Judge), 76
Mitchell, Harvey Bell, 102
Mitchell, John (Sheriff), 49–50
Moffitt, Robert, 44–45

Monida, Mont., 219
Monmouth, Ill., 128
Monroe, James (U.S. President), 18
Montcalm, W. T. "Billy" (alias of Z. G. Harshman), 149
Montezuma, N.C., 82–88
Montpelier, Id., 223, 225
Moody, Gideon C. (Judge), 121, 123
Moore, Asa, 194
Moore, Billy, 71
Moore, Carroll, 71, 77–79
Moore, David, 75–76, 78
Moore, George, 94
Moore, Jade, 71
Moore, James D., 63
Moore, Jesse, 71–72
Moore, John W., 64
Moore, Judson, 75–76, 78–79
Moore, Pat, 71
Moore, Thomas (Sheriff), 29, 33–34
Moorman, S. C., 166
Moran (robbery victim), 116
Morgan (Justice of the Peace), 104
Morgan, Ore., 146
Morganton, N.C., 66
Morgantown, Va., 25
Morrison, Joseph, 33
Morrison's Cove, Penn., 27–28
Morristown, Tenn., 66
Mosquito Creek Bottom (In.), 176
Moulton, Frank (Sheriff), 121
Mount Vernon, Wash., 153–154
Moyer, S. L., 185
Mud Lake, Id., 231
Munzon, Braulio, 15
Murray (Under Sheriff), 220
Murray, James, 26, 30
Murrayville (Murray), Id., 135
Nealon, Michael F., 166–168
Near City, Ore., 150
Nelson, Emil, 224
Nevins, Capt. James (Pinkerton Superintendent), 152–154
New Albany, In., 175–176
New Brunswick, N.J., 22
New Salem, Ill., 145
New York City, N.Y., 12
New York City, N.Y., 22
Newland, N.C., 85
Newland, W. C., 85
Newman, Paul, 12
Newville, Penn., 43–44
Nicholson, Joseph (Prison Superintendent), 123
Nittany Mountain (Penn.), 48
Noble, Madeleine M., 174, 176
Noble, Philander, 21, 23–26
Noblitt, Asa D., 223–224
Noe, William, 182

Nome, Alsk., 144
Norfolk, Neb., 165
Norgrath, Mr., 98
North Platte, Neb., 138
Northfield, Minn., 8
Norton, Bayliss, 69–70
Norton, Dillard, 69
Norton, Drury, 69
Norton, George, 69–70
Norton, Hack, 67
Norton, James, 69–70
Norton, Josiah, 69–70
Norton, Nancy Franklin "Granny" née Shelton, 69–70
O'Ley, Robert (Deputy Sheriff), 220, 222
O'Neill, Neb., 168
O'Rourke (Sheriff), 220
Ogallala, Neb., 138
Ogdensburg, N.Y., 24
Ohnhaus, Charles J. (U.S. District Clerk), 207
Old Woman's Forks (Wyo.), 117
Olsen, Pete W., 217–218, 226–227, 229, 231
Olympia, Wash., 149
Omaha, Neb., 119–121, 123
Omaha, Neb., 138
Orell, James, 207–208
Osborn, John, 26
Osborne, W., 133
Osceola, Mo., 4
Ouray, Co., 129
Overmeyer, C. R., 167–168
Overton, A. P. (Judge), 105
O'Reilley, Hazel E., 206
Palmer, John B. (Colonel), 67
Palmer, Wash., 150
Panola, Tx., 94
Parker, Glen (District Attorney), 208–209
Parker, W. H., 121, 126
Pass Christian, Miss., 216
Passmore, Enoch, 20
Patrick, Florence (Dr.), 202–203
Patterson, George W. (District Attorney), 205
Payne, William, 133, 136, 141
Pearson, R. C., 67
Pella, Ia., 128
Pelot, Cal, 222
Pelton, Clark (alias William "Kid" Webster), 116–120
Pence, Mary Lou, 195, 209
Pendelton, Peter, 43
Pendleton, Ore., 146, 161–162, 163
Peoples, Jim, 28–29
Perkins (U.S. Marshal), 120
Perkins, George, 68
Perkins, Marion, 223
Peró, Carlos, 15–16
Peró, Mariano, 15–16

Peter's Mountain (Penn.), 46
Petersburg, Penn., 41
Peterson, Charles F. (Assistant U.S. Prohibition Director), 206 Petriken, William, 54
Phelps, Alonzo, 206–209
Phelps, Sarah May "Billie", 206–209
Philadelphia, Penn., 22, 26, 34–35
Pine Grove Furnace, Penn., 24, 26
Pineola, N.C., 87
Pinkerton's Detective Agency, 8
Piper, John, 27
Pittsburg, Penn., 26, 37, 41
Place, Etta, 12–15
Pocatello, Id., 219, 231
Porter, Al, 224
Porter, Bryon (Sub–Asst. Commissioner, Freedman's Bureau), 92–94
Porter, Fanny, 15
Porter Township, Penn., 48
Portland, Ore., 138
Portland, Ore., 145, 151–154, 157
Potter, James, 47
Potter, Sam W. (Constable), 224
Potter's Mills, Penn., 47–48
Powell (outlaw), 118
Powell, Fredrick U., 184–196, 203
Powell, Mary Nora Keane, 185–203, 207–212
Powell, William Edwin "Bill", 185, 188, 196–197, 199, 203–209
Price, William, 37–38
Prichard, Andrew J., 131–132
Prichard Creek (Id.), 131, 135, 139
Princeton, N.J., 22
Prineville, Ore., 157
Pritchard, Adolphus, 72
Pritchard, Alfred, 61
Pritchard, Arthur, 61, 78
Pritchard, Belle, 87
Pritchard, Edna, 87
Pritchard, Elizabeth, 61
Pritchard, Estelle, 87
Pritchard, Harriet, 61
Pritchard, Henry, 61
Pritchard, James, 61
Pritchard, John R., 61, 70, 75, 77–79
Pritchard, Nancy, 61
Pritchard, Sarah Malinda see Sarah Malinda Blaylock
Promontory Point, Ut., 1
Quantrill, William Clark (Confederate Partisan Captain), 4, 65, 89
Quechisla, Bolivia, 15
Queenstown Heights, Ont., 24
Radamaker, Fred, 182
Rainbolt, John, 176
Ramsey, James, 37
Rankin, John, 54
Rapid City, S.D., 120–121

Ray, Betsy, 33
Raymond, John B. (U.S. Marshal), 121
Ray's Hill (Penn.), 31
Reamer, Christian, 36
Redford, Robert, 12
Reed, Robert F. (Police Chief), 231
Reid, James R., 26, 28
Reiley, John, 39
Reiniger, Conrad, 46
Reynolds, Hedge, 104
Reynolds, William B. (Sheriff), 104
Rich (Sheriff), 228
Richardson, Buelah, 191
Richardson, Elizabeth, 197
Richardson, Harry P., 189, 191
Richmond, Va., 183
Riddle, Samuel, 30, 32
Riddle, William, 48
Rigby, Id., 220, 222
Ringo, Johnny, 129
Rio Gallegos, Argentina, 12
Rio Pico, Argentina, 15
Rios, Timoteo (Police Inspector), 15–16
Risbell (Sheriff), 153–154
Ritner (Sheriff), 42
Robbins, Bob, 87
Robinson, William, 21–22, 24
Rochester, Wash., 147, 149
Roder, Peter, 49
Rodney, Caesar, 43, 45
Rogers, Carl (Deputy Sheriff), 224
Rollins, W. W. (Major), 73
Romero, Felix, 223
Root, Erastus (General), 21
Rose, Robert R., 218
Ross, Albert see Albert F. Sesler
Ross, Andrew, 189, 191
Rothrock, James, 54
Rowe, Alexander, 98–99
Rowe, James, 93–94, 97–99
Rowe, Mary, 93
Rowe, Thomas, 93
Rowley, James, 26
Roxbury, Penn., 27
Rupp (Roop), Jonas, 41, 46
Russelville, Tenn., 67
Sacramento, Cal., 142, 144
Saginaw, N.C., 84
Saint Joseph, Mo., 109
Saint Joseph, Mo., 8
Saint Paul, Minn., 116
Saínz, Julian, 15
Salem, Ore., 157
Salisbury, N.C., 67, 70
Salt Lake City, Ut., 229
Samish Flats (Wash.), 153
San Antonio, Tx., 15
San Bernardino, Cal., 128
San Diego, Calif., 144
San Felipe, Tx., 90

San Francisco, Cal., 144
San Francisco, Calif., 234
San Jacinto (Tx.), Battle of, 90
San Quentin Prison (Calif.), 105, 107, 150
San Vicente, Bolivia, 15–16
Sandy, Ut., 229
Santa Rosa, Calif., 105
Saskatoon, Sask., 233
Savage, Spoon, 220
Schettler, C. L. (Deputy Sheriff), 229
Schmidt, Antonio, 93
Schoaf, James, 27
Schofield, John M. (General), 66
Scott, Rube, 220
Scruggs (Deputy Sheriff), 225
Seattle, Wash., 150
Seattle, Wash., 3
Sesler, Albert F. (Albert Ross), 219
Sharkey, Tom, 144
Sharp, Joseph (Sheriff), 229
Sharp, William, 205
Sharpe, J. W., 31
Shelby, Tx., 94
Shelton, David, 69
Shelton, James "Old Jim", 69
Shelton, James, 69
Shelton Laurel, N.C., 69
Shelton, Rodrick "Stob Rob", 69
Shephard, William, 50–51
Shippensburg, Penn., 25
Shirleysburg, Penn., 37
Shoenberger, Peter, 46–47
Short, Luke, 129
Shoshone County, Id., 132, 137, 140–142
Shuck, Clabe (Sheriff), 176
Shull's Mill, N.C., 72–73
Sideling Hill (Penn.), 36–37
Sidney, Neb., 114
Silver Bow, Mont., 219–220
Silver City, N.M., 10
Silverton, Co., 129
Sink, Daniel, 103–104
Sinnemahoning Creek (Penn.), 48, 50
Smalley, Eugene V., 131
Smith, B. S. (Constable), 185
Smith, James, 26, 33
Smith, Joseph, 109
Smith, Mabel Blaylock, 87
Smith, Pegleg, 26, 30
Smith, Samuel, 50–51
Smith, Thomas "Bear River Tom", 141
Smith, Watson B. (U.S. Commissioner), 119
Smithers, B.C., 233
Smith's Fork (Wyo.), 224
Snake Spring, Penn., 38
Snow Creek Township, N.C., 79
Soda Springs, Id., 222
Spencer, Id., 219
Stanford, Leland, 1
Starr, Belle, 209

Statesville, N.C., 76
Steele, James, 138
Steele, James R. (Dr.), 139
Steele, Thomas, 138–140
Steven, Hugh, 46
Stevens, Henry L., 197
Stevens, Reese, 49
Stevenson, H. F., 152
Stillwell, Frank, 128
Stoffer, Fred, 231
Stoll, W. F., 133
Stoneman, George (Major General), 73
Stoner, Clarence, 214, 230–231
Stoner, Ellen Whitney, 214
Stoner, Grayce, 214
Stoner, John H., 224
Storey, William (Sheriff), 152–154
Stoystown, Penn., 22
Strawberry Plains, Tenn., 65
Stucker, Edward, 166
Suddreth, Lloyd, 87
Sullivan, J. R., 205
Sun River, Mont., 138
Sundance Kid (Harry Alonzo Longabaugh),
    4, 12–16
Swan Valley, Id., 222
Sweeney, C. T., 118
Sweeney, Charles, 133–134
Sybille Country (Wyo.), 185, 197
Tabitha (Counterfeit Engraver), 26
Tacoma, Wash., 149–150
Taylor, Frank S. see Charley Whitney
Taylor, Tex, 216
Taylor, Tom, 223
Tennyson, Charles, 175–176
Terry, Jake ("Cowboy Jake"), 150
Thacker, John N., 107
Thatcher, W. W., 107
Thompson, Ben, 138
Thompson, William "Texas Billy", 138
Tidball, V. J. (Judge), 201, 208
Tietze, Joe, 197
Tillson, Davis (Brigadier General), 73
Timberlake, John, 180
Tindell, John, 180
Tod, John, 33
Tombstone, Az., 127–129
Tompkins, Daniel (N.Y. Governor and U.S.
    Vice President), 21, 57
Tonopah, Nev., 144
Topeka, Ks., 110
Toplitz (Telegrapher), 140
Torres, Victor, 15
Trinidad, Co., 129
Trombley, Winn S. (Marshal), 229
Troutdale, Ore., 152
Troy, N.Y., 21
Trugillo, Joseph, 188
Tucker, Bill, 138
Tuckett, E. J. (Justice), 228

Tucson, Az., 128
Tupiza, Bolivia, 15
Twiss, Ulysses (Marshal), 225
Ukiah, Calif., 107
Uniontown, Penn., 30
Uyuni, Bolivia, 15
Valentine, Neb., 166–168
Van Buren, Ark., 128
Van Fossen, Walter, 229
Van Lear, William (Dr.), 39
Vance, Zebulon B. (Colonel), 63
Vanderbuilt, Cornelius, 2
Vanderbuilt, William Henry, 2
Vandorn, Milton, 166
Vandyke, Henry, 54
Vaughn, John C., 67
Vaughn, William R., 136
Victoria, B.C., 3
Villa Mercedes, Argentina, 14
Waco, Tx., 94, 101
Wagner, Con, 194
Wagner, Mont., 226
Walcott, F. M. (Judge), 167–168
Walker, Andrew, 49
Walker, John, 72–73
Walker, Jonathan Hoge (Judge), 21, 30–31
Walker, Medie née McHaarg, 72
Wall, James, 116–117
Wallace, Id., 135
Wallich, Samuel, 27
Walnut Bottom, Penn., 25
Walnut Street Prison (Philadelphia, Penn.),
    31, 34–35, 40, 48
Walter, A. D. (U.S. Attorney), 206
Wanless, A. D., 195
Wanless, Charles F., 195–196
Wanless, Frank, 195
Wanless, Marie, 195
Wanless, Mary, see Mary Powell
Ward, Alberson, 26
Ward, John H. (Sheriff), 227–228, 230
Ward, Marrion, 88
Warm Springs, N C., 66
Washington, D.C., 107
Waterford, Penn., 27, 47
Waterloo, Tx. see Austin, Tx.
Watson, Cattle Kate, 209
Wautoma, Wis., 226
Waynesburg, Penn., 37
Weaver, Henry, 27
Webb, Milton, 71–72, 78
Webster, William "Kid" see Clark Pelton
Weise, Fred, 168
Weiser, Id., 213
Wertz, 39
West, Isaac E., 123
West Point, In., 182
Westfield, Mass., 23
Whatcom, Wash., 154
White, B. T., 167–168

White Caps, 173
White, H. A. (Captain), 69
White, Hamilton I, 89–101
White, Hamilton II, 89–101
White, Hamilton III "Ham", 89
White, Henry, 133
White, Jeremiah, 89
White, Joseph, 70, 77–78
White, Noah, 75
White Rock, N.C., 69
White, Tabitha *née* Hutchings, 90, 92, 97
Whitefish, Mont., 235–236
Whitman, Jay, 208
Whitney, Avis Douglas, 213
Whitney, Bruce, 214, 216
Whitney, Charley Spraig, 213–218, 223–236
Whitney, Charlotte Lathrop ("Lottie"),
    213–214, 216
Whitney, Ethel, 214
Whitney, Florence, 214
Whitney, Frank, 117
Whitney, Fred H., 213–214, 216
Whitney, Helen, 214
Whitney, Hugh, 213–233
Whitney, Timothy, 213
Wichita, Ks., 128
Wickersham, F. S., 133
Wicondah Township, Ia., 108
Wilcox, Ariz., 129, 142
Wilkesboro, N.C., 73
Wilkie, G. D. (Reverend), 233

Wilkinson, James (General), 21
Williams, John (alias of Z. G. Harshman),
    150–151
Williams, John, 133
Willow Creek, Id., 222
Wilson, Hill, 28–29
Wilson, James Q., 17
Wilson, Ned "Big Ned", 194
Wilson, Thomas J. (Attorney), 176
Wilson, William, 14–15
Wiseman, Louis, 180
Womeldorf, Charles, 166
Wood Lake, Neb., 166–167
Wood River (Id.), 140
Woodbury, Penn., 27
Woodfin, John (Major), 66
Worth, Jonathan (N.C. Governor), 75–76,
    79
Wounded Knee, Wyo., 119
Wright, Thomas, 73, 75
Wyman, Phillip, 141
Yankton, S.D., 120–121, 123
Yeager, James, 182
Young, Harry Sam "Sam", 111, 114
Young, John, 33
Younger, Cole, 8
Younger, Jim, 8
Younger, John, 8
Younger, Robert, 8
Yund, C. C. (Sheriff), 188